P.F.M. FONTAINE

THE LIGHT
AND
THE DARK

A CULTURAL HISTORY OF DUALISM
VOLUME VIII

J.C. GIEBEN, PUBLISHER
AMSTERDAM

THE LIGHT AND THE DARK

P.F.M. FONTAINE

THE LIGHT AND THE DARK
A CULTURAL HISTORY OF DUALISM

VOLUME VIII

GNOSTIC DUALISM IN ASIA MINOR
DURING THE FIRST CENTURIES A.D.

J.C. GIEBEN, PUBLISHER
AMSTERDAM 1993

To my eldest grandson
Pieter Daniel Smidt van Gelder,
born July 29, 1978,
excellent grammar-school pupil,
enthusiastic flute-player,
able household manager

No part of this book may be translated or reproduced in any form, by print, photoprint, microfilm, or any other means, without written permission from the publisher.

© by P.F.M. Fontaine / ISBN 90 5063 093 6 / Printed in The Netherlands

"For all things are called
light and darkness"

Parmenides

CONTENTS

Preface xv

I PHILO BETWEEN JEWISH ORTHODOXY AND HELLENISTIC PHILOSOPHY 1

1. Alexandria, the Jewish metropole 1
2. What is known of Philo's life 2
3. Philo's writings 3
4. Philo and the Old Testament 5
5. Philo's idea of God 6
6. Philo's idea of the immutability of God 8
7. The encounter of Judaism with Hellenism 10
8. Philo as an unbiblical prophet 11
9. God transcending all knowledge 12
10. The problem of creation 14
11. The role of the intermediaries 14
    a. The intelligible world 14
    b. The Logos 15
    c. Monad and Dyad 17
    d. The Ideas 18
    e. Angels and logoi 18
    f. The Powers 19
    g. Why Philo needed so many intermediaries 19
12. Order and disorder 20
13. Philo's abhorrence of the material world 21
14. The Man of God 21
15. Philo's anthropology 23
16. The role of wisdom 25
17. Philo's attitude towards women 26
18. Philonic doctrine and the Gnosis 26
    a. A provisional summary 26
    b. The origin of evil 27
    c. An ambivalent idea of the cosmos 28
    d. The Man of God and the first Man 28
    e. Élitism 29
    f. The basic dualism 29

		g.	The significance of knowledge and wisdom	29
		h.	How Gnostic was Philo?	33
19.			Conclusion	34
20.			The pseudo-Aristotelian treatise 'On the World'	35
Notes to Chapter 1				37

II		HERMETIC SECRETS		45
1.			On hermetic scripture in general	45
2.			The mental landscape of hermetic literature	46
	a.		The demise of rationalism	46
	b.		The reassertion of the East	47
	c.		Another idea of the divine	47
3.			Hermes and Toth	49
4.			Hermes and the hermetic writings	50
5.			What hermetic writings are about	51
6.			The composition and the character of the Corpus Hermeticum	52
7.			The optimistic line	52
8.			Some shorter pessimistic passages	54
9.			The 'Poimandres'	55
	a.		The introduction	55
	b.		God and matter	56
	c.		The origination of nature	58
	d.		The function of the Logos	58
	e.		The Powers	59
	f.		The Demiurge and the Governors	59
	g.		The imprisonment of the Logos	60
	h.		Two cosmological architects	61
	j.		The screening off of God	62
	k.		The role of the 'Will of God'	62
	l.		The cosmological function of the planets	63
	m.		The role of Man	64
	n.		Anthropology	65
	o.		Humanity divided	67
	p.		The ascent of the soul	68
	q.		Preaching the message	69
10.			The World Girl	69
	a.		The general character of the tract	69
	b.		The celestial bodies	70
	c.		Knowledge and Ignorance	71
	d.		The optimistic creation story	71
	e.		The pessimistic creation story	72

	f.	Man as a 'Fremdkörper'	72
	g.	The possibility of redemption	74
	h.	The destruction of the earth	74
	j.	The saviours	75
	k.	The tract's main theme	75
	l.	Optimism and pessimism	76
	m.	Is the Korê a Gnostic treatise?	76
	n.	The dualistic elements in the Korê	77
Notes to Chapter II		77

III	A LIBRARY IN A JAR	85
1.	The site	85
2.	The discovery	86
3.	The Library	86
4.	The precarious vicissitudes of the Library	87
5.	Authors, translators, and librarians	88
6.	Why the collection was made	90
7.	Why the collection was stored away	90
8.	How the collection is composed	91
Notes to Chapter III		92

IV	SETH'S PROGENCY	94
1.	Did there exist a Sethian sect?	94
2.	Did the sect exist in Egypt or elsewhere?	95
3.	The extent of the sect	96
4.	Seth, the ancestor of the sect	96
5.	Cain, Abel, Seth	97
6.	The nature of the Sethian texts	98
7.	A threepartite universe	99
	a. The three roots	99
	b. Darkness's jealousy	100
	c. The saving of the Spirit	101
	d. The dualism of the lower and higher worlds	101
8.	Sethian cosmogony	102
9.	The creation of man	103
	a. The report of the Paraphrase of Shem	104
	b. Hippolytus' account	104
	c. The story as told in 'The Apocalypse of Adam'	105
10.	The unhappy brothers	107
	a. What Pseudotertullian has to say	107

		b.	Epiphanius on Cain and Abel	107
		c.	The relation in 'The Gospel of the Egyptians'	108
11.		Seth the Redeemer		110
12.		The role of knowledge		111
13.		The Sethian attack on the Bible and Judaism		113
14.		The attack on the New Testament		115
15.		The rejection of the world		116
16.		The end of the world		117
17.		The ascent of the soul		117
18.		The Archontics		118
		a.	The godhead	120
		b.	The heavens	120
		c.	Sabaoth	120
		d.	Cain and Abel	121
		e.	Seth	122
		f.	The Archontics and Christianity	123
Notes to Chapter IV				124

V	THE SERPENT AND ITS RETINUE: THE OPHITES AND RELATED SECTS			134
1.		Which sects may be called 'Ophitic'?		134
2.		The veneration of the snake		135
3.		About the Ophites in general		135
4.		The snake as the sect's patron		136
5.		Ophites, Naassenes, and Gnostikoi		137
6.		Trinity and quaternity of first principles		137
7.		The First Woman and Christ		138
8.		The downward course of the light and its escape		139
9.		Jaldabaoth		140
10.		The snake		141
11.		Jaldabaoth-Jahve and the creation of man		142
12.		The revenge of Jaldabaoth		143
13.		Humanity at risk		144
14.		The race of Cain and the race of Seth		144
15.		The Ophites and the biblical heritage		145
16.		Christ and Jesus		146
17.		Dualism galore		148
18.		The Ophians		148
		a.	The Ophian diagram	148
		b.	Gnosis and dualism in the Ophian system	151
		c.	Salvation	152

19.	Gnostic antinomianism: those of Cain		153
	a. Antinomianism		153
	b. The Cainite doctrine		155
20.	Gnostic antinomianism: those of Nicolas		156
	a. Nicolas and Nicolaites		156
	b. The bad reputation of the Nicolaites		156
	c. Nicolaite doctrine		158
21.	The Peratae, the 'crossers'		159
	a. About the sect itself and its name		159
	b. The three-rooted universe		160
	c. The shaping of matter		161
	d. The Fall		162
	e. Anthropology		163
	f. The Saviour		163
	g. The rejection of the doomed		164
22.	Justin's Baruch-book		165
	a. The author and his book		165
	b. The three powers		165
	c. The angels		166
	d. The creation of Adam and Eve		167
	e. Elohim deserts Eden		167
	f. Eden's revenge		167
	g. Baruch the Redeemer		168
	h. The secret mysteries		170
23.	The Severians		171
Notes to Chapter V			172

VI	THOSE OF BARBELO		181
1.	What are Barbelo-Gnostics?		181
2.	What Epiphanius had to report about the Barbelo-Gnostics		182
3.	Barbelo-Gnostic scripture		182
4.	What Barbelo-Gnostic doctrine explains		183
5.	The highest principle		183
6.	Barbelo		184
7.	Christ		185
8.	Cosmogony		187
	a. Adamas		187
	b. Sophia's wilful acting		188
	c. Jaltabaoth the Demiurge		189
	d. Jaltabaoth's cosmogonic activities		190
	e. Sophia repents what she has done		191

	f.	The creation of Adam	191
	g.	The Pneuma	193
	h.	The second Fall	194
	j.	Redemption	195
	k.	The counter-offensive	195
	l.	The fallen state	196
	m.	Eloim and Yave	197
	n.	The origin of Seth	198
	o.	A promise	198
	p.	The destiny of the souls	200
	q.	A bad, bad world	200
	r.	The Saviour	202
	s.	Dualism	202
9.		Other Barbelo-Gnostic sects	203
	a.	Which sects there were	203
	b.	The role of Barbelo	204
	c.	The two spheres	204
	d.	The two battling forces	205
	e.	Libertinism	206
Notes to Chapter V			209

VII   THE BASILIDIANS   213

1.		Basilides and his work	213
2.		The heresiologues on Basilides	214
3.		What remains of Basilides' writings	215
4.		The report of Irenaeus	217
	a.	The Pleroma	217
	b.	The heavens	218
	c.	The world	218
	d.	The God of the Jews	219
	e.	Christ	219
	f.	'Those who know'	220
	g.	Conclusions	221
5.		The Hippolytan version	222
	a.	Rootless nature	222
	b.	God the cause of this world?	223
	c.	The world-seed	223
	d.	The threefold Sonship and the Spirit	224
	e.	Two worlds	224
	f.	The Great Ruler of the Cosmos	225
	g.	The Son of the Demiurge	225

	h.	The lower archons	226
	j.	The third Sonship and his Gospel	226
	k.	The fate of the world	228
	l.	Some conclusions	228
6.	The Basilidian community	230
Notes to Chapter VIII	230

VIII THE VALENTINIANS   235

1.	The founder	235
2.	The literary output of Valentinus	236
3.	What Valentinus intended to do	238
4.	The first stage: the Gospel of Truth	238
	a. The necessity of Knowledge	238
	b. The Father and the Son	239
	c. The aeons	239
	d. Error	240
	e. What is wrong with the world	241
	f. Jesus the Christ	242
	g. The 'book'	242
	h. Sleep and awakening	243
	j. The true nature of Jesus	244
	k. The Gospel of Truth as a Gnostic tract	245
5.	Vintage Valentinianism	246
	a. The Depth	246
	b. Ennoia	247
	c. Emanation	248
	d. The Pleroma	249
	e. All the aeons	250
	f. The Fall	251
	g. Matter	253
	h. Uproar in the Pleroma	253
	j. Jesus, the joint fruit of the Pleroma	254
	k. Esoteric knowledge	255
	l. Sophia's offspring	255
	m. A glimmer of hope	257
	n. The Saviour	257
	o. Substances and bodies	258
	p. The Demiurge	259
	q. The creation of man	260
	r. Christ and Jesus	262
6.	A different view of the Demiurge and his work	267

7.	Heracleon's view	269
8.	The Tripartite Tractate	273
	a. The Father, the Son, and the Church	273
	b. The Logos	274
	c. The lower sphere	275
	d. The Logos, the Demiurge, and the world	276
	e. The creation of man	277
	f. A confusing moral perspective	278
	g. The Saviour	280
	h. The fate of mankind	281
	j. The Redeemer redeemed	282
	k. Christ all in all	282
	l. The Tripartite Tract and its relation to Christianity	283
9.	The extent of Valentinianism	284
Notes to Chapter VIII		

IX	GNOSTIC POLEMICS AGAINST JUDAISM AND CHRISTIANITY	296
1.	Were the earliest Fathers of the Church 'heresy-hunters'?	296
2.	Gnostic syncretism	297
3.	Gnostic polemizing	298
	a. The anti-Jewish attitude of the Gnostics	298
	b. Anti-Christian polemizing	299
Notes to Chapter IX		300

Graphs of Gnostic systems		303
I	Simonianism	303
II	Menander's system	304
III	System of Saturnilos	305
IV	System of Cerinthus	306
V	System of the Pseudoclementina	307
VI	The Carpocratian system	308
VII	The Sethian system	309
VIII	The Archontic system	310
IX	The Ophitic system	311
X	The Barbelo-Gnostic system	312
XI	The system of de Gospel of Truth	313
XII	Vintage Valentinianism	314

XIII	The Tripartite system	315
XIV	The system of Basilides (in the version of Irenaeus)	316
XV	The system of Basilides (in the version of Hippolytus)	317

| Bibliography | 319 |
| General Index | 331 |

PREFACE

1. The making of Wagner's 'Parsifal'

Wagner's opera 'Parsifal' was extremely long in gestation. When on July 26, 1882, it had its first night in the Festspielhaus at Bayreuth (under the Jewish conductor Levi), the composer had forty years of preparation behind him. Way back in 1843 he had already composed an oratorio called 'Das Liebesmahl der Apostel'; this was based on the idea that is equally central in 'Parsifal', Wagner's version of the Last Supper. At some moment or other the composer had become acquainted with Wolfram von Eschenbach's romance of chivalry, 'Parzival' (ca. 1210). Needless to say that Wagner transformed the bard's ideas in order to suit his own intentions. He even denigrated the medieval poet and his work. He found Wolfram an immature person who had understood nothing of the true and real contents of his own work.

In 1845 a few fragments for a future opera were sketched. Four years later Wagner began working on a drama to be called 'Jesus of Nazareth'; he never completed this. Although intensely occupied with other musical dramas, in particular with the Ring and with 'Tristan und Isolde', the Parsifal-theme kept him enthralled. The first drafts of a text date from 1857. But in a letter to Mathilde von Wesendonk, he sighed that he could not and would not go on with the project. "Today I take my leave of this senseless plan." He indeed abandoned it for about twenty years but took it up again in 1877 after he had completed 'Der Ring des Nibelungen'.

He then began writing, within the time of five weeks, the poem which was to become the libretto. In 1879 the composition was virtually ready, but it took Wagner another year and a half to refine the score so that it would perfectly match the special accoustics of the Festspielhaus. On January 13, 1882, Cosima Wagner could note in her diary that the opera was ready. When it was performed half a year later, the public saw and heard Wagner's last opera on the stage and at the same time the greatest triumph of his music.

2. An outline of the contents

The scene of the first act is the castle of Monsalvat surrounded by a sacred area, a 'haram', as the Moslims would call it. In the castle itself two holy objects are kept, the lance which pierced Jesus' side on the cross, and the chalice of the Last Supper, surnamed 'the Grail'; legend (but not Scripture) has it that in this chalice the blood that streamed from Jesus' side on the cross was caught.

Both the lance and the Grail have been brought to Monsalvat by King Titurel. When the opera begins he is still living, although very old; he has abdicated the throne in favour of his son Amfortas. This Amfortas, the reigning king, is an invalid; he is suffering from a festering wound in his side that will not close. Long ago he marched out from the castle to heathen country to fight the dark enemy of the Grail, Klingsor, the magician. During this expedition he was seduced by the wild woman Kundry. This enabled Klingsor to get hold of the Holy Lance and to injure Amfortas in his side. Now the king is lying on his sick-bed in the castle; only an 'innocent fool' (der reine Tor), enlightened by compassion ('durch Mitleid wissende'), will be able to heal him.

When Parsifal appears (from nowhere) in the sacred domain, Gurnemanz, an old knight and, so to speak, the historian of the knights of the Grail, tells him all this. The young man is allowed to witness the ritual in the castle hall but this does not make an impression on him; he is still too immature. Instead of trying to become a Grail knight, he prefers leaving the castle in order to combat Klingsor.

On his way to Klingsor's castle, in Act Two, he meets a crowd of adorable Flower Maidens who attempt in vain to seduce him. Now

Kundry appears, still Klingsor's willing servant; she discloses to Parsifal his descent and his name (which he did not know until then). Her learns that Gamuret, his father, fell in battle in Arabia before his son was born. His mother was called 'Herzeleide', Heart's Sorrow. She tried to guard her child from the fate of his father but time came that he left her and made his way into the world. This broke her heart and she died. The news of her death is announced to the young man by Kundry. She also explains to him the meaning of his name : 'Parsifal' is 'Fal parsi', the 'innocent fool'.

The wild woman almost succeeds in seducing Parsifal; she gives him a long and ardent kiss on the mouth. But then he too feels a wound, a wound in his heart, and he pushes her aside. Suddenly he realizes that he is destined to work redemption; Kundry will be the first to be saved by him.

On the battlements of his castle Klingsor appears who sees Kundry escaping him. This wicked man is a former knight of the Grail himself; incapable, however, of keeping his vow of chastity he has been expelled. Now he is burning to take his revenge on the knights. Discovering Parsifal he throws his spear - the Holy Lance - at him, but the young man succeeds in catching it. With the Lance he makes the sign of the cross over Klingsor's realm of evil which disappears into nothingness. Is it a sign of the times that in the last two performances I saw, one in the Music Theatre at Amsterdam and the other in the Flemish Opera at Antwerp, this sign of the cross was not made?

When the third act begins it is ten years later. Titurel has died in the mean time. King Amfortas is still an invalid but the possession of the Sacred Spear makes Parsifal his designated successor. When Parsifal arrives after his long absence, it is Good Friday, the appropriate day for the celebration of the Grail ritual. But Amfortas refuses to officiate, he desires to die, and the castle is plunged into the deepest gloom.

Gurnemanz informs Parsifal of this deplorable situation. Seeing the spear in the young man's hands, he understands how much he is changed. The old knight therefore creates him a knight and immediately after that anoints him as king. The first act of the new king is to deliver

Kundry of the curse; this he performs by baptizing her. This scene is accompanied, or rather carried, by the incomparably beautiful music of the 'Karfreitagszauber', the Good Friday Magic.

Parsifal now enters the castle hall (for which the cathedral of Siena served as the model). There the mourning ceremony for Titurel is taking place in the course of which Parsifal cures Amfortas by touching the ailing king's side with the Holy Lance. "Be whole, absolved, and atoned!" Amfortas silently cedes his throne to Parsifal who immediately changes the mourning ceremony into the Grail ritual. He takes the chalice from its shrine, shows it to the kneeling knights, and blesses them with it.

Wagner has always been great in closing scenes, the entry of the gods into Valhallah at the end of Das Rheingold, Wotan drawing the fire circle around the sleeping Brünnhilde's body in the final scene of the Valkyrie, the burning Valhallah tumbling down into the waters of the Rhine in the Twilight of the Gods, and here the majestic score of the last scene. When I heard it a few weeks ago in the Music Centre Vredenburg at Utrecht in a brilliant concertante performance under Edo de Waart, the public, utterly overwhelmed, forgot to applaud.

3. What 'Parsifal' is not

There has been much discussion on the fundamental meaning of 'Parsifal'. There were and are interpreters who detect a racist ideology in it. In their view Parsifal is the blond Aryan hero who delivered Jesus of his tainted Jewish blood. Protagonists of this theory had to admit that this racism was preached in veiled mystical terms. For this reason this opera should have appealed to Hitler who, just like Wagner, was fiercely anti-Semitic and a racist. However, it seems impossible for me to detect the supposedly racist background of this work; its hero is neither blond nor Aryan, and there is not even the slightest reference to anything Jewish. This theory is in fact' hineinterpretiert' into the opera, inferred as it is from the historical fact that Wagner indeed wrote some profoundly anti-Jewish tracts.

Another and more popular interpretation is that this opera must be understood as a Christian work. The French author Romain Rolland even went so far as to speak of 'the fifth Gospel'. It must be admitted that, seen superficially, the work contains a number of specifically Christian elements. There is much talk of redemption and salvation, there is a baptism, the sign of the cross is made, there is some sort of a eucharistic meal, the climatic scene takes place on Good Friday, and so on.

Then there are the two great symbolic objects, the Sacred Spear and the Grail. But exactly at this point doubt begins to set in. Jesus' side was indeed pierced by a Roman soldier with his lance, but nobody knows what happened to this weapon. That this soldier was called Longinus and that the spear was preserved as a sacred relic is pure legend. And wholly legendary is the chalice, the Grail : the Gospel authors do not mention that Jesus' blood was caught in a vessel.

In matters like these we begin to move away from the Gospel texts and from orthodox Christianity. It is significant, moreover, that Jesus Christ is not once mentioned by name in the libretto; isn't this a curious thing in a 'Gospel'? In fact he is referred to only rarely, and then as Saviour and Redeemer. Nothing at all is said of his life, with the exception of references to the Last Supper and his death on the cross.

Still more divergent from Christian orthodoxy is the eucharistic meal in the great hall of Monsalvat. Whereas, according to Roman-Catholic dogma, by means of the sacral and institutional repetition of Jesus' words at the Last Supper, bread and wine are changed into his Body and Blood, just the reverse takes place in the castle hall. At the end of Act I the squires and knights, assembled for the ritual, sing : "Blood and body of that holy gift ... now turn for your refreshment into the wine poured out for you, into the bread that feeds you today". How anybody can make a Christian drama out of this is a mystery to me.

4. The anti-female trend of this opera

The Knights of the Grail form a closed and secluded community with esoteric characteristics, centred around the symbols of Spear and Grail.

The sacred area in the middle of which Monsalvat is situated resembles an Indian (Buddhist) 'asrama' or hermitage, while, as Carl Suneson writes, "the Knights of the Grail represent Indian ascetes rather than Christian temple servants"[*]. The community is all-male, the knights having vowed chastity. The tenor of the libretto is strongly anti-female, even anti-sexual. The great representative of femininity is Kundry.

Wagner found her, or rather her name (Cundriê) in Wolfram's poem, for his Kundry is really an amalgam of the ambivalent traits of this Cundriê and of Mary of Magdalen : human and animal-like, wild and subdued, sinful and longing for forgiveness, all in the same person. When she first enters the scene, she looks like a witch with her long, loose hair and her girdle of snake skins. 'The wild woman', Gurnemanz calls her; "I never do good", she says of herself. And indeed, Amfortas is incurably ill just because he has sinned with this wild woman. Klingsor, her master, names her 'primeval witch, rose of hell' and says that she has formerly been Herodias, the murderous woman who instigated the death of John the Baptist.

So all that is bad is concentrated in Kundry, culminating in her sexual magic. "I well know the spell that forever binds you to serve me again", Klingsor assures her, or in other words, sex is the fatal instrument of the evil one. But when she tries her art on Parsifal she fails. The same happens to the Flower Maidens, who are also servants of Klingsor, when they attempt to overwhelm him with their erotic attractions. There is a radical opposition here between sex and eroticism on the one hand and purity and chastity on the other. When King Ludwig II of Bavaria asked the composer why chastity is needed for acquiring knowledge and pity, he only answered that this is 'a terrible secret'.

---

[*] Carl Suneson, Richard Wagner und die indische Geisteswelt. Leiden, 1989 (translated from the Swedish by Gert Kreutzer), p. 89.

5. The realms of the Good and Evil

The personification of this purity is Parsifal. It is remarkable that Wagner changed Wolfram's 'Parzival' into his own 'Parsifal'. According to the composer, the meaning of this name is 'the Innocent Fool'. That this a false etymology did not bother him at all. He found it in Joseph von Görres' edition of 'Lohengrin' (1813) in which this scholar suggests that 'Parsifal' is derived from the Arabic 'pars or parsh fal' i.e. the pure or poor fool [*]. It is because of his innocence, his purity, that he will ultimately replace Amfortas and become the new king of Monsalvat. Here we have the dualistic opposition of purity and impurity, of innocence and guilt, of sinlessness and sin that is so dear to the Gnostic heart.

Equally conspicuous is the radical opposition of Evil and the Good, made apparent in the absolute contrast of the realms of Klingsor and Monsalvat. The castle lies in a large clearing in a forest that is 'shady and solemn but not gloomy'; the clearing itself is a pleasant, open landscape with a background of gently rising flowery meadows. This landscape is at its most beautiful on Good Friday, for then the 'Karfreitagszauber' takes place. "Now all creation rejoices." And Parsifal exclaims : "Never did I see so fresh and charming the grass, the blossoms and the flowers, nor did they smell so sweet of youth or speak with such tender love to me". This beauty and this youthful force of nature must not surprise us because Monsalvat is 'the realm of the true faith'.

Klingsor, on the contrary, lives 'secluded in a valley' in the direction of a rich heathen land, by which Moorish Spain is meant. However, he has succeeded in turning the desert into a garden; natural beauty in this garden (tropical vegetation, luxurious display of flowers) is not the gift of the Creator but the product of black magic. In it "women of infernal beauty bloomed", the Flower Maidens. It is all artificial. When Parsifal has caught the Spear in its flight and made the sign of the cross with it over Klingsor's magic garden, his "castle sinks as if by an

---

[*] See Suneson o.c. 88.

earthquake". The garden swiftly withers into a desert; faded flowers are strewn on the ground. The triumph of the Good over Evil is complete.

6. Redemption

This brings us to a still more important theme, that of Redemption. When the play opens, the purity of the Grail Knights is not unsullied. Gurnemanz has to admit that Klingsor has succeeded in ruining 'full many of us'. His principal victim is King Amfortas who lies ailing in the castle. Hence the importance of water in this opera, the purifying element par excellence. Already in the very first scene we see Amfortas carried to the bath he has to take every day in order to find relief for his suffering. In Klingsor's garden there is no water whereas in the stage-directions for the Monsalvat area a spring is expressly mentioned. In the last act Gurnemanz and Kundry bring Parsifal to this well. Here the woman washes the hero's feet, and the old sage sprinkles his head with water from the fountain. "Then let him be free of stain, and the dust of lenghty wanderings now be washed from him." In other words, the water from the 'holy spring' washes away the whole past and prepares the hero for the future.

Redemption and salvation are key-words in this opera. The name of the castle is already a pointer, 'Monsalvat' = Mount of Salvation. At first there is only talk of relief for Amfortas, but then we hear from Gurnemanz that he is "anxiously imploring some sign of salvation". During the first ceremony in the castle hall the youths seem to answer him when they sing of 'the great Redeemer, the Saviour'. It is only after Parsifal's victory over Klingsor and the subsequent disappearance of his magic garden that Redemption becomes fully possible. It is destined for human beings but no less for nature. In fact, nature is redeemed before Kundry and Amfortas. This is the real significance of the Karfreitagszauber. "Thus all Creation gives thanks, all that here blooms and soon fades, now that nature, absolved from sin, today gains its day of innocence."

7. Parsifal the Redeemer

As the play proceeds it becomes increasingly clear that the Redeemer is not Jesus Christ but Parsifal. Or rather, the first Saviour was Jesus whose place is gradually taken over by the young hero. It takes a long time (the ten years of his wanderings in unknown regions) for Parsifal to recognize this role. During his passionate encounter with Kundry he says something remarkable. "The Saviour's lament I hear there, the lament, ah, the lamentation of his profaned sanctuary : 'Redeem me, rescue me from hands defiled by sin'." Here Jesus the Redeemer is declared powerless and the work of salvation incomplete; a second Redeemer is needed who will save the first one.

When Parsifal has pushed off Kundry, he at once knows that he is this second Redeemer. "I offer redemption to you in your sin", he says to her. When he enters the Grail precincts after ten years for the second time, he announces to Gurnemanz : "I dare think myself ordained". He is then duly anointed as king. He expresses his new self-consciousness to Kundry by telling her : "Believe in the Redeemer!". After having baptized Kundry, he performs his great task by touching Amfortas' side with the Holy Spear.

The opposition between Parsifal and Amfortas - the contrast is often overlooked - is of a dualistic nature. Amfortas succumbed to Kundry, Parsifal rejected her. Amfortas gambled away the Holy Spear, Parsifal regained it. Over against the effectual Parsifal who goes straight to the point stands the depressive, sickly Amfortas who feels inclined to give up everything. No wonder that the young hero becomes king in Amfortas' place.

7. Redemption and knowledge

Redemption and knowledge are closely interconnected. The Redeemer is someone who possesses knowledge. In the first scene Amfortas says that he awaits somebody who is 'enlightened through compassion' ('durch Mitleid wissend'); this person will be 'the pure fool' ('der reine Tor').

That the future Redeemer must be a 'fool' means that he must be bare of all common knowledge, whether of a practical or of a scholarly kind. What he needs is a very special, an esoteric knowledge. That Parsifal lacks all common knowledge is proved by the fact that he does not know who his parents are nor even his own name. "Such a dullard I never found before, save Kundry!", the astounded Gurnemanz exclaims. He does not realize yet that it is precisely this dullness that makes Parsifal capable of performing his redeeming work.

The erotic encounter with Kundry convinces him that it is not 'carnal knowledge' that he needs. As soon as he has snatched the Holy Spear from Klingsor's hands, he understands that redeeming knowledge will be his lot. It even dawns upon him that he himself will be the Redeemer. "But one weapon serves, only the Spear that smote you (Amfortas) can heal your wound ... O Blessed be your suffering that gave pity's mighty power and purest wisdom's might to the timorous fool (des reinsten Wissens Macht dem zagen Toren gab)."

8. A neo-Gnostic drama

The attentive reader will have remarked by now that with Wagner's opera 'Parsifal' we are in the presence of a (neo-)Gnostic work full of dualistic elements. The world of the opera is totally different from the ordinary walks of life, peopled as it is with a priest-king and his hieratic knights, with a magician and his demoniac female servants, and with Parsifal, 'der reine Tor'. When Parsifal returns to Monsalvat, he tells Gurnemanz that he left a very imperfect world behind him. "Through error and the path of suffering I came ...; battles and conflicts forced me from my path." But now he comes to bring perfection to the brotherhood of the Grail; Monsalvat will become the new and definitely healed world.

Life in the castle bears no resemblance whatsoever to our day-in day-out existence; it is wholly centred on the performance or non-performance of the sacred ritual. Parsifal who has scarcely any connection with ordinary humanity is virtually a Messiah, acting as a Redeemer and spending salvation. His redeeming power is the consequence of the knowledge he possesses. This is the most telling Gnostic element in this opera.

9. Hitler and Wagner's music

It was in the night of March 7, 1936. In the train that hastened on through the dark Ruhr region, spectrally illuminated by flaming blast-furnaces, Adolf Hitler sat. Germany's Führer had just experienced one of his great moments of triumph; he had visited the reoccupied Rhineland, everywhere applauded by enthousiastic crowds. Now he was returning to Munich and pensively leaning back in his seat he ordered that a record of the overture to 'Parsifal' should be played. In the deep silence that followed he said, as if to himself : "Aus Parsifal baue ich meine Religion" ('out of Parsifal I build my religion'), and then : "nur im Heldengewand kann man Gott dienen" ('only in a hero's garment can one serve God') [*].

Bring a hundred historians together and ask them whether they have ever seen Wagner's Parsifal. Ninety of them will tell you that they never go to an opera at all. Of the ten others eight will answer that they love opera but loathe Wagner. The remaining two may profess to be Wagner fans but the first, by some strange chance, has never seen Parsifal; the other has but it was twenty-five years ago, so he does not remember much of it. This explains why not one of the historians who occupied themselves with Hitler - Bullock, Fest, Maser, Toland, Görlitz, Gisevius, you name them - pays any attention to this remarkable utterance.

Hitler, it is well-known, was a Wagner fan if there ever was one. He simply adored this composer's music, just as he venerated the Wagner family. That sly and witty girl Friedelind, granddaughter of

---

[*] Hans Frank, Im Angesicht des Galgens. Deutung Hitlers und seiner Zeit auf Grund eigener Erlebnisse und Erkenntnisse. München-Gräfeling, 1953, p. 213.

Richard, twisted the great Führer of all the Germans round her little finger. Hitler's Wagner adoration is a sufficient reason for countless music-lovers to abhor Wagner as much as they detest Hitler. The usual comment is that both were rabid anti-Semites. It is generally considered that Wagner's musics tended to make Hitler hysteric and aggressive.

Instead, Wagner's music had a soothing, a relaxing influence on the Führer. The friend of his youth, August Kubizek, testified to this. "When he listened to Wagner's music he was a changed man; his violence left him; he became quiet, yielding, and tractable. His gaze lost its restlessness; his own destiny, however heavily it may have weighed upon him, became unimportant. He no longer felt lonely and outlawed and misjudged by society [*]. This is confirmed by Ernst ('Putzi') Hanfstaengl, Hitler's friend in Munich after 1919, a very wealthy and cultivated man, and a famous drawing-room lion. On Christmas Eve 1924 Hitler had Hanfstaengl play the record of the 'Liebestod' in 'Tristan und Isolde'. After this, Hanfstaengl declared, he was as if transformed; suddenly, he was relaxed, as so often when hearing Wagner, almost merry [**]. Would Hitler had listened more frequently to Wagner!

Hitler loved opera, in particular the operas of Richard Wagner. 'Lohengrin' was his first opera ever, in 1901 when he was no more than twelve years old. We know for certain that he saw Wagner's 'Rienzi' in November 1906 in the opera theatre in Linz; it made an enormous impression on him. During his first visit to Vienna, in May 1906, he made the acquaintance of 'Tristan und Isolde'. Visits to the famous opera houses of the Austrian capital during the first year of his stay there - 1908 -, made the list fairly complete, although other Wagnerian operas were to follow. Wagner never bored him; many a Wagnerian work he saw

---

[*] August Kubizek, Young Hitler. The story of our friendship. London (1954), p. 143 (shortened translation of 'Adolf Hitler, mein Jugendfreund". Graz, 1953).

[**] Ernst Hanfstaengl, Zwischen Weissem und Braunem Haus. Memoires eines politischen Aussenseiters. München, 1970, p. 163/164.

dozens of times. Some libretti he knew by heart; he could whistle or hum many Wagnerian motifs, as he often did.

Among his great favourites was Parsifal; it is ascertained that he saw it in the Festspielhaus at Bayreuth in 1933. Sometimes he acted as a Parsifal-exegete. During the Wagner festival of 1936 he was overheard remarking to Goebbels with whom he sat in the restaurant how much more beautiful Parsifal would be, if the Flower Maidens were to perform stark naked in it. This would become possible as soon as Nazism would have produced a superior human race [*].

10. Hitler's identification with Parsifal

What attracted Hitler so strongly in this opera? Parsifal did not know who his father was; his father had disappeared and died before he was born. The idea of a fatherless boy brought up solely by his mother struck a deep chord with him. He had not greatly loved the Alois Hitler to whom he owed his life; this gruff, unpleasant, authoritarian man died when his son was thirteen years old. Unconsciously he must have wished that the father had died much earlier so that he could have remained alone with the mother he adored. It could easily be argued that Klara Hitler's influence on the young man was very much greater than that of his father.

Hitler's relation to his beloved mother was not unequivocal. If it is true that he adored her, it is equally true that he manipulated her, sometimes in his usual brutal way. She knew all the time that she could not keep him, her one and only love. For she had never loved her callous husband Alois, twenty-three years older than she was, and whose third wife she became when she was already made pregnant by him. In the spring of 1907 it became clear that her son would be off to Vienna as soon as he could. Klara fell ill, cancer was diagnozed, and a breast was amputated.

---

[*] Friedelind Wagner, The Royal Family of Bayreuth. London, 1948, p. 129.

In spite of the condition of his mother, eighteen-year old Adolf departed for the capital in September 1907. His mother stood weeping at the top of the staircase of their house in Linz-Urfahr. But go he did. In October a neighbour notified him of the fact that his mother's condition was rapidly deteriorating. He returned and saw her die in December. When all was over, he returned to Vienna. In my opinion his mother lost the will to live when she recognized in her son the same heartlessness her husband had always shown her. Then she really became 'Heart's Sorrow'.

It is not impossible that Hitler never had a clear conscience about the way he had treated his mother. He had adored her, he continued to venerate her almost religiously (while forgetting his father), but he had also maltreated her. Was he not, at least partly, guilty of her death? Did it touch a sore spot in his heart when he heard Gurnemanz speak to Parsifal of "your mother whom you deserted, and who now frets and grieves for you"? And was this reproach not also directed at him : "You did not consider her woe, her desperate grief, when you finally did not return and left no trace behind"? And did not Parsifal's outcry : "Mother! Sweet, dear mother! Your son, your son it was who killed you!", also refer to him?

There is still more. Whereas father Alois did not believe in his recalcitrant son, his mother did, to such an extent that Helm Stierlin felt justified in calling Hitler 'the delegate of his mother' [*]. It is not, of course, as if she foresaw that her son would once become Führer and Reichkanzler of the German Reich. But she was convinced that he would become a great painter - this in contrast to her husband who had not for a moment believed in the artistic capacities of the boy. This comment of hers is deeply significant : "Adolf will find his way throug the world, without pardon (rücksichtslos), as though he was alone in the world" [**]. One feels compelled to state that Hitler inherited his identity from his mother, not from his father.

---

[*] Helm Stierlin. Familienperspektive. Frankfurt a.M., 1975. P. 73/74.

[**] August Kubizek, Hitler, mein Jugendfreund. Graz, 1953. P. 158.

In Parsifal's mother Herzeleide Hitler saw another woman who wanted for her son something quite different from what her husband had seen as his future. "To shield you (Parsifal) from like peril (as had felled his father - F.), she deemed it her highest duty's task. She strove to hide and shelter you safe afar from weapons and from men's strife and fury." It is Kundry who revealed this to the hero as well as what his name (= his identity) is. It was, indeed, his dying father who had chosen this name for his still unborn son, but it was transmitted to him by his mother through Kundry. "Parsifal? Once in a dream my mother called me that."

There is a period in Hitler's life that is strikingly similar to a time in Parsifal's life. After his first visit to Monsalvat, Parsifal disappears, only to return ten years later. It is not disclosed where he has lived all those years. But when he came back, he knew what he had to do and was ready to do it. It must not surprise us that precisely at that moment his name (his real identity) is revealed to him. Hitler left Linz for good in 1908. Then followed five empty years in Vienna plus an equally aimless one in Munich. Next came the four bloody years on the front. In November 1918, when Hitler was being treated in a military hospital at Pasewalk in Pomerania for a blindness caused by gas, it suddenly dawned upon him, almost in a vision as he later described it, that he had to become a politician. He then was ready to perform the (still unspecified) task his mother had had in mind for him. And just as Parsifal encountered a desperate situation in the castle, Hitler started his career in the chaotic turmoil of the German revolution years 1918-1919.

11. Hitler-Parsifal as the Redeemer

The many Christian, or rather pseudo-Christian, elements in this opera must have appealed strongly to Hitler. It is true that, since he was sixteen years old, he longer practised the Roman-Catholic faith in which he had been raised (by his mother, not by his non-practising father). But it would be a very grave misunderstanding to assume that he now became totally irreligious. Nothing would be more beside the mark! It was only in 1937 that he declared himself entirely rid of 'the religious notions of his early years'. It was only then that he could fully develop his new Parsifal-religion.

However, he always remained nostalgic for the solemn rituals of the Roman-Catholic Church. He rediscovered them in this opera : bread and wine, blood and water play a great role in it, just as the chalice of the Last Supper. Then there was Kundry's baptism and Parsifal's anointment as king. The most characteristic ritual element is, of course, the eucharistic feast in the great castle hall. It had a still greater impact that Parsifal more and more assumes the traits of a Messiah. It is not only that is he literally called 'redeemer', but a dove descends on him, reminding us strongly of what happened when Jesus was baptized in the river Jordan.

There are many proofs which show that Hitler too saw himself as a Messiah, a Redeemer, identifying himself with Jesus Christ and gradually putting himself in his place. He wanted, he said on Christmas Eve 1928 in Munich, "to bring to an end the work that Jesus had begun, but that he had not completed". "From our movement redemption emanates", he said in October 1923 [*], "this has almost become a new religious creed." One feels justified to detect identification with Jesus Christ in these words : "I will be crucified if it is believed that I have not fulfilled my duty", or when he wrote that "Christ had been the greatest fighter against world Jewry" [**].

Redemption from what? Adolf Hitler suffered all his life from the idea the that he had Jewish blood in his veins. The immediate cause of this fear was that Hitler's father Alois was an illegitimate child. Born in 1837, he was named Schicklgruber after his mother Maria Anna; it was only in 1887 that he could adopt the name Hitler (a corruption of the name of the man in whose family he had been raised, Johann von

---

[*] Joachim C. Fest, Hitler. Eine Biographie. Frankfurt a.M, 1973. P. 263.
[**] Adolf Hitler, Mein Kampf (I), 1924. P. 227.

Nepomuk Hütler). Alois' mother never disclosed the indentity of the begetter. Adolf did not know it neither did her grandson.

There ran persistent rumours that the man had been Jewish - rumours that, however false and tendentious, Hitler feared might be true. Since we perfectly know what he thought of Jews and Jewish blood, he must have felt oppressed and anguished by this idea. "We all are suffering from the disease of the mixed, tainted blood", he said to Hermann Rauschning *, "how can we purify and redeem this?" Since we may be certain that Hitler saw himself as the principal victim of this corrupted blood, we can infer that he applied the closing words of the Parsifal-drama : "our Redemeer redeemed" to himself. For he too needed redemption. He must have been fascinated by the opposition between the unadulterated blood of the 'pure fool' and the corrupted blood of King Amfortas. He even called this, in that same conversation with Rauschning, 'the real subject of this profound drama'.

12. Dualism

This brings us to another element in 'Parsifal', namely its dualism. There is hardly another opera of Wagner in which the composer demonstrated his dualistic philosophy of life so palpably as in his last one. The basic unbridgeable opposition is that between the sacred region of Monsalvat and Klingsor's magic garden. Connected with this opposition is that of the innocent Parsifal and the thoroughly evil Klingsor. This appealed to Hitler who thought just as dualistically as his venerated Wagner. It would have pleased him that Parsifal proved able to destroy his enemy, together with his realm, through the sign of the cross. Did he not possess a cross of his own that would annihilate this wicked world, the swastika?

---

* Hermann Rauschning, Gespräche mit Hitler. Zürich/New York, 1940. P. 216/217.

13. The role of knowledge

The essential question, not only in 'Parsifal', but also in Hitler's ideology, is how the redemption was to be achieved. Certainly, not as in Christianity by grace, by Jesus' expiatory death on the cross. This would have made Hitler dependent on God's grace and the redemptive deed of somebody else. No, redemption is brought about by knowing, by knowledge. Parsifal begins as somebody who is unknowing, even as a 'fool', but gradually he becomes 'knowing'. The first thing he discovers is who he is himself. For this drama is also the story of the discovery of identity, of a personal, a finished identity that Hitler himself so painfully missed.

In the final scene in which Parsifal is acting as the officiating High Priest, he says that he has now acquired 'purest wisdom's might' ('reinsten Wissens Macht'). Hitler understood perfectly well what that meant; identifying with his hero, he called the congregation of the Knights 'the brotherhood of the knowing' [*]. Speaking of 'knowledge' and of 'those who know', both Hitler and Wagner harked back to that ancient and powerful ideology of the first centuries of our present era, the Gnosis, Christianity's oldest and most obstinate opponent. With the spread of secularism since the days of the Enlightenment, the Gnosis again acquired control of the European genius.

The substantial elements of the Gnosis - election, élitism, dualism, ascent, utter rejection of this wicked world, victory over evil, and above all, redemption through knowledge - all return in Wagner's opera. It is for this reason that Jeziorkowski called it 'the Pontifikalamt (solemn High Mass) of the bourgeois Gnosticism of the end of the nineteenth century" [**].

---

[*] Rauschning ib.

[**] Klaus Jeziorkowksi, Empor ins Licht. Gnostizismus and Licht-Symbolik in Deutschland um 1900. In : Eine Iphigenie rauchend. Aufsätze und Feuilletons zur deutschen Tradition. Frankfurt a.M., 1987. P. 156.

14. The road to the Gnosis

In Chapter II of Volume VII I described the development through the ages of the terms 'gnosis' and 'gignooskein', the ordinary Greek words for knowledge and knowing. From Homer and Hesiod through all the poets and philosophers of the Hellenic and Hellenistic civilizations, these terms always denoted a special brand of knowledge. This knowledge has nothing to do with the sort of knowledge we can acquire by means of experience or study or training. The Greeks used several other words for for practical knowledge and the like. There always adhered a special aura to gnosis and gignooskein which lifted them out of the common range of meanings. This was an aura of intuition, sudden insights, revelation of mysteries, and sometimes of a knowledge with a special power, that of redemption.

In Chapter IV of Volume VI as well as in Chapter I of Volume VII I sketched the road to the Gnosis, the several stages that finally led to its dawning as a full-blown ideology in the first century AD. In the last centuries before the birth of Christ many elements of this ideology were already plainly discernible.

Of course, I emphasized naturally, first and foremost, that specific meaning of knowledge, a knowledge of a superior and uncommon kind, spontaneous, esoteric, and even divine. Connected with this is the élitism that was common to so many Hellenistic scholars and philosophers, that jealously guarding of the secrets of the guild against the vile curiosity of those who were doomed to remain unknowing. Some philosophical circles closely resembled secret societies with an esoteric character. In order to join them, the adept often had to undergo a ritual of initiation. Initiation was very much en vogue in that period; one need only think of the mystery religions that flourished in the Hellenistic and Roman worlds.

There was much esotericism in the schools and sects of the Hellenistic world. The general idea of those who considered themselves elect and initiated was that their insights were of a superior order, far beyond the ken of ordinary people, insights that were not derived from the world that is common to all of us but that were revealed to the chosen.

This almost inevitably led to a stern dogmatism and to the absolute incapability to see anything of value the spiritual positions of other persons or groups, even in those of similar schools of thought. By the same token we find mysticism, a predilection for mysteries, for number theories, for magic, for theosophic speculations. The consequence of this is the contempt in which rational history and all kinds of historical evidence are held. All these elements we find back in the Gnosis proper.

15. Is a definition of 'Gnosis' possible?

How comfortable it would be if only we had a clearcut definition of the concept 'Gnosis', so that, with its help, we could easily distinguish what is Gnostic from what is not! It should preferably be a simple definition, easy to handle, for instance one with only one lemma and no more than one or two sublemmata. But alas! such a yardstick does not exist. Gnoseologues do not agree on what is the main characteristic of the Gnosis. Is it the redeeming Knowledge? The Fall? The Saviour? The elect? The rejection of the world? The eschaton? Its dualism?

The problem is that not all systems dubbed Gnostic display all these features, and or tend to emphasize them in different ways. For instance, most systems fiercely reject the world and view it as doomed to destruction. But in other systems or a milder climate prevails; the present world, after the departure of the redeemed to the luminous upper world, is allowed to subsist, albeit in a state of blissful ignorance of the existence of a better world.

There is, however, one Gnostic element on which all scholars agree : its dualism. This does not mean that these scholars all consider dualism the distinguishing feature of the Gnosis. But to quote Karl Prümm : "One should always insist on a metaphysical foundation of dualism as the true characterization of what Gnosis is" [*]. To put it as

---

[*] Prümm, Gnosis 12, note 2 (see Bibliography).

succinctly as possible, all Gnostic systems are fundamentally dualistic. A long time after I had completed this preface I read Couliano's fine book on the dualistic Gnosis[*] (see Bibliography); I see that he takes exactly the same position. "The only correct **description** of Gnosticism consists in stating that it represents a group of **dualistic** systems ... **Dualism**, therefore, is the unique and the most general of the features that apply to Gnosticism in its entirety ... Gnosticism is **always** dualistic and makes use of **dualistic myths**" (his emphases).

Simple as this may seem, it, nevertheless, presents two problems. The first is that this thesis is not reversible : whereas Gnostic systems without exception are dualistic, by no means every dualistic system is Gnostic. In the volumes of this series that have appeared so far, we have reviewed many dualistic ideologies which could certainly not be regarded as 'Gnostic' does.

The second problem is far more formidable. The attentive reader will have remarked at once that the statement : all Gnostic systems are dualistic, is, in fact, a petitio principii, a circular argument. We start from the premise that we know what 'Gnostic' means; this we do by using the term 'Gnostic' in the beginning, instead of at the end of our argument. This is a false assumption : we still have to determine what 'Gnostic' is. Therefore, we are not allowed to use the concept 'dualism' to detect out Gnostic systems.

We can solve our first problem by defining what kind or kinds of dualism are meant in Gnostic systems (even granted that we presume to know what 'Gnostic' is). We saw in the Prümm text quoted above that this scholar qualified the term 'dualism' by adding 'metaphysical'. This is indeed correct but it is not enough. Gnostic systems are always poised on two kinds of dualism. First, there is metaphysical dualism : the upper world, the Pleroma, is essentially different from and opposed to the nether, material world, the cosmos. This is a horizontal dualism. Next there is anthropological dualism, one between the elect, the chosen, the redeemed, the Gnostic pneumatics, and the hylics, the matter-people,

---

[*] Couliano, Les gnoses 167/168 (see Bibliography).

who will not be saved. This is a vertical dualism, but only present in the nether world.

In both cases my definition of dualism applies : that of two opposed and irreconcilable principles or systems or groups of people or even worlds, with no intermediate terms connecting them, while one of them is seen as inferior to the other. In the first case, that of metaphysical dualism, we have to do with relative dualism since the nether world is dependent on the upper one; the cosmos does not lead a sovereign existence. Whether in the second case, that of anthropological dualism, the dualism is relative depends on the system we are dealing with. In some, even in most systems, the pneumatics and the hylics, the Gnostics and the others, the elect and the massa damnata, are opposed in the most absolute way. But in certain others it is possible for a hylic to become a pneumatic Gnostic. The Valentinians interpose a third group between the pneumatics and the hylics, namely the psychics, the soul-people. This does not really do away with the anthropological dualism, because the intermediate group is destined to disappear : psychics become either pneumatics or hylics.

We may be allowed to conclude that the term 'dualism' becomes more workable by terming it 'metaphysical-anthropological'. As far as I know, there are no non-Gnostic dualistic systems that are both horizontally and vertically dualistic, metaphysically and anthropologically. I think that in this we have a divining-rod useful for detecting Gnostic systems. If we do this we may avoid using the word 'Gnostic' right at the start of our argument. We could then say : any system with this double dualism differs basically from all others that do not contain it, whether dualistic or not, but is of one group with all others in which it occurs.

16. Gnostic dualism

However important and influential the Gnosis was in the history of mankind and as a subject of the history of religions, I should not concede it the ample space it is getting in this work if it were not viscerally dualistic. Gnostics prosper on radical oppositions; with them it is always either - or, with nothing in between. Metaphysically there is the opposition of the good God who, however, remains a 'deus absconditus', a hidden god, and the bad Demiurge with his helpers who created the world.

Then there is the ethical dualism of Good and Evil. Once again this a question of either - or; in Gnostic ideology there are, as in Jesus' parable, no fields where the wheat is growing together with the tares. If one is not entirely good, then one is entirely bad. This leads to yet another opposition, that of the 'massa damnata', the great mass of people who unwittingly go to their doom, and the few elect who will be redeemed by the possession of Knowledge. In fact, the Knowledge is the redemption.

The world in which we live, our factual, historical world, is evil from the time of its inception. As Peter Sloterdijk says, Creation and Fall are identical in the Gnostic vision; the world as such is fallen, wicked, doomed [*]. It cannot be saved, it cannot be recreated, there will be no new heaven and new earth, it will be destroyed. Hans Jonas has explained that the Gnosis must be not be seen as 'revolutionary' in the traditional sense of the word . According to modern political use of this term, 'revolution' signifies a radical endeavour to replace an existing socio-political situation that is judged unsatisfactory, by another, ideal or at any rate much better, situation. But in this kind of revolutionary activity the Gnosis proves totally uninterested.

It might, says Jonas, rather be called, 'reactionary', because this attitude with regard to the present world can easily urge people to refrain from attempts to ameliorate their situation. But if we see in 'revolution' an attitude that wants to lift the world off its hinges, then, he concludes, the Gnosis is eminently revolutionary [**]. The true Gnostic

---

[*] Peter Sloterdijk, Die wahre Irrlehre. Über die Weltreligion der Weltlosigkeit. In : Weltrevolution der Seele. Eine Lese- und Arbeitsbuch der Gnosis von der Spätantike bis zur Gegenwart. Herausgeber Peter Sloterdijk/Thomas H. Macho. 1991 Artemis & Winkler Verlag. P. 39.

[**] Hans Jonas, Gnosis I 148, where he spoke of an "Umwertung'.

may say, with a line of the German poet Friedrich Rückert : "Ich bin der Welt abhanden gekommen" ("I have done with this world"), and state as his ideal, with Rückert again : "Ich bin gestorben dem Weltgetümmel und ruh' in einem stillen Gebiet! Ich leb' allein in meinem Himmel" ('I am dead to the bustle of this world and repose alone in a tranquil domain living alone in my heaven') *.

For Gnostics, the world as it exists is something negative. This prompted Sloterdijk to speak of the Gnosis as 'negative psychology' - a psychology that develops into psychotherapeutics, in so far as it is an attempt to disengage the elect from the hypnotic power of the world. The 'pneuma', the divine spark in man, must be liberated and shown the way back to the primal godhead. Gnosis, knowledge, is in fact 'knowledge of the way'. But one can only set foot on this way if one realizes that man is utterly lost, imprisoned and hypnotized by this world as he is **. A corollary of this sentiment is the typical Gnostic individualism. Gnostics were only intent on freeing the divine spark in their own souls; they could not care less what happened to others. The idea of a 'people of God' that is current in Judaism and Christianity, or the related idea that we should love our neighbour like ourselves was completely alien to them.

Redeemed, fortified, and protected by Knowledge, the pneuma will unfailingly find its way back through all the spheres that envelop the world, past all the wicked archonts, even past the bad Demiurge, to arrive safely in the realm of the hidden God who, as the negation of all that exists, of all that we see and do and are, at the same time is an un-God.

---

* This poem was set to music by Gustav Mahler.

* Sloterdijk o.c. 46-48.

17. A short summary of what the Gnosis teaches

I hardly ever meet anyone who is knowledgeable about the Gnosis; this even applies to highly erudite persons, including classical scholars. Nearly all of my readers, therefore, will be treading in this volume on virgin soil. This is one difficulty, but it is fairly minimal when set against the deeply esoteric naturer of Gnostic writings being esoteric to a degree. They are not destined for laymen but only for the initiated; they are couched in opaque, sometimes impenetrable language. I have done my best to make Gnostic doctrine accessible to the reader; if the matter I am bringing sometimes will be found difficult to understand, I am afraid I cannot help it. I am, I believe, sinning by simplification rather than by making things more obscure than they are. I hope the reader will be helped by the graphs of the Gnostic systems to be found at the end at the book. Furthermore I will here set out the main lines that are common to all, or nearly all Gnostic systems.

It will, I feel, help the reader if he bears in mind that in the Gnosis a circular course is followed : it all starts from God, out of God, and returns to God, into God. The apex of the whole system is the prime godhead who has no name and is in fact unknowable; he is often called the Father of the All, although he is not the creator of the world. Under him is the Pleroma, or Fullness, the upper, celestial world, emanating from him but not containing him. This celestial world is peopled with celestial beings (powers, aeons, emanations) who are divine entities partaking in the essence of the prime godhead and are united with each other in a common identity. What kinds of aeons there are, and how many, differs from system to system, but usually their quality deteriorates the greater the distance from the first godhead. This explains why some cosmic or metaphysical catastrophe, usually called the Fall, or Error, is liable to take place in the lowest part of the Pleroma.

However different the reports about this catastrophe may be, they always amount to the fact that some part of the divine essence, of the Light, becomes enclosed in the nether world, the cosmos. This nether world is divided from the Pleroma by an almost impassable barrier.

Originally there is only formless matter there. Once again accounts differ as to how the cosmos is modelled from matter, but all of them take it for gratned that the cosmos was not the creation of the first godhead. Usually there is a world-maker in his own right, a Demiurge. Often he has co-rulers, the archons. At best, the Demiurge is ethically neutral, although invariably ignorant, which makes him bungle things, but more often he is wicked and evil-intentioned. The result is that the world is not a happy place to live in.

This would pose no problem at all, were it not for the sparks of Light that are imprisoned in matter, that is to say, in human bodies. In human beings this spark is called the Pneuma, the Spirit. These particles must not be destroyed together with the world. It is the task of the Saviour, sent by the prime godhead, whoever this Redeemer is, or whatever he is called, to collect these sparks of light and bring then back to the Pleroma whence they originate. For this it is necessary that at least a number of people should be saved from the grip of matter and the Demiurge; the means to effect this is Knowledge, knowledge of a superior kind that is, about the prime godhead and the Pleroma. Not many people want to become acquainted with it.

Those who accept the Gnosis are free from matter and imperfection and evil now; in fact they are already pleromic beings. What happens to them is that they realize that they once were god, part of god; this realization makes them god again. When they die, they leave soul and body behind, but their Pneuma, their Sprit, which is in fact the spark of Light, surges upwards through all the lower spheres, to become one again with the prime godhead.

17. How and why the Gnosis originated

Space is created for a religious or metaphysical dualism, for dualism, of the Gnostic type, for the Gnosis, when a dominating religion, an established and acknowledged religious system, begins to vacillate and loses its foothold in society. In foregoing volumes it has been related that this is what happened to the Olympian system. This process already started during the great classical period and accelerated in Hellenistic times. It is safe to say that in the last centuries before our era hardly any educated person still believed in the Homeric divinities, although, for reasons of socio-political expediency, their official cult still continued. The old faith had been relegated to the position of a literary heritage and a superstition that simple people still clung to.

But educated people no less than simple folk were also open to alternative religions, ranging from the mystery religions that were very much in vogue, to astrology, magic, and occultism. Or they underwent the impact of new philosophical systems, of the several philosophical doctrines of Hellenism, even including the most radical scepticism. Many of these trends, as Chapter III of Volume VI has amply shown, were dualistic to a degree, while gnosticizing tendencies too were not rare in this period.

The historical situation was not really conducive to stability. Though Alexander's great conquests had opened vistas of a new civilization, very little came of it. His successors relentlessly fought each other, his empire split up into inimical parts, every strip east of the Euphrates was lost. In the west loomed the Roman Empire, in the east its Parthian counterpart, both steadily encroaching upon the ever shrinking Hellenistic domain. There never originated a really Hellenistic culture, a harmonious amalgam of Hellenic and non-Hellenic civilizations; the Greeks proved viscerally incapable of overcoming their inveterate, age-old anti-barbarian attitude. In the process the polis, once the safe harbour of the Hellenes, lost almost all of its significance which was to lead to desorientation. The unavoidable result was an individualism which sometimes came perilously close to anarchism; the more respectable citizens retreated into self-complacency and political indifference. All this is described in Chapters I and II of Volume VI.

18. Two lines of transmission and where they converged

In Chapter I of Volume VII I described a great number of constitutive elements that went into the making of the Gnosis. These elements, I wrote, can be arranged along two lines of transmission, a western one starting from Greece, and an eastern one beginning in Iran and India. In the Hellenistic world, after the campaign of Alexander, when east and west became politically intertwined, these lines began to converge. We have no absolute certainty regarding the exact locality where these electric currents sparked off enough energy to give birth to the Gnosis. In all probability, to quote myself further, this happened in the Syrian region comprising Phoenicia, the hinterland east of Phoenicia called Coelesyria, Samaria, and Palestine. It was there that the great religions met and competed with each other : Judaism, Samaritanism, the Qumran sect of the Essenes, early Christianity, and pagan religions, including the official Olympian creed, the Hellenistic ruler cult, elements, moreover, of Egyptian and Mesopotamian religions, and the mystery religions. There indeed the situation was rife with syncretism. And the Gnosis is eactly this : a syncretistic religion, original but at the same feeding on many other creeds.

19. A Gnostic-dualistic spiritual climate

In fact, the whole spiritual climate of that time was Gnostic-dualistic to the core. Gnostic ideology, with its inherent dualism, began to take shape in the doctrine of Simon Magus, a Samaritan who was the contemporary of the Apostles, and in that of his successor Menander, another Samaritan, and perhaps also in the teaching of Saturnilos, a Syrian. Cerinthus, an independent Gnostic, came from Asia Minor, but he was a Jew. The Gnostic-dualistic texts of the so-called Pseudoclementina have in part a Judaeo-Christian background. The founder of the Carpocratian sect, Carpocrates, with his precocious son Epiphanes, originated a system that showed relations (albeit rather vaguely) with Judaism and early Christianity. These systems, all of them moving within a Judaeo-Christian ambit, are described more fully in Chapter III of Volume VII. With Carpocrates who was born in Alexandria we leave the Samaritan-Syrian orbit and move to Egypt. The present volume will be devoted to ideologies that originated in that country.

19. The position of Judaism and Christianity

It is a curious thing that Judaeo-Christian ideology proper has no part in these developments. In that wide sea of Gnostic-dualistic trends, tendencies, opinions, speculations, systems, the Old and New Testaments and the Talmud stand out like a rock. All three of them present fundamentally homogeneous views of life. However, one of my points is that there exist no systems that are seemlessly homogeneous from one end to the other. The Judaeo-Christian ones are no exception to this rule in that they too show rifts and fissures, antagonistic and even dualistic tendencies. The interested reader may find this elaborated for the Old Testament in Chapter II of Volume IV, for the New Testament in Chapter IV of Volume VII, and for the Talmud in Chapter VI of that same volume. In the end it was the Judaeo-Christian rock on which the Gnosis foundered.

20. The Gnosis on its course through the ages

Together with Christianity, but not in unison with it, the Gnosis competed for the hearts and minds of men. Great Gnostic schools of thought came into being, like those of Basilides, Valentinus, and Marcion, to mention only the most important. The last great Gnostic system was Manichaeism founded in the third century AD by the Iranian prophet Mani. It obviously touched a chord with people, the best-knowing adherent being Saint Augustine who around 370 was an ardent Manichee. It was already a sign of the changing times that Augustine converted to Christianity. The Gnosis steadily lost ground until it was finally superseded by the Christian faith.

But the Gnosis, with its visceral dualism, did not disappear from the scene. By no means! It subsisted underground, it continued its course through the ages in streams deep under the surface, to re-emerge suddenly from time to time. Such manifestations were, for instance, Bogomilism and Catharism during the Middle Ages. There were powerful gnosticizing elements in the German mysticism of Tauler and Meister Eckehardt, and still more in that of Jakob Boehme around 1600. From then on a neo-Gnosis began to develop, acquiring more and more momentum in the course of the last centuries. We need only think of modern science which has all the characteristics of mysteriosophic knowledge.

Is this neo-Gnosis slowly but certainly becoming a world religion, as Gilles Quispel dubbed it? Or rather, an anti-world religion? Will it attempt to, will it succeed in taking the place of orthodox Christianity which seems so very much on the wane? In the Preface of Volume VII I sketched the contrast between a neo-Gnostic ideology and biblical Christianity in the form of a comparison between the world of the High Priest Sarastro and that of the simple birdman Papageno. Seemingly the triumph is for Sarastro but Mozart's sympathies obviously were with Papageno. This volume I began with an analysis of Wagner's 'Parsifal' in which a neo-Gnostic ideology triumphantly appears. It tried to show how this creed was adopted by Adolf Hitler, the Gnostic dualist par excellence. He attempted to succeed where the great Gnostic prophets of Antiquity had failed, for he tried to make the triumph of the neo-Gnosis complete by breaking into splinters the rock on which the Gnosis had foundered sixteen centuries ago.

At the end of this work I have to thank some persons without whose help I could not have completed it. Dr. J.C.M van Winden, emeritus-professor of the Greek of Late Antiquity in Leiden State University, read and commented upon Chapter I and saved me from some errors. Dr. J.R. Dove, a retired associate professor of English and American literature living in Amsterdam, corrected, as always, my English courteously and accurately. We had many a chat 'over coffee', not only about this book but also about a great many other subjects. My daugher, Dr. Th.A.M. Smidt van Gelder-Fontaine, who has a family of four on her hands, besides having a job, and my other 'general reader', Dr. A. Budé, went through the whole text with their usual care and provided me with a number of clever and useful notes. To my great regret Dr. Budé has notified me that he is no longer able to act as a 'general reader'. I am deeply in debt to him for all he did for me in the course of so many years; let him remain assured not only of my immense gratitude but also of my lasting friendship. My wife Anneke brings up the rear; she always very carefully corrects the last version but one for typing errors; she was also a great help with the preparation of the diagrams of Gnostic systems at the end of the book. Finally, Mr. J.C. Gieben, friendly and businesslike as ever, saw this book through the press. To all of them I feel very grateful. But I alone assume full responsibility for the whole work, for its contents as well as for its typography and lay-out.

Volume IX is in preparation and will continue the argument on the Gnosis. After a final chapter on the Nag Hammadi Library it will shift the scene from Egypt to Asia Minor, to Marcion, the Mandaeans, and Mani and his Manichees.

P.F.M. Fontaine
Amsterdam (NL)

CHAPTER I

PHILO BETWEEN JEWISH ORTHODOXY AND
HELLENISTIC PHILOSOPHY

1. Alexandria, the Jewish metropole

The Jewish community of Alexandria in Egypt was the largest of all the Diaspora; it may have counted up to two hundred thousand souls. In the time that the town was a city of the Roman Empire, two of its five quarters were almost entirely inhabited by Jews. We do not know exactly how numerous its Jewish community was, but since Alexandria was one of the largest cities of the ancient world, the number of Jews within its confines must have been very large indeed. Apart from a well-to-do class of bankers and merchants, most Alexandrian Jews earned their living as artisans and shopkeepers. Their community was autonomous; its members were free to follow their own religious customs. The central synagogue was a very large building [1].

During the Ptolemaic period Alexandrian Jewry led an almost undisturbed existence, but things changed for the worse with the advent of the Roman era. The Hellenized Egyptians who had formed the ruling class under the Ptolemaeans were deprived of their power in favour of Roman officials. This meant that they now, as simple citizens, became the equals of the Jews who, in spite of their freedom, had always been considered second-class citizens. This led to friction between the two ethnic groups and to outbursts of anti-semitism on the part of the Egyptians.

Tension rose so high that in AD 38 armed 'Greeks' of Alexandria (= Hellenized citizens) fell upon the Jews in the town, slaughtering a great number of them, humiliating their elders in public, and desecrating their synagogues. These 'Greeks' profited from the permissive attitude of the Roman governor, Flaccus [2]. The Alexandrian rabble now demanded that statues of the emperor, Caligula, should be set up in the synagogues; Flaccus did not prove averse to this idea [3].

The persecuted Jews then decided to send an embassy to Rome of which the almost sixty years old Alexandrian philosopher Philo was the leader; he travelled to the capital in AD 46, the only established date of his life [4]. Although Flaccus was deposed, this did not mean that the emperor had become more cooperative. Quite the contrary! He even ordered a golden statue of himself to be erected in the Holy of Holies of the Jerusalem Temple. It was only his assassination on January 24, AD 41, that saved the Temple from this abomination. When they were in Rome, the psychopathic Caligula's persistent enmity drove Philo and his party almost to despair; they had every reason to fear for their lives.

As soon, however, as Claudius who was well known for his friendship towards the Jews became emperor, the Jews of Alexandria saw their chance and in their turn attacked the 'Greeks'. Order was only restored when Claudius reinstated the Jews in their old rights [5].

2. What is known of Philo's life

We have very little information about Philo's life [6]. It may be summed up in the terse communication that it spanned the period of (approximately) the years between 20 B.C. and A.D. 50; in consequence, he was a contemporary of Jesus Christ and of the Roman emperors Augustus, Tiberius, Caligula, and Claudius. Josephus, his fellow-Jew of a younger generation, mentions him only twice, saying merely that he wrote a lot on Jewish affairs [7], and that he was sent to Rome on an embassy [8].

He came from an extremely wealthy family, his brother being a rich banker; his clan entertained amiable relations with the Herodian princes as well as with the imperial court. This may well cause us to ask whether Philo was an orthodox Jewish believer. But orthodox or not - we shall have every occasion to study this question -, he practised the faith, at least in some important respects. It is certain that, if only once in his life, he visited Jerusalem and the Temple. He also attended the services in the synagogue on Sabbath days. Although he and his family were thoroughly hellenized, they considered themselves true to Jewish cult and customs [9].

Philo's reaction to the fateful news that Caligula wanted to place his statue in the Temple proves beyond all doubt that as a Jew he had his heart in the right place. "We stood speechless. Our nerves broke down ... Even if we got the permission for a second audience, what could we expect apart from inevitable death? So let it be, we shall know how to die. For a glorious death in defense of the Law is also a kind of life" [10].

The fact remains, however, that Philo had received such a solid grounding in Greek scholarship that, in regard to his erudition, he must be considered to have been thoroughly hellenized. His education had been that of a Greek of the upper layers of society : a profound training in Hellenic and Hellenistic literature, philosophy, and science. This is not to say that he did not know the Old Testament. On the contrary, he shows himself very well versed in it, but he read and studied it in the Greek translation, the Septuagint, which had originated in his native town. Alexandria was just the place where somebody with a marked taste for scholarship should have been born. Having replaced Athens, the town had become the greatest seat of learning in the Hellenistic world, rightly famous for its enormous library containing, it was said, all the works in Greek that had appeared so far. Small wonder that Philo's Greek is exellent. The reverse of the coin is that, in all probability, he did not know Hebrew [11].

3. Philo's writings

In default of a richly detailed biography relaying the story of Philo's life and containing deep psychological insights into his innermost mind, we have the large bulk of his writings, 38 works in all. The output of Philo is the first we possess more or less completely since the philosophical works of Plato and Aristotle. It must, however, be conceded that he does not often become personal in his works; there is no autobiography such as Flavius Josephus wrote one. Most of his books were handed down to us in Greek but some in Armenian translations [12].

According to Yehoshua Amir (Neumark), Philo's treatises can be divided into three groups. The first group involves an exposition of the Pentateuch as a legal code. Philo saw the five books of Moses not as the earliest history of mankind and the people of Israel, but as a law code. The second group is incomplete but contains "a philosophical interpretation of the Pentateuch ... completely disregarding their narrative content and transposing them by way of allegorization into a set of philosophical-mystical concepts". The third group consists of 'Questions and Answers to Genesis and Exodus' and has come down to us only in an Armenian translation. A number of philosophical treatises does not fall under these three headings are a number of philosophical treatises, among them the well-known one 'On the eternity of the world', two works on the troubles in Alexandria and the embassy to Rome which I mentioned already, and finally a disquisition on the contemplative life [13].

The scholarly and literary appreciation of Philo's work in the past centuries could not have been more divergent. To a great many authors he is a kind of genius and a profound thinker. Wolfson, singing his praise loudly, saw in him the man who had initiated the philosophy of the Schoolmen, not only those of Christianity, but no less of Judaism and Islam [14]. On the other hand, he bored Bousset to death [15], while in the view of other modern scholars he was pedantic, garrulous, and superficial [16]. The severest judgment on him has been passed by Festugière who maintained that it is not doubtful that Philo had no taste for wisdom (very probably the discipline of philosophy is meant - F.), and that he was not well grounded in philosophy. "One can read all Philo without encountering one original reflexion which denotes some personal experience ... It is always nothing but the conventional, the banalities of the handbook" [17].

4. Philo and the Old Testament

Yet in another passage Festugière seems to contradict this : "If anything is sincere in Philo, it is his love both of philosophy and the Bible. He possesses no genius but he is truly aspiring to wisdom" [18]. But as a Dominican priest Father Festugière should have known that the Bible, albeit the New Testament, says at the same time that no one is able to serve two masters. It is with philosophy and the Bible that we shall have to occupy ourselves; it remains to be seen which of these two Philo serves best. As Wilson states, "... in Philo, Judaism appears as both a philosophy and a religion, embracing in itself the best that others faiths could offer and speaking with an authority which they could not claim. It is not simply another mystery but, above all others, the only complete and perfect faith" [19]. The question is whether and in how far (Jewish biblical) religion and (Hellenic-Hellenistic) philosophy were really compatible with each other.

In the curious amalgam of religions and philosophical opinions that constituted Egyptian Hellenism, orthodox Judaism, strongly represented by Alexandrian Jewry, was a kind of 'Fremdkörper'. Regarding its main document, the Old Testament (in the original version), it cannot be maintained that it was 'hellenized' in any respect, although some of its later parts were written in Greek. However, the legalistic and formalized garb in which the Pharisees had dressed Judaism did not suit the educated Jewish class of the Egyptian metropole; they considered it too narrow and restricting and insufficiently open to other, mainly Helllenistic trends and influences.

What Philo, the main representative of Jewish scholarship, not alone in Egypt but in the Diaspora as a whole, intended to do was, to put it as neutrally as possible, to confront Judaism with Hellenism, without in the slightest respect diminishing Jewish faith and orthodoxy. In other words, he was not striving after a kind of syncretistic religion.

What he really desired to do was, in Wilson's words, "to make Judaism intellectually respectable by linking it with Greek philosophy" [20].

Philo certainly hoped to make the Jewish faith acceptable to pagans. He may have been encouraged by the existence of great numbers of proselytes, pagans who had been converted to Judaism. The philosopher would not have considered his attempt as hopeless in view of the widespread relativism and scepticism in the Hellenistic world; this made many people long for something more stable and definite, more sure of itself. He would also have taken into account the demise of the old Olympian gods and the unmistakable tendency towards monotheism in Hellenistic philosophy. Yet in such a confrontation between Judaism and Hellenism, casualties on both sides were inevitable.

Long before Philo started to publish, there had already come into existence a great work of hellenized Judaism to which I have already alluded, the Septuagint, that is, the translation of the Old Testament into Greek. It was not meant in the first place as an instrument of Jewish propaganda among the Gentiles but rather as a means to enable the Greek speaking Jews of Egypt to read the Bible. It was inevitable that certain Hellenistic mental concepts should filter through this translation into the Jewish mind. Wilson even speaks of 'syncretism of a sort' here. "In their Greek dress these (i.e. some fundamental) ideas (of Judaism) are not exactly what they were in the original Hebrew" [21].

5. Philo's idea of God

First of all, there is the name of God, not his generic name but his personal name [22], the tetragrammaton YHVH, usually vocalized as 'Jahve' and meaning 'I am who I am' or 'I am who am' [23]. The Septuagint renders this as 'egoo eimi ho oon' which transposes the personal colouring into a philosophical concept. This changes the character of God and widens the distance between him and mankind.

Philo often calls God 'ho oon' which means 'the being' but in the masculine form instead of the neutral one. "Observe the goodness of him who is" [24]. Twice he refers to the basic Exodus text. He first cites

Moses as asking after God's name and then goes on in this way. "First tell them that I am who is, that they may learn the difference between what is and what is not, and also that no name can be properly used of me to whom alone all existence belongs" [25]. But this is not at all what God said to Moses in the burning bramble. He said indeed 'I am who (I) am' but the rest is an amplification by Philo that betrays influence of Greek philosophy. We see the author philosophizing freely here thereby twisting the biblical text to suit his own insights.

The second time that he cites the Exodus text, Philo categorically states that "it is not the nature of him that is to be given a name but simply to be" [26]. Here Philo uses the neutral 'to on' thus making God still more of an abstraction. Max Pohlenz is certainly correct in writing that "the God whom Philo confesses is no longer the Jahve of the old popular creed" [27].

Another hellenistic element is that Philo never uses a personal name for God. One has only to read right through his treatise on creation [28], to say nothing of his other works, to see that he has always only one word for God, the Greek 'theos'. In this he follows the precedent of the Septuagint.

This must have vaguely suggested to Greek educated readers of both the Septuagint and Philo that there was a certain resemblance between the Olympian 'theoi' and the Jewish 'theos' [29]. Here we must take into account that the Hellenistic world had for a long time ceased to take the personal characteristics of the Homeric gods. All the gods together tended to blend into something more generic and abstract; this is often referred to as 'to theion' (neutral) = the divine, sometimes specified as 'Zeus', since this god's name was used in later times more as a generic term than one attached to a distinct personality.

Wilson draws our attention to the fact that Plutarch, in the opening phrases of his 'Isis and Osiris', in one breath uses the terms 'hoi theoi' (plural masculine), 'ho theos' (singular masculine), and 'to theion' (neutral) without discriminating between them. Immediately after this Plutarch submits the opinion that the finest thing Homer said about the gods was that Zeus was the greatest among them, thus clearly associating the supreme god closely with 'the divine' itself [30].

Just as in pagan Hellenistic authors, in Philo too this mode of name-giving points to 'a far-reaching depersonalization' [31], in his case of Jahve, and to the 'revitalizing of the abstract monotheism of Hellenistic philosophy' [32]. The Jewish philosopher put God at a far greater distance from creation and mankind than is the case in the Old Testament. This would doubtless have landed him in considerable difficulties had he wished to preserve intact the idea of God's immanence in the world, which is characteristic of Scripture.

6. Philo's idea of the immutability of God

Philo's problem becomes more apparent in his treatise on the unchangeability of God [33] (in fact only a small part of it relates to this unchangeability). Of course, Scripture does not see God as fickle and inconstant; his basic immutability is categorically expressed by that 'I am who I am' signifying that God is wholly identical with himself to the point of being entirely self-sufficient; he is always the same, with or without his creation. But the Old Testament (this is far less so in the New Testament) uses many anthropomorphic forms for God indicating that he can be in different moods. He can, for instance, become angry and then reconcile himself with man again, he can regret a decision and then, on human pleading, retract it. This anthropomorphism has kept many theologians occupied, among them Karl Barth in his 'Kirchliche Dogmatik' who really holds that God can change to a certain extent.

Now the perfect immutability of 'the divine' was a tenet of Hellenistic philosophy; hadn't Aristotle spoken of the 'unmoved prime mover'? In this view the divine is immovable and cannot be moved, neither in the physical nor in the affective sense. Philo finds himself faced with a painful dilemma here. As his cue he has taken Genesis 6:5-7 : "The Lord seeing that the wickedness of men had multiplied on earth and that every man intended evil in his heart diligently all his days, God had it in his mind (remembered) that he had created man upon the earth, and he bethought him. And God said, I will blot out man whom I made from the face of the earth". Even before starting to argue, Philo comes down on the 'careless inquirers' who believe that God can repent of something. "What greater impiety can there be than to believe that the unchangeable changes" [34]. Philo evidently is committing a petitio principii here by using a circular argument.

'To on', the Being, the Existent, he goes on to say, "does not experience repentance [35]; he is not susceptible to any passion at all" [36]. The Bible uses such anthropomorphic expressions as "a kind of elementary lesson, to admonish those who would not otherwise be brought to their senses" [37]. In other words, the anthropomorphisms are there to be of service to us but do not relate to God. Obviously not entirely satisfied with this explanation, Philo then plunges into a long and confused disquisition which only serves to show how much the problem is bothering him. He had, moreover, already been perorating lyrically on the quietude of the Sage, of the 'sophos', of the philosopher in the Stoic sense that is. The soul of the Sage is steadfast, harmonious, and consistent, 'resting in unruffled calm'. How "can you doubt then", he concludes, "that the Blessed One ... knows no change of will, but ever holds fast to what he purposed from the first without any alteration?" [38]. God is made here into a kind of Stoic super-philosopher.

Indeed, Philo took recourse to Stoic philosophy by referring to the four categories of existents, the inorganic, the flora, the fauna, and rational man. Rational man has been endowed with free will which he has misused. Philo now gives a slight twist to the original wording of Genesis by saying that God "had it in his mind and bethought him, not now for the first time but even from of old" that he had created man free [39]. By making God's thought something from all eternity and not of some specific historical moment, the philosopher delivers himself from the idea that God might repent of something and have second thoughts.

7. The encounter of Judaism with Hellenism

Summarizing what I have written so far, I could, to begin with, say with Heinemann [40], that the hellenized form of the Old Testament, the only form in which Philo knew it, exercised a certain influence on his trend of thought. When commenting on the Bible, the Torah, the Jewish Law [41], he did not study it objectively but rather tried to present it as advantageously as possible to Hellenistic sages. In order to attain this ideal, he permitted himself some, not always innocuous, sleights. He was not above omitting details that did not suit his paedagogical intentions. The way he handles scriptural data is sometimes uneven and occasionally even inaccurate. Probably he often quoted from memory. His tendency to project situations and conceptions of the Hellenistic world into the biblical sphere was responsible for many anachronisms.

In Philo we have an intriguing example of the encounter of Hellenism and Judaism. In Palestine itself, as we have seen [42], this encounter was the source of much friction and enmity, and finally even of a war between the Jews and the Seleucid princes. In Egypt the situation was different because large sections of the Jewish population had been thoroughly hellenized. Therefore Philo could optimistically believe that it would be feasible to harmonize the Jewish creed with Hellenistic philosophical tenets. But since Judaism and Hellenism were basically different, even in the last resort dualistically opposed entities, it should not surprise us that led to placing one of the two systems at a disadvantage [43].

Bréhier said that nothing illustrates better the confusion that reigned in Philo's innermost mind than his idea of God. Was God for him a Being without properties, the abstraction of all abstractions? Or was he the God of Abraham, Isaac, and Jacob, a father and sometimes a judge [44]? On the whole, Philo who doubtless thought of himself as a really pious man, tended towards the philosophical approach. I feel that Treitel's conclusion that "Philo's concept of God takes its distance from the strict Jewish concepts of God as they were taught on Palestinian soil" is justified [45].

8. Philo as an unbiblical prophet

However, Philo did not follow the Stoics always and in every respect! He rejects, for instance, the well-known argument, common to them, that God can be known from his works [46], the Creator inferred from his creation. But those who reason in this way "apprehend God by means of a shadow" [47]. They are "truly admirable persons ... and holy and pious worshippers of God in very truth". But they don't recognize his real nature [48]. And now Philo proceeds with a most remarkable statement. "There is a mind more perfect and more thoroughly cleansed, which has undergone initiation into the great mysteries, a mind which gains knowledge of the First Cause not from created things ..., but lifting its eyes above and beyond creation obtains a clear vison of the uncreated One" [49]. "The seekers for truth are those who envisage God through God, light through light" [50].

I have no doubt that the philosopher is speaking of himself in this passage. For elsewhere he writes about his own experiences, things that happened to him 'a thousand times'. Let me quote his own words. "On some occasions, after making up my mind to follow the usual course of writing on philosophical tenets ..., I have found my understanding incapable of giving birth to a single idea, and have given up ..., filled with amazement at the might of him that is, to whom is due the opening and closing of soul-wombs. On other occasions, I have approached my work empty and suddenly become full, the ideas falling in a shower from above and being sown invisibly, so that under the influence of divine possession I have been filled with corybantic frenzy and been unconscious of anything, place, persons present, myself, words spoken, lines written. For I obtained language, ideas, an enjoyment of light, keenest vision, pellucid distinctness of objects, such as might be received through the eyes as the result of the clearest shewing" [51].

This is a passage rich in disclosures. The philosopher begins with complaining that the ordinary method, the scholarly manner of philosophizing does not always give him what he wants. However, he did not turn to the Bible as every pious Jew would have counselled him to do.

Instead, he threw himself immediately on God who is the opener and closer of 'soul-wombs' ('mētrai'). Of course, not a female womb is meant but, indeed, as the Loeb translation has it, the womb of the soul. God is pictured here in the image of a midwife. Anyhow, an exclusively personal and intimate experience is described. God endows the philosopher with an insight that neither philosophy nor the Bible can give him.

In Philo's philosophical theology God is wholly transcendent, far beyond creation, and, in consequence, inaccessible to human beings. He can only be found in ecstasy. Isn't this a gnosticizing element? In any case, it is utterly unbiblical! Philo presents himself here as a privileged person receiving exlusive insights, and as an inspired prophet. In doing this he is putting himself outside, and perhaps even opposite, the main stream of Jewish piety. Rather than the prophetic giants of the Old Testament he resembles the self-appointed Gnostic seers.

9. God transcending all knowledge

In yet other respect Philo distances himself from Greek, in this case Platonic philosophy. Whereas for Plato the supreme and primary idea was that of the Good [52], Philo categorically declares that God, whom he calls 'the perfectly pure and unsullied Mind (Nous) of the Universe', "transcends virtue, transcends knowledge, transcends the Good itself and the Beautiful itself" [53]. "The superiority of God to the ideas consists ... in the fact that he is their creator" [54]. Plato would never have admitted that there was something or somebody beyond all Ideas, beyond the Idea of all Ideas!

In Plato, "the Ideas are exemplary of things, in consequence the Ideas must resemble things" [55]. For Philo, still very much a Jew, this was unpalatable : God does not resemble anything at all, for all things are corruptible, and God is, of course, wholly incorruptible [56]. "Like God there is nothing" [57]. But in his ardour to preserve God from the very tinge of Platonic or, indeed, of any other philosophy and thus avoid the charge of blasphemy, he entirely forgets what Genesis had said : that

God created man in his image and likeness. This means that there is a resemblance between God and man. But Philo sees this otherwise.

Let me use Bréhier's words to explain this. "This dissimilarity (i.e. of God and creation) above all finds its expression in the ideal of absolute sanctity and purity; because of his being holy God must be put far from and protected against every profane thing. He cannot soil himself by contact with the visible world; for this reason he remains separated from it by the intelligible world (about this intelligible world see below under 11 - F.). This violent, absolute, radical separation of the sensible and intelligible worlds is the primary characteristic of Philo's God" [58]. This, self-evidently, is the sheerest dualism.

Closely related to this notion of God's absolute transcendence, philosophical as well as psychological, is Philo's tenet that God is unknowable. He belongs to no genus, is not a species, possesses no qualities, and, therefore, cannot be defined. It is true that, for instance, by contemplating his creation we can infer his existence, but nothing at all can be predicated as regards his essence. God, he says, "is unnamable and ineffable and in every way incomprehensible" [59]. This "does not mean that God is not comprehended by the senses (which, of course, is not the case - F.) but rather as he explicitly states elsewhere, that 'he is not comprehended by the mind'" [60].

Wolfson, whom I am quoting here, says that neither Plato nor Aristotle said anything of this kind. It is a fact that "the conception of the ineffability or unnamability of God (is not) found in any other Greek philosopher before Philo" [61] (if this is correct, it would contradict Festugière's judgment on Philo). Philosophers, and scholars in general, prefer not to speak of unnamable and incomprehensible entities and concepts; their job is to describe and to define. As a philosopher Philo in this respect takes a position that is basically unphilosophical. True enough, we have the biblical prohibition against applying names to God. But this does not mean that he would be totally incomprehensible; the idea is that human beings may not appropriate him as the pagans do who try to arrogate their gods to themselves by using their names. Here Philo shows himself as neither really Jewish nor perfectly Hellenistic but rather as approximating the basic tenets of the Gnosis and of Jewish mysticism. The chasm he is opening between God and the human mind may be dubbed dualistic.

10. The problem of creation

Here a fundamental problem presents itself. If God and creation are so fundamentally dissimilar, who then created the universe? Philo, as may be expected, does not take the Gnostic line that the inaccessible God did not create the world but that some bad Demiurge was responsible for it. He leaves no room for doubt : God is the creator of all that is. He denies that the world is without beginning and everlasting. To postulate in God a vast (creational) inactivity is an impious falsehood, he says [62].

But then he goes on to declare that "the universal must consist of two parts, one part the active Cause and the other the passive object ... The passive part (i.e. matter) is in itself incapable of life and motion but, when shaped and quickened by Mind, changes into the most perfect masterpiece, namely this world" [63]. There is remarkable dichotomy of God and the world here, accentuated by the fact that Philo does not speak of 'God' but of 'cause' and 'mind'. This is more akin to Stoic philosophy than to biblical theology, also demonstrated by Philo's calling Moses the supreme philosopher [64].

11. The role of the intermediaries

a. The intelligible world

The first means Philo has for escaping from his aporia about creation is that God performed his creational work by using intermediaries and not doing it directly [65]. The most essential of these intermediaries is the intelligible world. God "assumed that a beautiful copy would never be produced apart from a beautiful pattern, and no object of perception could be faultless which was not made in the likeness of an original ('archetupos') discerned only by intellect. So when it was his will to create this visible world he first completely formed the intelligible ('noêtos') world, in order that he might have the use of a pattern ('paradeigma') wholly God-like and incorporeal ('asoomatos') in producing the material ('soomatikos') world as a later creation, the very image of an earlier (world = the intelligible one)" [66].

Once again we are confronted with a pregnant text. The, so to speak, two-layered universe of Genesis, consisting of the Creator and the world, has been replaced by a three-layered one, of God, the intelligible world, and the visible world. There is no longer an analogy between Creator and created, in particular man, but only between creation and its archetype which comes from God but is not God. It is also necessary to pay attention to the pair of opposites 'physical' and 'incorporeal'. Before the visible world is created, there has to be an incorporeal and intelligible one first. It is as though God feels that he alone is unable to create the concrete universe, that of beings and objects, and shuns it. "Philo", says Treitel, "did never attain to a uniform fundamental concept in which the duality of God and matter is dissolved because it makes proceed matter from God" [67]. Once again, it must be stated that we are in close vicinity of dualism, if not right in it.

From whatever angle we look at it, in Philo God steps back somewhat from his creation; the distance between the divine and the terrestrial becomes accentuated ever more sharply. God, while not creating directly, kept, so to speak, only the supervision of the creational work by "keeping his eye upon his pattern and making the visible and tangible objects correspond in each case to the incorporeal ideas" [68].

b. The Logos

In Philo's description of the primary, intelligible world the term 'logos' occurs often. This was, of course, quite customary in Hellenic and Hellenistic philosophy but alien to the Old Testament in the Hebrew original [69]. Perhaps one might say that Logos, with which is meant divine thought emanating from the supreme godhead, is in Judaism replaced by wisdom, by 'chokma', or 'sophia' in Greek [70]. In the several books of the Old Testament wisdom figures as a personalized entity that, while emanating from God, nevertheless is never wholly identifiable with him. We might describe it as God's creating spirit or power. The Logos as such we meet only in the New Testament, above all in the famous prologue of the Gospel of John; in his theology Jesus Christ is the Logos.

We have only to compare the Philonic indexes on the lemmata 'logos' and 'sophia' to discover which of the two is Philo's favourite term : more than thirteen pages of 'logos' in Leisegang against four on 'sophia', while in Mayer the lemma on 'logos' gets three-and-a-half columns as against barely one on 'sophia'.

The philosopher indicates the place of the Logos in the scheme of creation in this way. "It well befits those who have entered into comradeship with knowledge (epistême; the philosphers are meant) to desire to see what is (Being, to on), if they may, but if they cannot, to see at any rate his image (eikoon), the most holy Logos, and after the Logos its most perfect work of all that our senses know, even this world" [71].

Once again Philo presents to us the three-layered universe, but in this passage we hear of the Logos instead of the intelligible world. Obviously the concrete world has not been created by God directly but by the Logos. This conflicts with the biblical presentation, not only with the Genesis texts according to which God takes direct action, but with the Book of Wisdom too in which it is said that Wisdom (chokma) was with God when he created rather than that it itself was the really creating force. Seen from the view-point of God himself, the Philonic Logos-Image is his messenger, his angel, for the benefit of those who are not yet capable of seeing the true God [72]. It is a regularly recurring theme in Philo that most people, most philosophers included, are unable to find God himself and must remain content with his 'shadow'.

Like all philosophers of Antiquity Philo hit on the problem of the relationship of the One and the Many, in his case on the question how the multiple, the multiform concrete world could proceed from the One. Now the remarkable thing is that he deduced the Many not so much from the one God (as a biblical author would do) but from an intermediate form, the Logos-Image acting as the unitary principle or Monas. "God speaks in umixed Monads" [73]. It is as though this author suggests that God does not want to have anything to do with the multiple, that is with our world. There is dualism in this.

With regard to the material world the Logos has a different function, so much so that Philo could even speak of two Logoi. One he called "the archetypal Reason above us, the other the copy of which we possess (= the material world)" [74]. The extent to which the philosopher was skating on dangerously thin ice in his doctrine of intermediaries is illustrated by a curious passage in his treatise on the immutability of God [75]. It makes us think of his two Logoi. There he says that the cosmos is the younger son of God because it is observable by the senses; the elder is spiritual - this refers to the intelligible world or Logos - and is in possession of the right of primogeniture. This son is staying with God; the younger son obviously is an inferior being and distant from God. Probably horrified by his own temerity he then falls over backwards to argue that God is one (for he came very near the heresy of all heresies, that there are two gods, namely God and the Logos); the Logos, he says apologetically, is called God only in a figurative sense.

c. Monad and Dyad

The Logos "is in no way different from unity" [76]; it is the essential Monad. The Dyad, or twofold (containing, or even being, the principle of difference and division) "comes next to the Monad". It is derived from it but obviously feels itself, so to speak, in exile, for "it presses on to the ideal form which is free from mixture and complexity" [77]. We see this, for instance, in Moses, "whose twofold nature of soul and body was resolved by the Father (i.e. when he died) into a single unity, transforming his whole being into mind pure as the sunlight" [78]. This betrays dualism, here that of soul and body which, in Philo's opinion, do not constitute a unity.

The decisive difference between Monad and Dyad is that "the Monad is the image of the First Cause (= God), the Dyad of matter passive and divisible (= the material of which the cosmos is made)". This comes fairly close to a dualistic distinction, and this impression is strengthened by the phrase that follows : "Therefore one who honours the Dyad before the Monad should not fail to know that he holds matter in higher esteem than God" [79]. This is what became the undoing of Adam, who was "doomed to die when he touched the twofold tree (what is meant are the two trees, of life, and of knowledge, in Gen. 2:9 - F.), thus honouring the two before the One, and revering the created rather than the Maker" [80].

Speaking of the Monad-Dyad relationship, Philo repeats what he said elsewhere, that "they go wrong who are at pains to discern the uncreated and the Creator of all from his creation; (they) are on the same footing as those who try to trace the nature of the Monad from the Dyad, whereas observation of the Dyad should begin with the Monad which is the starting-point" [81]. This amounts to saying that God is not immanent in his creation.

d. The Ideas

A word must be said of the relationship of the Logos and the intelligible world. First we saw that the intelligible world is the intermediary between God and the concrete world, and then we saw that the Logos fulfils this role. Are they identical? They are, at least to a certain extent. The Logos summarizes and contains all Ideas (the stuff of the intelligible world); it is the Idea of Ideas [82]. The Ideas in their turn are the images of the concrete world [83].

e. Angels and logoi

We have not yet done with the intermediaries. Philo also often speaks of 'angels'. He calls them "holy and divine beings, the servitors and lieutenants of the primal God" [84]. Sometimes he identifies them with the 'logoi', for instance when he speaks of "the divine and holy Thoughts ('logoi') who are often called angels" [85]. But we can also find that the Logos itself is dubbed 'angel' [86]. Philo himself defines these logoi as "principles which are divine and are older than we and all that belongs to earth" [87]. These logoi, or principles (of creation), seem to be elements and/or emanations of the supreme Logos.

f. The Powers

We are not yet at an end. For Philo also postulated 'powers', 'dunameis'. 'Power' was a much used notion then, indicating lower-rank divinities. Of course, the philosopher would not hear anything of other deities than God alone, but all the same the idea of 'powers' came in handy for him to bridge the distance between the created world and the transcendent God which otherwise would have remained radically dualistic [88]. "Though transcending and being beyond what he has made, none the less he has filled the universe with himself, for he has caused his powers to extend themselves throughout the universe to its utmost bounds" [89]. Leisegang in his Philonic indices heads the numerous entries with (supernatural) powers as "forces by means of which God created the world and which penetrate and contain all nature". There are places where the philosopher identifies the powers with the logoi, the Ideas, and the angels.

g. Why Philo needed so many intermediaries

If the reader is getting somewhat confused, it is not his or her fault. Philo himself was not altogether certain of the functions and relations of these entities interposed between God and the world. The critical question is why he needed them and in such a great number. One gets the impression that the philosopher wanted to protect God against a charge that might be brought against him. It is as if he were erecting a shield between God and the world; the thicker this shield the better. Treitel concludes here that the basic dogma of the Judaistic doctrine, that of the unity and indivisibility of God, became severely damaged by theories such as divine powers serving as intermediate beings [90].

Philo's basic, metaphysical dualism becomes abundantly apparent once we tackle the question of cosmogony, in particular that of the origin of matter. Then we fully realize why he needed such a host of intermediaries, and above all the Logos. This is because it is impossible for him to bring God into close and direct contact with matter, with what is finite, and to see him as the Creator in the biblical sense of the word. "When out of that confused matter God produced all things, he did not do so with his own handiwork, since his nature, happy and blessed as it was, forbade that he should touch the limitless chaotic matter. Instead he made full use of the incorporeal potencies well denoted by their Forms to enable each kind to take its appropriate shape" [91]. This is tantamount to saying that the Forms are the real creators (although I assume that Philo would not have gone so far).

12. Order and disorder

We should not confuse sheer matter with the cosmos (or the corporeality of the world). The cosmos, highly organized as it is, is much more than matter; it could not come into being without the action of God, albeit this divine activity was exercised through the intermediaries, in particular 'through the instrumentality of the Logos'. But just as the cosmos possesses the possibilities of growth, it is also 'carrying the seeds of destruction within it' [92]. It bears the imprint of the Creator but at the same time it is tainted by the negativity of matter.

There is much that is imperfect in this world : "The whole substance of things only created to perish is one constant war" [93]. How can we reconcile the confused state of the world with the idea of a perfect God? "All the bounty of the Uncreated must be perfect and complete; it may not be that any of his gifts should be imperfect" [94]. The inference can be no other than that there are two principles at work in the world, one of order, another of disorder.

Or shouldn't we rather speak of a principle **and** a condition, a principle of activity and a condition of passivity? For as Zeller said : "When all workings and operations proceed from God, then for the second principle (viz. matter) only sheer passivity remains ... Philo's dualism that is the basis of his whole ideology forbids him to derive the finite completely from divine causality" [95].

13. Philo's abhorrence of the material world

Perhaps we might say that Philo was incapable of seeing matter as fully real [96], for his depreciation of matter goes so far as even to call it 'non-existent' [97]. And this world, once created out of matter, does not fill him with admiration either. Everything on earth is "in a constant and ceaseless state of flux", with the result that "we are incapable of observing anything with exactness" [98]. And once again the fundamental opposition : "With the divisive there is no turning; variableness belongs to the nature of the created" [99]. True enough, in the Old Testament too God is constant and the world changing, but there it is always assumed that there a real connection between God and matter or the world.

The point is not, of course, that for Philo matter (or the world or the cosmos) is some kind of divinity or some 'autonomous principle next to God'. This would give an ontological status to matter that, in Philo's view, it by no means deserves. "Matter possesses for Philo the status of an eternal constituent of reality with an existence (if that word can be used) in some way independent of God" [100].

14. The Man of God

One of Philo's favourite tenets is that of the Man of God, the 'anthroopos theou'. As is well-known there are in Genesis two creation stories that, since the eighteenth century, are ascribed to two different authors [101]. That they are substantially different was already common knowledge in Antiquity. Philo made use of there being two creation stories to fashion two notions of man.

Philo postulated that, proceeding from the Logos, there was a generic or ideal man who is incorporeal, intelligible, incorruptible, and neither male nor female. He believed that the creation of man as told in Gen. 1 referred to this image-man. Only after the creation of this entity came that of terrestrial man; this earthly, concrete man was an imperfect copy of the heavenly archetype [102]. In the second creation story, that of Gen. 2, God, acting in the manner of a potter, fashions a human form out of clay, later to be called 'Adam' = man of the earth ('adamah'). "There is a vast difference between the man thus formed and the man that came into existence earlier after the image of God (i.e. according to Gen. 1). For the man so formed (i.e. out of clay) is the object of sense-perception ... consisting of body and soul, man or woman, by nature mortal, while he that was after the (divine) image was an idea or type or seal, an object of thought" [103]. Once again we see Philo twisting a biblical text so that it may suit his particular philosophy. For Gen. 1 expressly states that the human beings created in the image of God were made male and female.

But this is not my point here. I want to emphasize that Philo, in this passage, obviously does not want to stretch the difference between his man of Gen. 1 and that of Gen. 2 so much that it becomes dualistic. All the same, the germ of dualism is already there. For the time being, Philo calls this "first man, earthborn, ancestor of our whole race, ... most excellent in each part of his being, in both body and soul excelling those who came after him in the transcendent qualities of both alike" [104].

There still is a tenuous organic link between the image-man and terrestrial man. "It is in respect of the Mind, the sovereign element of the soul, that the word 'image' is used. For after the pattern of a single Mind, even the Mind of the universe as an archetype (here the Logos is meant - F.), the mind of those who came successively into being was moulded" [105]. One might say with Bréhier here that "according to the idea that man is a microcosmos, there is nothing more similar to God in the world than intelligence in the human composite" [106]. Philo himself puts it like this : "The human mind evidently occupies a position in men precisely similar to that which the great Ruler occupies in all the world" [107].

15. Philo's anthropology

Speaking of Philo's anthropology, of the status of man in his philosophy, and of man's relation to God, we must bear in mind Zeller's remark that "the dualism of the Philonic system appears in his anthropology all the more evidently ... Of all the older systems on which Philo leaned for this part of his doctrine, no one came to meet his dualism so much as Platonism" [108]. The backdrop of his anthropology is that "to God we are aliens and sojourners (viz. in this world). For each of us has come into this world as into a foreign city, in which we before our birth had no part; in this city he (man) does but sojourn, until he has exhausted his appointed span of life" [109].

In principle, this not un-unblical; in fact, the philosopher cites Lev. 25:23 here which also speaks of 'aliens and sojourners'. But I think there is more than a shade of difference between what the Old Testament said and what Philo means. Texts like that in Leviticus signify that man should not get absorbed by this world and thus forget God. Philo, on the other hand, seems to imply that man does not really belong to this world.

The consequence of Philo's view on man is that we are "in the presence of two unharmonized types of thought" [110]. This made Drummond speak of Philo's 'higher anthropology', that of the ideal man; he does not mention a 'lower anthropology' but we are entitled to believe that there is one, referring to terrestrial man.

That these two anthropologies lead to confusion becomes all too evident in Philo's theory of the origin of the human soul. In his treatise on the Giants he is clearly following Plato by assigning pre-existence to the soul. "The air must needs be filled by living beings, though indeed they are invisible to us ... (There) is no reason why we should doubt that there are souls in the air, but they must be apprehended by the mind ... Now some of the souls have descended into bodies, but others have never deigned to be brought into union with any of the parts of the earth. They are consecrated and devoted to the service of the Father and Creator whose wont it is to employ them as ministers and helpers, to have charge and care of mortal man (the angels are meant - F.). But the others descending into a body as though into a stream have sometimes been caught in the swirl of its rushing torrent and swallowed up thereby, at other times have been able to stem the current, have risen to the surface and then soared upwards to the place whence they came. These last, then, are the souls of those who have given themselves to genuine philosophy, who from first to last study to die to the life in the body, (so) that a higher existence immortal and incorporeal, in the presence of him who is himself immortal and incorporeal, may be their portion. But the souls which have sunk beneath the stream are the souls of others who have held no count of wisdom. They have abandoned themselves to the unstable things of chance, none of which has aught to do with our noblest part, the soul or mind, but all are related to that dead thing which was our birth-fellow, the body" [111].

This revealing Philonic passage is as perfectly Hellenic as it is unbiblical. It is a Greek, a Pythagorean and Platonic idea that souls are pre-existent and descend into a body. But there seem to be in Philo perfect and less perfect souls, or souls of a higher and a lower class. The higher class, that of the angels, prefers to stay on high, near God. The others go downward and associate themselves with a body. The alliance of soul and body is an uneasy one, conjoining something living and something dead. A deep contempt of the body and of earthly things in general becomes apparent here; the relationship of soul and body is clearly dualistic in character. The metaphor used by Philo, that of a wildly streaming river, is in accordance with this. The souls drop into this stream, some are drowned, others are saved. There is no notion here of the continued existence of the whole human being; the body obviously is to be discarded, whereas the soul returns to its heavenly abode. Soul and body part ways with regard to their innermost desires. What the body strives after is 'irrational pleasure', whereas what the soul wants is 'the mind of the universe, even the godhead' [112]. Because we are flesh, "the divine spirit cannot abide" [113]. Man can only save his soul by dedicating himself to 'genuine philosophy'; in his opinion obedience to the Law is also philosophically living, since he or she who lives according to the Law lives in agreement with nature which is the will of God.

However this may be, with regard to the body our philosopher can only express himself in purely negative terms. The mind is all too often swamped by the inrush of what the senses have to offer. "The mind, swallowed up by the huge inpouring, is found at the bottom (viz. of the stream), unable so much as to rise to the surface and look out" [114]. The mind is 'like a prisoner in the gaol' [115]. Still more scornfully he expresses himself when he writes that the body "is wicked and a plotter against the soul and is even a corpse and a dead thing" [116]. This is unadulterated dualism of body and soul, of course; it will cause no surprise that we find the old soma-sêma simile (the body is a tomb) again : one is "buried in it as in a coffin or shell" [117]. It is categorically stated that "he whose abode is in the body and the mortal race should attain to being with God; this is only possible for him whom God rescues out of the prison" [118].

16. The role of wisdom

Consequently Philo is equally contemptuous of all that belongs to this world. "It behoves the mind that it would be let forth and let go free to withdraw itself from the influence of everything, the needs of the body, the organs of sense, specious arguments, the plausibilities of rhetoric, last of all itself" [119]. The body and wisdom are radical opposites. "All flesh destroys the perfect way of the Eternal and Indestructible, the way which leads to God. This way, you must know, is wisdom" [120]. "When the the light shines, darkness disappears" [121].

It is self-evident what an enlightened, a wise and 'knowing' person will have to do. "When the mind begins to know itself and to hold converse with the things of the mind, it will thrust away from it that part of the soul which inclines to the province of sense-perception". We also find in Philo that condescending attitude towards less privileged persons, so typical of Hellenistic philosopher. "It is impossible for one who is possessed by love for all that is incorporeal and incorruptible to dwell together with one who leans towards the objects of sense-perception doomed to die" [122]. "The wise person must die to the life in the body" [123]. For "the serpent, pleasure, is bad of itself' and therefore it is not found at all in a good man, the bad man getting all the harm of it by himself" [124]. And once again a categorical command : "(Wise men) are cutting away from their hearts and minds all that is near and dear to the flesh" [125].

17. Philo's attitude towards women

We should not be surprised that Philo should relegate women to as essentially passive role (a dualistic standpoint). "The man shows himself in activity and the woman in passivity; so the province of the mind is activity, and that of the perpective sense passivity, as in woman" [126]. That man is active and woman is passive is a song that will echo throughout the ages (it did not take its tune from the Bible), but Philo puts it into a philosophical context here. That man is active puts him on the side of mind, or even the godhead (the active principle in Philo); the passivity of woman allies her with matter - which is not only passive but also non-existent!

18. Philonic doctrine and the Gnosis

a. A provisional summary

There is no doubt that Philo was mainly in the stream of Platonic and Hellenistic, in particular Stoic philosophy; he also made an extensive use of biblical texts, though not rarely distorting them in his own curious fashion. What remains to be answered is whether there is a connection between Philonic doctrine and the Gnosis. In order to clarify this issue we must summarize what we have found so far.

God in Philo is unknowable; for our common, down-to-earth humanity he is a 'deus absconditus', a hidden God. There is no road leading from creation, by means of the contemplation of God's handiwork, to the Creator. On this point Philo does not differ from what the Gnostics held of God's knowability. There is, however, in Philo's system no bad Demiurge who is directly responsible for the creation of an evil universe. On the other hand, God and matter are very much apart, so far that is possible to say that matter is 'in some way independent of God'. Matter is neither a real entity nor a principle, still less some sort of deity. Philo judges it negatively : it is passive and formless, to the point of non-existence. It is not intrinsically evil, but it may be conducive to all that is evil.

b. The origin of evil

The cause of the presence of evil in this world is not in Philo, as in Gnostic systems, a fundamental error occurring during the gestation of the cosmos. Philo has not much to say of the Fall as it is described in Gen. 3; he does not really believe in its historicity but treats it, like everything else in the Old Testament, in an allegorical fashion. As Zeller wrote : "The Old Testament stories of a primeval situation and of the Fall have only a very external relation with his own system" [127].

The source of evil is humanity itself, especially its female half. As long as the first man was alone, he excelled in everything. But then woman was created, and immediately things went astray. "Woman became for him the beginning of a blameworthy life." For he desired her, "and this desire begat likewise bodily pleasure ..., the pleasures for the sake of which men bring on themselves the life of mortality and wretchedness instead one of immortality and bliss" [128].

What Philo is sharing with the Gnostics is a deep distrust of femininity and sexuality. He seems to adhere to the idea that the initial sin was of a sexual kind. But there is not one word of sexuality and carnal desire to be found in Genesis. The first sin consists in the fact that man and woman want to be the sole arbiters of good and evil. Here too Philo is swerving from the literal biblical text and its meaning. Anyhow, we see in the Philonic text the beginning of a general depravation, of a general sinfulness that is common to all humanity. This sinfulness consists in this that the soul allies itself with the body. Philo's contempt for all that is of this world also brings him close to Gnostic ideology.

c. An ambivalent idea of the cosmos

Philo's attitude regarding the cosmos is ambivalent. He does not believe in a creatio ex nihilo since he adheres to the classical Greek notion that nothing can originate from nothing (although he is somewhat inconsequent in suggesting that matter could even be non-existent); in consequence, God can only create the cosmos from something that is already there, i.e. matter. The cosmos cannot have come into being without God. But since the distance between God and matter is unbridgeable, creation can only take place by means of intermediaries. The idea of a hidden God not meddling directly with creation resembles Gnostic cosmogonic notions, but God's intermediaries are not, as in the Gnosis, the servants of an evil power, a Demiurge.

d. The man of God and the First Man

Philo's method of biblical exegesis is allegorical; he is not interested in the literal meaning of the text. This approaches him to Gnostic theosophy although he could lean on the Stoa too for allegorical interpretations, but he remains far from the florid mythology of the Gnosis. We find in him, however, an equivalent of the 'First Man', an archetype created by God after whom real man is modelled but who is, according to the Gnostics, profoundly spoiled by the Demiurge. In Philo there is the Man of God who is the prototype of the human beings of flesh and blood. Though those are not said to be utterly corrupted, they, or rather their souls, are seen as imprisoned in their bodies. With the Gnosis this philosopher shares the dualism of the spiritual and material elements in man.

e. Élitism

After death, souls can return to God. Obviously, the ascent to heaven will not be effected by everybody because one needs to be a 'philosopher' for this. In other words, the élitism that was rampant in the late Hellenistic world, with the philosophers as well as with the Gnostics, is detectable here too. In plain words it can be stated that a believer, in order to be saved, has to 'know' something that other less privileged people do not know, something fundamental.

A principal element of Philonic philosophical anthropology is the realization that the soul is imprisoned in the body. By no means everybody is ready to acknowledge this; on the contrary, most people prefer to indulge in material pleasure. Contempt for ordinary humanity is another thing Philo and the Gnostics have in common.

f. The basic dualism

"All such ideas", writes Wilson, "Platonic, Stoic, Orphic, Philonic, (and we might add Gnostic - F.) have as a basis a dualistic conception of the world as divided into regions of sense and spirit, of noumenal and phenomenal, real and apparent ...; man really belongs to the higher sphere, but has fallen or been banished to the lower. The body is a prison fom which the soul longs to escape" [129]. The basic dualism of Gnostic ideology, that of God and matter, soul and body, was also that of Philonic philosophy.

g. The signifance of knowledge and wisdom

All these resemblances and agreements do not, of course, make Philo into a proper Gnostic; it must be understood that he lived some time before the first flourishing of the Gnosis. But we are perfectly entitled to state that he was studiously 'gnosticizing'. One thing remains still to be studied, his use of terms of knowledge. Did he use them, in particular 'gnosis', in a way that resembles that of the Gnostics and is also in agreement with the idea the Stoa had of wisdom?

There is no doubt that knowledge and wisdom were very important concepts for Philo. This philosopher, as the very erudite man he was, was an admirer of all kinds of human knowledge, such as to be found in science and scholarship. But far above all such disciplines Wisdom soars, Sophia. The highest Wisdom is not human but divine. Wisdom, he says, is a daughter of God, "a true born and ever-virgin daughter ..., free from every defiling touch". Here Philo is in full agreement with the biblical Book of Wisdom.

But then he goes on to speculate in his own curious and somewhat confusing fashion. Sophia is not God, she "occupies a second place, and therefore was termed feminine to express its contrast with the Maker of the universe who is masculine and its affinity with everything else. For pre-eminence always pertains to the masculine, and the feminine always comes short and is lesser than it" [130]. This text reveals quite a number of things, Philo's predilection for contrasts, his opinion that what is feminine is of a lower order, and the idea that God does not have a direct affinity with 'everything else', with creation that is.

But now Philo stumbles on a problem that he tries to solve in a rather clumsy way. Wisdom generates in souls 'learning, instruction, science, prudence, beautiful and laudable actions'. Generating, however, means activity, and action, in his view, can only proceed from a masculine principle. Therefore, without batting an eye-lid, he declares wisdom to be 'not only masculine but even a father' [131]. He then ventures somewhat further along the same path. "The architect who made this universe was at the same time the father of what was born, whilst its mother was the knowledge possessed by its maker [132]. With his knowledge God had union, not as men have it, and begat created being. And knowledge, having received the divine seed, when her travail was consummated bore the only beloved son who is apprehended by the senses, the world (kosmos) which we see" [133].

This daring language with its sexual imagery must have sounded like blasphemy in the ears of the Jewish sages! Bréhier points out several (non-Jewish) ideas that are behind this curious presentation. We are surely not far from the idea of the 'hierogamos", the sacred wedding, the union of a male and female godhead (or of a godhead and a queen or priestess) that is well-known from Hellenic mythology. "The idea of a Bride-Mother is familiar for the Orphics", while the lineage too has Orphic traits [134]. I add that Philo is coming very close to the notion of a supreme god having a 'paredra', a female divinity next to him (like the divine couple Zeus-Hera) that is common to both Greek and Indian mythology. Furthermore, we find here the sexual imagery and the 'inclusive thinking' that is typical of Gnostic systems. If we take into account that the divine Wisdom in itself is by no means an un-Jewish concept, then we see Philo standing in the centre of many worlds. It shows how syncretistic the mental climate of this period was.

We are not yet at the end. For what is the relation between Wisdom and the Logos? Philo cannot lay claim to the title of systematic thinker! He uses his terms very loosely. In some passages Wisdom is the source of the Logos : "The divine Logos descends from the Fountain of Wisdom like a river" [135]. In others it is just the reverse : "The supreme divine Logos is the fountain of Wisdom" [136]. "The contradictions are undeniable", writes Bréhier, "Philo, on his part, does not attempt to hide them." They are there, not because he is incapable of surmounting them but because he is indebted to Hellenistic religious conceptions [137].

We have already seen how supremely important philosophy was to Philo, not so much as a fine field of study but rather as the means for the soul to soar upwards to God. God is benevolent enough to give to all people without exception an intuition of his existence. "God loves to give, and so to bestow good things on all, even on those who are not perfect (another proof of this philosopher's élitism - F.) ... There is abundance even for those who will derive no great benefit from it" [138]. "No soul is capable by itself of seeing its maker (but) the invisible Deity stamped on the invisible soul the impress of itself (so that) it should obtain an conception ('ennoia', intuition) of him who wrought it"

[139]. But, after all, such a preliminary idea is no more than a mere intuition; most people neglect and forget it. "Those who bear the burden ... cannot look up to the heavens as they revolve but (remain) rooted to the ground like four-footed beasts" [140].

However, God "clearly manifests himself to him that escapes from things mortal and mounts up into a soul from the encumbrance of this body of ours" [141]. Philo is speaking of a philosopher here, of a philosopher of a Stoic stamp (and not of a law-abiding Jew). The relation between Wisdom and philosophy, between sophia and philosophia, is of prime importance, for this is the tenuous link between the divine Logos and the human soul. "Philosophy is the practice or study of wisdom (sophia) and wisdom is the knowledge ('epistēmē') of things divine and human and their causes (a modern philosopher would not agree that his discipline is about 'things divine'; he prefers leaving this to theology - F.). Philosophy must be the servant of wisdom" [142]. The ascending soul of the philosopher must leave all behind, the body, the senses, and most of all its own self [143]. It is the higher form of philosophy that sets men free. Let me add that the idea of the ascent of the soul is a typically Gnostic notion.

In view of the climactic importance of knowledge-concept in his philosophy, it comes somewhat as a surprise that Philo only rarely employs the word 'gnosis'. In both lexica I mentioned the lemma 'gnosis' is extremely short whereas the list of 'epistēmē'-entries is much and much longer (in Leisegang ten columns against a mere ten lines for 'gnosis'). But on the few times when he uses the former he almost invariably makes it mean superior, higher knowledge. In doing so he remains within the tradition of Hellenistic philosophy [144]. He speaks, for instance, of "the search for the knowledge ('gnooseoos') of the best. And what is the best of all that is but God?" [145].

The goal of the mind's course is "the recognition ('gnoosis') and knowledge ('epistēmē') of God" [146]. Here gnosis and epistēmē are equated with each other [147] and also with sophia, for the road followed by the mind is that of Wisdom (sophia). It is even said that God has 'gnosis' of the things he has made [148]. Real knowledge is that "of him who in reality is" [149]. Gnosis is also 'acquaintance with piety' [150] and knowledge of 'what is just' [151]. Occasionally, however, gnosis may denote knowledge of the facts, in particular the facts of a juridical case [152]. But here too the insights of a judge are seen as superior to pedestrian knowledge.

h. How Gnostic was Philo?

To conclude this section, we must ask the question : how Gnostic was Philo [153]? In his book 'The Gnostic Problem' [154] and in a Kairos-article of 1972 [155], Wilson mentioned two options with regard to Philo's supposed Gnosticism. The first is that Philo forms part of the Gnostic movement, in other words that he was a Gnostic himself. Nobody less than Hans Jonas adhered to this option [156]. The other option, which Wilson favours, is that Philo is not an authentic Gnostic but rather a 'precursor' of the later Gnostic movement [157]. After considering the matter as accurately as I could, I must say that, on this point, I side with Wilson rather than with Jonas. "Philo is not a gnostic in the strict sense of the term, although he has affinities with Gnosticism" [158].

In what, according to Wilson, do Philo's affinities with the Gnostic movement consist? To begin with, there is 'the emphasis on the complete transcendence of the supreme God'. To this it should be added that the biblical tenet of God's immanence in the world is not to be found in Philo. His theology is a negative one, since it is humanly impossible to know God in his essence from his works. However, that God is not immanent in the world does not imply that he is as indifferent to it as the supreme godhead of the Gnostics. Secondly, the interposition of intermediaries between God and the world is Gnostic, but these are not 'as wicked and rebellious as the archons in the Gnostic myth'. Finally, there is Philo's 'general disparagment of the sense-perceptible world', a context which gives meaning to the ascent of the soul.

Let me bring forward a fourth point that, though not turning Philo into a Gnostic, nevertheless makes him predisposed to the Gnosis. Peter Sloterdijk wrote that those people are predisposed towards the

Gnosis for whom, in questions of truth, it is essential to be clever rather than pious [159]. This certainly applies to Philo's way of handling the Bible. His favourite way of treating it is to interpret the biblical pronouncements as allegories. Robert Musil, the Austrian novelist, once wrote that an allegory is "a spiritual relation ... in which everything signifies more than is reasonably due to it" [160]. Philo tried to harmonize biblical texts with Platonic and Hellenistic philosophical tenets giving them in this way a meaning the original Jewish authors never thought of. In doing so the philosopher showed himself a very ingenious rather than a pious Jew. For piety would have meant that he accepted the Old Testament as it stands, as, according to Jewish orthodoxy, the word of Jahve, and humbly wait what it would work out in him. For this Philo was too clever by half.

19. Conclusion

Philo was not only a clever man, he was also courageous, if not downright audacious. We see him manfully treading the tight-rope between Jewish orthodoxy and Hellenistic philosophy. It is not a wonder that he lost his footing, since the two are incompatible. The point is rather to which side he fell off. I believe that every line of my essay made it manifest that he swerved off in the direction of philosophy. The discussion I mentioned in the previous section on whether he was a Gnostic or a precursor of the Gnosis is already evidence enough that we are not confronted with a pious orthodox Jew.

My inference from Philo's heroic attempts to reconcile the irreconcilable is this. As I believe to have already demonstrated, in that period the choice was between dualistic and non-dualistic systems. Only the Old and New Testaments and the Talmud are non-dualistic [161]. All the others, Platonic and Hellenistic philosophical systems, Essenianism, Gnostic ideology, many philosophical parts of the Hermetica, the contents (as we shall see) of the Nag Hammadi library, Jewish mysticism, and the apocryphal gospels, are dualistic [162]. By attempting to twist the meaning of the texts to make them support his own essentially nonorthodox ideology, he inevitably became a dualist himself.

20. The pseudo-Aristotelian treatise 'On the world'

I feel this is the right place to throw in a word or two on a remarkable treatise that is not by Philo but shows a close affinity with important parts of his ideology. The tract I am speaking of here is entitled "On the world' ("Peri kosmou'); it is entered in the name of Aristotle. This philosopher, however, had nothing to do with it, the text being some three centuries younger than his authentic work [163]. An anonymous author (who in all probability was not a Jew), writing in the beginning of the Christian era, composed it and, to enhance its prestige, ascribed it to Aristotle [164].

The tract contains a description of the cosmos. It speaks of the universe, of ether, fire, and air; it then describes earth and sea and goes on with the natural phenomena like winds and rainbows. So far there is little or nothing that could interest us with regard to our theme; it is all rather conventional Hellenistic scholarship. But the work is preceded by a prologue that says that, whereas obviously most people shrink back from contemplating the truth that is in things universal, the philosopher alone strives to recognize this truth. While it is not possible to do this in the body, the soul can soar upwards, taking the intellect as its guide, and comprehend things very far removed in space; it may even apprehend things divine, and interpret them to mankind [165]. There is a double dichotomy here, that of soul and body, and that of the philosopher and the rest. This picture is familiar to us, not only from Platonic and Hellenistic philosophy but also from Philo.

The book becomes really intriguing when, in its closing chapters, it begins to speak of the position of God in the universe. Then the author's cosmogony and geography make place for theology. The earth and the things upon the earth, says the writer, seem feeble and full of confusion [166]; they are mutable and admit of many changes and conditions. By contrast, the celestial bodies always preserve the same order and never alter their course or move from it [167]. This means that the superlunary and sublunary regions are fundamentally different. This invites us to lift up our eyes and envisage the higher spheres.

The author wholeheartedly acknowledges God (he always writes 'theos', in the singular) as the Creator of all that is. "All things are from God and were framed for us by God, and no created thing is of itself sufficient for itself, deprived as it is from the permanence which it derives from him [168] ... Enthroned amid the immutable (i.e. the celestial bodies), he moves and revolves all things, where and how he will, in different forms and nature [169]". Must we conceive of this God as a person, such as he shows himself in the Bible? Absolutely not! "God and nothing else is meant when we speak of Necessity (Anankè)", says the author, taking his cue from Stoic theology and subscribing to late Hellenistic views on the dominant role of Fate [170]. "He is Fate ('heimarmenè') and Destiny and Moira and a number of similar things too" [171].

The author of 'On the world' shows himself to be of one mind with Philo by stating that the Creator does not personally administer the affairs of this earth. It must be considered beneath his dignity to see to the petty details of earthly and human existence. There is a long digression on the way oriental potentates governed their empires : this they did from afar [172]. This comment that it is said that the Great Kings' (of Persia) were 'invisible to all' is a revealing detail[173]. This is tantamount to contending that God is inaccessible. His function remains restricted to that of being 'the cause of permanence' [174] and preserving the harmony of all things [175].

There is no immanence of God in this world. "He has his seat not in the midst where the earth and this our troubled world are situated, but being pure himself he has gone up into a pure region, ... the furthest boundary of of the upper world, ... free from all gloom and disordered motion" [176]. One should note here the clearly dualistic opposition of heaven and earth, obviously comprising that of God and man. The farther a creature is from God, the more tenuous his bond with him is. "He has himself obtained the first and highest place and is therefore called Supreme. The heavenly body which is nearest to him most enjoys his power, and afterwards the next nearest, and so on successively until the regions wherein we dwell are reached. The earth and the things upon the earth are farthest removed from the benefit which proceeds from God" [177]. This pseudo-Aristotelian deity certainly does not find his delight in being among the children of men [178].

There can be no doubt that this anonymous writer is assuming a theological stance very much akin to that of Philo and the Gnosis. God is inaccessible and an abstraction or a philosophical concept rather than a person. Although he is the creator and sustains all that is, in the last resort he is not interested in what he brought forth. He belongs to the upper spheres and does not occupy himself with the nether spheres which are considered inferior and not worthy of his presence. However, the author was not a Gnostic. The most important Gnostic articles of faith are absent from his treatise : the wicked Demiurge, the utter rejection of the doomed world, the ascent to heaven by the chosen, and last but not least, the role of knowledge.

NOTES TO CHAPTER I

1. Isaiah Gafni s.v. 'Alexandria' in Enc.Jud. 2, 589/590.
2. Philo himself describes this pogrom in his Contra Flaccum 53-96.
3. Philo, Contra Flaccum 41-43.
4. Eusebius, Hist.eccl. 17. 1 says that, according to tradition, the philosopher met the apostle Peter when in Rome. Although Eusebius says that this is 'not improbable', it is almost certainly a legend.
5. See the article 'Antisemitism' (by Eds) in Enc.Jud. 3, 89/90. Philo himself described the events of AD 38-40 in his Legatio ad Gaium (= Caligula).
6. The little we know has been assembled by H. Leisegang s.v. 'Philon (Alex.)', PW XX (Stuttgart, 1950), 1-3.
7. Jos., Ant. 1.218.
8. Jos., Ant. 18. 259 sqq.

9. Goodenough, Introduction, Ch. IV, The Jew.
10. Philo, Legatio 189 and 192.
11. For the much debated question whether or not Philo knew Hebrew I refer the reader to the very thorough and detailed discussion in Nikiprowetzky, Le commentaire, Chap. 3 Les connaissances hébraiques de Philon. This scholar's conclusion is that the philosopher really did not know Hebrew. : "A whole sheaf of convergent indications are pleading forcefully in favour of this ignorance ... Our ultimate impression, therefore, is negative" 81.
12. 1. F.H. Colson and G.H. Whitaker eds. 10 volumes in the Loeb Classical Library, 1929-1962, + two volumes translated from the Armenian by R. Marcus, 1953 (see Bibliography). An earlier standard edition in Greek is that by Leopoldus Cohn and Paulus Wendland, Philonis opera, 1896-1915, in six volumes + one volume indices, 1926-1930 (see Bibliography). 3. A good translation into German (without the Greek) is that by Leopold Cohn, Isaak Heinemann, Maximilian Adler and Willy Theiler, 7 volumes, Berlin, 1962-1964 2 (1908 1).
13. Yehoshua Amir (Neumark), s.v. Philo Judaeus. Writings. Enc.Jud. 13, 410/411.
14. Already the title of Wolfson's book expresses this far-flung admiration : Philo. Foundations of Religious Philosophy (see Bibliography). This author called him ' a philosopher in the grand manner', Wolfson, Philo I, 114.
15. Bousset, Rel.d.Judentums, 454.
16. Nikiprowetzky, Commentaire 1/2.
17. Festugière, Rév.II. Le dieu cosmique, 533/534.
18. Festugière, Rév.II Le dieu cosmique, 553.
19. Wilson, Gnost.Probl. 36.
20. Wilson, Gnost.Probl. 31.
21. Wilson, Gnost.Probl. 32.
22. Strictly speaking, Jahve is a kind of generic name too, but throughout the Old Testament it is used as a personal name.
23. Ex.3:14.
24. Philo, Leg.All.III. 105.24.22
25. Philo, De Vita Mosis I.74-75.
26. Philo, De somniis I.230.
27. Pohlenz, Philon 435.
28. Philo, De opificio mundi.

29. "While the Hebrew form is incapable of a plural and asserts the unity of the divine Being by attributing to him personality and denying the divinity of all other beings, theos either admits of a plural or escapes plurality by avoiding the problem of personality. Thus the substitute of theos for Elohim involves some readjustment of thought", Dodd, Bible and Greeks 7.
30. Wilson, Gnost.Problem 51; the reference is to Plutarch, De Iside et Osiride 351 C-E.
31. Dodd, Bible and Greeks 7 : "Philo has not escaped this tendency".
32. Wilson, Gnost.Problem 32.
33. Philo, Deus imm.
34. Philo, Deus imm. 20-23.
35. Philo, Deus imm. 33.
36. Philo, Deus imm. 52.
37. Philo, Deus imm. 52.
38. Philo, Deus imm. 24-26.
39. Philo, De immut. Dei 49.
40. Heinemann, Philons Bildung, Par. 11, Zusammenfassende Untersuchungen, 511-574.
41. Heinemann, Philons Bildung 527, believes that Philo actually only knew the Torah (in Greek); he did not know the 'Oral Law', the Pharisaic lore (528).
42. See Vol. VI, Ch. II.11.
43. As Drummond, Philo, I,18, wrote more than a century ago : "These two positions, maintained by Philo without any sense of contradiction between them, were in reality incompatible. Moses did not teach the Platonic doctrine of ideas, nor could the deep utterances of a spiritual philosophy be found in the literal meaning of the stories of Genesis".
44. Bréhier, Idées 69.
45. Treitel, Gesamte Theol. 19.
46. We find it also in Paul, Rom. 1:18-21.
47. Philo. Leg.All.III.97-99.
48. Philo, De praem. et poen. 43-44.
49. Philo, Leg.All.III.100.
50. Philo, De praem. et poen. 46.
51. Philo, De migr.Abrah. 34-35.
52. See Vol. III, Ch. III.11b.

53. Philo, De opificio 8. See for this subject Wolfson, Philo I, 202/202.
54. Wolfson, Philo I, 204.
55. Bréhier, Idées 72.
56. Philo, Leg.All.II.3.
57. Philo, Leg.All.II.1; De somniis I.72.
58. Bréhier, Idées 73.
59. Philo, De somniis I.67.
60. Wolfson, Philo II, 111; Wolfson's quotation from Philo is from Deus imm. 62.
61. Wolfson, Philo II, 113.
62. Philo, De opificio 7.
63. Philo, De opificio 8.
64. Philo, De opificio 12.
65. It is difficult to find in Philo an expression suggesting that God is not the creator of the universe. We should in any case not conceive of the intermediaries as the real creators. In Philo's theology God remains the sole creator, but all the same the picture becomes somewhat ambiguous and open to misunderstanding by the introduction of intermediaries who are not found in Genesis. See Wolfson, Philo I, 269/270.
66. Philo, De opificio 16.
67. Treitel, Gesamte Theol. 19.
68. Philo, De opificio 18.
69. We should not think of Philo's Logos as being identical with the 'universal soul' or 'world soul' of Plato and Stoics, Wolfson, Philo I, 325/326.
70. Wolfson, Philo I, 258, says categorically that "wisdom ... is only another word for Logos, and is used in all the senses of the term Logos". I am not so sure of that.
71. Philo, De confusione 97.
72. Philo, De somniis I.238.
73. Philo, Deus imm. 83.
74. Philo, Rer.div. 230. Chapter V, Der philonische Logos of Farandos' book Kosmos und Logos (see Bibliography) was a great help in finding my way through the great mass of Philonic writings.
75. Philo, Deus imm. 31.
76. Philo, Deus imm. 83.
77. Philo, De Abrahamo 122.

78. Philo, De vita Mosis 2.288.
79. Philo, De spec.leg.III.180.
80. Philo, De somniis I.69-70.
81. Philo, De praem. et poen. 46.
82. Philo, De opificio 25.
83. Wolfson, Philo I, 289/294 aptly summarizes Philo's views on Logos, intelligible world, Ideas, wisdom, and powers, beginning with stating that it all started with Plato's Theory of Forms.
84. Philo, De Abrahamo 115.
85. Philo, De conf.ling. 28.
86. Philo, Leg.All.I.177.
87. Philo, De post. Caini 89.
88. Pohlenz, Philo 442.
89. Philo, De post. Caini 14.
90. Treitel, Gesamte Theol. 19.
91. Philo, De spec.leg.I (De sacrificantibus), 329.
92. Runia, Philo 455.
93. Philo, De somniis I.253.
94. Philo, De sacr.Ab. 57.
95. Zeller, Phil.d.Gr. III.2.2, 440.
96. Billings, Platonism 13.
97. Philo, De opificio 81.
98. Philo, De spec.leg.I.27.
99. Philo, De cher. 19.
100. Runia, Philo, 453/454; this scholar is somewhat contradicting himself by saying that "matter is a shadow reality that ultimately proceeds from God" and that matter is "in some way independent of God". By the same token he first firmly denies that in Philo there would be 'true dualism' (but what would 'untrue dualism' be?), strongly asserts that "Philo's thought is monistic", and then comes back on this by stating, with A.H. Armstrong, that "in Philo one might speak of 'monarchic dualism' (whatever that may be). There is much confusion of terms in this. We find here the common misunderstanding, which I always combat (Vol. I, pp. 63/64, Vol. IV, p. 298, Vol. V, pp. 20, 22, 24, 108, Vol. VI, pp. XXIV/XXV, 137/138, 202, Vol. VII, p. 210) that monism and dualism, as being opposites, exclude each other. In fact, a dualistic system can easily have a monistic starting-point; the dualism then sets in one level lower. Monis-

tic-dualistic systems occur far oftener than systems that are dualistic right from the start.

101. See Vol. IV, Ch. II.3.
102. Drummond, Philo II, 276.
103. Philo, De opificio 134.
104. Philo, De opificio 136.
105. Philo, De opificio 69.
106. Bréhier, Idées 121.
107. Philo, De opificio 69.
108. Zeller, Phil.d.Gr. III.2.2, 441/442. Several studies have been devoted to Philo's reliance on Platonism, for instance the already mentioned works of Billings and Runia (see Bibliograpy).
109. Philo, De cher. 120.
110. Drummond, Philo 277.
111. Philo, De gigant. 8-15.
112. Philo, De gigant. 40.
113. Philo, De gigant. 29.
114. Philo, Deterius potior 100.
115. Philo, De ebrietate 101.
116. Philo, Leg.All.I.69.
117. Philo, De migr. Abrah. 16. Baer, Philo's Use 14 writes : "One of the fundamental emphases of Philo's anthropology is the distinction frequently made between a higher and a lower part of man's being ... (This) basic distinction remains constant throughout his writings".
118. Philo, Leg.All.III.42.
119. Philo, Leg.All.III.41.
120. Philo, Deus imm. 142-143.
121. Philo, Deus imm. 123.
122. Philo, De migr. Abrah. 13.
123. Philo, De gigant. 14.
124. Philo, Leg.All.III.68.
125. Philo, De ebrietate 69.
126. Philo. Leg.All.II.38. On pp. 15/16 Baer, Philo's Use, prints a dual list of the elements in resp. man's higher and lower nature. The higher nature is a-sexual (that is, it does not contain the categories male-female); it is only in the lower nature that the categories male-female appear. On p. 42 Baer says : "Throughout his

writings Philo associates a great variety of evils with the female, and uses female terminology in close conjunction with (a number of) highly pejorative expressions."
127. Zeller, Phil.d.Gr. III.2.2, 450.
128. Philo, De opificio 150-152.
129. Wilson, Gnost.Probl. 45.
130. Philo, De fuga 51.
131. Philo, De fuga 52.
132. True enough, Philo employs the word 'epistēmē' here instead of 'sophia', but Philo, Rer.div.127-128 proves that these terms are interchangeable.
133. Philo, De ebrietate 30.
134. Bréhier, Idées 119.
135. Philo, De somniis II.242.
136. Philo, De fuga 92.
137. Bréhier, Idées 117.
138. Philo, Leg.All.I.34.
139. Philo, Det.pot. 86.
140. Philo, De gigant. 31.
141. Philo, Det.pot. 159.
142. Philo, De congressu 79.
143. Philo, Div.her. 68-69.
144. See Vol. VII, Ch. II.
145. Philo, De virt. 178-179.
146. Philo. Deus imm. 143.
147. The same in Philo, Leg.All.III.27.
148. Philo, De migr.Abrah. 42.
149. Philo, De somniis I.60.
150. Philo, De Abrahamo 268.
151. Philo, Spec.leg.IV.70.
152. Philo, De decalogo 148; Spec.Leg.IV.64.
153. In this way the question is put by Pearson in his essay 'Philo, Gnosis, and New Testament' (see Bibliography).
154. See Bibliography.

155. R. McL.Wilson, Philo and Gnosticism. Kairos 14, 1972, 213-219 quoted by Pearson in his essay on Philo and the Gnosis (see previous note).
156. Jonas, Gnosis u. spät-ant. Geist II.1, 38-53, 70-121.
157. Pearson, Philo and Gnosis 77.
158. Wilson in his Kairos-article 215; he states there that the philosopher "belongs mostly to Gnosis, not to Gnosticism". As I wrote earlier, I consider the distinction Gnosis-Gnosticism invalid, Vol. VII, Ch. I.1.
159. Sloterdijk, Wahre Irrlehre, Weltrev. I, 35.
160. Robert Musil, Der Mann ohne Eigenschaften, Rowohlt edition 1981, I, 407.
161. See for the Old Testament Vol. IV, Ch. II, for the New Testament Vol. VII, Ch. IV, and for the Talmud Vol. VII, Ch. VI.
162. See for Plato Vol. III, Ch. III, for Hellenistic philosophy Vol. VI, Ch. III, for early Gnostic systems Vol. VI, Ch. III, for Essenianism Vol. VII, Ch. V, and for Jewish mysticism Vol. VII, Ch. VI.
163. However, the authenticity of the text is recently defended by some scholars.
164. Festugière, Rév. II Le dieu cosmique, 479. Greek text ed. W.L. Lorimer. English translation E.S. Forster. See Bibliography.
165. Philo, De mundo 391a.
166. Philo, De mundo 397b.30-31.
167. Philo, De mundo 400a.21-24.
168. Philo, De mundo 397b14-16.
169. Philo, De mundo 400b11-13.
170. See Vol. VI, Ch. IV.20.
171. Philo, De mundo 401b7-14.
172. Philo, De mundo 396b6-7.
173. Philo, De mundo 398a14-15.
174. Philo, De mundo 398a3.
175. Philo, De mundo 400a3.
176. Philo, De mundo 400a4-9.
177. Philo, De mundo 397b24-31.
178. Prov.8:31.

CHAPTER II

HERMETIC SECRETS

1. On hermetic scripture in general

Towards the end of the Hellenistic era, that is to say in the period with which we are occupying ourselves in the present volume, a body of revealed wisdom came into circulation that, anonymous though it was, was attributed either to Iranian Magi, like Zoroaster, or to an Egyptian god (Toth-Hermes), or to some Hellenic sage, like Pythagoras.

Among these writings the collection that bears the name of Hermes, the so-called 'hermetic' literature, is not only the most important and voluminous but also the best-known. But whereas the writings themselves remain the almost exclusive province of experts, the word 'hermeticum' has become proverbial. In modern languages, this word, like 'hermetic(al)' in English, has come to mean mysterious', impossible to gauge, as in a 'hermetical art' such as alchemy, or in a 'hermetic secret', or, then again, it may simply mean closed, as in a 'hermetically' sealed vacuum. The reason for this modern usage is that ancient Hermetic scripture is mysterious indeed and difficult to probe (and was meant to be so). Since we have diverted our attention to Egypt, we shall restrict ourselves to the Corpus Hermeticum because this originated in the country of the Nile.

2. The mental landscape of hermetic literature

a. The demise of rationalism

In Volume I of his magisterial and voluminous work on the thrice great Hermes, the 'Hermes Trismegistos', Father Festugière, the learned Dominican, sketched a broad panorama of the mental landscape in which the Hermetic writings originated [1]. He begins his exposition with a theme that I myself have broached more than once already, the decline of rationalism in the Hellenistic world [2]. Hellenism, in the time of the arrival of the Romans, had lost much of its vigour. "It was like a wounded animal that had lost much blood" [3]. This scholar believes that one of the main reasons for this decay is that the Greeks did not experiment. Their philosophy and their science always remained purely speculative. "Greek rationalism had, so to speak, devoured itself. Because of the fact that reason gave itself free play without encountering its normal check in a better observation of concrete data, it was inevitable that that very dialectical power ... that had served to erect the building now was instrumental in destroying it" [4].

People became tired of discussion; the general intellectual climate was sceptical. With regard to religion, this worked out disastrously. There was no longer a common creed or generally accepted ethical rules. Imperial Roman religion, official and political as it was, proved incapable of filling the gap. In the first century A.D. Pliny came no further in his idea of God than to state that "it is God when a mortal helps another mortal" [5].

In this wasteland we perceive a remarkable revival of Pythagoreanism. "Belief in Pythagoras grew in the measure that the impact of reason became less ... The power of this new Pythagoreanism was that it was not a philosophy nor a coherent system of thinking on God, the universe, and man." Festugière calls it 'a religious order'; its members blindly followed the word of an inspired person [6]. A number of neo-Pythagorean sacred books, called 'hieroi logoi', began to circulate.

b. The reassertion of the East

Oriental prophets too were very much en vogue, perhaps even more than Hellenistic ones, because the Greeks had always tended to overrate the wisdom of the East. They honestly believed that "barbarians had been the teachers of the first philosophers of Greece" [7]. In their eyes oriental priests held the key to the mysteries [8]. In particular Egyptian priests enjoyed a great reputation of purity and wisdom. But Persian magi, Essenians, and even Brahmans were no less renowned. Against the backdrop of Roman decadence, they stood out as ascetic and as conversant with the divine. Egyptian priests and Chaldaean sages "knew how to enter into contact with supernatural forces, how to evoke them, and if need be, how to restrain them; furthermore, they knew the mysterious 'chains' that connect all the things of this world with the stars, and with the spirits that inhabit the stars" [9].

What an incredible spectacle this conjures up! Exactly in the time that the whole world seems to have gone Greek, the East reasserts itself with renewed vigour. But all those elements of Hellenistic civilization that once were considered so valuable - rationality, science, humanism - now were regarded with indifference. What people really wanted was Gnosis, oracles, apocalypses, and all this the East had to offer in abundance [10].

c. Another idea of the divine

The idea of the divine underwent a profound change. For the Greeks of the classical period religion had been a public affair; there was not much personal piety. The Olympian divinities were venerated in the official polis cult, publicly. With the demise of the Olympian gods the public cult lost its significance, although it was not abolished; however, it no longer satisfied the really religious spirits, if it had ever done so. The idea grew that the quest for the divine, the supernatural, was now up to the individual and should be performed in solitude. The gap between the public cult and true religiosity began to widen, perhaps so much so that we may think of it as dualistic.

I am thinking here of hermits, an entirely new phenomenon in the ancient world, people who turned their backs on public life, on the human community, and withdrew into the desert, to be alone with the godhead. Festugière says that the Greek language in this period was enriched with a number of neologisms all derived from 'monos' = alone, for instance, 'monoosis' = solitude, or 'monazein' = to live alone; the best-known of these terms is, of course, 'monastêrion' = monastery, which has survived in modern English [11].

It was the most consequent of the seekers for solitude (I am not speaking of Christians but of pagans) that went into the 'erêmia', the desert, where they became 'hermits'. Soon enough such hermits became highly popular, particularly in Egypt where there is no lack of desert and where the overpopulation of the Nile valley can get on one's nerves. People, even Roman soldiers, flocked to the hermits, disturbing their precious solitude, not to follow their example but rather to admire their way of life and to listen to their wise pronouncements that had the ring of oracles.

And oracles were what people wanted. We should not think here of oracles in the ancient sense - pronouncements made by a divinity regarding what was in store for a person who sought for guidance -, but in the sense we still give to it, that of definite statements on questions of morals and religion made by some religous teacher. Such a statement was also considered divinely inspired [12]. As I wrote earlier, the late Hellenistic age was prone to dogmatism [13]; oracular pronouncements have all the character of a dogmatic statement. This was what people needed who were fed up with and felt confused by philosophical scepticism and the ineffectiveness of official religion. Hermetic literature too was of this revealed, oracular, and dogmatic type.

3. Hermes and Toth

Greeks and Hellenized Egyptians gave the Hellenic name of 'Hermes' to the ancient Egyptian god Toth. This divinity was considered the inventor of chronology; later he was the scribe of Osiris, the god of life and death. In consequence he became the inventor of writing, and of all science and all the arts, to say nothing of magic. Its seems that the whole wisdom of Egypt was concentrated in him [14]. Toth was especially venerated in the town of Khomounou (now Achmouneim) in Middle Egypt, rebaptized by the Greeks as 'Hermopolis'. It was there that his star rose still higher. "The theologians of Hermopolis ... elaborated a cosmogony in which the principal part fell to Toth." He, or at least his voice, now became a sort of creator, perhaps showing, says Festugière, " some resemblance with the Greek Logos or the Sophia of Alexandrian Jews" [15], of Philo, for instance. As Voice he could make pronouncements of a dogmatic kind. "What he pronounces subsists in eternity" [16].

With the Greeks Toth became highly popular. The reason that they renamed him "Hermes' was not that their own god Hermes had been the inventor of the art of writing, for this invention was attributed by them to the Phoenicians. But Hermes no less than Toth was associated with all the arts and with liberal education; he was the inventor of the lyre. In medical magic he was knowledgeable too. Later, in Hellenistic times, Hermes, the messenger of the Olympian gods, was considered an interpreter, a herald of wisdom. He too was assimilated with the divine Logos. And then his identification with Toth was finally complete [17].

Now why was this Hermes-Toth called 'Trismegistos', the 'threefold great' - 'trismegistos' being a kind of superlative of 'megistos' (= greatest), the superlative of 'megas' (= great)? This epithet was given solely to Hermes with whose name it became so completely identified that 'Hermes Trismegistos' looks a single proper name [18]. Ancient authors propose different explanations for the epithet, for instance that Hermes was the Prime Author, Cause, and Demiurge of Creation [19]. That the explanations differ proves that nobody knew exactly what the origin of this 'trismegistos' was.

4. Hermes and the hermetic writings

The authorship of every ancient book of importance was ascribed to Hermes; if one wanted to enhance the prestige of a certain writing, it had to go under his name [20]. Probably there existed no books under the name of Hermes in Egyptian already in Pharaonic times, but under the Ptolemaeans, in the Hellenistic period, there originated an hermetic literature in the Greek language. This literature is a motley collection; all kinds of work form part of it (I shall come back to this). There has been much speculation on the question who were the authors of these books. Festugière points out that hermetic literature forms part of a widely spread genre, a literary mode; what is called 'hermetic' in Egypt is elsewhere ascribed to Jewish, Chaldaean, Iranian, or Indian brotherhoods. In all probability there existed in Alexandria a community of Hermes. The tracts of the Corpus are partly the literary rendering of what the disciples were taught there orally. We must, however, not think of a kind of Hermetic Church : there was no cult with priests and sacrifices, but prayers were said and hymns sung [21].

A genre like this is wholly in keeping with the spirit of the times. It is a genre that does not seek scientific knowledge for its own sake; it rather wants to conduct the reader to the godhead. Whatever their subject, such books are no more than pseudo-scientific; they want to appear mysterious and use the jargon of the mystery-cults.

What makes it utterly impossible to attribute the body of hermetic writings to any specific religious group is that it presents two totally opposed and irreconcilable doctrines. The one is that the world is all good, the other that it is essentially bad. In the last case it cannot possibly be the work of God, or of the prime godhead, because he, hidden and unknowable as he is, shuns contact with matter. The mortal who wants to reach him must fly this world and live in it as a stranger [22].

5. What hermetic writings are about

All kinds of disciplines went pell-mell into the making of the body hermetic. First, there are a number of astrological treatises. As a substitute-religion, astrology had become very popular during the last centuries B.C. [23]. A great many pseudo-sciences were based on it: astrological medicine, alchemy, magic, the divinatory arts [24]. Hellenistic astrology saw celestial bodies as animated and conscious beings; they were able to exercise a benign or malign influence on the lives of men. A person well versed in astrology could even predict the future.

Next there are treatises on medicine and botany, two disciplines that were closely connected with astrology because of the supposed influence of the stars on nature and the human body. From there to the occult sciences it is not a great step. Works like these claim to explore the secrets of nature, the knowledge of which would bestow marvellous therapeutic and magic powers on its possessors [25]. The logical sequel to these writings are, of course, those on alchemy and magic, alchemy having the status of a mystical religion.

In addition to the former group there is a body of writings that may be dubbed 'literary fiction' [26]. We should not think here of the manner of working of the modern novelist, since the anonymous authors of such fiction claim to have been favoured with a revelation. We are confronted by a wisdom or knowledge not resulting from study or human experience but coming from another world, from on high, from a god; we are justified in speaking of 'gnosticizing' with regard to these works. Such revelations may come to the receiver when he is in a state of ecstasy or dreaming; he may even have a conversation with a divinity or signs from heaven may reach him. The transmission of a revelation always goes from a superior to an inferior, from a sage to a prince, from a prophet to a layman, or from a father to a son [27].

The tractates of this group have a philosophical character. Or perhaps we should call them 'theosophical' since religious subjects have pride of place in them. They are all centred on the themes God-cosmos-man. Whereas we use to style the whole body of writings mentioned so far 'hermetica', the literary or philosophical or theosophical hermetica, the most intriguing group, is given a name of its own, the 'Corpus Hermeticum'. For our subject they are the most important.

6. The composition and character of the Corpus Hermeticum [28]

The collection originated in several stages during a period roughly circumscribed as between 100 B.C. and A.D. 100 [29]. It consists of seventeen treatises or 'logoi', the term 'logos' denoting that they are revealed wisdom, for they pretend that conversations of Hermes Trismegistos himself with his son Tat were revealed to some anonymous author [30]. There is no telling who made a 'corpus', a collection out of these seventeen or when [31]. Although there is not much that is genuinely Egyptian in it [32] - its character is rather Greek -, it presents itself as Egyptian wisdom. It does not contain a uniform ideology and is by no means free from crass contradictions [33].

7. The optimistic line

As I said above, there are two stances in the philosophical hermetica. To put it as briefly as possible, the world is good, and the world is bad [34]. I do not want to convey the impression that, in my opinion, dualism is always and everywhere the order of the day. Although it is an integral part of the picture, the non-dualistic stream usually is by far the strongest. In order to keep the perspective straight I shall devote a few paragraphs to non-dualism in the Corpus. For even if it is true that the mentality of the time was generally dualistic and gnostic, there remained some islands of non-dualism.

In the non-dualistic tracts the world is considered beautiful; order reigns everywhere. This is manifested by the regularity of the seasons and the harmonious structure of the earth itself and of all living beings, above all of man. In the supralunar sphere we see the stars, the planets, and all the celestial bodies move according to fixed laws. This admirable ordering presupposes one who created it. Contemplation of the world leads naturally to the knowledge and adoration of God [35].

Let me give a few illustrations from one of the optimistic tracts, the 'Asclepius' [36]. "God loves his creation because it is full of the goodness of all beings" [37]. He is the creator of all that is, of the heavens, of the human soul, and of all beings in the world; these are all governed by their creator [38]. There is no talk of a wicked Demiurge. Man is dually (not dualistically) composed of soul and body; with the soul he admires the things of heaven, with the body he cares for the terrestrial things and governs them [39]. He has a privileged position in creation and is superior to all other beings because of his intellect which makes him analogous to God [40]. The fact that he is mortal (only partly, for his soul is immortal) does not make him inferior [41]. Nowhere do we find a condemnation of procreation and sexuality nor are there any anti-female utterances. Evil exists but not as a sovereign or autonomous power; it will disappear as soon as the hour of God has come.

Ten of the tracts of the Corpus Hermeticum are in this optimistic vein [42]. In one of these procreation is not only judged positively but even declared holy. God is Father because he has created everything. Therefore, "wise people regard the procreation of children as the most important function of life and the most holy". To die childless is considered a great sin [43]. Another treatise implicitly rejects the notion of a hidden God. Of course, God is invisible but he makes himself visible through his creatures [44]. If one desires to know God, he or she need only consider how marvellously creation is made [45]. There is no dualism of God and cosmos : "One should never sever the Creator from things created" [46].

However, even in these predominantly optimistic writings there are some curious dualistic slips. Absolutelynothing, with the exception of God himself, may be called good, even however little. "For they (human beings) are body and soul, and (therefore) have no place that can contain the Good" [47]. Another point is that tract no. 5 seems to dilute the notion of an immanent God into a sort of pantheism. "Nothing in the whole world exists that is not him. He himself is by the same token all that is and all that is not ... He is multiform, or better, omniform, he has all the names" [48]. There are more passages with a pantheistic colouring [49]. Festugière speaks of a 'cosmic mysticism' here [50]. So much for the optimistic vein.

8. Some shorter pessimistic passages

Four tracts are decidedly pessimistic and show dualistic characteristics [51]. One of these, no. 7, is entitled 'The greatest evil among men is ignorance about God'. The Greek word for 'ignorance, 'agnoosia', makes us think of the Gnosis. This text even speaks of "the undiluted doctrine (logos) of ignorance" which "inundates all the earth and corrupts the soul imprisoned in the body" [52]. The author hardly has sufficient terms of abuse for the body : tissue of ignorance, support of malice, chain of corruption, murky jail, living death, sensible corpse, the tomb you carry with you, the thief who lives in your house, the one who hates what you love and loves what you hate [53]. What your enemy (the body) fears is that you will lift up your eyes, contemplate the beauty of truth, and then come to hate you (the body) [54]. This is all that this short treatise has to say but it is as clear as daylight that this is vintage dualism, that of body and soul, of man split into two.

Dualism is also to be found in the hermetic fragments collected by Stobaeus in his anthology in the first quarter of the fifth century [55]. One of these maintains that there is no truth on earth but only in the celestial bodies. In our human constitution, mixed as it is, there is no truth at all. At best terrestrial things are copies of truth but this applies only to a small number of them; the rest are lies. It is possible that some human beings may have a notion of truth, but only if God accords it to them.

Things below are incapable of receiving the Good since they are perishable, dissoluble, movable, always in a state of alteration, ever changing from one form to another. Since such things are not even true with regard to themselves, how can they reflect any truth whatsoever? For everything that changes is a lie. And since man too is changing all the time, to the extent that he becomes unrecognizable to those who knew him earlier, what truth can we find in him? Only the sun never changes and remains always identical with itself. Therefore it not only rules over all the things on this earth but it produces them. After the One and the First he is the true Demiurge [56].

Quite a number of aphorisms in Stobaeus are blatantly dualistic. "God is good, man is bad. There is nothing good on earth, nothing bad in heaven. Nothing in heaven is slave, nothing on earth is free. Nothing is unknowable in heaven, nothing is knowable on earth. There is no communication of celestial beings with those on earth, but there is communication of terrestrial beings with those in heaven. All that is in heaven is irreproachable, all that is on earth is open to reproach. Earth is without reason, heaven is reasonable. What is God? An immovable good being. What is man? A changeable bad being" [57].

9. The 'Poimandres'

a. The introduction

I have kept the best-known, most intriguing, and most Gnostic of all the hermetic treatises to the last. It is the so-called 'Poimandres' which means 'Shepherd of Men' [58]. The anonymous author begins to relate how once upon a time a figure of an enormous size appeared to him introducing himself to him as 'Poimandres, the Mind (Nous) of the Absolute Power' [59]. This Poimandres tells the author that the Light that was before Nature is 'the Nous your God' and that he himself is this Nous. This means that we are in the presence of a divine revelation and that we are to be instructed with regard to things beyond the ken of human beings. As soon as the author has said that he above all wants to know (gnoonai) God, he falls into a state of ecstasy and is blessed with a vision [60]. It is at once clear that true knowledge of God is impossible when we are in our normal humdrum state.

The author thus presents himself as a highly privileged person, exclusively blessed with a special revelation directly coming to him from the supreme godhead. The only sensible thing people can do is to listen to him. In this way he situates himself squarely in the venerable élitist tradition of Greek philosophy. But he is not really a philosopher since he has not discovered what he knows by dint of hard thinking. It has been revealed to him in a state of ecstasy. For, infinitely far away from creation, from the cosmos, hidden in mysterious heights, unapproachable, unknowable, God resides. He is called the Nous of Absolute Power; this means, he is seen primarily as mind. The consequence of this is that he can be reached only by those (few) who have received the right knowledge.

b. God and matter

From the very first there exists a marked duality, even a dualism, between, on one side, the primal God and, on the other, the dark, serpent-like mass of unspecified matter; there obviously is no connection or relationship between them. For this reason Jonas described them as two 'first principles' [61]. However, as he also points out, they are not coeval. It all begins with the Divine Light from which or in which shortly afterwards Darkness develops and sinks downward. This implies that we should not think of radical or absolute dualism, that of two coeval and equally sovereign first principles, but of relative dualism in which one principle is to some extent dependent on the other. Jonas remarks that the fact that the "Darkness appears **after** the Light and must have arisen **out** of it (his emphasis) (is) contrary to the Iranian type of dualism" [62].

"Whence came that (the Darkness), if it was not there from the beginning? ... This would be precisely the question of questions", put here by Jonas, "which all non-Iranian dualism must finally face ... (The) principle is that a break or darkening within the divinity must somehow account for the existing division of reality" [63]. Even the most attentive reading of the 'Poimandres' will not supply us with an answer to the question why this occurred. It remains unexplained, it is there, it just happened, no more can be said of it.

The author describes his first God, the Nous, as the Absolute Power or Sovereignty ('authentia') and as being unlimited ('aperioristos'). Nevertheless, he carries Darkness, at least as a potentiality, in himself. What does this mean? That God is not whole? And how are we to understand the idea that Light generates Darkness? Normally this can only mean that the Light goes out or becomes less brilliant. But to suggest this is obviously not the author's intention! I assume that he, perhaps unconsciously, was ready to put up with this irregularity if only he could stick to his basic dualistic conceptions.

That Darkness could proceed from Light is, however illogical this may seem, a consequence of the inveterate tendency of the Gnostics to think in contrasts and their innate incapability of conceiving of fundamentally homogeneous entities. Even their God does not escape this tendency. Although he is not dual himself, he nevertheless brings forth his dualistic counterpart.

What really intrigued the Gnostics was the evil world, the wickedness of mankind, as they saw it. Whose fault was this? Not of mankind! Mankind was the victim; they located the origin of evil as far up as possible, even not shrinking from seeking it in the bosom of the godhead itself. That they were unable to offer an explanation did not bother them at all. The author of this work and Gnostics in general were really interested in explanations on this theogonic level. For they were not scholars, philosophers, or theologians; essentially they were mythologists, myth-makers; as such they found the answers in myths which were their own explanation.

However this may be, radical or relative, Iranian or non-Iranian, explainable or left unexplained, logical or illogical, the dualism of God and matter is conspicuous. The author wanted to make it perfectly clear that the two are basically, dualistically different (although he does not speak of 'matter' but of 'Nature'; both terms are evidently identical). We know that matter stood in a very bad odour with the Gnostics. In their bipolar world God is at one end, matter at the other, separated by a deep chasm, an almost unbridgeable abyss. Matter is described here in utterly negative terms : it is dark, horrifying, tortuous and serpent-like.

c. The origination of Nature

Darkness, however, is not wholly passive. It is capable of acting autonomously, without any intervention from the first God, which is proved by the fact that it brings forth, of its own accord, humid nature; how this could happen is left entirely unexplained. I interpret 'humid nature' as the raw material of the cosmos, as yet formless and unorganized but ready to be worked upon. We might see it as something passive that is awaiting the coming of an active principle. Perhaps this is the import of a cryptic wailing that, according to the text, arises from humid nature. Festugière translates this 'boê' as 'cri d'appel', as a 'summons'. I believe that he is right in this, because the Greek author very probably means that humid nature is appealing to somebody or something not to leave it in this quandary indefinitely. This proves that matter possesses a kind of consciousness because it seems to realize that it is in a poor condition.

d. The function of the Logos

Nature's lament is heard by the first of the three 'successive divine creations or emanations' [64], the Logos, or the Word (the others being the Demiurge and Man). "The luminous Logos that issued from the Nous is the Son of God" [65]. The luminous Logos issues from the Nous (God)'; it is, therefore, an hypostasis of God. The existence of the Logos is necessary in order not to make the first God directly responsible for creation. Out of the Light the Holy Word (Logos hagios), responding to the cry from below, descended into the obscurity, the primeval state of nature [66]. The Logos 'comes over' humid nature which means that it enters into 'an intimate union' with it. The murky and indefinite mass that Nature still was is kept moving by the breath of the Logos [67]. Basing himself on this description, Jonas believes that the author was acquainted with the first biblical creation story in Genesis, in the Septuagint version, of course [68].

The union of Logos and Nature results in a work of separation, the lighter elements, fire and air, being separated from the heavier ones. Air and fire soar upwards; this constant talk of upwards and downwards is typical for the Poimandres. Acting from within nature the Logos keeps the lighter elements firmly in their place, for left to their own devices, they would (I guess) continue their flight upwards. On no account must any material element, however light it may be, enter the celestial sphere. As it is, fire becomes 'the outer circumference' [69] of the cosmos. Poimandres describes this to the visionary as the archetypal form of the cosmos.

e. The Powers

The divine Nous is male and female at the same time, as well as Life and Light [70], containing in itself an incalculable number of Powers ('dunameis') [71]. What we see here is the first idea of a cosmos; Poimandres expounds this as a 'the archetypal form, the principle preceding the infinite beginning' [72]; the future visual world is already archetypically prefigured in the Nous by the Powers [73]. Once again we are, just as in Philo, confronted by a model of the cosmos, although it must be admitted that this 'model' is still very formless. The will of God (i.e. of the God-Nous himself), taking the archetypal model of the beautiful cosmos as its guide, then fashions the concrete universe [74]. We shall have to come back to this 'Will of God'.

In other words, Nature has arrived at the point that everything can be generated. The author is now able to perceive the countless number of 'Powers', of elements that will go into the construction of the cosmos. My speculation is that the constitutive elements of the cosmos were thought to be potentially present in the still unspecified Nature.

f. The Demiurge and the Governors

We are now plunging right into the most authentic Gnostic mythology. The Nous-God brings forth a second Nous, a Demiurge, god of Fire and Breath; Zielinski called the triad Nous Father-Nous Demiurge-Logos 'the hermetic Trinity' [75]. This Demiurge "fashioned seven Governors who encompass the sensible world with their circles, and their government is called 'Heimarmenê' (Destiny)" [76]. These 'Governors' are the seven 'planets' according to the ancient conception, namely the sun, the moon, and the five planets that are visible with the naked eye. The ancient world, and in particular Hellenism with its belief in astrology, was always very much inclined to ascribe a decisive influence on the course of events to celestial bodies. The 'Governors' will steer human existence with an iron hand, but in this context their real task seems to be to shield off the primal God, the Nous, from the world.

g. The imprisonment of the Logos

The interference of the Logos with Nature has the dire consequence that it gets so involved with it that it remains stuck in it. This makes it all the more evident why the first God does not meddle with Nature and matter. Having taken pity on helpless matter and having started the process of differentiation, it became so deeply immersed in Nature that the Logos is unable to escape upwards. It is clearly very dangerous for an intellectual power, even for pure intellect, to mix too much with matter, with what is only natural.

It is only when the Demiurge has appeared and has sealed off the natural world from the upper regions that the Logos succeeds in leaving Nature. It is as though the Logos needed a rescuer from its sorry plight, a rescuer that is nothing else than its exact likeness. This escape looks like a prototype of the flight of the human soul. The soul too has to make good its escape by passing through the spheres of the planets. The result of the departure of the Logos is that the nether sphere remains deprived of reason; with the Logos no longer present in it, Nature immediately reverts to a state of mere matter, just as the body, after the soul has left it [77].

The Logos, after having separated the first elements, fire and air, from the indefinite obscure mass, flies upwards and unites itself with the Nous-Demiurge with which it is of the same substance [78]. If the bewildered reader now asks whether the Logos and the Demiurge are one entity or two, the answer is that this is a fine specimen of the inclusive thinking that is so typical of Gnostic ideology.

h. Two cosmogonical architects

At the first creational level below the primal Nous, therefore, we meet not one but two beings or entities, the Logos and the Demiurge. Both proceed from the first God and are in essence united with him, with the consequence that they are of the same substance. In this concept there is, for once, no dualism; the two entities are not opposed to each other or to God. This Demiurge is not the evil counterpart of the Nous Father. At a somewhat later stage Logos and Demiurge join hands to collaborate in unison, so much so that they manifestly are only one entity.

Why then were two cosmogonic architects needed, if they have the same origin, are substantially the same, and, finally, merge into another? One answer could be that, when the planetary spheres are being created, the Logos is still deep down in the material world. An other answer could be found in the different functions of Logos and Demiurge. By his action within the material world the Logos supplies the element from which the planetary sphere are fashioned, fire; the Demiurge then takes over and creates the planets and their orbits. The task of sealing off is especially entrusted to the Demiurge, because it is he who fashions the planets. The planetary sphere is also the sphere where imperfection and even malevolence begin.

The Nous Demiurge, indeed, is an hypostasis of the Nous Father, but this notwithstanding, he is the creator of the planetary spheres, the Governors of the material world which, as the offspring of Darkness, are the source of evil and imperfection, and as such, opposed to the first God. This explains why a second Nous is needed : the pure Nous Father must in no way be associated with the material creation.

j. The screening off of God

If we follow the downward road, from the first principle to the actual creation, we do not, as we have seen, arrive immediately at the cosmos, the world, and mankind. In no way! Between the first world and our world, us that is, several stages are interposed. God is so solidly screened off from mankind that more than ordinary knowledge is needed to have cognizance of him. Hence the author, as somebody who 'knows', is able to pray to the holy God "who wants that people know ('gnoosthēnai') him and who is known ('ginoosketai') by those who belong to him" [79].

k. The role of the 'Will of God'

The 'Powers', which are the potentialities within Nature or their archetypal constitutive elements, are of themselves incapable of forming an orderly world, a cosmos. For this the intervention of the 'Will ('boulē') of God' is required. This Will that appears only once receives in itself the Logos and taking the archetypal world (that of nature surrounded by fire) as its model, fashions an orderly cosmos out of the elements. It is the Logos in her (the Will is female) that enables her to work according the archetype.

But what is this mysterious Will of God? Not, of course, what Jews, Christians, and Moslems understand by it! The fact that it is female proves that it (she) is not the primal God, for he (it) is androgynous. We must also remember that the divine Logos descended into Nature, that Nature took it in. The speculation of Jonas with regard to this difficult point is that the Will of God is an alternative to the Darkness of the beginning. "The main support of my (Jonas') argument is the role of the Logos in both instances. As the humid nature, after the Logos has 'come over her', separates into the elements (the lighter ones, that is - F.), so the female Will of God, having been 'received' into the Logos, organizes herself according to her elements" (that is, she materializes those elementary potentialities that were left in her after air and fire had broken out of her - F.) [80].

Nevertheless, I don't think that wholly identical cosmogonical processes are meant by the author of 'Poimandres'. The text remains mysterious to the point of obscurity but is not repetitive. The passage with the Will of God represents a second stage; in the first one the Logos works on a still utterly passive and undifferentiated nature, in the second Nature has acquired some sort of consciousness (proved by the fact that she can now imitate the archetypal model and acts creationally herself). "The Boulē is more of an independent agent that is the humid nature" [81]. It must not escape attention that all the time there is no talk of the primal God.

1. The cosmological function of the planets

What the Logos and the Demiurge do unitedly together is to send the heavenly bodies on their way around the earth by initiating the rotative movements of the planetary sphere. It is the endless circular movements of the planets which set the creational process going. One could think of a potter's wheel. Sea and earth are separated and the living beings all originate [82]. The text is confusing here. First it says that the rotation brings forth the mindless animals made out of the lower and heavier elements, but one sentence further on it states that, after earth and water had been separated, it was from the earth that the animals came.

What is probably more important is that the planetary spheres, once sent rotating, appear to possess a creational drive of their own. Since we have already seen that the Will of God too acts as a creational agent, the whole thing looks rather muddled. For who or what is, when all is said and done, the real creational agent? But I don't think that the author was interested in answering this question. Questions that seem logical to others look quasi-logical to the Gnostic mind. What the author really wanted to convey is that the first God remains at immense distance from the process of creation; as long as he could keep his God out of this, he did not really bother who were the actual makers of the world.

We should not overlook the fact that the planets are made out of fire and breath, that is to say, out of elements that, light though they are, are in the last resort material and hence belong to the nether world. Furthermore, they are 'Governors', they govern the world in such a way that their management is dubbed 'Destiny' ('heimarmenè'). This means that the higher powers deliver the cosmos, the world, and mankind to fatality. The Logos now having fled from it, the world is without reason.

Jonas says that "we may ... suspect that the gifts of the planetary powers ... might have their fatal aspects". He admits that "the immediate context contains nothing to bear out this suspicion" [83] but then we have to remember that, as we shall see, the liberated soul has to pass through the planetary spheres, leaving behind at every sphere part of its bad nature. This implies that the quality of the nether material sphere, the planetary one included, is infinitely inferior to that of the higher powers.

m. The role of Man

The first Nous, the Father God, brings forth an archetypal Man with whom he becomes enamoured (which means that the Nous is in love with his own image) and to whom he entrusted all his works [84]. Just as his Father, this archetypal Man is androgynous; that he should not be confused with a common mortal is proved by the fact that he does not need sleep [85].

Man is the third hypostasis of God. As an entity he stands on one line with the Logos and the Demiurge, with this proviso that he was brought forth after the completion of the world (minus mankind). We must see him as 'an emanation of his (God's) own substance'; he is God's 'own representation' and not, like Adam, "formed of clay, (he) is Life and Light purely" [86]. The Demiurge calls him 'brother' but his ontological status is higher than that of the Demiurge and his authority is greater because he is to have full power in the creational sphere.

Once again the author saddles himself with a problem. Man wants to create but the creational process is almost finished. There is no indication that he created anything at all. He shows a resemblance to the Logos in this that he too descends into mindless Nature. If we remember the fate of the Logos, we can imagine that Man, by his downwardly directed urge, runs the same risk of becoming confined within Nature. It is said that each one of the planets gives Man part of its own character. As we have seen that the properties of the planets are not wholly positive, we may assume that some negative qualities accrue to Man during his downward voyage. This is consistent with the fact the soul during its ascent sheds its bad habits by ceding them to the Governors. The Gnostics saw "the planetary constituents of the soul as **corruptions** (Jonas' emphasis) of its original nature contracted in its descent through the cosmic spheres" [87]. The dualistic message is clear : no being or entity of a higher origin can mix with the matter of Nature with impunity.

n. Anthropology

We now come to the anthropological part of the tract. Seeing what the Demiurge had already achieved, the archetypal Man wanted to have his own creation. Following Zielinski, we might dub this 'the First Fall' since Man desired to have more than was due to him [88]. He entered the demiurgical sphere where he assumed full authority, while the Governors (the planets) acknowledged him as their master [89]. That the orbit of the planets really served as a shield is shown by the fact that Man has to break through it in order to push his way downward to lower Nature. Fond of erotic imagery as the Gnostics were, the author now relates how Man falls in love with Nature who embraces him [90].

The union of Man with Nature is presented in the form of the Narcissus motif. Nature saw the beautiful reflection of Man in the water (when his shadow fell over it) and fell in love with him. And Nature's love was answered by Man. Let us turn to Jonas for an explanation. "The Poimandres version (i.e. of the Narcissus motif - F.) ... adroitly combines three different ideas : that of the Darkness becoming enamored of the Light and getting possession of part of it; that of the Light becoming enamored of the Darkness and voluntarily sinking into it; that of a radiation, reflection, or image of the Light projected into the Darkness below and there held fast" [91].

The intermingling of the Model-Man with Nature is the reason why (ordinary) man is 'double', mortal because of the body (the contribution of Nature), immortal because of the essential Man [92]. It is a favourite topic of the Gnosis that man is constituted of two differing and not concordant parts. Another of their tenets is that sexual love is degrading. Here we see that the essential Man, although being immortal and having power over everything, undergoes the condition of mortals even to the point of becoming a slave [93]. This really constitutes a Fall, the moment that creation definitely became derailed; it is the second and decisive Fall.

All this is a mythical way of relating of how soul and body came together, although they are by no means of the same sort. But why is this archetypal Man needed? Let us not forget that the Logos has left Nature and that it is now mindless, soulless. In one way or another the presence of soul and mind in it must be explained. They can only arrive from beyond the natural world, since this is unable to generate something spiritual itself. It is manifest that what is described is a Fall of something higher into something lower. Jonas adds that Man was committing an error, "in that he was ignorant of the lower elements". He is half excusable because these elements were clothed in his own reflection [94]. So much is certain that 'the submersion of a divine emanation in the lower world' goes to the detriment of the divine.

What follows is announced by Poimandres as 'a mystery kept hidden to this day'. From the coupling of Nature and essential Man seven androgynous beings are born with their natures corresponding to those of the seven planets [95]. In these seven primeval human beings, Essential Man, composed as he is of Life and Light (let us remember that the divine Nous too is Life and Light), transforms himself into soul and mind, Life becoming soul and Light turning itself into mind [96]. This implies that there are authentically divine elements in the primal human beings. The real task of essential Man seems to have been to endow these creatures that partly originate from Nature with these higher elements.

What is related so far comprises the first world-era, the era of androgynity. It ended by the will of the Father. All animals, and also the human beings, all of them up to this point androgynous, were divided into males and females. It is not explained why this should be so. But we should keep in mind that Man was subdued by Nature because of his erotic desire. No wonder that henceforward sexuality becomes dominant on earth. All the hitherto androgynous beings are now split up into males and females. Their Eros, says the text explicitly, will be the cause of their death.

God gives them the command to be fruitful and multiply; for once the author shows himself acquainted with the Book of Genesis, since he is obviously referring to 1:22. Just like Philo, he handles Scripture in an arbitrary way, for he adds a text not to be found in Genesis : "Man endowed with mind shall recognize that he is mortal and that the cause of death is love" [97]. I do not doubt that sexual love is meant. Jonas wrote that it was "ultimately love which drew Man into Nature" [98]. The reason of the Fall, therefore, is erotic attraction. As Festugière said, to 'know' the causes of life and death, and, in particular, that man is really immortal, is one of the two central themes of the Gnosis (the other being the knowledge of God) [99].

o. Humanity divided

The author's next subject is the (dualistic) division of mankind into two groups. Some who 'know' themselves will attain the Supreme Good. Others who cherish their bodies - bodies consequent on the error of love - remain in obscurity and suffer in their senses the dispensation of death [100]. Here we have several Gnostic themes at the same time : apart from the already mentioned split of mankind, there is the depravity of sexuality, the opposition soul-body, and the knowledge that sets one free. Those who prefer to remain ignorant are for this reason deprived of immortality.

What is their sin? It is their failure to realize that the first cause of the existence of the body is that hateful obscurity which was the prime condition of the material world; hence death feeds on it [101]. The knowing ones, on the other hand, are aware of the fact that they also issue forth from the Life and the Light brought into Nature by the Primal Man who, in his turn, received those gifts from the Father. This passage makes it abundantly clear that the division among mankind is fiercely dualistic in nature, and that this is caused by the eventuality of knowing and not-knowing, i.e. by gnosis. In fact, the author several times uses forms of the verb 'anagnoorizein'.

The Nous promises to protect the chosen against the nefarious operations of the body by barring its evil influences from entering the soul [102]. The vicious ones he delivers into the hands of an avenging demon; they will be left a prey to all the evil and passions of which they are insatiable [103].

p. The ascent of the soul

The final sections of the Poimandres are devoted to another beloved Gnostic theme, the ascent of the soul. The road back to God can only be travelled by the pure of heart who 'know'. During the ascent of these souls to heaven they strip themselves of everything untoward and are then free to return to the first God and be united with him.

At the moment of death man, who basically is a compositum, is dissolved into his constituent parts. The body, being material, is given over to dissolution. Each of the senses returns to its source (among the elements that is), with the exception of the irascible [104] and the conscupiscent sense that sink down into dumb Nature [105]. And now man, that is to say his soul (this refers, of course, only to the souls of the elect) is ready to soar upwards. Passing through the spheres, it successively sheds all its vicious proclivities, like the power to grow and to decrease, the arrogance of dominion, the appetite of wealth, and so on [106]. Thus purified, the soul enters into the Ogdoas which is the sphere of the fixed stars, where perfect order and regularity reigns. With those who are already there he begins to exalt the Father and to mount upwards still more. In mounting all the redeemed souls become Powers and enter the godhead. And then the author utters the great word : "Such is the good end of those who have attained gnoosis : to become God" [107].

q. Preaching the message

In the concluding sections the author relates how he begins to preach this message to the people. "O nations, earthborn men, you who have abandoned yourselves to drunkenness, sleep, and ignorance, stand back from all this ... After having heard me they joined me unanimously ... But some soon had enough of me, for they were engaged in the way of death. But others threw themselves at my feet and implored me to instruct them ... And I became the guide of humanity and taught them the doctrine how and by which means they would be saved ... For in myself the sleep of the body had become the vigil of the soul, the occlusion of the eyes a veritable vision ... And all this happened because I had received from my Nous, that is from Poimandres, the Word of Absolute Sovereignty" [108].

10. The World Girl

a. The general character of the tract

Among the hermetic writings one finds a text with the curious title 'Korê Kosmou', the Girl of the World, the World Girl. It has been preserved for us by Stobaeus in his anthology, but not in its entirety although he certainly presents almost all of it. First of all, who is this 'World Girl'? Several scholars believe her to be the Egyptian goddess Isis, since the whole tract is a revelation from her to her son Horus [109]. The tract opens in this way : "After having said this, Isis etc.", and the hymn that in all probability formed the conclusion of the tract is missing

[110]. Very probably its author will remain forever unknown but there can be little doubt that he was an hellenized Egyptian.

The literary genre is that of a revelation given by the goddess Isis to her son Horus; however, Hermes too is playing a major role, since he 'knows' ('gnous') all [111]; he is mentioned as the composer of 'sacred books' (= the hermetic tracts) [112]. The mythological background is manifestly Egyptian, although a number of Hellenic divinities are present too. There is one phrase that proves that the author knew the Old Testament, at least the Book of Genesis : "God spoke and it was" [113]. He also made use of Plato's 'Timaeus'. The fact that the text is not really clear and consistent in all its parts is explained by its being composed out of material of different provenance and periods [114]. Admittedly this a very difficult and often baffling text in which several traditions have been interwoven, sometimes rather clumsily. Luckily the provenance of the different parts of the text need not occupy us. Bousset wrote in 1921 that up to then nobody had succeeded in presenting a convincing analysis of it [115]. I wonder whether we have got much further by now.

b. The celestial bodies

In the beginning there was only God and the Chaos. The upper and nether worlds were intermixed, and matter was still formless. Everything below God was in the grip of Ignorance. But then God enabled the gods to know him; it is not disclosed who these gods were or from where they came, but there can be no doubt that they were the stars [116]. At their request God created the cosmos. He begins with the upper regions where the stars were placed.

The same domain became the abode of the souls, the 'psuchai'. The Korê differs from the biblical creation stories in the fact that at a certain moment we see God working as an alchemist, mixing substances, murmuring secret incantations, shaking and boiling the concoction [117]. Out of this potion he fashions myriads of souls, all eternal, which have their abode in the celestial ranges of the cosmos; it is their task to make the 'cylinder' (the cosmos that is) revolve according to a fixed order [118]. After their creation the signs of the Zodiac were fashioned. Herewith the upper world was complete.

The first categorical statement of the text is that 'multicircled heaven' is superposed on lower nature [119]. Here the heavenly bodies are meant; their character is divine, they are eternal, they are perfect, they encompass the whole world, they govern lower nature over which they have sovereign authority. It is expressly stated that they are beyond the ken of human intelligence [120]. Once again one descries the dualistic distinction of the higher and the lower worlds. They have quite another status than in the 'Poimandres', more Platonic, since in the 'Korê Kosmou' they form no part of the lower world. It is not said who created the celestial bodies nor that they were created at all; they are obviously coeval with the supreme godhead.

c. Knowledge and Ignorance

Lower nature is very much afraid of the heavenly bodies; it does not know God and is enveloped by Ignorance ('agnoosia') [121]. "In the primal Chaos the as yet formless matter grows" [122]. Here too 'knowing' and 'not-knowing' are the important themes. For a long time Nature was sterile and inactive; it brought forth nothing at all. Now God decides to reveal himself to the 'gods', that is to the celestial bodies; he performs this by distributing to them the light that is in himself [123]. The 'gods', therefore, 'know'; first and foremost they know who is God. Be it noted, however, that initially even the gods do not know who God is!

d. The optimistic creation story

Then it is the turn of the nether region, the lower world. The heavenly bodies presented a request to God the First Father to the effect that the initial chaos might be organized into a cosmos. God acceded to their request [124]. In a later section it is God himself, here called the Monarch, who convokes the gods and announces to them that the chaos must disappear [125]. The souls now take part in the cosmogonical process; taking the signs of the Zodiac, that is the archetypal animals, as their model, they fashion the animal species. (Here the author forgets that the earth has not yet been created.

For what now follows one should keep in mind that God is acting as his own Demiurge; he is really the creator of the world in the direct sense. In this respect the Korē is much nearer to Jewish and Christian conceptions than the Poimandres. However, about the manner in which God fashioned his creation the reports diverge somewhat. For our purpose it is not necessary to go into details with regard to the cosmogony. It is sufficient to state, with Festugière, that this part of the story is optimistic. "God who is essentially energy in the act of bringing forth, is unable to stand it that creation does not resemble him, that it remains inactive, and that it is not the object of praise" [126].

e. The pessimistic creation story

But soon the tone ceases to be optimistic. The souls do not remain content with their functions and their fixed places in the established heavenly order. They desire to leave their departments and move about, for "to stay attached to a single residence they consider a death". In leaving their appointed sections they transgress the divine commandments [127]. Therefore, God decides to punish the rebellious souls by incorporating them into human bodies; these bodies were expressly created with this end in view [128]. The task of creating them is entrusted to Hermes who is described as the sacred Mind (Nous) of God's Nous; once again it is overlooked that the earth does not yet exist.

f. Man as a 'Fremdkörper'

Although God rejoices in his work and even declares the earth sacred [129], man seems to be the exception, a 'Fremdkörper' on the face of the earth. He, or rather his body, his material part, obviously is considered far inferior to the souls, even as something malicious; the descent of the souls into bodies evidently is a severe punishment. Man is a strange and uncomfortable mixture of divine and material elements. Here we have a clear example of the Fall according to the Gnostics : the imprisonment of the soul in the body. It deserves attention that the Fall takes place after the creation of the visible world but before that of man. It is a cherished Gnostic notion that the Fall occurs in the upper spheres.

The divinities, in complete agreement with the supreme God, all contribute to the misery of mankind, although they have also some wholesome gifts in store for him. The sun declares itself ready to give more heat, the moon brings forth Terror, Silence, Sleep, and Memory (which we learn are disadvantageous), Kronos begets Justice but also Necessity, that is the iron rule of the law. Zeus shows himself afraid that there would be endless wars - in which he was not far wrong - and therefore engenders Fortune, Hope, and Peace. But Ares has already made mankind happy with Strife, Rage, and Quarrels. Aphrodite in her turn alleviates the troubles of humanity by presenting it with Desire, Lust, and Laughter - which, as we know, are mixed blessings. Finally, Hermes takes pity on man by conferring Wisdom (Sophia), Temperance, Persuasion, and Truth upon him [130].

God confides to Hermes the task of fashioning the human body. For this he uses the residue of the mixture out of which the souls were made. This having become totally dry, he mixes it with a large quantity of water. In other words, the body is matter rather than anything else. The Monarch is content with the result and orders the souls to enter into the bodies [131]. The souls protest loudly against being forced into the bodies, like captured animals being driven into their cages [132]. One of them gives vent to the feelings of all of them by declaring that they are brutally separated from the upper spheres in order to undergo no end of miseries. "We who had a blessed life together with the gods, are going to be imprisoned in ignoble and base tents" [133]. It is categorically stated that the souls no longer belong to God; they are unhappy and feel condemned [134]. There are two dualistic separations here : that of God and the souls, and that of soul and body.

g. The possibility of redemption

The distracted souls now implore God to set a limit to their sufferings. The Monarch graciously accedes to their request. But as Bousset aptly remarks, it seems to be entirely forgotten that the fall of the souls had already been accomplished [135]. For a group of the souls, so they are told, is obviously without blemish and may continue to inhabit the heavenly sphere! A second group will sin only slightly and may in due time return to heaven, while leaving their bodies behind. But the third group, the really bad souls, will be banished forever into animal bodies; they will have to roam from one animal body to another [136].

The author adheres to the doctrine of rebirth. The final aim is the separation of soul and body but before it comes to this the souls will have to change their earthly abodes. The best will enter into the bodies of just kings, philosophers, legislators, prophets, etcetera. But now follows a passage that seems to contradict what the author had said about the fate of the bad souls. Now we read that the souls of the just assume animal shapes, and moreover the animals in question will be considered the most excellent, like lions, eagles, or dolphins [137]. This is a plain absurdity!

It is only after all this that the cosmogonical task is taken up again. Sun and moon are created, and the earth with all that belongs to it. At last human beings have their own abode. But in spite of all that has happened, there is still general ignorance.

h. The destruction of the earth

Now a horrible spirit arises from the earth; it is Momus, the embodiment of criticism. And he pronounces words that will rejoice the hearts of modern ecologists. For he indicts mankind for doing untold damage to the earth. Man, with his indiscreet eyes and his garrulous tongue, pries into everything that does not concern him. He pulls out the roots of the plants, dissects animals, even human beings, fells the woods, travels to the limits of the earth, and penetrates into the most inaccessible sanctuaries of nature. And he does all this with carefree arrogance [138]. There is a dualistic distinction between man and his terrestrial habitat.

Totally ruled by Ignorance, the souls, making use of their bodies, urge them to attack one another, the strong destroying the weaker [139]. But then the elements rise in protest and petition God because of the savage behaviour of mankind. Fire complains that it is misused, air that it is polluted, water that it is soiled, and Earth that it is disfigured [140]. Man threatens the very structure of the cosmos.

j. The saviours

God answers the bitter complaints of the elements by appointing Isis and Osiris as the saviours of the earth. They make an end of the initial anarchy, erect temples, inaugurate sacrifices, and give laws to the mortals [141]. After having brought order to the world, the two gods return to heaven.

k. The tract's main theme

However many incoherences there may be in this text, says Festugière, there can be no doubt that its real theme is the opposition 'agnoosia-gnoosis', Ignorance-Knowledge [142]. In the lower world Ignorance is the dominant (negative) force, while Knowledge is at home in the upper spheres. But initially not even the gods possess Knowledge (of God); God himself has to impart it to them. It is clear that the knowledge in question is a divine gift. It is expressly stated that the human race is incapable of understanding [143]. The great guardian of Knowledge is Hermes, the Mind of God; he is the one who knows and has written sacred books containing a secret doctrine [144]. This secret knowledge has been passed on by Hermes to the ancestors of Isis and by them to her [145].

Being in sympathy with the mysteries of heaven, Hermes is able to communicate the hidden knowledge to mankind. He has put it down in writing but then has hidden it in order that each new generation born into the world will seek it [146]. For the time being, because of the general depravity nobody proves interested. But later, when general disorder is reigning among men, the saviours of mankind, Isis and Osiris, are taught by Hermes all the secrets of his writings and the secret ordinances of God.

It is clear that there is a dualistic opposition between Ignorance and Knowledge. Ignorance is the common lot of creation in general and of mankind in particular. Knowledge is divine, a gift of God, and being secret and hidden, it has to be revealed. Without this gnosis there would be no order on earth. A subtheme of this main theme is the incapability of mankind to manage its own affairs. Its only capacity, when left to itself, is to pollute the earth and to be at each other's throats.

l. Optimism and pessimism

Another main theme, distinguished by Festugière [147], is the duality of the creational motifs, one optimistic, one pessimistic. The first is that of cosmogony, of all that exists; the second refers to the destiny of the souls. In the cosmogonical part order and beauty are the keywords. The famous question 'what is wrong with the world?' may be answered with 'nothing is wrong with the world'. Even with regard to the creation of human beings, a vague optimism is dimly shining through; God's resolve to make them is even announced to an assembly of the gods [148].

The tone is getting pessimistic when the gods present their gifts; many of these are plainly unpleasant. Then the souls, although created by God himself, have to descend into human bodies, and all is now wretchedness. Order is finally restored by a direct divine intervention.

m. Is the Korê a Gnostic treatise?

Is this an authentically Gnostic treatise? Yes and no. Gnostic without any doubt is the opposing of Ignorance and Knowledge, although it must be admitted that the term 'gnoosis' itself does not occur. It is equally Gnostic in that the Knowledge in question is of a higher sort and in possession of the gods; mankind is clearly incapable of 'knowing'. Also Gnostic is the notion that soul and body have a different origin and contract an uneasy alliance. And nothing could be more Gnostic than the idea of the imprisonment of the soul in the body.

On the other hand, some typically Gnostic tenets are not sustained. There is no trace of a rejection of the whole cosmos as a bad and utterly lost thing. There is also no wicked Demiurge who is responsible for creation. God himself is the real creator and acts with intermediaries. But there is one notable exception : the human race is created by Hermes who, after all, is a god too, even the Nous of God. God himself obviously takes his distance from mankind. The judgment on humanity is predominantly negative. Finally, there is no ascent of the souls through the spheres back to God. But perhaps the return of Isis and Osiris at the end, with their mission accomplished, entails a promise to mankind.

n. The dualistic elements in the Korê

There are, to conclude, so many dualistic elements in the 'Korê Kosmou' that this tract fits admirably into the line of dualistic treatises we have already perused. It must be conceded, however, that its dualism is not of the most radical sort. First of all, there is a marked duality between the upper and nether spheres. Then there is the opposition of soul and body, the most marked of the dualisms in this tract. Furthermore, man is constantly at war with nature, or with his environment, as we would put it. Finally, there is the running fight between Knowledge and Ignorance.

NOTES TO CHAPTER II

1. Festugière, Rév. I L'astrologie et les sciences occultes.
2. See for instance Volume VI, Ch. IV.10.
3. Festugière, Rév. I L'astrologie 7.
4. Festugière, Rév. I L'astrologie 8.

5. Pliny, N.H. 2.18.
6. Festugière, Rév. I L'astrologie 14/15.
7. Festugière, Rév. I L'astrologie 23.
8. Festugière, Rév. I L'astrologie 27.
9. Festugière, Rév. I L'astrologie 37.
10. Festugière, Rév. I L'astrologie 41/42.
11. Festugière, Rév. I L'astrologie 45.
12. Festugière, Rév. I L'astrologie 59.
13. See for instance Vol. VI, Ch. III.4b.
14. Festugière, Rév. I L'astrologie 67/68.
15. Festugière, Rév. I L'astrologie 68.
16. Inscription from the first century A.D. on the walls of the temple of Dendera, quoted by Festugière, Rév. I L'astrologie 69.
17. Festugière, Rév. I L'astrologie 71-73.
18. Festugière, Rév. I, L'astrologie 73/74. 'A syncretism of Thoth and Hermes', says Fowden, Eg.Herm. 22.
19. Quoted by Festugière, Rév. I L'astrologie 74.
20. Festugière, Rév. I L'astrologie 74.
21. Van den Broek/Quispel, Corp.Herm. 25/26. Idem in Tröger, Mysterienglaube 54/55 : "Wenn in CH XIII eine Opfer-Praxis eindeutig abgelehnt wird ..., dann darf man die oft gestellte Frage nach einem Kult getrost verneinen, und das trifft unserer Meinung nach für die Hermetik überhaupt zu." And this is what this same scholar says respecting a possible Hermetic community : "Man wird sich die Hermetiker als Esoteriker vorzustellen haben, die in kleinen Kreisen zusammenkamen, um sich in die Gnosis einzuüben und bei Gebet und Gesang mit einander Gemeinschaft zu halten. Dabei hielten vielleich fortgeschrittene Brüder Vorträge und Fragestunden für die Neulinge und führten sie so in die religiösen Geheimnisse ein. Die hermetischen Traktaten können auf diese Weise als 'vervielfältigte' Referate entstanden ... sein." G. van Moorsel, Myst. of Herm.Trism. 129 : "So we can do very well without the idea of a Hermetic church, but Hermetic **conventicles** (his emphasis) are the obvious thing to think of." (P. 130) In these conventicles hymn-singing was very important; "it is part of the cosmic contemplation". Fowden, Eg.Herm. 149 : "Our philosophical texts imply an actual historical milieu that was dedicated to the spiritual life. Instruction and initiation were group experiences, even when, at the highest levels, they involved only the spiritual guide and a solitary pupil; and those who participated in these encounters instinctively expressed their solidarity and joy through prayer

and hymnody, and in such comradely gestures as embraces and the sharing of food. But they knew nothing of the special priesthoods, cult-places and ceremonies that were essential to the conduct of mystery religions."

22. Festugière, Rév. I L'astrologie 81-84.
23. Vol. VI, Ch. IV.22.
24. Festugière, Rév. I L'astrologie 91.
25. Festugière, Rév. I L'astrologie 200.
26. Festugière, Rév. I L'astrologie 309.
27. Festugière, Rév. I L'astrologie, Ch. IX.
28. Fowden, Eg.Herm., The texts 1-11, is useful here.
29. The 'philosophical' Hermetica could be of a somewhat later date, late first tot late third centuries A.D., Fowden, Eg.Herm.14.
30. The innocent reader will be surprised to see that the last logos is numbered 18; this is because no. 15 has been deleted as not belonging to the Corpus proper.
31. The Corpus Hermeticum has been published with French translations by Nock and Festugière under the title 'Hermès Trismégiste' in four volumes (see Bibliography). Since shortly the Dutch readers may dispose of an excellent translation, publishe in an elegant volume, 'Corpus Hermeticum', introduced, translated, and annotated by R. van den Broek and G. Quispel (Amsterdam, 1990).
32. Iversen, Eg. and Herm. doctr. 29 writes that "in the running debate the importance of Iranian, Platonic, Stoic, Gnostic, Manichaean, Jewish and even Christian influences on the texts and their origin have been differently assessed and judged by their various advocates, while at the same time there has been a marked tendency to underestimate and downgrade the possibility of an influence from Egyptian sources". He himself adopts 'an Egyptological approach'. His conclusion on p. 54 is that "while its origin (i.e. of the Corpus) and the sources from which its singular doctrines were drawn remain debatable, its association with genuine and well-established Egyptian concepts and notions can hardly be denied or disputed". But my compatriot G. van Moorsel has this to say about 'the Egyptological approach' : he values the attempts of the last years to do justice to the non-Greek elements in Hermetism, but "nevertheless it must be said that the philosophical substructure of Hermetism, however electic it may be, links up directly with the points in question of Greek philosophy", thesis VIII of his doctoral dissertation Myst. of Herm.Trism.

33. G. van Moorsel, Myst. of Herm.Trism. 13 : "It is impossible to outline the Hermetic doctrine for the very simple reason that there is no such doctrine (his emphasis) ... The Hermetica are, 'dogmatically' speaking, a farrago, a Gordian knot, or, rather, a complicated draught."

34. Tröger, Mysterienglaube 5/6 presents a useful review of how the tracts have been classified by modern scholars : 1. Reitzenstein : pantheistic and dualistic; 2. Zielinski (1905/1906) idem; 3. Bousset (1914) : monistic-optimistic (the older part) and dualistic-pessimistic (the younger one); 4. Bräuninger (1926) : hellenic and oriental; 5. Quispel (1951) pantheistic-optimistic-monistic and pessimistic-gnostic; 6. Colpe (1961) dualistic and monistic-optimistic. Tröger does not mention Nock-Festugière. He himself groups the tracts in this way : a. hellenistic-pantheistic (V, VIII, IX, XIV); b. dualistic-oriental-gnostic (I, IV, VI, VII, XIII); c. mixed : IX, X, XII, Asclepius.

35. Quoted from Festugière, Rév. II Le dieu cosmique X/XI.

36. This treatise have come down to us in a Latin translation; of the original Greek text only a few fragments are extant. This Greek text bore the title 'Logos teleios'. It is unknown who wrote it and who made the translation (which was already utilized by St. Augustine shortly after 400). It is printed with a French translation in Nock-Festugière (Eds.), Herm.Trism. III.

37. Asclepius 8.

38. Asclepius 3.

39. Asclepius 8.

40. Asclepius 6-7.

41. Asclepius 9.

42. Nock-Festugière (Eds.), Herm.Trism.III.nrs. 2,5,6,8,9,10,11,12,14,16.

43. Nock-Festugière, Herm.Trism.III.2.17.

44. Nock-Festugière (Eds.), Herm.Trism.III.5.2.

45. Nock-Festugière (Eds.), Herm.Trism.III.5.3-5.

46. Nock-Festugière (Eds.), Herm.Trism.III.5.8.

47. Nock-Festugière (Eds.), Herm.Trism.III.2.14.

48. Nock-Festugière (Eds.), Herm.Trism.III.2.9-10.

49. See Festugière, Rév. II Le dieu cosmique. 59-71 La veine panthéiste.

50. Festugière, Rév. II Le dieu cosmique 55.

51. Nock-Festugière (Eds.), Herm.Trism.III, nrs. 1,4,7,13.

52. Nock-Festugière (Eds.), Herm.Trism.III.2.1.

53. Nock-Festugière (Eds.), Herm.Trism.III.7.2.
54. Nock-Festugière (Eds.), Herm.Trism.III.7.3.
55. Stobaeus, Anthologium III, 436-441. Nock-Festugière (Eds.), Herm.Trism.III, Exc. IIA.
56. Stobaeus III.11.31.
57. Stobaeus, Anthologium I 274-277, 1.41; Nock-Festugière (Eds), Herm.Trism. IV. Exc. XI.
58. Nock-Festugière (Eds.), Herm.Trism. I, no. 1. The reader will find a shortened English translation in Jonas, Gnost. Rel. 148-151, and a German translation in Werner Foerster (Herausg.), Die Gnosis I 141-161 (see Bibliography). The title 'Poimandres' was sometimes used to indicate the whole Corpus Hermeticum. Reitzenstein, Poimandres, concludes his Ch. I on 'Alter des Poimandres' with the statement (p. 36) that the original version of the tract must be dated before the beginning of the second century A.D.
59. Nock-Festugière (Eds.), Herm.Trism.III.1.1-2. 'Absolute Power' is an approximative rendering of 'authentia', which is a Gnostic term.
60. Nock-Festugière (Eds.), Herm.Trism.III.1.3-4. Fowden, Eg.Herm. XV : "Truth, for the Hermetists, was not an object of scholarly enquiry that might adequately be discussed in the pages of a philosophical treatise, but a seen and catalyctic force in their personal lives."
61. Jonas, Gnost.Rel. 179.
62. Jonas, Gnost.Rel. 173. I feel we should specify this 'Iranian type' somewhat by thinking in particular of Zervanism. Jonas spoke here of 'primary dualism' which he did not detect in the cosmogony of Poimandres. In my view there is most certainly 'primary dualism', but if Jonas really meant 'radical dualism', then he is right.
63. Jonas, Gnost.Rel. 171.
64. Jonas, Gnost.Rel. 154.
65. Nock-Festugière (Eds.), Herm.Trism.III.1.6.
66. Nock-Festugière (Eds.), Herm.Trism.III.1.4-5.
67. Elements like these made Reitzenstein, Poimandres, assume that an original pagan version was worked over by a Christian author. In his Chapter II, 'Analyse des Poimandres' he mentions what according to him are interpolations into the main text.
68. Jonas, Gnost.Rel. 147.
69. Jonas, Gnost.Rel. 171.
70. Nock-Festugière (Eds.), Herm.Trism.I.1.9.

71. Nock-Festugière (Eds.), Herm.Trism.I.1.7.
72. Nock-Festugière (Eds.), Herm.Trism.I.1.8.
73. Zielinski, Hermes 324.
74. Nock-Festugière (Eds.), Herm.Trism.I.1.8.
75. Zielinski, Hermes 324.
76. Nock-Festugière (Eds.), Herm.Trism.I.1.9.
77. Nock-Festugière (Eds.), Herm.Trism.I.1.10.
78. Nock-Festugière (Eds.), Herm.Trism.I.1.10.
79. Nock-Festugière (Eds.), Herm.Trism.I.1.31.
80. Jonas, Gnost.Rel. 171.
81. Jonas, Gnost.Rel. 171. Zielinski, Hermes 325, and Reitzenstein, Poimandres 39-45 both identified the Will as the Egyptian goddess Isis; in Reitzenstein's opinion the Boulè must be seen as the paredra of the Nous (39).
82. Nock-Festugière (Eds.), Herm.Trism.I.1.11.
83. Jonas, Gnost.Rel. 156.
84. Nock-Festugière (Eds.), Herm.Trism.I.1.12.
85. Nock-Festugière (Eds.), Herm.Trism.I.1.15.
86. Jonas, Gnost.Probl. 155.
87. Jonas, Gnost.Rel. 157.
88. Zielinski, Hermes 327.
89. Nock-Festugière (Eds.), Herm.Trism. I.1.13.
90. Nock-Festugière (Eds.), Herm.Trism.I.1.14.
91. Jonas, Gnost.Rel. 161.
92. Nock-Festugière (Eds.), Herm.Trism.I.1.15.
93. Nock-Festugière (Eds), Herm.Trism.I.1.15.
94. Jonas, Gnost.Rel. 164/165.
95. Nock-Festugière (Eds.), Herm.Trism.I.1.16.
96. Nock-Festugière (Eds.), Herm.Trism.I.1.17.
97. Nock-Festugière (Eds.), Herm.Trism.I.1.18.
98. Jonas, Gnost.Rel. 152.
99. Festugière, Herm.Trism.I, p.23, note 47.
100. Nock-Festugière (Eds.), Herm.Trism.I.1.19.
101. Nock-Festugière (Eds.), Herm.Trism.I.1.20.
102. Nock-Festugière (Eds.), Herm.Trism.I.1.22.

103. Nock-Festugière (Eds.), Herm.Trism.I,1.23.
104. Translation of 'thumos'.
105. Nock-Festugière (Eds.), Herm.Trism.I.1.24.
106. Nock-Festugière (Eds.), Herm.Trism.I.1.25.
107. Nock-Festugière (Eds.), Herm.Trism.I.1.26.
108. Nock-Festugière (Eds.), Herm.Trism.I.1.27-30.
109. Wilhelm Bousset s.v. 'Kore Kosmu', PW XII (Stuttgart, 1921). Reitzenstein, Poimandres 144-146, thought that it was the pupil of the eye of Osiris since this eye really is Isis who is hidden in the eye of the god. Zielinski, Hermes 356, however, opted for 'Jungfrau der Welt'.
110. Stobaeus, Anth. I Ekl. 44.927-981 (pp. 385-407). Reprinted in Nock-Festugière (Eds.), Herm.Trism.IV.23, to be cited by me as KK with the section numbering of the French edition.
111. KK 5.
112. KK 8.
113. KK 11 = Gen. 1.
114. Festugière, Herm.Trism.III, CL says that the author was working on two older texts, one with Isis as its speaker and one that is older with Hermes as spokesman. There are, however, several theories on the structure of the KK (Zielinski, Reitzenstein, Scott, Ferguson), all different, of which Festugière gives a useful review in Herm.Trism.III, CLXVIII-CLXXVIII. "As many opinions as scholars", he sighs. I sigh with him.
115. Bousset s.v. 'Kore Kosmu', PW XII (Stuttgart, 1921), 1387.
116. Because they circulate along the dome of heaven, KK 9. This is a curious inconsequence since there has been no creation so far. But it is apparent that the upper region as such, the 'ouranos', is already in existence, KK 9. See Festugière, Herm.Trism.III, CLXXXII/CLXXXIII.
117. KK 14. Zielinski, Hermes 367 spoke of 'a chemical process'.
118. KK 16.
119. KK 2.
120. KK 2 and 50. It was of the irregularities of the text that the cosmogonic theme of section 2 is taken up again in section 50.
121. KK 3-4.
122. Norden, Agnostos Theos 67.
123. KK 4.
124. KK 9.
125. KK 50.

126. Festugière, Herm.Trism.III, CLXXXI.
127. KK 24.
128. KK 25.
129. KK 51-52.
130. KK 29.
131. KK 30.
132. KK 33.
133. KK 34.
134. KK 36.
135. Bousset s.v. 'Kore Kosmu' PW XI (1921), 1388.
136. KK 37-49.
137. KK 42.
138. KK 43-46.
139. KK 53.
140. KK 54-61.
141. KK 64-65.
142. Festugière, Herm.Trism.III, CLVI.
143. KK 5.
144. KK 8.
145. KK 32.
146. KK 5.
147. Festugière, Herm.Trism.III, CLXXXI.
148. KK 27.

CHAPTER III

A LIBRARY IN A JAR

1. The site

Although there is a railway station and a railway bridge spanning the Nile, I don't think that the average tourist travelling to Luxor, some sixty miles farther upstream, will interrupt his journey at Nag' Hammâdi. It is only a small town with (in 1976) some thirteen thousand inhabitants, situated on the west bank of the river, circa three hundred and fifty miles from the Mediterranean (as the crow flies). What the town has to offer are some factories for wool, sugar and aluminium; in the river there is a dam. That is all.

Even archaeologists are not greatly interested in this region, although it has a very long history. Long ago the region was not unimportant. The nearby township of Hiw was several times the capital of Upper Egypt in Antiquity and during the Middle Ages. The locality of Nag Hammadi corresponds more or less with that of an ancient town that was called Shenesit in Coptic and Chenoboskion in Greek. A Roman garrison was stationed just opposite on the other bank of the river. In the beginning of the fourth century A.D. Chenoboskion was no more than a hamlet. In the vicinity a few Christian hermits lived in a religious community.

About 318 they were joined by a young convert to the Christian faith, Pachomius. This was an energetic young man, much given to organizing. He became the author of the very first monastic rule and the founder of eleven monasteries. In the close vicinity of Nag Hammadi, in the midst of the sugar plantations, there are three villages in which Coptic Christians are very numerous still. One of these, Es-Sayyad, is supposed to be situated on almost the same spot as Chenoboskion. On its outskirts two monasteries can be found, with in-between a plot of uncultivated land. Coptic reports say that it is there that Pachomius lived and worked; a cave is shown that, according to legend, once was an hermitage.

2. The discovery

Further on, beyond the plantations, the imposing rock wall of the Gebel al-Tarif rises up. On its eastern slope, not far from the hamlet of Hamrah Dwm, some pharaonic tombs of the sixth dynasty can be seen [1]. In December 1945 an Egyptian farmer was looking there for natural nitrate to be used as fertilizer for his fields (or so he says). Let us give all the honour due to the long Arab name of this twenty-six year old man : he was called Muhammad (son of) 'Ali 'al-Shamman (son of) Muhammad Halifah; he was accompanied by his brother Khalifah. Muhammad saw a corpse lying in one of the tombs and a jar standing at the side of the deceased (or so he said). He lifted the jar out of the tomb, carried it a few yards down the slope, and broke it. In it he found a number of very ancient bound books. Having wrapped the find in his tunic, he mounted his camel and rode back to 'Al-Yasr, the village where he lived [2].

3. The Library

The lucky farmer had no idea that he just discovered the now famous Nag Hammadi Library. It consists of twelve books, or codices (plus eight leaves from a thirteenth), bound in leather and containing fifty-two manuscripts on papyrus. Six of these are duplicates, six others were known already, either in Coptic or in Greek, which leaves us with a total of forty hitherto unknown texts. They would have originally numbered 1068 pages but since some are missing the present count is 1014. Several manuscripts are in a bad shape. They are in Coptic [3], in the Sahidic and Subachmimic dialects. All the codices are now in the Coptic Museum of Cairo but this does not mean that they went straight from the village of 'al-Qasr to the Egyptian capital. Quite the contrary!

4. The precarious vicissitudes of the Library

It is rumoured but not confirmed that the mother of the two brothers, an illiterate widow, burned part of the manuscripts in her oven. Equally illiterate neighbours and members of the family bought the rest for a trifle [4]. Some of them scented that there might be money in this. Let me restrict myself to the adventures of the most famous of the codices, Codex I, surnamed 'the Jung Codex' [5]. The family of the finder sold this precious codex to Fikri Jibra'il who kept a shop at 'al-Qasr. An antique dealer of Cairo, Phocion J. Tano, a Cypriote, had already in March 1946 been able to buy eight codices from an inhabitant of 'al-Qasr who had come to the capital on the instigation of an antique dealer from the nearby city of Qena. Guessing or hearing that there was more, this Tano went to 'al-Qasr where he bought nineteen leaves and fifty fragments of Codex I but failed to buy the rest because the price was too high.

In June 1946, however, forty-one leaves plus the leather cover of the codex were delivered to the antiques shop of Joseph Albert Eid, a Belgian living in Cairo. This man was knowledgeable enough to send photocopies of some pages to the École biblique of Jerusalem where they were identified as belonging to an ancient Gnostic document - "the first scholarly achievement in the study of the Nag Hammadi codices" [6].

On a day in the autumn of 1947 Eid was visited by Togo Mina, the director of the Coptic Museum, and Jean Doresse, a French scholar, with his wife Marianne. The result of this visit was a report on Codex I that was presented to several learned academies in Europe. Eid, having purchased more leaves from Codex I, put the whole lot on sale with the intention to export them, thereby dodging the official restrictions on the export of Egyptian antiques. The leather cover he sold separately. It went its own way and was finally bought in 1973 by the Institute for Antiquity and Christianity at Claremont (California).

The sensational news of the discovery, "surpassing in scientific interest such spectacular discoveries as the tomb of Tout-Ank-Amon", was presented to the world on June 10, 1949, in a press release by the Coptic Museum. After this, with the codex still on sale - Eid had died in the meantime -, Doresse on the one side and two scholars, Henri Puech and Gilles Quispel on the other, were in the race for its purchase; the question, of course, was who would be the first to collect the sum required to buy it from Eid's heirs. Puech and Quispel acted on behalf of the director of the Jung Institute at Zürich in Switzerland, Dr. C. Meier, who in his turn commissioned the Swiss ambassador in Cairo to act as his deputy there.

A rich American provided the necessary funds and thus, on November 15, 1953, the Jung Institute came into the possession of Codex I; this is why it is called the Jung Codex (although Dr. Carl Jung, the famous psychologist, never had anything to do with it). It was sent from Cairo to Utrecht (NL) where Quispel then taught and brought by him to Zürich where the invaluable document was handed over to Dr. Meier. Later the heirs of Dr. Jung returned it to the Coptic Museum in Cairo where it arrived on October 12, 1973, and where it still is to be found, along with the other codices.

5. Authors, translators, and librarians

The reader is, of course, eager to know who wrote these books, who made a library of them and for whose use, and who stored them away in such a desolate spot and why. To answer these questions we have very little to go by; the results of the investigations are very disappointing. What we know for certain is that the Nag Hammadi books were written originally in Greek and then translated into Coptic. Some tracts, we know from other sources, existed in Greek or in Latin. These include, for instance, some sections of the 'Asclepius', mentioned in Chapter II, and a very short passage from Plato's Republic [7]. The title of 'The Prayer of the Apostle Paul' is actually written in Greek but the rest in Coptic.

It is not probable that all the Nag Hammadi Codices (NHC) were translated by one translator or by a specially appointed group of translators in order to serve a specific clientele. There was no preconceived plan to organize one Coptic collection. They were translated one by one, at different times, and, as James Robinson said, "not always by a translator capable of grasping the profundity or sublimity of what he had before him" [8]. Many translations are transcriptions of Greek originals which in their turn were transcriptions of older documents. This means that, though the Library as such dates from the fourth century A.D. [9], most texts are much older, from the second century A.D. probably, or perhaps even from the first in some cases. But it is impossible to date the texts with exactitude.

The consequence of all this is that the texts were assembled and made into a collection by someone or by a community. We can imagine these books standing on the shelves of a reading room. Where? On the inside of the cover of Codex I the word 'Chenob' = Chenoboskion was found, which proves that the collection originated there (it is the only mention of this name in the whole library). "Personal names, titles, forms of address, and the like that are present in the cartonnage tend to indicate that it (the library) came from the Pachomian monasteries founded in this region up and down the Nile during the first half of the fourth century", says Robinson. The nearest of these monasteries, that where in all probability Pachomius' hermitage had been, was only at an hour's walk distance from where the jar was found [10]. The Christian monks of this institution obviously wanted to be able to consult these texts, when needed. They acquired them to have them at hand. These monks must have been non-hellenized Egyptians, not capable of reading Greek.

6. Why the collection was made

Why was this collection made? Robinson explains this in the following words. "The focus that brought the collection together is an estrangement from the mass of humanity, an affinity to an ideal order that completely transcends life as we know it, and a life-style radically other than common practice"[11]. And indeed, the texts contain much that must have strongly appealed to world-forsaken monks.

Is this sufficient to explain the presence of this largely Gnostic collection in a Christian monastery? Yes, says Robinson, "those who collected this library were Christians and many of the essays were originally composed by Christian authors. In a sense this should not be surprising since primitive Christianity was itself a radical movement"[12]. The problem, however, is that the texts in question are mainly Gnostic and partly hermetic, and by means orthodox-Christian. Not one Bible book was found in the jar, neither of the Old nor of the New Testament. Among the writings there is no liturgical or devotional book of Christian provenance nor a work by an early Father of the Church.

7. Why the collection was stored away

The jar was not found at the site of a monastery but at some distance from it in a desolate spot on the slope of a mountain. This looks as if somebody wanted to dispose of it. Who this person was, or who these persons were, and why he or they did this, is anybody's guess. Could it be that, like the Dead Sea Scrolls, the documents were stored away to save them from destruction or desecration by enemy soldiers? But we do not know of a foreign invasion or a civil war in this region in the period when the library was hidden.

What we know, however, is that in this period orthodoxy was beginning to win the day; there was a heresy hunt for Gnostic books, most of which were destroyed. Their contents survived only fragmentarily in the form of quotations and descriptions by the early Fathers of the Church. More specifically, we have a letter published by archbishop

Athanasius, patriarch of Alexandria, at Easter 367, condemning heretics and their "apocryphal books to which they attribute antiquity and give the name of saints". Theodore, abbot-general of the Pachomian religious community, had it translated into Coptic and deposited in his monasteries. This makes it evident that it was found necessary to combat Gnostic tendencies among the monks. Robinson whom I am quoting here, supposes that the Gnostic library of Nag Hammadi was stored away at "the approach of Roman soldiers who by now have become Christian" [13]. It is probable that their officers made their men search the whole neighbourhood for heretic books. But whatever may have happened, through the discovery of the Nag Hammadi Library we have a large collection of authentic Gnostic books at our disposal.

8. How the collection is composed

The forty original texts in the Nag Hammadi Library are of of the most different provenance. I mentioned already that curious erratic block, a small part of Plato's 'Republic' [14]. Then there are some few hermetic writings (probably the Plato fragment was also considered hermetic). I also mentioned the Asclepius fragments earlier. Finally, we have the large body of Gnostic texts coming from such different groups as the Sethians, the Barbelo-Gnostics, the Archontics, the Ophites, and the Valentinians. Among these texts we find a great many apocryphal Gospels, Acts, and Apocalypses [15].

The hermetic texts are assembled in Codex VI. That they were much in use is proved by the circumstance that birds' feathers serving as book-markers are found between the pages [16]. Since Chapter II has already given a fairly extensive survey of hermetic scripture, in particular of its Gnostic and dualistic elements, I will be brief here. In addition, Codex VI contains a treatise that has no name but is called 'The Discourse on the Eighth and the Ninth' [17]. The proof that it is hermetic is the appearance of the name of Hermes Trismegistos.

The treatise is a revelation by Hermes to some initiate. The cosmos, as the reader will remember, is surrounded, and by the same token, sealed off from the celestial world by the spheres of the seven 'planets'. It is only beyond and above these spheres that immortality is to be acquired. The great difficulty, of course, is how to come there. This is only possible through the possession of secret knowledge contained in holy books. Those who possess this knowledge must keep silent about it [18].

The elect who are equipped with this knowledge may pass through the seven spheres and attain the eighth. Here the lower and imperfect world is left behind and the realm of the divine is reached. One stage higher is the ninth sphere. The soul is now in the world of eternal bliss. Probably there is also a tenth sphere where God himself is dwelling. The initiate, having received light, life, and love, and is able to see the highest sphere by means of an ecstatic vision. Words fail him; he can only express himself in sounds [19].

NOTES TO CHAPTER III

1. A photo of the spot in Doresse, Livres secrets, opposite p. 137.
2. This description is based on Doresse, Livres secrets 146-151, Robinson, The Jung Codex, and Dart, Laughing Savior, Part I. There is also a good account in Pagels, Gnost.Gospels, Introduction. The story was told in 1978 in full detail by Robinson, From the cliff (see Bibliography).
3. Coptic is Egyptian written with Greek letters (+ six additional signs for sounds that do not occur in Greek).
4. NHL, Introduction by Robinson 23.
5. Related by Robinson in his articel 'The Jung Codex'.
6. Robinson, Jung Codex 19.
7. Rep. 588b-589b. For this see Painchaud, Fragment.
8. Nag Hamm.Libr. Engl., Introduction 2.
9. In the covers receipts were found dated 339 and 342, Rudolph, Gnosis 47.
10. Nag Hamm.Libr. Engl. Introduction 16.
11. Nag Hamm.Libr. Engl., Introduction 1.
12. Nag Hamm.Libr. Engl., Introduction 3.

13. NHL, Introduction 20. Säve-Söderbergh, Holy Script., however, arrives at the following, what he calls 'heretical', conclusion. "I have great difficulty to find any other explanation for the existence and character of the library as a whole than that it was brought together for heresiological purposes (i.e. with a view of combating the Gnostics - F.). It would then also be plausible to assume, that the heretical books were disposed of in a jar, buried in the desert, once they had served the purpose they had been collected for." In my opinion, this leaves unanswered the question why, in that case, the collection was not locked away in a special ward of the monastery's library, or perhaps even safely destroyed, instead of hiding it somewhere with the risk that, however desolate the spot might be, someone would find it and use it for the opposite purpose.

14. NHC VI.5 (=NHL 290/291), in "an extremely inept and inaccurate translation", says James Brashler.

15. Useful schematic reviews of the codices and their contents will be found in Doresse, Livres secrets 164-167, Rudolph, Gnosis 49-53, and Dart, Laughing Savior, Appendix. The reader will find books and articles published about the tractates of the library in Scholer's bibliography (see Bibliography); a list of publications after 1969 appears annually in 'Novum Testamentum'.

16. Doresse, Lives secrets 256.

17. NHC VI.6, NHL in Engl. 292-297.

18. NHC VI.6.63.

19. NHC VI.6.56 and 61 : "Zoxathazo a oo ee oo eee oooo ee oooooo ooooo oooooo uuuuu ooooooooooooooo Zozazoth".

CHAPTER IV

SETH'S PROGENY

1. Did there exist a Sethian sect?

If there ever was an elusive subject, it is the Gnostic Sethian sect [1]. However, whether or not such a sect existed, in Egypt or elsewhere, is a moot point among scholars. Some, with a reputation to lose, deny it; others, equally renowned, are convinced of it [2]. The sect is sometimes seen as a branch of a larger group, the Ophites (who venerated the Serpent), together with Barbelo-Gnostics and others. It is true that it is by no means easy to distinguish sharply between the different sects; it may be asked whether sharp distinctions would do justice to the historical situation.

But I for one would not dismiss out of hand the testimonies of one Latin [3] and three Greek Fathers of the Church, Pseudotertullianus, Irenaeus, Hippolytus, and Epiphanius [4]. All three cite the Sethians as a separate sect and devote long chapters to their doctrine (although it must be admitted that Irenaeus does not draw a line between the teachings of the Sethians and those of the Ophites [5]). This is corroborated by two lesser authors of the fourth century, Didymus of Alexandria, a professor, and Serapion, bishop of Thmuis in Lower Egypt; both expressly cite Sethians as a separate sect to be distinguished from others [6].

Finally, we should not pass over a personal testimony by Epiphanius. As a young man, he wrote, he was in Egypt about 330; he thought he had met Sethians there (although he adds he might have met them in some other country). "We have discovered some things about it (this sect) with our own eyes." They were nearing their extinction then, he said [7]. Therefore, I believe that we should concur with Erik Petersen's assertion that the Sethians were "a Gnostic sect that, identifying itself with the posterity of Seth, put the patriarch Seth at the centre of its speculation" [8].

2. Did the sect exist in Egypt or elsewhere?

Did this sect exist in Egypt only, or both in Egypt and elsewhere? Although Epiphanius keeps open the possibility that there were Sethians outside Egypt, not one of our sources says as much. Neither Irenaeus nor Epiphanius mentions a location. Didymus and Serapion, who spoke of Sethians, were both of them Egyptians. Finally, the Seth in question, the third son of Adam and Eve, is sometimes confused with the Egyptian godhead Seth, which could only happen in Egypt. I think that the scanty evidence we have points to Egypt as the home country of the Sethians, whereas there is no indication whatsoever of their existence elsewhere [9].

On the other hand, there is little or nothing in Sethian scripture, as preserved in the Nag Hammadi Library, that sounds authentically Egyptian. Hippolytus saw the Orphic mysteries as the source of Sethianism; he concluded that they give rise to certain important elements of the doctrine, like the maternal womb, the serpent, and the navel [10]. But many, many names were borrowed from the Old Testament (Adam, Cain, Abel, Seth, and so forth), and from the New Testament (Jesus Christ). In one of the texts we meet the name of Dositheus, a Samaritan Gnostic [11], to whom a revelation is ascribed. I believe that the usual Gnostic predilection for syncretism is at work here; Sethian doctrine seems to refer at the same time to Judaism, Christianity, Hellenic mysteries, and Samaritan Gnostic sources [12].

3. The extent of the sect

Basing himself on the theory that such an important body of writings as the Sethian documents must have a 'a basis in a group of human beings', and that, regarding the general character of Sethian scripture, this basis should not be thought of as 'being artificial and short-lived', Schenke came to the conlusion that "we have before us the genuine product of one and the same community of no small dimensions" [13]. This is, of course, entirely conjectural, which does not mean that this supposition could not be correct; but all kinds of evidence with regard to the extent of the Sethian movement are sadly lacking.

4. Seth, the ancestor of the sect

It will not do to dub 'Sethian' every Gnostic and Nag Hammadi document in which the name of Seth occurs [14]. The hallmark of the true Sethians is that they consider themselves the progeny of Seth, the third son of Adam and Eve. When Abel had been slain and Cain had fled, Seth was born to them, 'in the likeness and image' of Adam; Genesis states once again expressly here that Adam was created 'in the likeness of God' [15]. This was said neither of Cain nor of Abel. It looks as though Seth occupied a privileged position in the lineage, intimately connected as he is not only with his father Adam but even with God. Among the Jewish people traditions were current about the exceptional virtue of Seth and his progeny. Josephus said that "Seth cultivated virtue, excelled in it himself, and left descendants who imitated his ways ..., being all of a virtuous character". Moreover, they discovered the secrets of astrology and inscribed them on two pillars [16].

The Sethians claimed to be the descendants of Seth. They "boast that they descend from Seth the son of Adam, and glorify him and ascribe to him everything that seems virtuous and the proofs of virtue and justice and everything else of this kind" [17]. They held that Adam revealed many secrets to his son Seth. "And his son taught his seed (the Sethians) about them. This is the hidden knowledge of Adam, which he gave to Seth, which is the holy baptism of those who know the eternal knowledge" [18]. With this point we plunge right into medias res : the Sethians are in possession of a special and secret knowledge. In the Gospel of the Egyptians, itself a 'God-written, holy secret book', written by Eugnostos (= 'him who knows well'), a gospel in which not Jesus but Seth is the protagonist, it is said that the great Seth wrote a book and placed it "in the mountain that is called Charaxio"; it will be produced "at the end of the times and eras and reveal everything to those that dwell with them (= the celestial beings) in love" [19].

5. Cain, Abel, Seth

Let us first see how the Sethians themselves saw their origin. The reader should not expect anything too biblical [20]! One text says that God created Adam out of the earth along with Eve. She (Eve) "taught me (Adam) a word of knowledge of the eternal God. And we resembled the great angels, for we were higher than the God who had created us and the powers with him whom we did not know" [21]. Two things strike us here : Eve knew more than Adam, and still more, the Creator God is inferior to them. In the report by Irenaeus, Adam and Eve are expelled from Paradise in a deplorable condition, mentally as well a physically. But then Prunicus (Pruneikos) takes pity on them; this androgynous being is the same as Sophia, the Wisdom [22]. "By the providence of Prunicus Seth was generated, and also (his sister) Noreah; from them the rest of mankind was descended" [23].

Pseudotertullianus relates that, according to Sethian doctrine, both Cain and Abel were created by angels (he makes no mention of Adam and Eve as their parents). After both brothers had come to grief, the 'Mother' (= Sophia) saw to it that Seth was born to replace Abel; the Sethians hold that Christ is identical with Seth [24]. The real ancestor of Seth in this account is Wisdom.

We find the identification of Seth with Jesus Christ also in Epiphanius : "They (the Sethians) assert that he is Jesus" [25]. After the death of Abel, "the one called Mother and Female (= Sophia, the Wisdom) prevailed ... and caused Seth to be born and put him into her own power, implanting in him a seed of the power from on high and the spark that was sent from on high for the first foundation of the seed ... For this reason, then, the race of Seth is set apart and taken up from this world, since it is an elect (race) and separated from the other race (= the rest of mankind)" [26]. "From Seth, from his seed and descending from his race there came the Christ himself, Jesus ..., and he is Seth himself" [27]. We have a first glimpse of dualism here, that of the two races in mankind, the elect and the rest.

6. The nature of the Sethian texts

Hippolytus wrote that those wanting to know what Sethianism is about should turn to the 'Paraphrasis Seth'; "all their secrets are expressed in this book" [28]. The problem, however, is that there is no 'Paraphrasis Seth' in the Nag Hammadi Library but, instead, a 'Paraphrasis Shem' [29]. There is, of course, discussion on the question whether the text mentioned by Hippolytus is identical with the Nag Hammadi book [30]. There are two good reasons for assuming this identity. The first is that what the Nag Hammadi document has to say is substantially the same as we find in Hippolytus, the second that in Codex VII the 'Paraphrasis Shem' is followed by 'The Second Treatise of the Great Seth' [31].

We must not think of Sethian texts as scholarly theological essays. They usually announce themselves as revelations or as secret books : "the teaching of the mysteries ..., of the mysteries and the things hidden in silence ... taught to John, (the) disciple" [32], the already mentioned holy, secret book of the Egyptians, the revelation of Adam taught to his son Seth [33], the revelation of Derdekeas to Shem [34], and more of this kind.

It is made abundantly clear that we are brought in touch with a very special knowledge and insight, utterly, dualistically different from all other sorts of knowledge. This peculiar character is also accentuated by the veiled language in which these texts are written; often they are mysterious and opaque to the point of incomprehensibility. It will be evident that this sets the Sethians at a great distance from the common run of mankind. They alone, the initiated, 'know', and, in consequence, are able to understand these texts.

However, the wilfulness and individualism that are so characteristic of Gnostic scripture are given free reign here too; the reader should not expect a uniform doctrine. In the following sections I will be sinning against the intentions of the Sethians by presenting their doctrine in a much more coherent form than that to be found in their books. But I feel I have no choice; either it must be done this way or else there will be no understanding at all [35].

7. A threepartite universe

a. The three roots

In the beginning there was Light and there was Darkness. "The Light was mindful of attentiveness and reason ... And the Darkness was wind in waters; he possessed the mind wrapped in chaotic fire" [36]. This is the usual dualistic picture " Light above and Darkness below, utterly different from each other. So far so good. But there is yet a third Power or root, or principle, the Spirit (Pneuma), 'a gentle humble light'. The Spirit was between Light and Darkness. All three roots are sovereign powers : "They reigned each in themselves, alone" [37]. This means that we see a tripartite universe consisting of three separate parts; the Spirit is keeping Light and Darkness apart. Elsewhere, the Light is described as "Father of All, nous (mind) in the heights above the below, voice of Truth, untouchable Logos, (ineffable) Voice, (incomprehensible) Father" [38]. Here the incomprehensibility and hiddenness of the primal godhead is stressed.

The gentle Pneuma is not breath or air but rather an odour, a fragrant perfume. Light and odour by their nature can penetrate into everything and are, therefore, also present in the Darkness [39]. Darkness as a root is disorderly; its crookedness consists in its lack of perception and its ignorance, because it thought itself self-sufficient supposing there was nothing above it. That is, it knew nothing of Light and the Spirit. It made such a stir with its waters that the frightened Spirit coming to see this became nauseated by the sight of the chaos [40].

b. Darkness' jealousy

Seeing the luminous Spirit hovering above him, Darkness became jealous and wanted to equal the Spirit, that is to say, to become light itself although this would have been impossible. But now "the exalted, infinite Light appeared (and) wished to reveal himself to the Spirit". It looks very much as though even the Spirit did not know initially who or what the Light was. This is because the Light is ineffable and incomprehensible, the favourite Gnostic notion of the hidden God, the unknown God. The Light, therefore, did not appear in person to the Pneuma but as his 'son' who announces himself as 'the ray of the universal Light' [41].

This 'son' is no one less than the Derdekeas who is revealing the secret doctrine to Shem, the privileged person of the Paraphrasis. This Derdekeas - his name may mean 'child' or 'son' - is a typical Gnostic redeemer figure. His task will be to save the 'mind' of Darkness from the region of chaos and bring it back to the great Light. This 'mind' is the last remnant of divinity in the chaos, the well-known 'divine spark'. When the redeemer can succeed in this, "Darkness will become dark to himself, according to the will of the Majesty" [42]. What the Majesty (= the Light) intends to effect is the total separation of the upper and nether regions. The dualism of Light and Darkness, initially not so obvious must now become complete.

Because Darkness has a 'mind', that is understanding or intelligence, it realizes full well that, bereft of this mind, its own spark of light, it will remain utterly dumb and dull. Therefore, it fights back with all its might seeking not only "to keep in its possession the brilliance and the spark of light" but also trying to draw down as much of the light of the Spirit as it can and to transfer it into its own element, the waters - and not without success [43]. What the Darkness really wants to acquire is 'the likeness of the mind and to resemble the Spirit' [44]. We see, as it were, Darkness aping the pure higher Powers and trying to act as a creative potency.

c. The saving of the Spirit

Derdekeas, the divine Redeemer, by the will of the Majesty does his utmost to salvage the Spirit and all the Light from the nether regions. "The Spirit gazed up at the infinite Light in order that his light might be pitied ... When the Spirit had looked, I (Derdekeas) flowed out - I, the son of the Majesty -, like a wave of light ... And at my wish the Spirit arose by his (own) power. His greatness was granted to him that he might ... depart from the burden of Darkness ... And the Spirit rejoiced because he was protected from the frightful water ... And the Spirit honored the exalted Light ... For the image of the Light was unseparable from the unbegotten Spirit" [45].

In this way the threefold division of the initial Powers gradually turns into a bipartite one, the Spirit now associating more and more with the infinite Light. The dualistic division does not become wholly complete, since Nature has succeeded in keeping to itself a small part of the light. Nature, which can be seen as an emanation or manifestation of Darkness, "possesses (something) of the power of the Spirit and the Darkness and the fire" [46]. I believe this is needed to explain why there is a spark of light in human beings too.

d. The dualism of the lower and higher worlds

Whoever has the courage to plod through the unscrutable, talkative, and repetitive Paraphrase of Shem will be struck by the negative terms in which the lower region is described and by the sexual imagery that is just as negative. For Darkness and Nature I note the following words : chaotic, abasement, disorder, crooked, evil, nauseating, putrid, vile, ignorant, bitterness, wickedness, dark, burden, frightful, harmful, blind, impurity, impure practice, guileful, and still more of this kind. It is the same with the sexual imagery. "From the Darkness the water became a cloud, and from the cloud the womb took shape ... And when the Darkness saw it he became unchaste. ... he rubbed the womb ... It was a seed of Nature from the dark root" [47]. That Nature was 'aroused to unchastity' was the fault of Darkness [48]. The "unclean femininity of Nature was strong". The 'womb' is the enemy of the mind; it, or she, is dead set against the idea that there should be any mind in Nature : "The wrathful womb came up and made the mind dry" [49]. And more in the same vein.

The dualistic character of this ideology becomes fully apparent if we compare these terms to those used for the higher powers : attentiveness and reason, faultless Light, exalted, infinite Light, incorruptible, universal, greatness, great Power, perfect Light, immeasurable mind, beautiful garment of light. And more of this. But no sexual imagery!

8. Sethian cosmogony

Having discussed the relations between the three initial Powers or entities, we now come to the cosmogony proper. Each of the three sovereign principles or roots disposes of a number of lesser powers or capacities. As Hippolytus tells us, they are 'innumerable times innumerable in number', and each of them possesses a mind and intelligence. They are restful as long as they remain on their own terrain. But as soon as one root comes into contact with one of the others a strong movement originates from the collision. The clashes are countless, and equally countless are the images and prototypes springing forth from them. These images are the models of all that is.

Derdekeas, the son of the Majesty, now descends to nature and lays before her "a great request that heaven and earth might come into being, in order that the whole light might rise up". It clearly is his intention to liberate the light from the grip of Nature. But as a pure spirit Derdekeas is unable to effect this and therefore puts on 'the beast' which in all probability means that he assumes a physical shape. "For in no other way could the power of the Spirit be saved from bondage except that I appear to her (Nature) in animal form" [50].

The cosmic Demiurge, however, is not Derdekeas ; in other words, no higher power is involved in the creational work. It is Nature that, by blowing on the wild waters, creates the heaven and then the earth from 'the foam of heaven'. The new earth brings forth all kinds of food for the animals [51].

Part of the story is told in sexual terms, of copulation, of impure intercourse, of a womb, and of 'an unclean penis' that, appearing from nowhere, 'rubs the womb' [52]. Hippolytus adds that "heaven and earth are shaped like a womb having the navel in the middle ... If anyone wishes to visualize this shape, let him carefully examine a pregnant womb ... In it there sprang to life ... the innumerable multitudes of living creatures. And in all this infinite number which exists under heaven in the different living creatures there is inseminated and distributed, together with the light, the fragrance of the Spirit" [53]. In every living being, therefore, there is a particle of light. Nevertheless, this is nothing to rejoice in. "After the forms of Nature had been together (= had copulated), they separated from each other ... being astonished about the deceit that had happened to them. They grieved with an eternal grief" [54].

The creational process is sketched in negative terms. Wild winds and demons play their role in it. But there is hope, an ultimate promise. Derdekeas will 'make Nature desolate'. He will give mind (the mind that is in Nature and Darkness but does not really belong to them) power over the winds and demons to keep some order in the cosmos. The mind loathes 'the unchastity of Nature with Darkness' which is the origin of all that is. And in the end Nature will be destroyed [55]. We see here the unbridgeable opposition of Mind and Nature, of higher and lower, and, in prospect, their final battle.

9. The creation of man

Since the Sethian accounts of the creation of man do not agree with each other, it is preferable to treat them one by one.

a. The report of the Paraphrase of Shem

First of all, we will confine ourselves to the Paraphrase of Shem that doubtless is the main document. This text is very short on the creation of man, and not exceptionally clear. The author obviously wants to hurry on to the elect. "The winds, which are demons from water and fire and darkness and light, had intercourse unto perdition. And through this intercourse the winds received in their womb foam (= semen) from the penis of the demons. They (the winds) conceived a power in their vagina ... When the times of birth were near, all the winds were gathered from the water which is near the earth. They gave birth to all kinds of unchastity ... Barren wives came from it and sterile husbands. For just as they are born, so they bear" [56]. Mysterious language replete with sexual imagery! And deeply pessimistic too! But the question is whether, with the exception of the elect, this applies to the whole of mankind. This is not said in as many words, but I believe it is the implication. If this is correct, then mankind has a dark, chaotic, and uncouth origin (but some light too has gone into its creation).

b. Hippolytus' account

Hippolytus' account, although not essentially different, is somewhat more explicit. "From the water there has come, as a first derivative principle, a fierce and violent wind which is the cause of all generation. For by making a turbulence in the waters it raises swelling waves from it." Once again we meet the obstretic imagery, for the swelling of the water is compared to the swelling of the pregnant womb. "The generation of the waves, as if it were some urge to swell in pregnancy, is the origin of man or of the mind, whenever it is stirred to excitement by the urging of the spirit ... This swelling wave receives in itself the offspring of the female being" [57].

Here too the origin of man is seen as chaotic, coming not from above but from below. It is not wholly clear who the female being is, but in all probability it is Nature, because we learn from the same passage that Nature was swelling in pregnancy. Her 'offspring', anyhow, is man. In view of this constant talk of wombs and pregnancy and female beings I ask myself whether Jonas was right in assigning the Sethian doctrine to the male group of the Gnostic movements. True enough, its main character, Seth, is male, but the feminine element is far from inconspicuous [58].

All this makes it evident that man is no more than a natural being, and cannot boast a divine origin. No superior being or power collaborated in his creation. Man as such is a being that belongs to 'below'. He is "begotten from water by the impulse of nature and by the movement of the wind" [59]. Wind and water, two formless and aimless elements, are the 'parents of man'. "The wind of Darkness, the firstborn of the waters ... produces man" [60].

But some hope, however slight, remains. "There was a ray coming from above, from that perfect light held fast in the dark, dreadful, bitter, filthy water" [61]. "It is (a) perfect god, brought down from the unbegotten light above and from the Spirit" [62]. Here we take up again the theme of the light that is held captive in matter. "This is the mind which takes form in its different patterns ... (It is) put into human nature as into a temple (= as a statue of the godhead in a sanctuary - F.)." But the light is scattered and fragmented, "like salt among the changing things" [63].

This "tiny spark, a detached fragment of the light from above is intermingled in the variously compounded bodies" [64]. It "impatiently seeks to be freed from its bodies and cannot find its release or escape" [65]. This is a radically dualistic picture : body and light live uneasily together, without belonging to each other; the sooner the combination is dissolved the better.

c. The story as told in 'The Apocalypse of Adam'

In 'The Apocalypse of Adam' [66], Adam tells his son Seth how "God created me and your mother Eve out of the earth". They seem to have had a kind of pre-existence since he adds : "I went about with her in a glory which we had seen in the aeon from which we came forth. She taught me a word of knowledge of the eternal God" [67]. This makes Eve into a more privileged person than Adam since she possesses a superior knowledge that he does not have. The text goes on : "And we resembled the great eternal angels for we were higher than the God who had created us and the powers with him whom we did not know" [68]. Two gods come into play here, an eternal God and a Creator-God, a Demiurge (a term that is not used in this tract). This amounts, needless to say, to a fundamental metaphysical dualism. It is not explained why, incidentally, the Demiurge is able to create a being who is more than himself.

Then comes the Fall. As is usual in Gnostic texts, it is not the fault of the first human beings but of the Demiurge. "God (the second one, that is), the ruler of the aeons and the powers, divided us in his wrath", that is, he broke the organic bond between them and transformed them into two separate individuals. "We became two aeons" [69]. It is not specified why he did this, but the implication must be that the Demiurge is essentially evil. "After those days the eternal knowledge of the God of Truth (the first God) withdrew from me and your mother Eve. Since that time, we learned about dead things, like men" [70]. The spiteful addition 'like men' is highly significant : mankind is fundamentally ignorant about the things from on high and occupies itself only with the worthless things from here below, the 'dead things'.

"Then we recognized the God who had created us (the Demiurge) ... and we served him in fear and slavery". But the eternal God obviously pitied them, for Adam was visited by three (unidentified) heavenly persons; he was unable "to recognize (them) since they were not from the powers of the God who had (created us). They revealed to him that a son of him and his wife (by whom Seth is meant) will come to possess eternal knowledge" [71]. There is no mention of Cain and Abel in this document.

10. The unhappy brothers

a. What Pseudotertullian has to say

The two unhappy brothers, however, figure prominently in the relation by Pseudotertullianus. He says that they were created by 'angels'. Much contention arose between the angels because of them. Obviously some angels were good and others bad. After Abel had been murdered, they (here probably only the good angels are meant) did want not the power that is above all power which they call 'Mother' (knowledge presumably) to get lost. Therefore Seth was born instead of Abel. This implies that Abel was the original bearer of that knowledge; I suppose the suggestion is that Cain who was ignorant slew his brother out of jealousy.

At the birth of Seth the angels who had created Cain and Abel withdrew from mankind, since, according to the text, mixtures of angels and human beings are improper. In this way the new seed, Seth and his progeny that is, would be preserved pure and unvitiated. So we have one pure and privileged race, the Sethians. But the bad seed of the ignorant will not perish either; it is the progeny of Cham, Noah's son, so that, "after the Flood, evil will live on and occupy the whole earth" [72]. Although the Pseudotertullian relation does not excel in clarity, its basic assumption is that the message it proclaims is 'knowledge'. Mankind is dualistically divided into two races, the knowing and the ignorant, equivalent with the good and the bad.

b. Epiphanius on Cain and Abel

What Epiphanius has to tell is only slightly different (no wonder, if he is really dependent on Pseudotertullianus), but it may clarify some points. It is not stated by him that angels created Cain and Abel; in this report they are the sons of 'two men' ('anthroopoi'; Adam and Eve are not mentioned by name). However, the angels quarrelled over the brothers. From the beginning there were two opposed races of men, their ancestors being the two brothers. And Abel was killed. "But the power on high prevailed (over the angels), the one they call the Mother and Female". This is Sophia, knowledge or wisdom (the word Sophia is not used). "She took thought and caused Seth to be born and put him in her own power, implanting in him a seed from the power from on high (from knowledge) and a spark that was sent from on high for the first foundation of the seed and of the institution (of the world) ... (In this way) destruction should come upon the powers of the angels who made the world and the two men in the beginning"[73].

This is an illuminative text. The creation of the world and of mankind obviously was a bone of contention between good and wicked powers; from the very beginning everything is dual. Mankind does not begin with Adam and Eve, but with two human beings, one of whom begets Cain and the other Abel. Those two initial human beings were not created by God but by 'angels'. There is in this passage no talk of God as the Creator, or of a Demiurge, but instead of a higher power who is female and in all probability is Wisdom. She only intervenes when things have already gone wrong and then makes a new start with mankind. A new race is created, the Sethians, 'the institution of justice and the election of the (elect) seed and race'. This race must not only represent and incorporate the good but even entirely foil the intentions of the wicked angels towards the world. The battle that rages in heaven is reproduced on earth.

c. The relation in 'The Gospel of Egyptians'

The story of the origin of Seth and his posterity is related differently but basically in an identical fashion in 'The Gospel of the Egyptians'. It is a revelation (in all probability by Seth himself) about the Great Invisible Spirit, the prime God that is, "whose name cannot be uttered ..., the Father of the Silence ..., unrevealable, unmarked, ageless, unproclaimable ..., self-begotten, self-producing, alien". This is the deus absconditus et ignotus of the Gnostics. "Three powers came forth from him, the Father, the Mother (Barbelo), (and) the Son"[74]. Each one of these, in his or her turn, brings forth an 'ogdoad', a subgroup of eight lesser but not inferior powers.

The whole story is told in densely veiled, highly esoteric language. Let me give only one instance of this in order that you, innocent reader, may see what I went through on your behalf. "The second ogdoad-power, the Mother, the virginal Barbelon epitioch()'ai, meneneaimen (who) presides over the heaven, karb(), the uninterpretable power, the ineffable Mother. (She originated) from herself (); she came forth, (she) agreed with the Father (of the) silent (silence)" [75]. The text is damaged and could be restored only partly; the non-English words, being neither Coptic nor Greek, are untranslatable. This passage, along with countless others in the same vein, shows that texts like these were intended neither for my eyes nor for yours.

A whole pleroma (fulness) of heavenly powers originated in this way; they bear strange names like Domedon Doxemedon, Ainon, Yoel, Esephech. Important beings in this pleroma are 'the great Christ' [76], the Logos, "the great self-begotten living (word), the true (God), the unborn physis ..., who (is the) son of the (great) Christ, who is the son (of the) ineffable silence" [77], and Mirothoe, "the living power, the mother of the holy, incorruptible ones (= in all probablity the Sethians), the great power ... And she gave birth to him whose name I name saying ien ien ien ea ea ea three times" [78].

The one who is meant here is Adamas. "For this one (Adamas that is) is (a light) which radiated (from the light; he is) the eye of the (light). For this is the first man [79], he through whom and to whom everything became, (and) without whom nothing became ... Then the great Logos, the divine Autogenes (= self-begotten), and the incorruptible man Adamas mingled with each other. A Logos of man came into being through a word" [80]. A few remarks are necessary. Man as such is connected with the highest powers by a chain of supernatural beings. But Adamas is not the same as the biblical Adam; he too is supernatural. Here also we have the ideal prototype of man that is common in Gnostic ideology; this time it is 'the Logos of man'.

Now "the incorruptible man Adamas asked ... a son of himself, in order that he (the son) may become father of the incorruptible race (= the Sethians), so that, through it (the race), the silence and the voice may appear, and, through it, the dead aeon may raise itself, so that it may dissolve" [81]. Thus the task of the elect is sketched : they must effect the victory over the world (= the dead aeon) and bring about the triumph of the luminous powers from on high.

"And thus there came forth, from above, the power of the great light, the Manifestation. She gave birth to the four great lights, Harmozel, Oroiael, Davithe, Eleleth [82], and the great incorruptible Seth, the son of the incorruptible man Adamas ... And the Father nodded approvingly; the whole pleroma of the lights was well pleased" [83]. Seth, therefore, is not as in Genesis the third son of Adam and Eve (Cain and Abel are not mentioned in this Gospel). Instead, he is the son of the archetypal Adamas and the 'Manifestation' who is an emanation or perhaps even a personification of the prime God. Seth, in consequence, does not have a normal human origin but an extraterrestrial, supernatural one; a line of higher luminous beings connects him directly with the highest Father.

To his posterity it is promised that they "will by no means taste death" [84]; they are "the incorruptible, holy race of the great Savior, and those who dwell with them in love, and the great, invisible, eternal Spirit, and his only begotten Son, and the eternal light, and his great, incorruptible consort, and the incorruptible Sophia, and the Barbelon, and the whole pleroma in eternity" [85]. No wonder then that Seth is thought to be the guardian of the highest esoteric knowledge.

11. Seth the Redeemer

"It might be postulated", writes Pearson, "that a constitutive feature of 'Sethian' Gnosticism is the notion of Seth as a heavenly redeemer, who can manifest himself in a variety of earthly incarnations, such as Zostrianos, Zoroaster, Melchizedek, Jesus Christ, etc." [86].

I mentioned already that, according to Pseudotertullianus and Epiphanius, Sethians equated Seth with Jesus Christ. In the Gnostic tractate 'Melchizedek' [87] this mysterious King of Salem [88] is clearly identified with Jesus Christ. There also 'the congregation of (the children) of Seth' is mentioned, "who are above the (thousands of) thousands and (myriads) of myriads (of the) aeons" [89], and almost in the same breath "(the) race of the High Priest (=Melchizedek) (which is) above (thousands of thousands) and (myriads) of myriads of the aeons" [90]. This can mean hardly anything else than that the races of Seth and Melchizedek are one and the same.

This leads Pearson to say that "we should entertain the possibility that in 'Melchizedek' the priest-savior Melchizedek is regarded as an earthly incarnation of the heavenly Seth" [91]. Elsewhere this scholar adds that "Melchizedek sees that the role of Jesus Christ as suffering savior and triumphant victor is his own future role" [92]; the King of Salem is "envisaged as performing the final work of salvation in the form of the crucified and risen Jesus Christ" [93].

In 'Zostrianos', the longest (but heavily damaged) Nag Hammadi text, Zostrianos must probably be equated with Seth; references to him abound throughout this text. Zostrianos too acts as a Saviour. He preaches to the 'erring multitude' in these words " "Know those who are alive and the holy seed of Seth. Do not be (...) disobedient to me ... Strengthen your sinless (elect) soul ... The Father of all invites you ... Do not baptize yourselves with death nor entrust yourselves to those lower than you instead of those who are better. Flee from the madness and the bondage of femininity and choose for yourselves the salvation of masculinity ... Release yourselves and that which has bound you will be dissolved ... The gentle Father has sent you the savior and given you strength ... Look at the Light. Flee the darkness" [94].

12. The role of knowledge

The decisive expedient by means of which salvation is to be effected, it goes without saying, is knowledge. 'Zostrianos' is very explicit on this.

"Adamas is the (perfect) man because he is the eye of the self-begotten (= the Light), an ascending knowledge of his, because the self-begotten God is a word of the perfect Mind of the Truth. The son of Adamas, Seth, comes to each of the souls, because he is knowledge sufficient for them" [95]. Here Seth does not only bring knowledge, he is the personification of knowledge. This is the prototype of salvation : a Gnostic should not only adhere to knowledge intellectually, he must identify himself with it, become it.

Zostrianos the prophet received his insights from a 'messenger of the knowledge of the eternal Light' [96]. Of what he knew he "wrote three tablets and left them as knowledge for those who come after me, the living elect" [97].

Towards the end of 'The Second Treatise of Seth' it is stated that "I (Seth) was among those (= the Sethians) who are united in the friendship of friends forever, who neither know hostility at all, nor evil, but who are united by my Knowledge in word and peace which exists in perfection with everyone and in them all. And those who assumed the form of my type (= who identify themselves with Seth - F.) will assume the form of my word (= will speak my language - F.). Indeed, these will come forth in light forever ... , since they have known in every respect (and) indivisibly that what is One ..." [98]. In 'The Three Steles of Seth' it is the 'Fatherly God' who is the source of redeeming knowledge : "salvation has come to us; from thee is salvation, Thou art wisdom, thou knowledge; thou art truthfulness" [99].

The glory and beauty of Knowledge is starkly contrasted with Ignorance. "Many in the race of Nature will seek the security of the Power (= the Light). They will not find it, nor will they be able to do the will of Faith. For they are seed of the universal Darkness ... Those who do not share in the spirit of Light and in Faith will dissolve in the Darkness, the place where repentance will not come" [100]. Zostrianos states categorically that the perceptible world is ignorant [101].

13. The Sethian attack on the Bible and Judaism

In 'The Second Treatise of Seth' a sharp attack on the Bible and Judaism occurs. It begins by saying that "Adam was a laughing-stock since he was made a counterfeit type of man ..., as if he had become stronger than I (Seth) and my brothers (the Sethians). We are innocent with respect to him, since we have not sinned" [102]. There are clearly two dualistically different races of men here, the Adamites who have sinned and the Sethians who have not. As in a litany, the same incantation is repeated for Abraham, Isaac, and Jacob - 'counterfeit fathers' -, David who was a laughing-stock in that his son was named the Son of Man (Jesus Christ is meant - F.), Solomon a laughing-stock because he was Christ (= he believed he was wise, but wise is Seth-Christ alone - F.), the twelve prophets since they have come forth as imitations of the true prophets; "neither (Moses) nor those before him, from Adam to Moses and John the Baptist, none of them knew me or my brothers" [103].

After having thus disposed of all the prominent figures of the Old Testament, the author shifts his attack to Jewish customs. "They (the Jews) had a doctrine of angels (negatively meant - F.) to observe dietary laws and bitter slavery, since they never knew truth nor will they know it. For there is a great deception upon their souls making it impossible for them to find a Nous of freedom in order to know him (the Gnostic Christ), until they come to know the Son of Man (not the New Testament Jesus is meant but the Gnostic Christ - F.)" [104].

Fierce, antinomian polemizing against the Old Testament becomes apparent in a passage where the Sethian author is glorifying the Sodomites. He bluntly states that the Majesty will appear "in place that will be called Sodom ... But you (Shem), proclaim quickly to the Sodomites your universal teaching, for they are your members ... The Sodomites, according to the will of the Majesty, will bear witness to the universal testimony. They will rest with a pure conscience in the place of their repose, which is the unbegotten Spirit. And so as the things will happen, Sodom will be burned unjustly by a base nature (= the God of the Jews)" [105]. Sodomites with a pure conscience, that, of course, is a travesty of the Genesis story!

Then it is the turn of the Jewish God, here called 'Archon', and elsewhere the 'Cosmocrator', the Demiurge. He is considered a laughing-stock because he said : "I am God, and there is none greater than I. I alone am the Father, the Lord, and there is no other beside me. I am a jealous God, who brings the sins of the fathers upon the children for three or four generations ... He was in empty glory. And he does not agree with our Father, for he was a laughing-stock and judgment and false prophecy" [106]. This means a total, a dualistic rejection of Judaism; there is no knowledge and no salvation in it.

14. The attack on the New Testament

The New Testament is rejected in the same scornful way. The archons (the forces of evil) "have proclaimed a doctrine of a dead man (= the New Testament Jesus) and lies so as to resemble the freedom and purity of the perfect assembly ... For they do not know the Knowledge of the Greatness that is from above" [107]. This is clearly directed against the Christian community in which the author evidently saw a rival for his own sect. He claims Christ for himself. The Son of the Majesty, the Son of Light, the heavenly Seth, wanting to become the Son of man, came down from above. "I (Seth) visited a bodily dwelling. I cast out the one that was in it first (= Jesus of Nazareth), and I went in ... I am the one who was in it (the body), not resembling him who was in it first. For he was an earthly man, but I, I am from above the heavens ... I am a stranger to the regions below" [108]. And now he may say : "I am Christ, the Son of Man, the one from you who is among you" [109]. The Jesus whom we know from the Gospels is pushed aside here; he does not count. Not only his place, even his body, is taken over by a Christ who shows little affinity with human existence.

The Gnostic Christ did not die on the cross. "I did not succumb to them (the Jews) as they had planned ... I was not afflicted at all ... And I did not die in reality but in appearance ... For my death which they think happened, (happened) to them in their error and blindness, since they nailed their man unto their death ..., for they were deaf and blind ... It was another, their (the Jews') father, who drank the gall and the vinegar; it was not I ... It was another, Simon (of Cyrene), who bore the cross on his shoulder. It was another on whom they placed the crown of thorns. But I was rejoicing in the height over all the wealth of the archons and the offspring of their error, of their empty glory. And I was laughing at their ignorance" [110].

This Sethian Christ is an anti-Christian Christ. The passion stories of the Gospels are dismissed in the most scathing way, with the consequence that the Redemption does not take place through the cross of Jesus Christ [111]. Christians are condemned as people who do not 'know'. We are in the presence of a variant of the docetist heresy here, which claims that, although Jesus Christ was real enough, he suffered only in appearance, that is in the person of Simon of Cyrene. The real Jesus himself was snatched away in time. Simon Magus and later Basilides were of the same opinion [112]. Gnostics could not stand the idea that celestial beings should have suffered so ignominiously.

The author of the 'Paraphrase of Shem' polemizes against Christian baptism. Baptism is wrong because it is done with water, and throughout this whole document it is held that the waters are evil. "They (the Christians) are deceived by manifold demons, thinking that through baptism with the uncleanness of water, that which is dark, feeble, (and) disturbing, he (the Spirit) will take away their sins. And they do not know that from the water to the water there is bondage and error and unchastity, envy, murder, adultery, false witness, heresies, robberies, lust, babblings, wrath, bitterness" [113]. Christians are unfree because they trust too much to the forces of Nature.

At this point we must ask ourselves what these authors, in particular the author of 'The Second Treatise', had in mind when penning these passages. It is as clear as sunlight that the latter distances himself firmly from both Judaism and Christianity; he is creating a dualistic opposition between these creeds and Sethianism, with that of Knowledge and Ignorance in the background. It is possible that the author of 'The

Second Treatise' was either a Jew (he shows a firm grasp of the Old Testament) or a lapsed Christian, more probably a Christian (he was acquainted in detail with the New Testament), and that he wanted to belie his spiritual origin.

It is also possible, but not in contradiction to what I have just said, that the sect as a whole had an intuition (in which they were right) that Judaism and still more Christianity would become the staunch and hardheaded opponents of the Gnosis. If I am correct in this, then this was a world-historical moment, for this was the start of the running battle between Christianity and the Gnosis that was to continue for many centuries, even to the present day.

15. The rejection of the world

In the 'Paraphrase of Shem' the world, the cosmos, is a creation of Darkness. "His mind dissolved down to the depths of Nature. It (Nature) mingled with the power of the bitterness of Darkness ... And when Nature had taken to herself the mind by means of the dark power, every likeness took shape in her" [114]. In other words, as Frederik Wisse said, "the mind of Darkness is the prime tool of Darkness to accomplish his evil schemes in the world" [115]. "The root of Nature, which was below, was crooked, since it was burdensome and harmful" [116]. Especially the body is evil. "No one who wears the body will be able to complete these things (= to attain salvation - F.) ... The bondage of the body is severe ... (But) when his (the believer's) mind separates from the body, then these things may be revealed to him" [117].

In 'The Second Treatise' the cosmos is the realm of the wicked archons, in particular of the Cosmocrator, the Jewish God, who is a lesser god, far below the Majesty. In general, the Sethian texts, just like all other Gnostic documents, express nothing but contempt for earthly existence and for humanity as such. Although the authors often use sexual imagery, they do not like sexuality. The first beginning of everything is androgynous rather than a-sexual. "Great is the first aeon, male virginal Barbelo, the first glory of the invisible Father, she who is called 'perfect'"[118]. This is, as Rudolph says, because the double sex is an expression of perfection [119]; it is 'pleroma', fulness. That there are two sexes on earth is, in consequence, a loss of pleroma, an imperfection, even a source of confusion.

The Sethian hatred of sexuality directs itself not so much to the males but rather to femininity. Zostrianos takes all the wrong things, the body, the world itself, femininity, and the Demiurge in his stride in one phrase. He separates himself "from the somatic darkness in me and the psychic chaos in mind, and the femininity of desire in the darkness ... I reproved the dead creation within me and the divine cosmocrator of the perceptible world"[120]. Perception of higher things is only possible after having shed everything that is of this world.

16. The end of the world

This bad, bad world will be destroyed in the end. In the 'Paraphrase of Shem' we find a Sethian apocalypse. "Evil times will come. And when the era of Nature is approaching destruction, darkness will come upon the earth. The number (i.e. of the elect) will be small. And a demon will come up from the power who has a likeness of fire. He will divide the heaven, (and) he will rest in the depth of the east. For the whole world will quake. And the deceived world will be thrown into confusion. Many places will be flooded ... Many places will be sprinkled with blood ... And the stars will fall from the sky ... And in the last days the forms of Nature will be destroyed with the winds and all their demons; they will become a dark lump, just as they were from the beginning"[121].

17. The ascent of the soul

As is usual in Gnostic doctrine, for the Sethians too, it all ends with the ascent of the souls of the elect. Even if they will be overpowerd by the forces of evil for a time, they will be saved in the end. "Blessed are they who guard themselves against the heritage of death, which is the burdensome water of darkness. For it will not be possible to conquer them (the elect) in a few moments, since they hasten to come forth from the error of the world. And if they are conquered, they will be kept back from them (= the other elect) and be tormented in darkness until the time of consummation (= the end of the world). When the consummation has come and Nature has been destroyed, then their minds will separate from the Darkness. Nature has burdened them for a short time. And then they will be in the ineffable light of the unbegotten Spirit without a form" [122].

Or listen to what Seth-Christ has to say at the end of 'The Second Treatise'. "O perfect and incorruptible ones, because of the incorruptible and perfect mystery and the ineffable one (= the Majesty). But they (the Sethians) think that we decreed them (=gave them their destiny - F.) before the foundation of the world in order that, when we emerge from the places of the world, we may present there the symbols of incorruption from the spiritual union unto knowledge. You (= the non-believers) do not know it because the fleshly cloud (= the body) overshadows you. But I (Seth) alone am the friend of Sophia. I have been in the bosom of the Father from the beginning, in the place of the sons of truth, and the Greatness. Rest then with me, my fellow spirits and brothers, for ever" [123]. Here we see, once again, the dualistic opposition of the two races of men, the predestined knowers and the ignorant, of corruption and incorruptibility, and of body and spirit.

All will be fulfilled through and in the union with the ineffable Greatness. "We bless thee ..., for thou didst unite the all through them all, for thou hast empowered us ... (Thou) hast saved, thou hast saved, thou hast saved us, O crown-bearer, O crown-giver! We bless thee eternally. We bless thee, once we have been saved, as the perfect individuals, perfect in account of thee, who is complete, who completes the perfect through all these" [124].

18. The Archontics

I feel we should conclude our disquisition on the Sethians with a few paragraphs on the Archontics. Puech points out that apparently they were once an independent sect. There are, however, many similarities between their doctrine and that of the Sethians. Epiphanius, our sole source for them among the early Fathers of the Church, says as much [125]. According to this source, Archontics were "not current in many places, but only in the province of Palestine". However, he adds that they had won adherents in Lesser and Greater Armenia. This was the work of a certain Armenian called Eutactus; Epiphanius scathingly remarks that he should rather be called 'Atactus' = disorderly (Eutactus means 'orderly'), because of his way of life.

This man visited Palestine on his way back from Egypt around 361 and there learned the doctrine from an old Archontic called Peter who lived in the village of Kaphar Barucha, three miles from Hebron [126]. "And when he (Eutactus) returned to his native land (where he lived near Satagh), he infected many of the inhabitants of Lesser Armenia and corrupted several rich men and a senator and other respectable figures; and through these eminent men he destroyed many in the region" - thus Epiphanius, who reveals himself as not well disposed towards the Archontics [127]. Puech concludes that 'Archontic' (from the 'Archontes', the rulers of the seven 'planets') in all probability is the Palestinian name for the Egyptian Gnostics [128].

Like all other Gnostics, the Archontics were literate people; their doctrine found expression in many books. "These men have fabricated some apocryphal books for themselves ... And they pile up other books for themselves, being accustomed to add to the pile whatever they read" [129]. Their own books comprise 'The Great and the Little Symphony', the so-called 'Allogeneis' (= with another origin = the seven sons of Seth), the 'Ascension of Isaiah', and the visions of the prophets Martiades and Marsianos who were in heaven for three days [130]. Only scant fragments of these books have been preserved; not one of them is present in the Nag Hammadi Library. Epiphanius writes that "the whole system can be understood from the book entitled 'The Symphony' [131].

a. The godhead

It all starts with a dual pair of godheads, the Father and the Mother. They obviously are uncreated, coeval, and equivalent. The Father is called 'Father of All, God on high, the good God' [132], but also 'the incomprehensible God, and the unnamable Power' [133]. This godhead, once again, is the hidden and ineffable God of the Gnostics. His paredra, his consort, the Mother, is not inferior to him. She is 'the Supreme Mother, the Power on high, the Luminous Mother enthroned in the highest heaven' [134].

b. The heavens

The duality of the godhead becomes dualism in the bipartition of the heavens. There are two heavens. The first and the highest is the Ogdoas, the eightfold heaven; the second one is the sevenfold heaven, the Hebdomas. In both celestial systems there are 'archons', rulers, or ruling powers, one for each heaven. "And each archon has ranks (of subordinates)." In the Ogdoas "the radiant Mother is the highest of all in the eighth (heaven)" [135]. There is not much further talk of the ineffable Father. One might say that the universe has a supreme female ruler.

There is a qualitative difference between the Ogdoas, the superior heaven, and the Hebdomas, the inferior one. The lower down we get the worse it becomes. The dividing line runs between both systems. In the inferior heaven each of the archons rules his own sphere; they are also called 'Principles and Existences' [136]. Each archon disposes of the services of angels who are brought forth by himself [137].

c. Sabaoth

The supreme archon in the lower sphere is 'Sabaoth', "who is the dominant power in the seventh heaven and overpowers the others" [138]. He is thought to be the god of the Jews; it is he who has given the law [139]. Sabaoth is not good like the supreme Father, but perhaps he is not really bad either; anyhow, he belongs to the left-hand power [140]. It is not quite clear what is meant by this 'left-hand power'. In Antiquity the left signified something unfavourable. Perhaps we might think here of the English expression 'a left-handed compliment'. Such a compliment is an ambiguous one; on the surface it sounds pleasing, but in reality it is a sly dig. Could it be that this power is opposed to the Mother [141]? Or is it perhaps the material, earthly element, as opposed to the pneumatic one [142]? However this may be, Sabaoth is the Jewish God, and by this statement on the part of the author of this text nothing friendly is meant.

Sabaoth has a son; he is the Devil. "Being from the earth he opposes his own father; his father is not like him" [143]. So we have a descending succession of beings, the lower the worse. The highest Father is all-good (but unknowable); Sabaoth, in the apex of the nether region, is neither good nor bad. His son, the devil, the grandson of the highest Father, so to speak, is depraved to the core. The whole universe falls apart into two halves. The upper half is the spiritual, pure, immaterial sphere of the Ogdoas where the Father and the Mother reign. There is nothing but good there. The nether sphere is that of the seven archons of the Hebdomas. There we find the material world created not by the Father on high but by the archons with Sabaoth at their head [144]. The two heavens do not really belong together but are kept connected by the pivotal figure of Sabaoth who is of both worlds. Nevertheless, the picture is thoroughly dualistic.

d. Cain and Abel

"Now the Devil ... came to her (Eve) and had intercourse with her as a man has with a woman, and begot with her Cain and Abel" [145]. Their satanic origin explains why they were unable to get on peacefully with one another. The Archontic story flatly contradicts the biblical one. "On this account one rose up against the other, because of the jealousy they felt for one another, not because Abel pleased God at all ..., but they invent another tale which they tell. It says, since they both were in love with their own sister, for this reason Cain rose up against Abel and killed him. For they (the Archontics) say they were natural offsprings of the Devil's seed" [146]. It is part of the antinomian mentality of the Gnostics to quote the Bible and, at the same time, distort it (Genesis does not mention daughters of Adam and Eve born before Seth). "When they (the Archontics)", says Epiphanius, "wish to deceive men, they produce evidence from the Holy Scriptures" [147].

e. Seth

After this "Adam had intercourse with his own wife and begot Seth, his own natural son." Since the origin of Seth differs from that of his half-brothers Cain and Abel, he is also called 'Allogenes' = differently born [148]. This doubtless indicates a privileged position for Seth in the story of salvation. Out of fear that he too might be slain, "the power from on high (very probably the Mother is meant - F.) came down together with the angels who serve the good god and caught up Seth ... and carried him up to some higher sphere and cared for him some time" [149]. From this we may infer that Seth in the upper world received insights and knowledge that are not be had on this earth.

"After a long time they (the angels) carried him back again to this world and made him spiritual and invisible (?)" [150]. This 'invisible' is Wilson's paraphrase of the Greek 'soomatikos' = corporeal. Now what is corporeal is not invisible, of course, but what in all probability is meant is that the spiritual Seth had a body only in appearance, just as the Docetists say of Christ. Through his sojourn in heaven Seth has become fully 'allogenes', a privileged person. No longer "the Demiurge has power over him, nor yet the powers and authorities of the (same) god who made the world ... He no longer served the maker, the Demiurge, but had knowledge of the unnameable power, the good God who is above, and served him." He now is a prophet and a Redeemer. He "gave many revelations discrediting the maker of this world and the authorities of this power" [151]. Seth and his seven sons, the 'Allogeneis', the ancestors of a privileged spiritual race, are said to be the authors of a number of books [152].

f. The Archontics and Christianity

The Archontics reject the Christian creed and customs. "They condemn baptism, even though some of them were previously baptized" - which proves that there were lapsed Christians among them. "They reject participation in the sacraments and (deny) their value, as extraneous and introduced in the name of Sabaoth" [153]. Dualistically thinking as they are, the body is nothing to them, it is only an appearance. They are all 'pneumatikoi', spiritual people, people of the spirit, like their ancestor Seth. "There is no resurrection of the flesh, only of the soul" [154].

It is essential that an Archontic keeps his distance from the Christian Church; he must "shun the baptism, the Church, and the name of Sabaoth" [155]. What is baptism against the possession of knowledge! It does not work salvation as gnosis does, the knowledge acquired by the Archontic from the teachings of Seth [156]. This will enable him or her after death to pass through the seven echelons of the Hebdomas. The journey is dangerous, for the inferior powers try to sap the juice of the soul and make it powerless in this way. "The soul is food for the (inferior) powers and authorities, without which they cannot live, since it (the soul) lives from the dew which comes from above, and this gives them strength" [157]. This means that the soul has an origin totally different from that of the body; the soul is from above, the body from below. The inferior powers try to encroach upon the superior world by appropriating its capacities to themselves.

To effect the journey back, the soul of the Archontic needs a number of pass-words, the 'apologiai'; it has to speak these pass-words to each of the seven archons of the Hebdomas in order to get safely through [158]. After this the saved soul enters the upper world of the Ogdoas and becomes united with the Father and the Mother from whom it came [159].

NOTES TO CHAPTER IV

1. Wisse, Stalking Those Elusive Sethians (see Bibliography).

2. Rudolph says : "Zieht man die Originalquellen heran, so gibt es kein eindeutiges Indiz für die Existenz einer gnostischen Gemeinschaft, die sich als 'Sethianer' titulieren und ein eigenes System besassen". Wisse goes further than Rudolph in stating that "the heresiologists (= the early Fathers of the Church) beginning with Hippolytus believed in the existence of a Sethian sect through a misunderstanding ... I see the various theological systems described by the heresiologists in detail as artificial constructs used by an 'orthodox' hierarchy to show the error of their rivals. Gnostics were not system builders. So we should not expect to find a system in their literature." Rudolph, Die 'Sethianische' Gnosis, with the ensuing discussion in Redisc. of Gnost. I (see Bibliography). But here I remember that Epiphanius, while still a young man and not yet an author and an 'heresiologist', met people calling themselves 'Sethians', as he explicitly states. At the other end of the spectrum we meet Hans-Martin Schenke, Phen. and Sign. (see Bibliography) who does not doubt the existence of a Sethian sect. 591 "I believe, on the basis of the texts in our group, that it will be possible also to determine what Sethian and Sethianism does and does not mean, and also where the statements of the Church Fathers are right and where they are wrong." It must be added that Hans Jonas too believes in the separate existence of a Sethian sect, Gnosis u. spätant. geist I, 342.

3. The report by Pseudotertullianus, Adv. omnes haer. is thought to be the oldest one on the Sethians, with Epiphanius dependent on it.

4. Michel Tardieu, Les livres 210 dismisses out of hand what the 'heresiologists', viz. the early Fathers of the Church, had to say on the existence of Sethian sects : "Laissons aux hérésiologues leur catégories, et revenons aux textes des Gnostiques eux-mêmes, pour apprécier le dosage des sources, la continuité des parallèles, la diversités des formes de pensée, logiques ou non, et leurs constantes".

5. Ir., Adv.haer. 1.30; Hipp., Ref. 5.19-22; Epiph., Panarion 39.

6. Didymus, Epistola Judae, PG XXXIX, 1813 C; Serapion, Against the Manichees, II.20.

7. Epiph., Panarion 39.1.2.

8. Erik Peterson s.v. 'Sethiani', Enciclopedia cattolica. Città del Vaticano, 1953. Pp. 433/434.

9. E.F. Scott s.v. 'Sethians', Enc.of Rel.and Eth. 6, 239, said they "took their stand on Iranian dualism; perhaps they were a Zoroastrian sect". Bousset, Hauptprobl. 122 sqq., was equally

convinced that Sethianism had an Iranian origin. In his Exkurs VII, Zoroaster-Seth, he even speculated on the identification of Seth with Zoroaster. As there is really nothing in the Nag Hammadi texts to corroborate this, Bousset has to refer to a passage from Pseudo-Chrysostomos, Opus imperfectum in Matthaeum, PG 56, 637/638 (fifth cent.) This passage says that 'far away in the East, on the Ocean', there existed a sect going by the name of Seth, handed down form generation on generation. The name of Zoroaster, however, is not mentioned here neither is it specifically stated that Persia is meant. Then there is a tradition found in the 'Bee' of Solomon of Basra (quoted by Bousset) saying that Zoroaster prophesied the birth of a child from a virgin, his crucifixion, and his resurrection. This, of course, is a purely Christian tradition, but then Zoroaster adds : "He will come from my family, I am him, and he is me and I in him". Once again there is no identification Zoroaster-Seth here but instead one of Zoroaster with Jesus Christ. Now according to the biblical genealogy, Jesus Christ is a descendant of Adam via Seth, Adam's son. This could suggest an identification of Zoroaster with Seth, both ancestors of Jesus. There is also a passage in Epiph., Panarion 39.3 that says that Jesus Christ was born from Seth "according to the seed and the succession of the generations; not according to usual generation (Epiphanius is quoting Sethian doctrine now - F.) but miraculously he (Jesus) appeared in the world; he is Seth himself, this Christ who visited the human race". Bousset o.c. 382 is, of course, right in stating that in this text we see the relationship between Seth and Jesus just as we see it in the 'Bee' between Zoroaster and Jesus. But I doubt whether this is sufficient to conclude that Zoroaster and Seth are identical. There is no Sethian text that expressly says this. There is a distance of about three centuries between the Sethian texts and those quoted here. Could it not be that Bousset stumbled on the well-known pitfall that all dualisms are somehow connected with Iranian dualism?

10. Hipp., Ref. 5.20.

11. See Vol. VII, Ch. III.1b.

12. Schenke, Phen. and Sign. 592 : "It would seem to be an oversimplification of the problem if, a priori, only Judaism were to be taken into account as a possible background or source or field of origin".

13. Schenke, Phen. and Sign. 592.

14. Seth is a popular figure in Gnostic literature. See Pearson, Figure of Seth (see Bibliography).

15. Gen. 5:3-4.

16. Jos., Ant. 1.68-72. How Seth figured in Jewish and Christian literature is described by Klijn, Seth in Jew. and Christ. Lit.; Klijn also treats Seth's role in Samaritan literature (Ch. II).

Stone has a report on the Seth tradition in Armenia (see Bibliography). Seth also appears in several non-Sethian texts, see Klijn o.c. 112-117, and also pp. 90-107 on the Nag Hammadi Library in which texts Seth frequently occurs.

17. Epiph., Panarion 39.1.3. We have a translation of this and similar texts in Foerster, Gnosis. Ed. Wilson.

18. Apocalypse of Adam, NHL V.5.85. Morard, L'Apocalypse 35, thinks that this treatise can be read as an 'anti-baptismal polemic'. (35) "The absence of Christian allusions that one remarks in the present text would explain itself by the author's belonging to that sectarian milieu that attached importance only to the salvation of the soul by gnosis and rejected all participation in the sacraments." The reader who looks for a full documentation on this subject (which is not really important for my theme) will find this in Sevrin, Le dossier (see Bibliography). His conclusion (181) is that the Sethians knew some form of spiritualized baptism that is identified with gnosis. This notion "is superimposed on a dualistic anthropological doctrine that opposes people illuminated by the gnosis to those the evil works of whom make their ignorance apparent." With regard to the date of this text, Morard, Apocalypse (text edition) 7 has this to say : "Nous pencherions donc ... pour les débuts du second siècle". On p. 17 of the text edition the reader will find a very useful scheme of the doctrine presented in the Apocalypse.

19. Gospel of the Egyptians. NHC III.2.68 and IV.2. It occurs twice in the NHL. This Coptic Gospel, also named 'The Holy Book of the Great Invisible Spirit', should not be confused with the apocryphal Greek Gospel of the Egyptians, Böhlig, NHL 195.

20. Morard, Thématique 288 says : "The utilization of the Old Testament and of Jewish literature are ... indeniable, but starting from the first datum, the construction of the text and above all the interpretation are totally different." In view of this, I find her remark that the Apocalypse is 'soldily rooted in the Jewish milieu' rather puzzling. She cites, among others as proofs, the revelation of divine secrets to Adam and the transmission of these to his son Seth. Where do we find these elements in Jewish orthodoxy?

21. Apocalypse of Adam, NHC V.5.64.

22. Ir., Adv.haer. 1.30.3.

23. Ir., Adv.haer, 1.30.9.

24. Pseudotert., Adv.omn.haer. 2.

25. Epiph., Panarion 39.1.3.

26. Epiph., Panarion 39.2.4-6.

27. Epiph., Panarion 39.3.5.

28. Hipp., Ref. 5.22.

29. NHC VII.1.
30. See for the question of whether or not the two Paraphrases are identical, Bertrand, 'Paraphrase de Sem'. His conclusion (153) is that they are not really identical but nevertheless very similar in the most important respects. "Il me semble que, quel que soit le poids des différents entres les deux traités, et il est lourd, la nature de leurs ressemblances force à admettre qu'ils sont de quelque manière apparentés. Ce qui emporte ma conviction, ce n'est pas le nombre des rapprochements, c'est la pertinence avec laquelle chacun d'eux est en situation. Il ne s'agit pas d'analogies banales, mais de groupes cohérents de parallèles précis ... Ce qui est évident, c'est qu'aucun d'eux ne dérive de l'autre. Il faut donc leur supposer un ancêtre commun."
31. NHC VII.2.
32. Apocryphon of John, NHC II.1.1.
33. Apocalypse of Adam, NHC V.5.64.
34. Paraphrasis Shem, NHC VII.1.1.
35. Several scholars have expressed themselves on the singular difficulty of these texts, in particular of the 'Paraphrase of Shem'. Fischer, Paraphrase des Seem, for one, gives the following explanation for its incredible denseness. "(255) Die Paraphrase des Seem sträubt sich auf eine ganz besondere Weise gegen ein Verstehen, obwohl die Schrift umfangreich und inhaltsreich ist und sogar ganz ausgezeichnet erhalten ist ... (259/260) Die Verschlüsselung und ihr Prinzip ist das eigentliche Problem. Die mythologische Welt, in der Verfasser seine Schau schildert, ist in sich so fremd und eigenartig, dass man zwar da und dort durch motivgeschichtliche Forschungen ein Paar Bausteine des Mosaiks zusammenfügen kann, aber nicht das Ganze wirklich durchleuchten ... (264) ... dass eine logische Ordnung nicht vorliegt, ja, dass man den Eindruck gewinnen muss, dass der Verfasser eine solche Ordnung gar nicht erstrebt. Der ... Rahmen einer gnostischen Weltgeschichte ist offensichtlich fast bis zur Unkenntlichkeit überfremdet. Alle Namen, an die man sich halten könnte, sind getilgt, die eigentlichen Vorgänge des Entstehens und Werdens sind verschleiert. Was übrig bleibt, sind Bilder, die je für sich eine ganz besondere Daseinserfahrung gnostischen Weltgefühls ausdrücken ... (266) Die Schrift will nicht in erste Linie verstanden werden, sondern auf der Grundlage einer gemeinsamen Geisteshaltung meditativ weitergesponnen werden."
This corresponds entirely with my own experience. When I opened the 'Paraphrase of Shem', at first I did not understand a single word of it. For four days I laboured on this text without coming any further. It was only when I discovered that the author endlessly repeated himself, as Fischer says, that I managed to fit some pieces of the mosaic together, that I at last felt that I had the beginning of the thread of Ariadne in my hands.

Barbara Aland, Die Paraphrase, while not agreeing with Fischer that this text is 'meditative', for the rest is of the same opinion. This text "(76) erscheint dem Leser aber wirr, ohne verständlichen Zusammenhang und Aufbau, reich an Bildern und dunklen Anspielungen ... Den Schlüssel zum Verständnis des Textes bietet, wie mir scheint, der Titel der Schrift : 'Die Paraphrase des Seem', ergänzt durch die einleitenden Worte 'Paraphrase über den ungezeugten Geist' ... Es geht um den ungezeugten Geist, d.h. jenen, der nicht dem Zeugen als Charakteristikum der Finsternismacht unterliegt, also jenen Geist der vom Licht stammt, der aber in das Dunkel gefallen ist und aus dem Dunkel wieder befreit werden muss. Dieser bekannte gnostische Zentraltopos wird im ganzen folgenden Text in jeweils immer neuen Bildern und Wendungen wiederholt und umschrieben, d.h. mit anderen Worten : er wird 'paraphrasiert' ... (81) Der Autor fügt 'Variation' and 'Variation' über immer das gleiche Thema der Gefangenschaft und Befreiung des Lichtes." But Aland has to admit that the term 'paraphrazing'is then used with a somewhat other meaning than is usual. "(76)' Paraphrase' meint also in unserer Schrift in erster Linie nicht die umschreibende Wiedergabe eines bestimmten vorgegeben Textes, sondern die einer grundlegenden Einsicht und Überzeugung."

36. Paraphr.Shem, NHC VII.1.1-2.
37. Paraphr.Shem, NHC VII.1.1-2.
38. Thought of Norea, NHC IX.2.27.
39. Hipp., Ref. 5.19.
40. Paraphr.Shem, NHC VII.1.2.
41. Paraphr.Shem, NHC VII.1.4.
42. Paraphr.Shem, NHC VII.1.4.
43. Hipp., Ref. 5.19.6.
44. Paraphr.Shem., NHC VII.1.5.
45. Paraphr.Shem, NHC VII.1.6-10.
46. Paraphr.Shem, NHC VII.1.20.
47. Paraphr.Shem, NHC VII.1.4-5.
48. Paraphr.Shem, NHC VII.1.7.
49. Parpras.Shem, NHC VII,1.18-19.
50. Paraphr.Shem, NHC VII.1.19.
51. Paraphr.Shem, NHC VII.1.20.
52. Paraphr.Shem, NHC VII.1.21-22.
53. Hipp., Ref. 5.19.11-13.
54. Paraphr.Shem, NHC VII.1.22.

55.	Paraphr.Shem, NHC VII.1.22-23.
56.	Paraphr.Shem, NHC VII.1.23-24.
57.	Hipp., Ref. 5.19.13-14.
58.	Jonas, Gnosis u. spätant. Geist, I, 143.
59.	Hipp., Ref. 5.19.15.
60.	Hipp., Ref. 5,19.19.
61.	Hipp., Ref. 5.19.17.
62.	Hipp., Ref. 5.19.15.
63.	Hipp., Ref. 5.119.15.
64.	Hipp., Ref. 5.19.16.
65.	Hipp., Ref. 5.19.15.
66.	NHC V.5, in NHL introduced and translated by George W. MacRae.
67.	NHC V.5.64.
68.	NHC V.5.64.
69.	NHC V.5.64.
70.	NHC V.5.65.
71.	NHC V.5.65-66.
72.	Pseudotert., Adv. omn. haer. 2.
73.	Epiph., Panarion 39.5.2-5.
74.	NHC III.1.41. Claude, Trois stèles 4 : "Le chiffre trois référait directement aux trois hypostases, l'Autogène, Barbélo, et l'Inengendré, cette triade divine du monde plēromatique."
75.	NHC III.2.42.
76.	NHC III.2.54-56.
77.	NHC III.2.60.
78.	NHC III.2.49.
79.	NHC IV.2.61.
80.	NHC III.2.49.
81.	NHC III.2.51.
82.	Harmozel = the light of the first aeon, ruler over grace, truth, and shape; Oroiael = the light of the second aeon, ruler over foresight, observance, and memory; Davithe = light of the third aeon, ruler over insight, love, and appearing; Eleleth = the light of the fourth aeon, ruler over perfection, peace, and wisdom.
83.	NHC III.2.51-52.

84. NHC III.2.66.
85. NHC III.2.68-69. There is yet another treatise that perhaps speaks of Seth, although he is not mentioned by name in it. It is NHC XI.3, the 'Allogenes', in NHL XII.3. introduced by Antoinette Clark Wire and translated by John D. Turner and Orval S. Wintermuth. 'Allogenes' means 'one of another race'. But as the introduction , NHL 403, says, this "is a common name in this period for semi-divine revealers". However, Pearson, Seth in Gnost. Lit. 486/487, thinks that "it is reasonable to regard the Nag Hammadi tractate Allogenes as a 'Sethian' book, and to assume that the revealer 'Allogenes' is to be understood as a manifestation of Seth himself".
86. Pearson, Seth in Gnost. Lit. 498. There is only one mention of Zoroaster in a Sethian text. NHC VIII.1. Zostrianos, in NHL introduced and translated by John H. Sieber, ends 132 like this : "Zostrianos. Words of truth of Zostrianos. God of Truth, words of Zoroast(er)"; perhaps Zostrianos is identified with Zoroaster here; Zostrianos in his turn may possibly equated with Seth.
87. NHC IX.1, in NHL introduced by Birger A. Pearson and translated by Sören Giveresen and Birger A. Pearson. According to Pearson, Introd. 399, "The obvious Sethian Gnostic element ... may be secondary".
88. Gen. 14:18-20; Ps. 110:4; Hebr. 5:1-11, 7:1-14.
89. NHC IX.1.5.
90. NHC IX.1.6.
91. Pearson, Seth in Gnost. Lit. 498.
92. NHL 399.
93. Pearson, Seth in Gnost. Lit. 498.
94. NHC VIII.1.131-132.
95. NHC VIII.1.30.
96. NHC VIII.1.3.
97. NHC VIII.1.130.
98. NHC VIII.1.67-68.
99. NHC VII.5.123.
100. NHC VII.1.35.
101. NHC VII.1.130.
102. NHC VII.2.63.
103. NHC VII.2.63-64.
104. NHC VII.2.64.
105. NHC VII.1.29; see also NHC III.2.56 and 60.

106. NHC VII. 2.64-65.
107. NHC VII. 2.60-61.
108. NHC VII. 2.51-52.
109. NHC VII. 2.65.
110. NHC VII. 2.55-56.
111. Tröger, Der zweite Logos, on the role of Christ in Sethian doctrine : "(268) Die Frage nach dem 'Cur Deus homo' ist gegenstandlos. Gott **wird** (all emphases are Tröger's) nicht Mensch. Der Mensch wird Gott, wird **wieder** Gott ... (270) Der gnostische Erlöser kommt nicht in die an sich gute und nur vom Menschen pervertierte Welt des Schöpfers um das Böse zu bannen, Sünde zu vergeben und den Menschen in seiner Gänze vor Gott zu stellen, sondern er kommt nur zur Sammlung des Lichts aus der Fisternis, den gefangenen Menschen heimzuholen, ihn zu erwecken, ihm den Weg zu bereiten - das ist seine Mission. Dazu braucht er kein Leiden, kein Kreuz, keine Auferstehung ... Und der seiner Herkunft nach göttliche Mensch hat einen solchen Erlöser auch gar nicht nötig ... Wie soll nun aber die Gnosis ... mit dieser Aporie, mit dem Paradoxon des leidenden Christus und dem Ärgernis des Kreuzes fertig werden? ... Wie kann sich überhaupt eine christliche-gnostische oder gnostisch-christliche Richtung bilden, wo doch Christentum und Gnosis in ihrem Wesen so verschieden sind? Oder sind sie es gar nicht? ... Die Antwort lautet im Hinblick auf die christologische Frage : durch den **Doketismus** ... 271 Das ist im Prinzip die Lösung die sich einem Gnostiker anbietet : die scharfe Trennung von Christus und Jesus ... Um zwischen beiden dennoch eine Beziehung herstellen zu können, grift man zur Vorstellung eines **Scheinleibes** ... 276 Nur selten hat ein vom Christentum beeinflusster Gnostiker diese radikale Differenz (i.e. von Christus und Jesus - F.) so deutlich empfunden wie der Autor vom Zweiten Logos des grossen Seth."
112. Ir., Adv.haer. 1.23.3. and 24.4.
113. NHC VII. 1.37.
114. NHC VII. 1.4-5.
115. NHL 308.
116. NHC VII. 1.7.
117. NHC VII. 1.34-35.
118. NHC VII. 5.121.
119. Rudolph, Gnosis 89.
120. NHC VIII. 1.1.
121. NHC VII. 1.44-45.
122. NHC VII. 1.48.

123. NHC VII.2.69-70.
124. NHC VII.5.120-121.
125. Epiph., Panarion 40.7.5. The reports in other ancient sources, Aug.; De haer. 1. Theodor., Haer.fab.comp. 1.11 (303); Johannes Dam., De haer. 85.40, are dependent on him. Puech s.v. 'Archontiker', Reallex.Ant.Christ. 1, 365.
126. Epiph., Panarion 40.1.1-3. This Peter was a priest but had been suspended by bishop Aetius because he was a Gnostic heretic, Epiph., Panarion 40.1.5.
127. Epiph., Panarion 40.1.8-9.
128. Puech s.v. 'Archontiker', Reallex,Ant.Christ. 1, 635.
129. Epiph., Panarion 40.2.1.
130. Epiph., Panarion 40.2.2, discussed in Puech s.v. 'Archontiker', Realllex.Ant.Christ. 1, 636/637.
131. Epiph., Panarion 40.2.3.
132. Epiph., Panarion 40.5.2, 40.2.8, 40.7.9, 40.7.1, 40.7.3.
133. Epiph., Panarion 40.5.2 and 40.7.3.
134. Epiph., Panarion 40.2.8, 40.7.1, 40.2.3.
135. Epiph., Panarion 40.2.3.
136. Four times in Epiph., Panarion 40.2.5, 40.2.7, 40.4.1., 40.7.1.
137. Epiph., Panarion 40.2.3 and 40.2.5.
138. Epiph., Panarion 40.2.6 and 40.5.8.
139. Epiph., Panarion 40.5.1 and 40.2.8.
140. Epiph., Panarion 40.5..2.
141. Cf. Ir., Adv.haer. 1.30.8.
142. Cf. Ir., Adv.hear. 1.5. See Puech s.v. 'Archontiker', Reallex.Ant.Christ. 1, 638.
143. Epiph., Panarion 40.5.1-2.
144. Epiph., Panarion 40.8.6.
145. Epiph., Panarion 40.5.3.
146. Epiph. Panarion 40.5.4.
147. Epiph., Panarion 40.5.4.
148. Epiph., Panarion 40.7.1-2.
149. Epiph., Panarion 40.7.1-2.
150. Epiph., Panarion 40.7.2.
151. Epiph., Panarion 40.7.3.

152. Epiph., Panarion 40.7.4-5.
153. Epiph., Panarion 40.2.6.
154. Epiph., Panarion 40.2.5.
155. Epiph., Panarion 40.2.8.
156. Epiph., Panarion 40.2.8
157. Epiph, Panarion 40.5.7.
158. Epiph., Panarion 40.2.8 and 8.6.
159. Epiph., Panarion 40.2.8

CHAPTER V

THE SERPENT AND ITS RETINUE :
THE OPHITES AND RELATED SECTS

1. Which sects may be called 'Ophitic'?

We now come to that part of the Gnostic movement that goes by the name of 'Ophitism'. It probably had its beginnings in the second century A.D. It is possible, as E.F. Scott writes, that "the name of 'Ophitai' propably belonged to one particular sect, but was extended to a large group of sects whose practices appeared to resemble those of the Ophites". Apart from the original and most authentic Ophites, he cites as 'Ophitic' the following Gnostic sects, : the Cainites, the Perates, the Sethians, the 'Gnostics' of Irenaeus, the Naassenes, the Barbelo-Gnostics, the Severians, and the Justinians. What binds these sects together is the 'ophis', or snake, which is a regular feature of their ideology. However, as Scott also states, in the doctrines of some of these sects "the cult of the serpent ... had a quite subordinate place" [1].

This is a sufficient reason not to speak in this context of the Archontics, the Barbelo-Gnostics, and the Sethians. Just as in the case of the Sethians not every text in which the name of Seth occurs is Sethian in the proper sense of the word, it will not do to dub every document that speaks of a snake or serpent as 'Ophitic'.

2. The veneration of the snake

The serpent occupies a prominent place in ancient mythology; veneration of the serpent, the snake cult, is not rare. It is perhaps difficult for an inhabitant of a country like mine, the Netherlands, where we have only one poisonous snake, a small one, the viper, to sympathize with the point of view that in all lands where the bite of a snake can bring sudden death, there exists great fear of such dangerous animals. There is every reason to pacify these bearers of evil.

On the other hand, the snake is seen as an exceptional animal provided with mysterious and occult properties. Doesn't it shed its hide and don a new one? This means that it is able to renew its life. And doesn't it crawl along the earth in its full length? This means that, more than any other living being, it is in intimate contact with Mother Earth, the element from which all natural life sprouts. Furthermore, it is an animal that is capable of biting its own tail, thus forming a circle, the symbol of perfection. Therefore, the serpent is not only a sign of death and evil but also of life, hope, and perfection. It knows all the mysteries. In many mythologies it is a primeval being, the real origin of the cosmos [2]. For this reason, Gnostics, who were much given to mysteriosophy, or at least this was the case with quite a number of them, fostered a predilection for the 'ophis', the snake.

3. About the Ophites in general

In one of the very few monographs on Ophitism, or perhaps the only one, Adolf Hönig explains that the Ophitic doctrine (which is, like love, a many-splendoured thing) is like a snake itself. Its enemies saw it as the worst possible doctrine, the deepest pit into which the human spirit could sink; for its adherents it was the zenith of knowledge and spiritual elevation. And just as a snake suddenly darts forward, while nobody knows where it comes from, so Ophitism with incredible suddenness stands complete before our eyes. "Strong, well-armed, the hand raised for the war of destruction against the existing religious and social institutes, all of a sudden it is there in the foreground of ecclesiastical history, and we ask in vain for the history of its infancy and for the name of its fatherland." This scholar deduces from the bitterness with which it was fought and from the fact that so many Christian apologists combated it, that this doctrine was powerful and wide-spread and counted numerous adherents [3].

4. The snake as the sect's patron

In the absence of specific Ophitic texts in the Nag Hammadi Library we have to turn to reports of the early Fathers of the Church. Leisegang is of the opinion that what Hippolytus has to say on the Naassenes is well suited to give us an idea of what Ophitism is about. Their name is derived from the Hebrew word 'nahas' = snake, in Greek corrupted to 'naas'. "The priests and advocates of this doctrine were first of all those who are called 'Naassenes'" [4]. The Hebrew background of the sect's name may point to an origin in Palestine but, on the other hand, its change into 'naas' suggests a Hellenistic environment which would suggest Egypt, Alexandria for instance.

The use of a basically Semitic name does not refer to heathen mythology but rather to the Old Testament where the snake as a more than ordinary animal appears as the seducer in the Paradise story or as the brazen serpent procuring healing for the afflicted [5], a most alluring symbol, since it is at the same time a sign of sin and death, and of life and health.

Epiphanius tells a story of how the Ophites themselves venerated the snake. They kept a serpent in a chest feeding it with bread; they venerated this animal, because they claimed it granted them knowledge. During their rituals they placed bread on a table, then brought the chest in, opened it, and let the snake crawl out. It mounted on the table and coiled itself around the bread. "This they believe to be the most perfect sacrifice." In addition to this Epiphanius heard from someone that "they not only break and distribute this bread ..., but that they even kiss the serpent. It has become innocuous either through the effect of their songs or by means of a devilish artifice ... This is what they call Eucharist" [6].

5. Ophites, Naassenes, and Gnostikoi

Another intriguing element is that, according to Hippolytus, the adherents of the snake cult first called themselves 'Naassenes' but later 'Gnostikoi', "alleging that they alone knew the deep things". This is a clear proof that by no means all the Gnostics called themselves so. Hippolytus goes on in this way : "Many (others) have split off from them and divided the heresy into many factions, though it is really one, by presenting the same (story) under different names" [7]. This suggests that Hippolytus thought that the Naassenes formed the very first Gnostic sect [8]. However this may be, I feel that, for clarity' sake, it would be preferable to lump the Ophite and Naassene doctrines together [9].

6. Trinity and quaternity of first principles

According to Irenaeus [10], there existed in the depth, the 'bythos', a primal light, "blessed and incorruptible and boundless, which is the Father of All and is called the First Man" [11]. From him the Ennoia (Thought) proceeds "whom they call the Son of the one who emits him, and he is the Son of Man, the Second Man. Below (or after) these is the Holy Spirit" [12]. Here we have a trinity of primary entities or principles. That Ennoia, or Thought, is male is curious since the Greek word itself is feminine [13].

Below 'the Holy Spirit on high' we find a quaternity of material principles, Water, Darkness, Abyssus, Chaos, "over which they say the Spirit hovers". The trinity and the quaternity obviously are both coeval as well as from eternity.

In spite of some references to the creation story in Genesis, we are worlds removed here from the Old Testament. In Genesis God, and nobody else, is the creator of this world. But to Gnostics like Ophites and Naassenes this idea is repellent. Since the physical, perceptual world is no good, it is inconceivable to them that the Father would have created the cosmos directly. We have two male principles, the First Man who is the Father, and the Second Man who is Thought and who is to all intents and purpose identical with the Logos. Why are there **two** male principles? This is to enable the Father not to be wholly and solely responsible for creation but to act with and through the Logos.

7. The First Woman and Christ

The Naassenes call the Spirit 'the First Woman' [14]. Now the sexual element comes into play. "The First man rejoiced with his son at the beauty of the Spirit, that is the Woman, and illuminated her; he begot from her an incorruptible light, a third male, whom they call Christ, the Son of the First and the Second Man and the Holy Spirit the First Woman, since both the Father and the Son lay with the Woman, whom they call the Mother of the Living" [15].

Since the Woman is 'below' or 'after' the two men, she is somewhat inferior to them; she is incapable of acting of her own accord but, in order to become the fountain-head of all creation, she has to be 'illuminated'. The product of the divine radiation is 'Christ' who, of course, is not Jesus of Nazareth, but somebody like the Messiah of orthodox Jewry [16]. It looks very much as though the Ophites wanted to improve on the original Genesis report.

"The First Woman was unable to carry or contain the greatness of the light, ... she was overfull and bubbling over at the left side, and their only son Christ, as being on the right and lifted up into the higher parts, was at once caught up to the Imperishable Aeon" [17]. We have a second duality here, that of the right and left sides of the Woman - the first being that of the two males and the Woman. Just as there is a qualitative difference between these males and the Woman, there is also one between her two sides. The Woman herself, the Spirit that is, is on the dividing line between the upper and nether worlds but belongs essentially to the higher one.

As always with Gnostics, duality soon enough turns into dualism. Mother and son, the Woman and Christ, have their abode in the higher spheres. "This is the true and holy Church, which is designation and unification of the Father of All, the First Man, and his son the Second Man, and of Christ their son, and of the afore-mentioned Woman" [18]. We find here the idea of the so-called 'invisible Church' that only exists in heaven, or only ideally, which is not at all identical with any Christian Church on earth. This is in accordance with much Protestant doctrine but not with Catholic teaching.

8. The downward course of the light and its escape

Because the Woman is not wholly perfect, she proves incapable of containing the divine Light with which the Father so profusely endows her. It streams down from her left side, and this suggests a decline. This down-going light is called 'Left and Prunicus (the Lewd) and Sophia and Man-Woman' [19]. On its downward course it evidently becomes less radiant and somewhat corrupted in the process. This emanation of the light is needed to explain why matter, which by itself is inert and powerless, starts to move. "She went down straight into the waters when they were still, and set them in motion, wantonly stirring them to the depths, and she took on a body from them" [20].

This 'she' who plunged into the waters is not the First Woman (who has returned to heaven) but the light that emanated from her, the Sophia who is now seen acting on her own accord. Things are going ever worse, for Sophia takes on a body and becomes physical, and this is negatively meant. "Everything rushed to her and clung to her, and encircled her; if she had not had this (trace of light), she would perhaps have been completely swallowed up and submerged" [21]. A running fight is developing between the light and matter (the 'everything that clung to her'), with the latter for some time to come on the winning side.

The encapsulated light, wanting to return to its origin, begins to struggle. "Being tied and severely weighed down by the body, because it was of matter, at last she got a saviour (of the light), and tried to feel up from the waters and rise up to the Mother; but she could not because of the weight of the body surrounding (her). Being in a very bad way, she devised means of hiding that light which was from above, for fear that it would also be harmed by the inferior elements just as she was herself. When she received from the trace of light within her (with her 'saviour' this light is meant - F.), she leapt up and was carried up to the height, and there she spread out and made this visible heaven from her body; and she remained under the heaven which she made, which still has the appearance of a watery body. Since she had a craving for the light above, and had acquired power through all things, she laid aside her body and was set free from it" [22].

What is the meaning of this text? First the luminous Sophia has grown entirely opaque; she has become wholly physical and inferior, not much better than the material elements by which she has let herself be engulfed. But she retains a spark of light within her physical body which spark, if I am interpreting the ancient text correctly, does not organically belong to her material constitution. This spark acts as a dynamic force creating an upward surge. Nevertheless, too much matter, in the shape of water (the most formless element), is clinging to her so that she is unable to effect her return in one rush.

First, she has to shed her body which she does by fashioning it into the vault of heaven. Only then can she find her way back to the world above. What we see portrayed here is the ideal prototype of the ascent of the human soul. In every human being there is a spark of light encased in the body. It can only return to the luminous world above if the body is radically done away with.

9. Jaldabaoth

On her return to the Light Sophia leaves a son behind her. How she came to this son is not explained; it obviously is a piece of parthenogenesis. The name of this son is 'Jaldabaoth', a name often occurring in Gnostic texts which does not imply that we know what it means. Most scholars derive it from 'jalda bahuth' = Son of Chaos [23]. This Jaldabaoth has "a breath of incorruptibility left in him by his mother (Sophia), and through this he acts"[24]. It appears that Sophia did not take away all the light with her; in her son too this spark of light is a dynamic force. Jaldabaoth produces a son, and this son another son, and this another, and so on, till there are seven generations, all brought forth without the intervention of women. They form a hierarchy, the oldest being the worthiest and the most powerful[25]; they constitute the seven celestial spheres[26].

According to Irenaeus, these seven, all of them invisible, are "heavens and virtues and powers and angels and creators ... (and they) rule things heavenly and earthly"[27]. The dualistic distinction between the upper and nether spheres is becoming ever more apparent. The creation and management of the cosmos is left entirely to lesser and not wholly benevolent demiurges; no being from above interferes. The dynamic force that is left in the demiurges is used for acting against the intentions of their all-mother Sophia. The main and real Demiurge is Jaldabaoth who "despising his mother, made sons and grandsons without anyone's permission"[28].

10. The snake

It is a well-known theme in Gnostic ideology that the inferior powers quarrel among each other (it is part of their inferiority); here the progeny of Jaldabaoth turns against him, obviously jealous of his precedence. Angered by their resistance, he fashions 'from the dregs of matter lying below' a being, another son, the Nous. This Nous is made in the shape of a snake; in its turn it becomes a Demiurge, for "thence came spirit and soul and all worldy things". Nothing good arose from it, only 'forgetfulness, malice, jealousy, and death'. This Nous-serpent is so abysmally bad that he even "perverted his own father (Jaldaboath) by his tortuousness"[29].

It is evident that the creational process has taken a decisive turn for the worse; it is now entirely dominated by evil. Epiphanius adds here that Jaldabaoth originated "from the imbecility and ignorance of his mother (Sophia)", who was stupid enough to let herself be taken prisoner by matter. The serpent, who was, so to speak, her grandson, was 'the source of all knowledge for mankind' [30] - a kind of knowledge that, in Gnostic view, is the sheerest ignorance.

11. Jaldaboath-Jahve and the creation of man

Seduced by the Nous, the world-spirit who is the personfication of evil, Jaldabaoth begins to boast that he is "Father and God and above me there is no one" [31]. Taking his cue from Is. 45:5, he is identifying himself with Jahve here. Epiphanius states this in as many words : "They (the Ophites) contend that Jaldabaoth is the God of the Jews ... and also that of the Christians, and therefore the common God of all that is" [32]. But whereas the Judaeo-Christian God really is the highest and omnipotent one, Jaldabaoth is an inferior divinity who mistakenly believes that he has no betters.

So we have the pair Jaldabaoth-Nous/Serpent of which, as Hönig says, Jaldabaoth represents physical evil and the snake moral evil [33]. Jaldabaoth's mother Sophia loudly protested against her son's preposterous claim but in order to make a diversion he decided to fashion a human being. The identification with Jahve becomes complete when he uses the biblical words of Gen. 1:26 : "Come, let us make a man in our image". But curiously enough, the idea for this really came from Sophia who in this way hoped to strip her son of what he possessed of divine powers by bestowing them on man. "Sophia contrived so as to empty him also of his trace of light, so that he would not be able to rise up against those above him by the power he had" [34].

The six beings that were the offspring of Jaldabaoth now fashioned a human being, 'a man of enormous breadth and length'; he lay like a worm wriggling on the ground incapable of standing upright. The six carried him to Jaldabaoth who blew the spark of light into him, in this way unwittingly emptying himself of his power. "But this man thus got Nous and Enthumesis (thought) ... and he at once gave thanks to the

First Man, forsaking his creators" [35]. It is, as Epiphanius writes, the spark of light that enables man to transcend and ignore the Demiurge. I see in this story a inversion of the report of the Fall in Genesis. There too man, wishing to acquire knowledge and insight, rebels against his Creator but there the result is only that he loses his superior status. Here the reverse is happening. Knowledge enables man (that is, the Ophitic Gnostic) to reach back to the prime godhead.

12. The revenge of Jaldabaoth

The jealous Jaldabaoth, wanting to get his power back by emptying man of it, fashioned a woman 'from his Enthymesis (thought)' [36]. Of old it has been an apple of discord to whom this 'his' refers, to Jaldabaoth or to the human male. Hönig, following Baur, thinks that it refers to the male. The Ophites obviously modelled their story upon that of Genesis; for this reason it would only be logical that the woman came forth from the male [37]. I should like to remark that the text does not mention Adam's rib or side; perhaps the Ophites found this detail too physical. So much is certain that the woman is an instrument in the hands of the wicked Jaldabaoth, to be turned against the male [38].

The six powers below Jaldabaoth admired the beauty of the woman, called her 'Eve' [39], and "lusting for her begot from her sons, and called them angels" [40]. Sophia-Prunicus, however, tried to frustrate the evil intentions of Jaldaboath with the help of the snake; this animal persuaded Adam to eat from the tree of knowledge, thereby transgressing Jaldabaoth's command [41]. What Adam and Eve, as the prototypes of the enlightened Gnostics, acquire by eating from the tree is the redeeming knowledge which gives them a more than human dimension. The serpent is the guardian of that knowledge.

But Jaldabaoth does not admit that he is beaten. He expels the first human beings from Paradise [42]. That means, says Foerster, that the portion of light remains 'imprisoned' in them [43]; Jaldaboth sees to it that they, although they now possess knowledge, are incapable of using it [44]. They "previously had light, clear, and as it were, spiritual bodies.

But when they came here (in the present world), they turned into something more opaque and thick and sluggish. The soul too has become lax and limp" [45].

13. Humanity at risk

At first it seems as though the serpent, working as the guardian of knowledge against Jaldabaoth, is on the side of the luminous Powers. But soon enough the contrary becomes apparent. Jaldabaoth casts down the rebellious snake into the pit; there he lords it over the angels and begets (with the angels) six sons who with their father constitute an Hebdomad. "These ... are the seven demons of the world, always opposing and resisting the human race, because on their (the humans') account their (the demons') Father (Jaldabaoth) was thrown down" [46].

The human race has many enemies; all the powers from below are laying snares for it. But Sophia came to its help; "she pitied them and restored to them a whiff of the sweetness of the trace of light". Another pivotal phrase follows. "Through this they (the human beings) came to recollect who they themselves were, and they knew that they were naked and had material bodies; and they knew that they were burdened with death. They became patient, knowing that the body is their garment (only) for a time" [47]. This too is a prototype of the Gnostic attitude. Ophites, like other Gnostics, do not want to be either in or of this world.

14. The race of Cain and the race of Seth

Cain, followed by Abel - although this is not said explicitly -, was born as the first son of Adam and Eve. He was so utterly corrupted by the Snake and his sons that he killed Abel; it is suggested that it was this homicide that brought death into the world. Then Sophia-Prunicus saw to it that Adam and Eve begot another son, Seth, and a daughter, Norea (of whom Genesis knows nothing at all); these two became the ancestors of the rest of mankind (it is to be supposed that there was also a race of

Cainites) [48]. They, it may be assumed, form two distinct and opposed races of men, the one tending to heaven, the other clinging to the earth. Theodoretus adds that Sethians and Ophites see in Seth 'a divine power' [49].

But first all went wrong for everybody. Even the race of Seth and Norea was "plunged by the lower hebdomad into every kind of evil and rebellion against the higher, holy hebdomad", with Sophia all the time struggling to preserve that precious spark of light in man [50]. Jaldabaoth attempted to destroy mankind by the Flood, but Sophia succeeded in saving Noah and his family by means of "the trace of light that came from her" [51].

15. The Ophites and the biblical heritage

The text then proceeds with seven-league boots through Old Testament history. A new race originated after the Flood, again with the spark of light in it. Abraham was elected by Jaldabaoth who made him promise that his seed would serve him; this gives Jewry a nefarious origin. It was Moses who gave them the Law and called them 'Jews' [52]. Then came Samuel, Joshua, and the prophets; it was their task to extol their father and god, Jaldabaoth of course [53]. If it is true, as indeed seems probable, that Ophitism has a strong Jewish background, then its adherents took care to distance themselves as far as possible from their origin.

Perhaps it is somewhat contradictory, at least in the view of us moderns, that the prophets of Israel not only proclaim Jaldabaoth but that Sophia too speaks through them. She makes them reveal "many things about the First man, the Imperishable Aeon, and about that Christ who according to them (the Ophites) is above, and she forewarned and reminded men of the imperishable light and the First Man and the descent of Christ" [54]. The proximity of Ophitism to Judaism is also proved by the circumstance that, according to this doctrine, Scripture not only contains much that is utterly wrong and false but at the same time the core of the essential and redeeming knowledge. The New Testament element in this is that it is centered on the person of Christ.

16. Christ and Jesus

Two men were born, 'one from the barren Elizabeth (John the Baptist), the other from Mary the Virgin (Jesus)'. This was arranged by Sophia but brought about "through Jaldabaoth who did not know what he was doing" [55]. As is usual in Gnostic texts, Jesus of Nazareth is not exactly the same person as Christ. Whereas Jesus is an earthly man from an earthly mother, Christ was sent down from heaven at the request of the First Woman by the First Man. He descended through the seven heavens of the lower hebdomad, that of the archons, and "emptied them of their power", that is, of all the sparks of light that were in their possession. In Christ "the whole trace of light flowed together".

Having arrived in this world, Christ united himself with Sophia who all the time had slaved to preserve some of the light in the lower world. Then they took up their abode in Jesus who, "being born from a virgin by the activity of a god, was wiser and purer and more just than all men" [56]. Theodoretus supplies an intriguing item, namely that Christ entered the womb of Mary in the shape of a serpent [57]. The Ophites showed themselves knowledgeable about the New Testament too, but in order to use it for their own ends, they felt free to distort its meaning.

Many of Jesus' disciples did not realize that Christ was working through him. Christ proclaimed the unknown Father and confessed himself openly as the son of the First Man. He was, therefore, the bearer and herald of the essential knowledge; for this reason, he incurred the hatred of Jaldabaoth and his party. They contrived his execution; that is to say, Jesus was crucified, not Christ. Christ and Sophia escaped in time to return to the Imperishable Aeon [58].

Theodoretus states categorically that in Ophitic doctrine "Jesus is really someone else than Christ" [59], Why this duality, if not dualism? In the Ophitic Christ-Jesus we have a hybrid and uncomfortable combination of the celestial and the terrestrial. This exemplifies the profoundly dualistic stance of this sect. They are in need of a Redeemer, a bearer of the saving knowledge. But their abhorrence of all that is corporeal, terrestrial, physical prevents them from seeing this saviour in

Jesus of Nazareth, such as the Gospels proclaim him. A human being, in their view, cannot organically unite himself with the divine. By the same token, the divine Christ can never identify himself with someone who is human. His divine status makes it impossible for him to suffer and to undergo death.

The Ophites accuse the Christians of ignorance and misunderstandings with regard to Jesus. According to them, Jesus did indeed rise from the grave, for "Christ sent a certain power into him, which raised him in the body. This body was one of soul (psychê) and spirit (pneuma), for what was worldy (i.e. the physical body) he left in the world (i.e. in the tomb)". His disciples, however, were stupid enough to think that he had risen in a real, physical body. No wonder, for "they did not know Christ himself" [60]. The risen Christ lived for another eighteen months after his resurrection. Only to "a few of his disciples whom he knew to be capable of such great mysteries he taught these things (about himself), and thus was taken up into heaven, where Christ sits on the right hand of the father Jaldabaoth, so that, after they had put off the worldy flesh, he may take to himself the souls of these who knew him" [61].

It will probably surprise the reader to find Christ back, not in the highest heaven at the side of the supreme Father of all, the First Man, but next to Jaldabaoth who by no means is a benevolent entity. But Christ's connection with him is only a temporary measure. Jaldabaoth, incurably ignorant as he is, does not even know that Christ is near and continues working against him.

Foerster asks himself whether Jesus is really necessary in this system [62]. I think that Jesus in Ophitic doctrine is acting as the forerunner of those souls that will be able to perform the ascent; he is the guarantee that such an ascent is possible, at least for a few. As soon as he has joined Christ, Jesus gathers, 'enriches himself with', the holy souls. This reduces Jaldabaoth's power; he proves incapable of sending these souls down into the world again. He only succeeds in sending back the inferior souls. At last all the elect are gathered around Christ and Jesus and are "taken up into the aeon of Imperishability" [63].

17. Dualism galore

There is no apocalypse; it is not related, at least not by our sources, what will happen to Jaldabaoth, the cosmos, and mankind. But even so there is dualism galore : that of the upper and nether worlds, of the elect and the rejected, of knowledge and ignorance, of soul and body; the whole gamut is there. There is also the determined rejection of orthodox Christianity. Let me end by quoting Foerster's final conclusion : "What we find again and again in Gnosis is also present here : the eschatological hope, which is not anticipated by any ecstasy; the fact that no philosophical efforts, but only a secret revelation, the bearer of which is in this case Christ, is able to lead to what is above; and the content of this revelation, the unknown God" [64].

18. The Ophians

a. The Ophian diagram

Origen is the only author to mention a sect called 'Ophian'. It goes without saying that, in all probability, these Ophians were identical with the Ophites. However, the description this Father of the Church gives of them does not agree in every respect with what Irenaeus reported about the Ophites. So there is some reason to see the Ophians as a sect closely related to the Ophites but not exactly the same [65]. We find Origenes' report in his book 'Contra Celsum', which dates from ca. 248. As the title indicates it is directed against Celsus, a scholar who in 178 wrote a book on Christianity called 'The True Discourse' ('Alēthēs Logos'); the new religion was thought to be important enough then to fight it vigorously. The book itself has disappeared; what we know of it comes from Origen.

Celsus, although he shows himself fairly knowledgeable about Judaism and Christianity, makes little or no difference between orthodox Christians and Gnostics [66]. This enables him, in the course of his attack on the Christian Church, to present a certain diagram that, says this

Father of the Church, was "in part based on misunderstood information about the insignificant Ophian sect" [67]. He then goes on to describe this diagram, without fully understanding it. "Although we (Origen) have travelled through many parts of the earth, and everywhere inquired for those who claimed to know anything, (we) have found no one able to explain the diagram" [68]. Even today it presents great difficulties to scholars. As Foerster writes, "it is probably impossible to get a 'system' directly from it" [69]. However, Leisegang, in his book on the Gnosis, presents us with a beautiful reconstruction of it [70]. The original has got lost.

Very probably the diagram, such as Celsus saw it, had a spherical shape, in accordance with the ancient idea that the universe must be a perfectly round globe. On the inside of this globe, close to its outer rim, we find the divine realm. It consists of two concentric circles, that of the Father and that of the Son. Inscribed into these two white circles there is a smaller one connecting them as a ring or a kind of knot. It is called 'agapê' = love, a female entity [71]. "The divine realm, therefore, represents a trinity of two male and one female spiritual beings who mutually determine and pervade each other"; Leisegang adds that Agapê is the personified urge of love that is drawing the Son downwards [72].

This suggests a connection with the one lower region which is the sphere of Life. This too consists of two concentric circles, the upper one being yellow, the colour of the light, and that of the other one blue, the colour of darkness. Into these two circles another smaller circle is inscribed connecting the two bigger ones. This obviously is the core, the essence of Life. Within this smaller circle we detect a rhomboid figure which is 'the Providence of Sophia'. Life and Sophia are closely related, for we find some important terms inscribed here : 'Nature or Sophia', 'Gnosis', and 'Synesis' = Insight [73]. This means that in the life sphere elements are stored that will make possible an authentically spiritual life.

One stage further down, but still within the intermediate region of Life, Wisdom, and Knowledge, we see the circle of the Zodiac; in this Paradise is located. It is rectangular and contains the Tree of Life and that of Knowledge of good an evil. This location of Paradise signifies that it is not situated on earth.

Descending still further, we reach the third sphere, that of the physical, perceptible cosmos. It is enclosed by 'Leviathan', the fabulous animal, a kind of sea-serpent, that we know from several Old Testament texts too [74]; biting its own tail, it encircles the cosmos. This dragon with its unfavourable reputation - in the Bible it is a symbol of pre-cosmic chaos - here is the soul which permeates the universe [75]. It is "the Lord of the world and the expression of the calamitous nature of the cosmos" [76]. This world snake divides the lower region from the two higher and purer ones; it is suggested that it will not be easy to pass from the earth to the divine realm.

Then follow seven concentric circles, of the five planets, the sun, and the moon, with that of the sun being the middle one, and that of the moon the lowest and smallest. The text does not speak of 'planets' but of 'archons', or 'rulers', and gives them fantastic names like Thantabaoth and Thaphabaoth. This is done in order to make clear that these archons really are demons, with the head of a dog or a bear, or with the shape of an ass, or hissing horribly [77].

The chief archon, the highest one, is identified with the planet Saturn. He is shaped in the form of a lion and is also called Michael [78]. In all probability he is the God of the Jews, elsewhere called 'Jaldabaoth' [79], the 'cursed god' [80], the one who has created this world [81]. From the sphere of the moon we do not immediately reach the earth but first pass the sphere of Behemoth [82], another primeval monster, the incarnation of evil. The encirclement of earth and cosmos by two fatal monsters implies that a human soul attempting to surge upwards to the father risks a highly hazardous journey.

Only then do we reach the earth itself; underneath it lies the underworld, the Tartarus [83]. Our earth, therefore, is situated in the pit of the great, all enclosing globe, encircled by a great number of spheres that from high to low become ever more narrow and horror inspiring. The distance between the sphere of the Father and the earth, or rather mankind, is enormous and almost unbridgeable. The seven planetary spheres together form a 'face of wickedness'[84] that the saved soul will have to pass. The nether, inferior world is effectively sealed off from the upper spiritual world by the Ogdoad, the seven planetary sphere plus Leviathan. It is to be expected that, if any, only highly privileged persons will be able to escape from this existence.

b. Gnosis and dualism in the Ophian system

Having arrived at this point, let us see how Gnostic and dualistic this system is. The highest god, the Father, remains at an immense distance from the nether world which he did not create. He does not show himself interested in this world. The sphere of Leviathan is the frontier between the higher and lower worlds; the difference between both worlds is dualistic because they are very strictly kept apart and also because the lower world is decidedly inferior. There is only one thing the true soul can do : escape and leave it all behind.

One of the most characteristic Gnostic elements is also there, the ascent of the soul. It is by no means given to everybody to return to the celestial realm. Only once is the word 'gnoosis' mentioned, in a passage where Celsus, obviously quoting the Ophians, says that Jaldabaoth really deserves being cursed since he himself cursed the serpent that taught the first human beings the knowledge (gnoosis) of good and evil. It is for this reason that they call themselves 'Ophians' = snake-people [85]. It is implied but not stated in as many words that this knowledge has a redeeming power. What, however, is conspicuoulsy failing is the figure of the Redeemer.

Gnostic systems are never radically dualistic in this sense that they would acknowledge two absolutely contrasted and differing worlds with not the slightest link between them. More than once I have argued that this brand of dualism is extremely rare. In respect of the Gnosis, radical dualism is utterly impossible since the souls of the elect must be able to depart from this world and attain the upper one. The question now is how this safe passage can be effected. In reviewing what Celsus-Origen have to tell us we must constantly keep in mind what Foerster wrote : "The language of these formulae is consciously kept enigmatic, although the riddle is soluble to the initiates" [86].

c. Salvation

There is talk of a 'seal' that in all probability is the symbol of life; it is not specified in what this seal consists. Somebody who is, as we may assume, an initiate and is, therefore, called 'father', imprints this seal on a novice who thereby becomes initiated in his turn and is now called 'young' and 'son'. "I am", he says, "anointed with the white unguent of the tree of life" [87]. It is clear that this 'young son' now forms part of the narrow circle of the elect and will be saved.

Although there is no specific condemnation of the body, at death it must be left behind; its place is the Tartarus. Only the soul, the pneuma, may go upwards. No longer encumbered by the body, the soul immediately attains the sphere of Behemoth which is equivalent to the atmosphere of the earth. Then the soul begins its journey through the planetary spheres and along their archons; for every archon it possesses a formula serving as a watchword that enables it to pass unscathed. For instance, this is what has to be said to Astaphaios (Venus) : "Astaphaios, ruler of the third door, overseer of the first source of water, see me as an initiate who has been cleansed by the spirit of the maiden. Let me pass since you are the essence of the world. Grace be with me; yes, Father, be it with me". To Horaios (the moon) it says : "Horaios, you who fearlessly overcame the barrier of fire, and obtained authority over the first gate, let me pass, since you see that the symbol of your power is made weak by the mark of the tree of life, taken (away) similarly by the image of the Innocent. Grace be with me; yes, father, be it with me" [88]. And so on.

With Leviathan safely behind it, the soul reaches the sphere of the Zodiac, attains the circle of Love, enters the pure, spiritual realm of the Father and the Son, and becomes part of the eternal Light. With this its salvation is completed.

19. Gnostic antinomianism : those of Cain

a. Antinomianism

The Cainite sect is a fine example of Gnostic antinomianism; it is, as Bareille has it, 'a clearly antinomian heresy' [89]. 'Antinomianism' is a term borrowed from the juridical sphere; it there denotes a law that is worded so as to make it impossible for both parties to appeal to it. In a wider context it then came to mean contradictions between laws ('nomoi') of all kinds. Kant was the first to use it in a non-juridical sense, namely for contradictions occurring in metaphysics [90]. Antinomies in his philosophy are presented as pairs of theses and antitheses. However, without the existence of the term itself, philosophical antinomies were already known to Zeno, Plato, and Aristotle.

But the philosophical postulating of antinomies is something quite different from a general tendency to turn against the law, not so much against the laws of the state but rather against authoritative biblical, ethical, and religious propositions. As far as I can see, antinomianism of this kind did not occur in classical and Hellenistic times, with one notable exception. It is told of the philosopher Diogenes (404-323 B.C.) that "it was his habit to do everything in public, the works of Demeter and Aphrodite alike" [91]. Since it is added that he behaved indecently in public, what can this mean other than that he urinated, defecated, masturbated, and perhaps even copulated in public, that is on the agora of Athens? If this is correct, than Diogenes is the father of antinomianism.

It was only in the period around the birth of Christ that antinomianism became a phenomenon of some importance. I feel this had something to do with the general negative and dualistic character of the times. Paul, for instance, had to reprehend people who, from his opposition to Mosaic Law, drew the conclusion that one should "do evil that good may come from it, as some libellously report me as saying" [92]. "Do not turn your freedom into licence for your lower nature" [93] - texts proving that there were people, even among Christians, who believed that 'anything goes'.

It was, however, only with some Gnostic sects that antinomianism became part and parcel of an ideology. We have already met an instance of this in the Sethian glorification of the Sodomites. This must be seen as a world-historical moment since antinomianism had come to stay and would play a significant role in many later movements. Antinomianism is overtly dualistic since it squarely opposes itself to orthodox doctrine and established law and custom; in general, it is violently opposed to Judaism and Christianity and attempts to turn essential biblical tenets into their reverse.

A little gem of antinomianism is this. Tertullian, around 200, mentions a woman, perhaps called Quintilla, belonging to the Cainite sect but very probably considering herself a Christian, who taught peculiar things about baptism [94]. Tertullian would not have fulminated so fiercely against her and her adherents if they had not been Christians; he censured this woman for arrogating to her self the right to teach in church [95]. She and others agreeing with her taught that baptism was not necessary at all. Abraham found grace in the eyes of the Lord not because he was baptized (for he wasn't) but because of his faith [96]. It was added that Jesus himself never baptized [97]; baptism was thought to be an institution of John the Baptist [98]. These anti-baptists denied that even the apostles were baptized [99]. Furthermore, it was incredulously asked how an immersion into simple water could make one pure for eternal life [100]. If one now knows that, according to Roman-Catholic doctrine, baptism is 'the first and most necessary sacrament', it will be evident that Quintilla was busy turning orthodox doctrine upside down.

One more remark should be made here, for it is in line with our main argument. I suspect that the real reason for the antinomian rejection of baptism was that it was thought that a material element that was not always capable of cleansing someone completely - Tertullian himself admitted that some catechumens emerged from the baptismal font no cleaner than they went into it [101] - that such an element was able to purify a person from his spiritual guilt. This is a dualistic element for, as was common in Gnostic circles, it denied the analogy between the natural and supernatural worlds.

b. The Cainite doctrine

Cainites apparently were popular with the early Fathers of the Church who cited the Cainites, although differently spelled, in some ten of their treatises, in most cases only shortly. In the Cainite system Sophia, Wisdom, is the highest and strongest godhead. But there is also a lower and weaker power. This second god the Cainites call 'hystera', the maternal womb; it is the creator of heaven and earth, that is of the lower, perceptible world [102]. From the very first there is dualism. Eve did not have her sons from Adam but Cain she had from Sophia and Abel from the Demiurge [103]. For this reason, says Pseudotertullian, "they glorify as if conceived by some potent power which operated in him (Cain)" [104]. Consequently they call themselves Cainites.

Cain did not slay Abel out of jealousy because his brother was the more pious one of the two, but he comitted his deed in order to prove that the principle he came from was the superior one [105]. Others of the same race were Cham, the Sodomites, Korah, Datan, Abiram, and Esau [106]; all these people are in bad repute in the Old Testament - Cham as the son who derided his father Noach [107], the Sodomites as homosexuals and rapers [108], Korah as a rebel against Moses, Datan and Abiram as usurpers of the priesthood [109], and Esau (with his supposed progeny Edom) as the eternal deviant [110].

According to Pseudotertullian, Cainites, in contrast to orthodox Christians, had also a high opinion of Judas, "saying that he is admirable and great because of the benefits which he is claimed to have brought to the human race ... For Judas, they say, observing that he (Christ) wanted to subvert the truth, betrayed him that the truth might not be overthrown". Cainites were not of one accord about the significance of Christ, since in another version of the doctrine he is the Redeemer. When the powers of this world tried to prevent him from suffering and thus achieving salvation for mankind, Judas intervened by betraying him "so that the work of salvation might not be delayed" [111]. Judas, as the bearer of the really effective knowledge is, therefore, the true successor of Cain, the Son of Wisdom [112].

There were several books of Cainite wisdom in existence, for instance, 'The Ascent of Paul' and 'The Gospel of Judas' [113].

20. Gnostic antinomianism : those of Nicolas

a. Nicolas and Nicolaites

Yet another vivid example of antinomianism is the doctrine of the Nicolaites. Irenaeus reports that they had as their teacher a certain Nicolas, "one of the seven who had been the first to be ordained deacons by the apostles themselves in Jerusalem" [114]. The Acts of the Apostles indeed mention among those seven 'Nicolas of Antioch, a former convert to Judaism' [115]. It seems, therefore, that Nicolas first was a pagan, then became a Jewish proselyte and later a Christian, to end as a Gnostic prophet; in respect of religion he had a chequered career which lets transpire some of the spiritual confusion of the times. If this is correct, we may assume that Nicolas 'flourished' around 50 A.D.

Nicolaites are twice mentioned by name in the Revelation of John. The Christians of Ephesus are praised because they "hate the practices of the Nicolaites" [116] but those of Pergamum are censored because they tolerate in their midst "some who hold the doctrine of the Nicolaites" [117]. This means that, towards the end of the first century A.D., they had a foothold in the Greek cities in the west of Asia Minor. But already Tertullian, writing ca. 200, speaks of them as a thing of the past [118]. Obviously this sect was not longlived.

b. The bad reputation of the Nicolaites

The author of the Book of Revelation accuses the Nicolaites of fornication and of eating food sacrificed to idols. Probably they are to be equated with other deviants of the Pergamum Church, people who "hold to the teaching of Balaam who taught Balak to put temptation in the way of the Israelites" [119]. Clement of Alexandria quotes people who say that they follow Nicolas by contending that one should yield to the impulses of the flesh; one could triumph over the passions by indulging in them, just as others, among them a certain Aristippus of Cyrene, are said to have taught. But this Father of the Church excuses Nicolas of this charge by stating that, on the contrary, this noble man had made clear that one should withstand the sexual urge [120].

Somewhat further on Clement explains how Nicolas' bad reputation came about. He had a very beautiful wife of whom he was very jealous. When the apostles reproached him for this, he, to prove that he was not jealous at all, put her in the middle of the congregation and declared that whoever wanted might marry her. But this, writes Clement, did not mean at all that Nicolas invited the congregation to fornication! He always remained entirely faithful to his wife; his daughter died as a virgin, and his son remained single [121]. Theodoretus adds that Nicolas' gesture of publicly renouncing his wife was misunderstood by people who thought that he had advocated common possession of women [122]. But others, like Saint Jerome, were equally convinced that all that was shameful and reprehensible in the Nicolaite sect came from Nicolas himself [123].

Whether or not the deacon Nicolas was innocent of what was imputed to him, and whether or not he was the founder of the sect that bears his name, the fact is that the Nicolaites had a reputation for licentiousness, for instance, of practising communal possession of women [124]. Even Clement reproaches them for their profligacy [125]. "They say it is of no importance to commit adultery" [126]. Irenaeus has this to say about their allegedly depraved way of life, stating that he had read this in their own books that were in his possession. Nobody, according to Nicolaite doctrine, can be saved who does not fulfil the works of the womb (with which no doubt sexual acts are indicated - F.). In every sinful and shameful act an angel urges them to commit impurity; they invoke him saying : "O you angel, I do your work'. This, they sustain, is the perfect knowledge : to err without fear in such acts that should not even be mentioned [127]. So much for their antinomian way of life.

c. Nicolaite doctrine

Filastrius reports that, although Nicolas first was a companion of the apostles and of his co-deacon Stephen, the first martyr, he later fell into error and fallacies. He then professed the same things as the Gnostics [128]. There are two worlds, one good, one bad. This is the most fundamental tenet of metaphysical dualism. Both worlds have their own supreme rulers. There is, writes Irenaeus, one (inferior) god who created this world, the Demiurge, that is, and another, superior god who became the father of Christ. This Christ, who is impassible himself, descended onto Jesus (who is a son of the Demiurge); later, after the passion and death (of Jesus, not of Christ), he (Christ) returned to the pleroma, the upper and perfect spiritual world where he came from. The lower, physical, material world finds itself at an immense distance from the invisible and ineffable beings of the pleroma; the cosmos, our world, does not belong to the pleroma, the All, the Fulness [129]. All this, it goes without saying, is the sheerest dualism.

In the lower world there were in the beginning only Darkness and depth ('bythos') and water; the Spirit divided these elements from each other, and land and water were separated. But then Darkness threw itself on the Spirit. It seems that this obscure text must be understood in this way that Darkness overpowered and raped the Spirit. The result was the 'mêtra', the womb, or 'hystera' which brought forth four aeons [130]. And "thus came about the right and the left, light and darkness". What this passage wants to make clear is, I guess, why, in spite of all, there is light in the world of the Demiurge.

One of the aeons, says Epiphanius, was particularly disgraceful, for he slept with the Womb. From their copulation the gods, the angels, mankind, and seven demoniac spirits, but also the (Jewish) prophets originated [131]. The Nicolaite idea of mankind is wholly pessimistic; it belongs to the nether world and enjoys the company of demons. This whole ideology is fiercely anti-Bible.

21. The Peratae, the 'crossers'

a. About the sect itself and its name

With the Peratae [132] we are returning not only to the serpent but also to the three-rooted initial stage of the universe. Our one and only source for this Gnostic sect is Hippolytus. As its founders he mentions a certain Euphrates and Celbes from Karystos [133]; probably a Greek city at the southern tip of Euboea is meant [134]. If this is correct, it is the first time that we enounter a Greek from the metropolis in a Gnostic text.

It is impossible to say where the Peratic sect was at home. Many of the names they used in their astrological mythology have a Greek ring or are decidedly Greek, like 'Achilles'. But Hippolytus suggests that their astronomical system itself is Babylonian [135]. Furthermore, there are references to Egypt, while the Bible too was used by them, in particular the Pentateuch. No wonder then that Hippolytus calls Peratic lore 'many-splendoured'; he suggests that 'the astrological sect' (of which nothing further is known) was its forerunner [136]. It remains unclear whether this was an important sect; if one reads what Hippolytus has to say of it, one would not think so : "(This sect's) slanders against Christ have remained hidden for many years; it is now resolved to publish their secret mysteries" [137].

The name of the Peratic sect can point to an Hellenic background, since 'peraoo' is a Greek verb signifying 'to cross over' ('peras' = frontier). They call themselves 'crossers' for the following reason. Nothing, they hold, which belongs to this world (which is one of becoming, not of being) "can escape the destiny laid down for things that come into being ... Whatever comes into being is also completely destroyed" [138]. But the initiate is fully knowledgeable about 'the routes by which man has entered this world', which implies that he also knows the routes by which to escape from it. The Perates "are the only ones who can pass through and cross over (perasai) destruction" [139]. This is a familiar picture by now : mankind doomed to destruction from which only an élite possessing the redeeming knowledge will escape.

A comparison is made with the exodus of the Israelites from Egypt and their dry crossing of the Red Sea. "Departing from Egypt means departing from the body, for they consider the body a miniature-Egypt" (which, of course, is entirely negatively meant). The crossing of the Red Sea is seen as the prototype of the crossing of 'the water of destruction', that is, of being saved. The Egyptians, on the contrary, were drowned because they were ignorant. "All the ignorants are Egyptians." Here we see two of the most prominent dualistic distinctions made by the Gnostics : that of body and soul (the body is 'Egypt' and has to be abandoned), and that of the knowing and the ignorant (who will not escape destruction). Arriving in the desert, just like the Israelites after having made good their escape from Egypt, means having escaped from the process of becoming, that is having become a people of a different order [140].

b. The three-rooted universe

With this we are already at the end, at the redemptive stage. Let us return to the beginning. Initially the Peratic universe is 'one, having three parts' [141]. Hippolytus' next communication is not really clarifying. He speaks of a single principle which can be divided into an infinite number of divisions, 'like a great source' [142]. We may assume, with Hans Jonas, that in reality the fundament of the all is meant from which the threefold division sprang [143]. If this is correct, then the Peratic system is originally monistic.

The first, and most important, element of the trias is the 'perfect goodness' which is paternal, the Father, the supreme god [144]. He is unoriginate. The second element is self-originate and also good, being 'like an infinite number of powers'. The third divine element is the 'particular' ('idikon'); it has an origin [145]. This suggests a 'genetic sequence' [146]. We can understand this passage best when we think of the

Platonic theory of forms which this system resembles : the Good is the Idea of all Ideas, then come the Ideas themselves, and finally the concrete things that correspond to the Ideas or Forms.

Plato, however, did not personify the Good into a Father. Anyhow, the unoriginate and self-originate worlds are the superior ones; the 'particular' world, the material, perceptible world, by contrast, must be seen as inferior (although this is not said in as many words) but it contains 'the seeds of every kind of power', signifying that higher elements are present and active here below too [147].

Further on in his disquisition Hippolytus recapitulates what he had said before on the three-rooted system in other terms. "The universe is Father, Son, and matter'; each of these three has innumerable powers in itself" [148]. The three roots, or main principles, are portrayed here as autonomous, separate from each other, and rich in possibilities. "Midway between matter and the Father sits his Son, the Word (Logos), the Serpent, who is always moving towards the immovable Father and towards the movable matter" [149].

c. The shaping of matter

The mediation by the Son between the Father and matter is presented in the simile of the snake that slides to and fro and turns up where one least expects it. This makes admirably clear why a mediator is needed : the Father and matter are so utterly different that in itself there is no contact whatsoever possible between them. This also shows that Gnostic dualists saddled themselves with a problem by opposing the higher and lower powers so radically; an intermediate power was postulated in order to explain how something could happen in or to matter.

What happened to matter is this. The Son "turns toward the Father and receives the powers in his person, and when he has received the powers, he turns himself towards matter, and the matter which is without quality or configuration is imprinted with the forms (or ideas) from the Son, which the Son printed off from the Father ... The Son by his own power transfers the characters of the Father to matter" [150].

d. The Fall

Hippolytus has clearly stated that all three parts of the trias were divine : 'three gods, three words, three minds, three men' [151], which would imply that the lower, particular world too is divine. But in all probability something has gone wrong. Hippolytus vaguely speaks of "the defection of good powers to the bad and of alliances of the good and the bad" [152]; this suggests something of a Fall. Our world obviously is not so good and divine as it first seemed; there are bad powers in it against which the good powers descending into it can hardly hold their own.

One of the Peratic books, writes Hippolytus, speaks of 'the power that comes from chaos'. This is 'the power of the absymal darkness' that gives the world its first shape, 'consolidating what is unstable'. "Its name was the Thalassa (the Sea). To this power ignorance gave the name of Kronos (= Time)" [153]. This Kronos "cannot be escaped by anything belonging to the world of becoming." For he "presides over the whole process of becoming, so as to make it subject to destruction; and there is no coming-into-being without the interference of Kronos" [154]. The nether world is the realm of changeability and transitoriness, clearly marked off from the higher world.

It is difficult to find out who or what is responsible for what went wrong with the world. In any case something went wrong between the original Peratic documents (which have all got lost) and Hippolytus. This ancient scholar called the wisdom of the Peratae "exceedingly subtle ... which it is difficult to describe in full, so twisted is it through its evident dependence on astrology" [155]. So much is certain that the Fall must not be attributed to man; it is not human but cosmic or metaphysical. Perhaps it was Kronos' fault. Elsewhere, however, it is stated that "the gods of destruction are the stars which bring upon those who come into being the necessity which belongs to changeable generation" [156].

Then again we read in another passage of a Demiurge, "the ruler ('archoon') and artificer ('Dēmiourgos') of matter, who taking up the characters distributed by the Son has reproduced them in his world, who (the Demiurge) is a murderer from the beginning [157]; for his work makes for corruption and death" [158]. It seems that the Demiurge has nothing original to contribute; he can only mangle the forms brought down from above by the Son-Serpent, but this he does effectively.

All in all, we are presented with a perfect Gnostic cosmological picture : initially from high to low all was for the best, but something went wrong; somebody spoiled the noble intentions of those on high.

e. Anthropology

Man is a microcosmos in the macrocosmos (a favourite Hellenic notion). The Peratae compare "the brain itself to the Father, because of its immobility, and the cerebellum with the Son, since it moves and has a serpentine shape". The cerebellum draws the spiritual and life-giving substance from the brain and transmits it through the pineal gland down the marrow of the backbone to the body [159]. This picture looks innocent enough but betrays dualism since it suggests a fundamental difference between the brain and the rest of the body.

f. The Saviour

As is common in Gnostic systems, there is a Saviour, but it is somewhat hard to determine exactly who he is, and still more how he saves. Much is made of the Serpent. Moses showed the children of Israel "the true perfect serpent ... There is no one who can save and deliver those who depart from Egypt, that is, from the body and this world, except only the perfect serpent who is filled with (all) fulness. The man who sets his hope on him ... will not be destroyed by the serpent in the desert, that is, by the gods of generation" [160].

Somewhat unexpectedly it is added that "the universal serpent is the wise word of Eve" [161]. It is also "he who appeared in the last days in a human form". The identification Son-Serpent-Christ is made by quoting Jo. 3:14 : "And as Moses lifted up the serpent in the desert, even so must the Son of Man be lifted up". "He is the great beginning of whom Scripture tells" [162].

The mission of Christ is spelled out as follows. He "came down from on high, from the unoriginate being ... (as) a three-natured man ... having three bodies and three powers, possessing in himself the complexities and powers proceeding from the three parts of the world ...; in him is all the godhead of the trias" [163]. "No one can be saved without the Son, or ascend (without him) who is the Serpent" [164]. But, as goes without saying, only the elect will be redeemed. "He brings up from this world those who are awakened and have become characters of the Father, bringing them across to that world from this as real beings out of unreality ... By the Serpent there is drawn back again from the world the fully formed perfect race (= the Perates)" [165]. The dualistic distinction of the higher and lower worlds is rendered here in terms of real and unreal. It is not explained how the Peratae become 'perfect, fully formed, and awakened', but we may safely assume that is through Knowledge, although the term 'gnoosis' is used nowhere.

g. The rejection of the doomed

It is wholly in keeping with Gnostic ideology that in Peratic doctrine the majority of mankind is left behind. "The things that conspired against what was brought down from on high are abandoned, punished, and rejected." It is admitted that Jesus said that he did not come into the world to destroy it, but that the world through him might be saved [166]. But what he really meant was that the two superior parts of the universe would become entirely free from corruption. The third part, however, the 'particular' one, our world, that is, is doomed to perdition [167]. Hippolytus' relation shows to perfection that what begins as monistic may end as dualistic.

22. Justin's Baruch-book

a. The author and his book

Another three-rooted system is presented in the book 'Baruch' by a Gnostic called Justin. This author should not be confused with Saint Justin the Martyr, a Christian philosopher who was executed in Rome in 165. Of the Justin who concerns us here we know hardly anything at all; perhaps he was an Egyptian who probably lived in the second century A.D. By rendering the contents of the Baruch-book I am trespassing in an unforgivable way, because it contains hermetically sealed doctrine. Justin made his followers swear to keep his mysteries secret [168]. We are following here the bad example of Hippolytus who, once again, is our only source. It cannot be a matter of doubt that this Father of the Church knew the original text (this text has disappeared in its entirety); he is evidently often quoting verbally.

b. The three powers

"There were three unbegotten powers of the All, two male, one female." The first power is male and is called 'the Good'; he knew all things in advance. The second power is male too, being 'the father of all things created'; he possesses no foreknowledge. The third power is female and a curious mythological figure since she is "down to the groin a young woman but a serpent below"; she too is "without foreknowledge, irascible, of double mind and double body" [169]. The snake is the symbol of agile mobility capable of mediating between higher and lower. The name of this snake-girl is 'Edem' and also 'Israel' [170]. 'Edem' must very probably be read as 'Eden' and be thought of as 'the earth' [171]. "These ... are the powers, roots, and springs of all things, from which the things that are come into being; and there was nothing else" [172].

c. The angels

The Father, who is also called 'Elohim' (one of the names of the Jewish God), became desirous of Eden, the serpent-girl, when he saw her. "Eden was no less desirous for Elohim, and the desire brought them together in heart-felt love" [173]. Once again we find the Gnostic predilection for sexual imagery. Theirs is a fateful union, because, as Haenchen writes, not only all evil results from it but the world as such too [174]. We should not conceive of Eden as the material principle, although she represents the earth, but rather as 'psuchê', whereas Elohim is 'pneuma'. Justin says precisely this, adding that pneuma and psyche are irreconcilable oppositions [175]. How could the Father be so imprudent? Because, as we saw, he is 'without foreknowledge', just as the girl. They have no idea what they are doing. I suppose this is the fundamental explanation why mankind is ignorant.

The girl Eden then bore twenty-four angels, twelve male and twelve female. Only the names of five 'paternal' angels have been preserved; some of these are biblical, Michael and Gabriel, and then 'Baruch' who is equated with the tree of life in Genesis [176]. The names of the twelve 'maternal' angels are all preserved; they have a nefarious ring, Babel, Bel, Naas, and others. 'Naas' (= Nachas, Hebrew for 'snake') stands for the tree of the knowledge of good and evil. We are plunging right into Gnostic mysteriosophy here, for this, says Hippolytus, is Justin's interpretation of Moses' words : "Moses spoke to them in veiled language, because not all can comprehend the truth" [177]. "The company of all the angels together is the Paradise" [178], that is, the origin of mankind is to be found in them.

Half of the angels have a positive nature, and the other half a negative one. This means that the future of mankind does not augur well. It should also be remarked that the negative angelic half is female; the female root Eden-Israel has a choleric character. "Of these twenty-four angels the paternal assist the Father in everything according to his will, and the maternal their mother Eden" [179]. It is evident that the cosmos will have a dual character. Dualistic too? Not initially!

d. The creation of Adam and Eve

In Paradise Father Elohim and Eden-Israel still live in 'mutual good pleasure'. Elohim's angels (not Elohim himself, and still less the primal root, 'the Good', which has receded into eternal silence) created Adam; they made him out of the upper part of the body of Eden, that is out of 'the human civilized parts of the earth' (let us not forget that Eden symbolizes the earth). From her lower (snake-like) parts the animals are made. Still acting in unison with her, Elohim planted in Adam the 'pneuma', or spirit, and Eden the 'psuchê', or soul. "And he becomes, as it were, a seal and love-token and eternal symbol of the marriage of Elohim and Eden." Eve was created in the same way [180]. But they did not live happily ever after!

e. Elohim deserts Eden

After the creation of the first human pair Elohim returned to heaven wishing to survey from there what he had performed. Perhaps something might be lacking. But then he made an unexpected discovery. At the limit of heaven he "beheld a light better than the one he had created"; he now wanted to enter the highest heaven (where this light shone). Having acknowledged that the Good was better and higher than he himself (for the Good was this light), he was allowed to go in and even sit at the right hand of the Good. His angels he must leave behind, since they have to manage the world. He is now out of the reach of evil, and the Good orders him to leave the creation to Eden [181]. This is the breach, the final and dualistic divorce of Elohim and Eden, for "Elohim, held fast by the Good, came down no more to Eden" [182].

f. Eden's revenge

For a time Eden hoped that Elohim would come back to her, but in vain. Then, deserted for good as she is, she "commands Babel (who is Aphrodite) to effect adulteries and divorces among men, in order that, just as she herself had been separated from Elohim, so also the spirit of Elohim might be pained and tormented by such separations and suffer the same as the abandoned Eden. And Eden gives great power to her third angel Naas, that through him the spirit of Elohim might be punished"[183]. "A stream of wickedness ... travels for ever unceasingly around the world, according to the will of Eden"[184].

Once again it is shown that the Fall, the introduction of evil into the world, is not the fault of mankind but is effectuated by some non-human power. The 'spirit of Elohim', that obviously is still present in men, must be understood as being identical with the 'spark of light' of other Gnostic texts. But Eden's revenge rests on a misunderstanding. For, says Elohim, "if she had known that I am with the Good, she would not have punished the spirit in men because of the paternal departure from thence"[185]. What is meant is that Eden's vengeful action is aimless, since Elohim no longer dwells on earth. Anyhow, so much is evident that mankind is not better off for being solely in maternal care now!

g. Baruch the Redeemer

Father Elohim, seeing what was happening, sent down his third angel, Baruch, "to the assistance of the spirit which is in all men". He took his stand in the middle of Paradise, enjoining upon men to eat freely from every tree in it, with the exception of the tree of knowledge of good and evil [186]. It will be remarked that, in contrast to the Genesis story, the tree of life obviously is included in the general permission.

Once again, things went wrong. Naas, the personification of the tree of knowledge, as the reader will remember, committed adultery with Eve, and after that used Adam 'as a boy' : here is yet another Gnostic who cannot do without explanations of a sexual kind. "From that time both good and evil held sway over men, springing from one origin, that of the Father." He should not have gone and left a moral vacuum behind him! "By departing from Eden he made a beginning of evils for the spirit of the Father that is in men." However, there is hope, as always in Gnostic systems : "By ascending to the Good the Father showed a way for those who are willing to ascend" [187]. The usual dichotomy in mankind is appearing here : it is suggested that not everybody is 'willing to ascend'. The first mission of Baruch has been effectively frustrated by Naas.

Later Baruch was sent to Moses; "through him he spoke to the children of Israel, that they might turn to the Good". But for the second time, Naas, the embodiment of evil, slyly intervened by inserting his own words into the message of Moses [188]. This too is a favourite Gnostic theme : that the original biblical message is salutary enough, but that is has become obscured and adulterated by later accretions of a demoniacal character. The result is that "the soul (psuchê) is ranged against the spirit (pneuma), and the spirit against the soul, for the soul is Eden and the spirit Elohim, both being in all mankind, male and female alike" [189]. Man is shown as dualistically torn apart by the warring factions of higher and lower, good and evil, spiritual and material. The implication is that the existence of the sexes is something of a lower order.

A third attempt is made. Baruch is sent to the prophets that "through the prophets the spirit which dwells in men might hear and flee from Eden and the evil creation, as the Father Elohim fled" [190]. For the first time it is unambiguously stated that the world is objectionable. The beginning of the road to salvation is to flee the world. But for the third time in succession Naas succeeds in spoiling the good intentions of Elohim. He "seduced the prophets through the soul which dwells in man along with the spirit of the Father, that they were all led astray and did not follow the words of Baruch which Elohim commanded" [191]. That the biblical prophets are rather ignorant or even misleading is yet another well-known Gnostic theme and stock-in-trade of their anti-biblical polemizing. Furthermore, it could not be more clearly stated that man is a dualistic being with a double origin, one part going back on Elohim and another on Eden.

A fourth attempt. The Gnostic were not particular in the choice of their mythological themes. It must, therefore, not astonish us that the man who now appears on the scene is a pagan, nobody less than Hercules [192], "that he might he prevail against the twelve angels of Eden, and liberate the Father from the twelve wicked angels of the creation". His works are equated with the famous twelve Herculean labours [193]. However, when he was near succeeding, he was seduced by Omphale [194] who is the same as Babel or Aphrodite, and stripped of his power. Babel-Aphrodite "put upon him her own garment, that is, the power of Eden, the power below" [195]. Thus Hercules' labours were of no avail. The implication is that sexual love incapacitates for achievements of a higher order.

The fifth and final attempt! "In the days of Herod the king, Baruch was sent, dispatched again by Elohim, and coming to Nazareth he found Jesus, the son of Joseph and Mary, tending sheep, a boy of twelve years old," explained to him why and how all previous attempts had misfired, and ordered him to "proclaim to men the things concerning the Father and the Good, and go up to the Good, and sit there with Elohim, the father of us all." Jesus obeyed and he preached. Naas, trying to seduce him too, did not succeed this time. Furious about this, he caused Jesus to be crucified. But Jesus finally foiled him. Leaving his body behind on the cross, he abandoned his psuchê, yielded his pneuma into the hands of the Father, and thus joined the Good [196].

h. The secret mysteries

Those who had become acquainted with these mysteries had to swear an oath that they would keep them secret. As all other Gnostics, these too separated themselves from the rest of mankind, the uninitiated. Their oath ran as follows : "I swear by him who is above all things, to preserve those mysteries and to declare them to no one, neither to turn back from the Good to the creation". Whoever had sworn this oath had become a redeemed, an exempted person : he goes 'into the Good' [197].

23. The Severians

Very little is known of the sect of the Severians, and nothing at all of its supposed founder, a certain Severus. Severians postulated a good God in the highest heaven; he is ineffable. There is also a lower divinity, presiding over the powers; his name is partly (says Epiphanius) Jaldabaoth, partly Sabaoth. It is not explained whether this means that this godhead is dual or androgynous. Anyhow, his, or their, son is the devil. This devil is expelled from heaven by the celestial power (the good God must be meant) and falls on the earth. There he assumes the shape of a serpent and, stimulated by desire, has intercourse with Earth as with a woman. From his seed the wine sprang forth.

The idea behind this communication is that a vine resembles a snake; it coils itself around the stick just as a serpent does. The text expatiates somewhat more on this similarity and concludes that wine confuses the spirit, makes passionate and garrulous, and allures people into amorous adventures. For this reason, the sect abstained from wine. Sexuality is obviously seen in an unfavourable light too. Must I add that dualism is rampant in this doctrine [198]?

Eusebius adds that the Severians accept the Law (the Pentateuch), the Prophets, and the Gospels; they expound, he says, Scripture in their own sense. They reject, however, the Acts of the Apostles (this means they did not associate with the young Church - F.) and the Letters of Paul whom they cover with maledictions [199]. Epiphanius writes that the Severians "make use of some apocrypha but also in part of the publicly read books (the canonical Bible books are meant - F.), hunting out only those things which, distorting them to their own taste, they handle in a completely different manner" [200].

Their rejection of women and sexuality could not be more radical. "They say that woman also is a work of Satan ... Hence those who consorts in marriage, they say, fulfil the work of Satan. Even in regard to men, half is of God and half of the Devil. From the navel upwards ... he is the creation of the power of God; from the navel down he is the creature of the evil power. hence ... everything relating to pleasure and passion and desire originates from the navel and below" [201]. If this is not dualism, I don't know what it is.

NOTES TO CHAPTER V

1. Scott s.v. 'Ophitism'. Enc.Rel.Eth. 9, 499/500.
2. See Lurker s.v. 'Snakes', Enc.Rel.13, 370/374.
3. Hönig, Ophiten 3.
4. Hipp., Ref. 5.6.3.
5. Num.21.6-8.
6. Epiph., Panarion 37.5.5-7; Pseudotert., Adv.omn.haer. 2.1. Filastrius, Div. haer. liber 1.1, says that they venerated the serpent because it brought us (mankind) the beginning of the knowledge of good and evil. Zacharias, Sat. cult 36 says that the Christian Church attributed the snake "almost exclusively to Satan. The Ophitic serpent-image and its cult is a complete antithesis and counterbalance to the ecclesiastical Imago Christi and the liturgy belonging to it. The Ophite communion is thus a forerunner of the true cult of Satan."
7. Hipp., Ref. 5.2. and 5.6.4.
8. In Ref. 8.20.3 Hipp, refers to the Ophites as a sect obviously different from the Naassenes, 'not worth to be refuted'. But we may safely assume that Ophites and Naassenes are identical, the more so because because ophis and nahas both signify 'snake, Hönig, Ophiten 29.
9. The ancient sources are : Ir., Adv.haer. 1.30.1-15 (he takes Sethians and Ophites together); Hipp., Ref. 5.6. 3 sqq.; Epiphanius, Panarion 37; Theodoretus, Haer.fab.comp. 1.14 (306-309) (taking Ophites, Ophians, and Sethians together); Pseudotert., Adv.omn. haer. 2.1-4; Origenes, Contra Cels. 6.24-38, who calls the Ophians 'a very insignificant sect' and states that his opponent Celsus misunderstood their doctrine.
10. Hönig, Ophiten 29, thinks that Ir. worked backwards in time so that his last section on the Gnostics, his description of the Ophitic system, Adv.haer. 1.30.1-15, refers to the earliest known form of the Gnosis. Actually, Ir. ends not with the Ophites but with the Cainites, but they are probably a variant of the Ophitic system.
11. Ir., Adv.haer. 1.30.1; Theodor., Haer.fab.comp. 1.14.10.
12. Ir., Adv.haer. 1.30.1; Theodor., Haer.fab.comp. 1.14.10.
13. Foerster/Wilson, Gnosis 84.

14.	Although 'pneuma', spirit, is neuter in Greek, it is feminine in Hebrew; the 'hovering' of the Spirit clearly refers to Gen. 1:2.
15.	Ir., Adv.haer. 1.30.1; Theodor., Haer.fab.Comp. 1.14.11.
16.	See Hönig, Ophites 33/34; this scholar cites a Midrash text in which the 'Spirit hovering over the waters' is equated with the coming Messiah.
17.	Ir., Adv.haer. 1.30.2; Theodor., Haer.fab.comp. 1.14.11.
18.	Ir., Adv.haer. 1.30.2; Theodor., Haer.fab.comp. 1.14.11.
19.	Ir., Adv.haer. 1.30.3; Theodor., Haer.fab.comp. 1.14.11-12.
20.	Ir., Adv.haer. 1.30.3; Theodor., Haer.fab.comp. 1.14.12.
21.	Ir., Adv.haer. 1.30.3; Theodor., Haer. fab.comp. 1.14.12.
22.	Itr., Adv.haer. 1.30.3; Theodor., Haer.fab.comp. 1.14.12.
23.	Foerster/Wilson, Gnosis I, 85.
24.	Ir., Adv.haer. 1.30.4.
25.	Ir., Adv.haer. 1.30.4.
26.	Epiph., Panarion 37.3.6.
27.	Ir., Adv.haer. 1.30.4.
28.	Ir., Adv.haer. 1.30.5.
29.	Ir., Adv.haer. 1.30.5.
30.	Epiph., Panarion 37.5.1.
31.	Ir. Adv.haer. 1.30.6.
32.	Epiph., Panarion 37..3.7.
33.	Hönig, Ophiten 39.
34.	Ir., Adv.haer. 1.30.6.
35.	Ir., Adv.haer. 1.30.6.
36.	Ir., Adv.haer. 1.30.7.
37.	Hönig, Ophites 41.
38.	Don't we find an exact parallel of this in Wagner's 'Parsifal', where the wicked Klingsor incites Kundry to seduce Parsifal, but in vain?
39.	In Gen.3:20 it is Adam who gives her this name.
40.	Ir., Adv.haer. 1.30.7. This is the well-known theme of celestial beings copulating with human females, see also Gen.6:1-4, and my commentary in Vol. IV, Ch. II.11b.
41.	Ir., Adv.haer. 1.30.7.
42.	Ir., Adv.haer. 1.30.8.

43. Foerster/Wilson, Gnosis 85.
44. There is a curious illogicality here. Only a few lines higher it is said that Adam, as the first human being, got nous and thought from the First Man and was thus able to forsake his creators. Why then has he to eat from the tree in order to have knowledge and thus recognize the highest Power, Hönig, Ophites 41?
45. Ir., Adv.haer. 1.30.9.
46. Ir., Adv.haer. 1.30.8.
47. Ir., Adv.haer. 1.30.9.
48. Ir., Adv.haer. 1.30.9.
49. Theodor., Haer.fab.comp. 1.14.18.
50. Ir., Adv.haer. 1.30.9.
51. Ir., Adv.haer. 1.30.10.
52. The term 'Jew' came in use only after the division of the original unitary kingdom into Juda and Israel, that is after 900 B.C.; it then denoted a citizen of Juda, a 'Judaeus', or later an inhabitant of the Persian province of Judea.
53. Ir., Adv.haer. 1.30.10-11.
54. Ir., Adv.haer. 1.30.11.
55. Ir., Adv.haer. 1.30.11.
56. Ir., Adv.haer. 1.30.12.
57. Theodor., Haer.fab.comp. 1.14.20.
58. Ir., Adv.haer. 1.30.13.
59. Theodor., Haer.fab.comp. 1.14.19.
60. Ir., Adv.haer. 1.30.13.
61. Ir., Adv.haer. 1.30.14.
62. Foerster/Wilson, Gnosis 86.
63. Ir., Adv.haer. 1.30.14.
64. Foerster/Wilson, Gnosis 87.
65. Foerster/Wilson, Gnosis, too treats Ophites and Ophians in separate sections.
66. It is a riddle to me how Celsus managed to confuse the Ophian doctrine with the Christian creed; they are absolutely dissimilar. Bousset, Hauptprobl. 323, says this : "Es ist nun ausserordentlich bemerkenswert, dass wir bei einer Reihe dieser Sekten noch ganz deutlich konstatieren können, dass hier im Grunde eine Religion vorliegt, die mit der christlichen nichts oder fast gar nichts zu tun hat, oder nur mit einem ganz dünnen Firnis überdeckt ist. So ist bei den Ophiten des Celsus-Origenes kaum eine Spur christ-

lichen Einschlages zu entdecken." Origen himself emphatically protested that contentions, such as brought forward by Celsus, "never were brought forward by Christians", Or., Contra Cels. 6.26. See also his 6.29 where he rejects Celsus' assertion that some specific Ophian doctrines were Christian. He adds that the Ophians admitted no one to their meetings who had not cursed Jesus first, 6.28.

67. Or., Contra Cels. 6.24.
68. Or., Contra Cels. 6.24.
69. Foerster/Wilson, Gnosis 94.
70. Leisegang, Gnosis, opp. p. 32; it is reprinted in Rudolph, Gnosis 76. Another attempt at reconstruction is to be found in Sloterdijk/Macho (Eds.), Weltrev. d. Seele I, 194.
71. Or., Contra Cels. 6.27 and 28.
72. Leisegang, Gnosis 169.
73. Or., Contra Cels. 6.38.
74. See Vol. IV, pp. 99 and 152.
75. Or., Contra Cels. 6.25.
76. Rudolph, Gnosis 77.
77. Or., Contra Cels. 6.30.
78. Or., Contra Cels. 6.30.
79. Or., Contra Cels. 6.31.
80. Or., Contra Cels. 6.27, 28, 29. and 33.
81. Leisegang, Gnosis 173; Bousset, Hauptprobl. 351 : "Jaldabaoth is Saturn".
82. Or., Contra Cels. 6.25.
83. Or., Contra Cels. 6.25.
84. Or., Contra Cels. 6. 31.
85. Or., Contra cels. 6.28.
86. Foerster/Wilson, Gnosis 94.
87. Or., Contra Cels. 6.27.
88. Or., Contra Cels. 6.31.
89. G. Bareille s.v. 'Cainites', Dict.théol.cath. 2, 1307 (Paris, 1923).
90. J. Klein s.v. 'Antinomie', Rel. in Gesch.u.Gegenw. 1, 451/452 (Tübingen, 1957).
91. DL 6.69.
92. Rom. 3:8.

93.	Gal. 5:13.
94.	Tert., De bapt. 1.1.
95.	Tert., De bapt. 1.3 and 17.4.
96.	Tert., De bapt. 13.1.
97.	Tert., De bapt. 11.1.
98.	Tert., De bapt. 10.
99.	Tert., De bapt. 12.
100.	Tert., De bapt. 2.1.
101.	Tert., De bapt. 2.1.
102.	Ir., Adv.haer. 1.31.1; Epiph., Panarion 37.1.4-6.
103.	Epiph., Panarion 37.2.6; Filastrius, Div.haer. 2, he adds that the second god is the devil.
104.	Pseudotert., Adv.omn.haer. 2.
105.	Epiph., Panarion 37.2.7.
106.	Epiph., Panarion 37.1.3 and 37.2.4.
107.	Gen. 9:20-22.
108.	Gen. 19:1-14.
109.	Num. 16:1-30. There was even a Gnostic legend that Datan and Abiram were spirited away by angels to save them from the wrath of Moses, Epiph., Panarion 38.2.4.
110.	See Vol. IV, Ch. II.15g.
111.	Pseudotert., Adv.omn.haer. 2.
112.	Theodor., Haer.fab.comp. 1.15.
113.	Ir., Adv.haer. 1.31.1; Epiph., Panarion 38.2.5. The Cainites cite Paul as a privileged source of wisdom since he said that he ascended into the third heaven and there heard ineffable words, 2Cor.12:4.
114.	Ir., Adv.haer. 1.26.3.
115.	Acts 6:5.
116.	Ap. 2:15.
117.	Ap. 2:15.
118.	Tert., De praescr. 33.
119.	Ap. 2:14. Balak, king of Moab, summoned Balaam, a non-Jewish prophet from Mesopotamia, to curse the Israelites which he refused to do, Num. 22-24. But in Num. 31:16 it is suggested that it was on the advice of Balaam that "the Moabites set about seducing the Israelites into disloyalty to the Lord", viz. by having intercourse with pagans.

120. Clem.Al., Strom. 2.20.117.5-118.5.
121. Clem.Al., Strom. 3.4.25.6-26. Epiph., Panarion 25.1.4-5, says that Nicolas renounced his wife but in spite of his vow returned to her later since he was incapable of resisting his intemperance.
122. Theodor., Haer.fab.comp. 3.1.
123. Hier., Ep. 14.9.
124. Theodor., Haer.fab.comp. 3.1.
125. Clem.Al., Strom. 3.118.3-5.
126. Ir., Adv.haer. 1.26.3.
127. Ir., Adv.haer. 1.31.2.
128. Fil, Haer. 33.
129. Ir., Adv.haer. 3.11.1.
130. Fourteen, says Epiph., Panarion 25.5.2.
131. Epiph., Panarion 25,5; Fil., Haer. 33.
132. Leisegang's disquisition on the Peratae proved very useful, Gnosis 142-151.
133. Hipp., Ref. 5.13.9.
134. There is yet another Karystos, far less well-known, on the Peloponnese, near the sources of the Eurotas.
135. Hipp., Ref. 5.13.12.
136. Hipp., Ref. 5.17.1.
137. Hipp., Ref. 5.12.1.
138. The phrase beginning with 'whatsoever' is a Sibylline oracle, Orac.Sibyll. fr. 3c.
139. Hipp., Ref. 5.16.1.
140. Hipp., Ref. 5.16.4-5.
141. Hipp., Ref. 5.12.1.
142. Hipp., Ref. 5.12.2; the confusing thing is that he says that this principle is part of the treefold division.
143. Jonas, Gnosis u. spätant. geist I, 341.
144. Hipp., Ref. 5.12.2; it is also possible to suppose that the first element is identified with the fundamental principle itself, see Foerster/Wilson, Gnosis 284, note.
145. Hipp., Ref. 5.12.2-3.
146. Jonas, Gnosis u. spätant. Geist I, 341.
147. Hipp., Ref. 5.12.5.
148. Hipp., Ref. 5.17.1.

149. Hipp., Ref. 5.17.2.
150. Hipp., Ref. 5.17.3 and 5.
151. Hipp., Ref. 5.12.3.
152. Hipp. 5.13.12.
153. Hipp., Ref. 5.14.1-2.
154. Hipp., Ref. 5.16.2-3.
155. Hipp., Ref. 5.17.1.
156. Hipp., Ref. 5.16.6.
157. Here Jesus' words in Jo.8:44 are quoted where he speaks not of a Demiurge but of the Satan.
158. Hipp., Ref. 5.17.7.
159. Hipp., Ref. 5.17.11-12.
160. Hipp. Ref. 5.16.7-8.
161. Hipp., Ref. 5.16.8.
162. Hipp., Ref. 5.16.10-12.
163. Hipp., Ref. 5.12.5.
164. Hipp., Ref. 5.17.8.
165. Hipp., Ref. 5.17.8 and 10.
166. Jo.3:17.
167. Hipp., Ref. 5.12.6-7.
168. Hipp., Ref. 5.24.1.
169. Hipp., Ref. 5.26.1. Hipp. refers here to a story told by Herodotus in 4.8.10, but does not say in as many words that Justin himself was making the same reference. It is a story about Heracles who, somewhere in Scythia, lost his horse. Searching for it, he found instead a girl whose upper half was human and whose nether half had the shape of a serpent. She would help him to his horse if Heracles was prepared to have intercourse with her. He consented, she became pregnant and bore three sons. See Jonas, Gnosis u. spätant. Geist I, 336, note 3; Leisegang, Gnosis 156-64; Haenchen, Baruch 301, note 2, believes that Just. borrowed this story from contemporary astronomy and astrology.
170. Hipp., Ref. 5.26.2.
171. Haenchen, Baruch 301. While the Jewish God as the Demiurge is a normal feature in Gnostic systems, Eden is new; she must be a creation of Justin himself, Haenchen, Baruch 325.
172. Hipp., Ref. 5.26.2.
173. Hipp., Ref. 5.26.2.

174. Haenchen, Baruch 301.
175. Hipp. Ref., 5.26.25.
176. In this Gnostic Baruch-book the biblical prophet, an aristocrat from Jerusalem who was the secretary of Jeremiah for twenty years around 600 B.C., is revalued into an angel. The historical Baruch was a witness of the downfall of Jerusalem in 586 B.C. and for this reason seemed exactly the man to preach penitence and consolation to his people. Following Haenchen, Baruch 313 further, we see that "in the beginning of the 2nd cent. A.D. the so-called 'Syrian Baruch Apocalypse' (= 2 Baruch) originated". In this pseudepigraphic book Baruch is the receiver of a revelation not only about the destruction of Jerusalem by the Romans but even about the end of the world. A third Baruch-book followed, and then a fourth (pseudepigraphic), equally in the second century A.D. In this so-called 'Greek Baruch Apocalypse' Baruch visits the heaven during his life thus becoming a celestial being and, by the same token, a heavenly revealer.
177. Hipp., Ref. 5.26.3,4, and 6. No such words allegedly used by Moses can be found in the Pentateuch. Throughout all its five books he is speaking unambiguously enjoining upon the people of Irsael to observe the ordinances of the Lord in unmistakable terms. The nearest guess I can make is Deut. 29:29 where Moses says : "There are things hidden, and they belong to the Lord our God" but these things obviously are hidden also to him.
178. Hipp., Ref. 5.26.5.
179. Hipp., Ref. 5.26.5.
180. Hipp., Ref. 5.26.7-9.
181. Hipp., Ref. 5.26.14-18.
182. Hipp., Ref. 5.26.5.
183. Hipp., Ref. 5.26.20-21.
184. Hipp., Ref. 5.26.13.
185. Hipp., Ref. 5.26.37.
186. Hipp., Ref. 5.26.21-22.
187. Hipp., Ref. 5.26.23-24.
188. Hipp., Ref. 5.26.24-25.
189. Hipp., Ref. 5.26.25.
190. Hipp., Ref. 5.26.26.
191. Hipp., Ref. 5.26.26.
192. Haenchen, Baruch 304/305, with note 1 on 305, believes that the Hercules-episode is a later insertion. One could indeed read straight from 26.26 to 26.29 and omit 27 and 28.

193. Hipp., Ref. 5.26.27.
194. In the Greek Heracles-myth the hero is sold by Hermes to Omphale, queen of Lydia, as a slave; in her service he performs many great feats.
195. Hipp., Ref. 5.26.28.
196. Hipp., Ref. 5.26.29-32.
197. Hipp., Ref. 5.27.1-2.
198. Epiph., Panarion 45.2.
199. Eus., Hist.eccl. 4.29. This communication has probably been inserted by another hand into the bishop's disquisition on Tatian. Same communication in Theodor., Haer.fab.comp. 1.29.
200. Epiph., Panarion 45.4.1.
201. Epiph., Panarion 45.2.1-3.

CHAPTER VI

THOSE OF BARBELO

1. What are Barbelo-Gnostics?

Yet another branch of Gnostic sects is formed by the Barbelo-Gnostics. To quote Leisegang : "Under this definition all those sects should be taken together which put the figure of Barbelo or Barbero in the centre of their doctrines and their cult ... Among them are to be counted the Nicolaites, Phibionites, Stratiotics, Levitics, Borborites, Coddians, Zacchaeans, and Barbelites" [1] (of the Nicolaites I have already written in Chapter V).

The first question is who or what this Barbelo is. There exists no satisfying explanation of the etymology of this name. Could it perhaps be a corruption of the Greek 'parthenos' = virgin, as Theodoretus seems to suggest [2]? Bousset asserts that he is convinced of this [3], since one Barthenos appears as the wife of Noah in Epiphanius [4]. But others derive it from the Hebrew 'bar-baal' or 'barbhe Eloha' = in the four is God [5]. These four could be the Ophitic tetras : Father, Son, Pneuma, Christ, or that of the (Ophitic) Book of Baruch : the Good, Elohim, Eden, Baruch. However, assuming that Bousset is right, then 'Barbelo' is a female mythological person, a 'power on high', whom others, according to Epiphanius, call 'Prunicus' [6] and who in all probability is identical with 'Sophia'.

2. What Epiphanius had to report about the Barbelo-Gnostics

Our oldest communication about Barbelo-Gnostics is the report of Irenaeus, but it is more interesting to listen first to Epiphanius. It is true that his report comes almost two centuries later than that of the bishop of Lyons, but he had first-hand knowledge of them. It must have been about 335 that he, as a young man of about twenty, travelled from Cyprus, where he was born, to Egypt, wanting to study the life of the monks there since he was of an ascetic cast of mind. In the country of the Nile he ran into a Gnostic group that, to all intents and purposes, was that of the Barbelo-Gnostics. Feeling initially attracted to this sect, he served an apprenticeship with it; he must have studied diligently since he shows himself well acquainted with their teachings, writings, and customs. Some of their books, he says, were put into his hands. And the brothers introduced him into the secret doctrine of the sect. Although Epiphanius does not say as much, the supposition seems justified that he actually was a member for some time.

There was more to be had than doctrine alone. Attractive women tried to seduce him treating him to the grossest obscenities. But thank God, he writes, he did not fall into their trap, and the scales fell from his eyes. He fled, pursued by the laughter of those loose women. He went to the bishop and there denounced the brothers who, at least nominally, were members of the Church. The end was that eighty of them were expelled [7]. The fact that Irenaeus knew them in the second century and Epiphanius in the fourth proves that the sect must have enjoyed a long life. Irenaeus spoke of "a multitude of Barbelo-Gnostics appearing like mushrooms out of the ground" [8].

3. Barbelo-Gnostic scripture

Until the discovery of the Nag Hammadi Library, Irenaeus' report on the Barbelo-Gnostics was the oldest we had. However, this Father of the Church drew his information from an original Gnostic document that, in consequence, must have been prior to 185 A.D., the approximate date of

Irenaeus' anti-heresy book. There can be little doubt that this Gnostic work was (to a large extent) identical with the so-called 'Apocryphon of John', a volume of the Nag Hammadi Library. Two centuries later Epiphanius quoted texts from a number of other Barbelo-Gnostic books, the 'Book of Jaldabaoth', the 'Apocalypse of Adam', the 'Gospel of Eve', the 'Books of Seth', the 'Book of Noreah', the 'Prophecies of Barcabbas', the 'Gospel of the Apostles', the 'Interrogations of Mary', the 'Gospel of Philip', and the 'Gospel of Completion' [9]. "They have lots of books", he writes. Some of these documents, like the Apocalypse of Adam and possibly the Seth and Noreah books, are to be found in the Nag Hammadi Library, while others are perhaps identical with already known apocryphal works. But a considerable part of Barbelo-Gnostic literature is lost.

4. What Barbelo-Gnostic doctrine explains

In the 'Apocryphon of John' [10] the risen Jesus, sitting on the Mount of Olives, is imparting secret knowledge to his favourite disciple, John, in the form of a supernatural revelation [11]. The apparition announces himself as the Father, the Mother, and the Son. "I am the unpolluted and incorruptible one. Now (I have come to teach) you what is (and what was) and what will come to (pass), that (you may know the) things that are not revealed ..., (and that you may tell them to your) fellow-spirits who are (from) the unwavering race of the perfect man" [12]. In other words, a secret doctrine is being propounded, destined for an élitist Gnostic sect. Wisse explains that "the Apocalypse of John supplies answers to two basic questions : what is the origin of evil? and how can we escape from this evil world to our heavenly home?" [13].

5. The highest principle

First of all, we are instructed who, or what, is the highest principle in the celestial order. This principle, the unity or Monad, has no one above him, he is "the Father of All, the Holy Spirit, the invisible". He must not be called a god, as there is no one above him, nor does anyone lord it over him [14], as it is the case with the Old Testament God (in the view of the Gnostics). In this way the author relegates the gods of all other inferior systems, Hellenic as well as Jewish and Christian, to inferior places. The fact that they let themselves be called 'gods' shows that they are of a lesser sort.

This highest principle is the cause of all that lives. "He is an aeon-giving aeon, (life)-giving Life, a blessedness-giving Blessed one, knowledge-giving Knowledge, goodness-giving Goodness", etcetera [15]. But he himself is no part of existence. "He is not one of (the existing ones, but he is) far superior ...; his essence does not belong to the aeons nor to time." This means that he is uncreated and as such essentially different from anything else, for "he who belongs to (an aeon) was first constructed" [16].

The first principle, on the contrary, cannot be understood in creational terms. "He is not corporeal (nor) incorporeal; he is not great (and not) small. (It is) not possible to say, 'what is his quantity' or 'what (is his quality)." Terms are applied to him that all suggest an immense distance, the impenetrable region in which he lives : perfect, illimitable, unsearchable, immmeasurable, invisible, eternal [17]. He is, in particular, unnameable and ineffable; "no one could comprehend him to speak (about him)". The author bends over backwards to describe the absolute otherness of the first principle. He really is the Gnostics' 'deus absconditus et ignotus'. There is, of course, nothing Jewish or Christian in this concept; on the contrary, "the highest deity", as Wisse says, "is defined in terms of an abstract Greek perfection which excludes all anthropomorphism and all involvement in the world" [18]. This means that dualism is round the corner.

6. Barbelo

It will be clear that the ineffable Father is fundamentally unwilling, perhaps even through lack of capacity, to occupy himself with the work of creation. For this a new entity is needed. This being is the female Barbelo, "(the) image of the invisible, virginal Spirit who is perfect" [19].

She may be seen as the female counterpart of the Father, and as an abstract emanation from him who is almost identical with him. There is once again something of the Narcissus-motif in the way she was generated ('created' would not be the correct term). "He (the Father) (gazes upon) his image which he sees in the spring of the (Spirit). (He) puts his desire in his light-(water, that is) the spring of the (pure) light-water (which) surrounds him ... And she (Barbelo) came forth, (namely) she who had appeared before him in (the shine of) his light." In consequence, it is no wonder that "the light (is the likeness of the) light, the (perfect) power" [20].

With this Barbelo we come one stage further in the creational process. She is effusively described as "the womb ('mêtra') of everything (= the effective creational power), for she is prior to them all (= to all created things); (she is) the Mother-Father, the first Man, the holy Spirit, the thrice-male, the thrice-powerful, the thrice-named androgynous one" [21]. This is a proof of the Gnostic predilection for inclusive thinking; what is meant is that Barbelo is all-perfect, and by the same token she is an expression of the Pleroma, the fulness : Barbelo contains all that will be in herself. Every form of existence is already archetypically present.

From the eternal Father she requested and received several great gifts, like eternal life and truth. Perhaps the most important of these gifts is 'foreknowledge' [22]. In another version of the Apocryphon it is called 'the First Knowledge' [23], and Irenaeus spoke of 'Prognosis" [24]. This means, she 'knew', with a knowledge she had directly from the Father.

7. Christ

However well provided Barbelo is, she is still not capable of creating without an impulse from the Father. This impulse is a spark of the pure light that surrounds him. But even when this spark was relayed, she still "did not equal his greatness" [25]. Nobody, that is, except the eternal Father, is entitled to the fulness of his perfection and wisdom. This spark, says Irenaeus, "is the beginning of all illumination and creation" [26].

A somewhat different version suggests that we must think of Barbelo's creational work as a conception. "Barbelo gave birth to a blessed spark of light." What was born from her is Christ, "the Only-begotten ..., the first-born son of the All" [27]. He is an incarnated light, "brought forth ... by the first power of his (the Father's) Pronoia who is Barbelo" [28]. "And he (the Father) anointed it (the spark of light) with his goodness, so that it became perfect and there was no deficiency in it (and it became) Christ. And he revealed himself to him" [29]. This means that Christ possesses intimate and personal knowledge of the Father.

Christ, therefore, is an emanation from an emanation (Barbelo); he proceeds indirectly from the Father, the first principle. The cosmogony of the Apocryphon is a chain of emanations. These emanations, however, form a descending line : Barbelo is already somewhat inferior to the Father, while Christ is less than Barbelo and the Father ('does not equal his/her greatness').

Christ wanted a 'fellow-worker' whom he requested from the Father; this companion was granted to him, the Nous (Mind), or, as Irenaeus says, the Logos [30]. This Nous-Logos represents the creative power; "the mind (Nous) wanted to perform a deed through the word (Logos) of the invisible Spirit" [31]. In other words, the Father-Spirit delegates his creational competence to Christ. "Because of the word (Logos), Christ the divine autogenes, created everything ... And the invisible, virginal Spirit placed the divine Autogenes (= self-begotten) of truth over everything. And he subjected to him every authority and the truth which is in him, that he may know the all which has been called with a name above every name. And they will mention that name to everyone that is worthy of it" [32].

A few remarks must be made. Christ is called autogenes, self-begotten, although he is not, like the Father, self-originated. I take it that he is called so in order to stress that he has no human origin. It is a favourite Gnostic tenet that Christ, as distinct from Jesus of Nazareth, has only a heavenly origin. Then there is markedly biblical ring to this text. Christ the Logos reminds us of the prologue of the Gospel of John, just as it reminds us of Paul's Letter to the Galatians 1:22 where all authority is ascribed to him, of his Letter to the Philippians 2:9 where it is asserted that his name exalted above all names. And thirdly there is the admonition to disclose the name, i.e. the essence, the hidden meaning, only to those "who are worthy of it", that is, to the Gnostics.

8. Cosmogony

a. Adamas

Still, the author remains extremely vague about actual creation. There are still more emanations. Christ is 'the light' and from him four more lights, or aeons, or angels emanate; they are called (H)armozel, Oriel, Daveithai, Eleleth. Each of these commands three lesser aeons that are actually abstractions, like form, perception, understanding, etc.; to Eleleth, Sophia belongs. There are twelve aeons in all, "and these twelve aeons belong to the Son, the Autogenes" [33]. A notable difference between the cosmogony of Genesis and that of the Apocryphon, indeed that of the Gnostics in general, is that, whereas the reports of Genesis are concrete, matter-of-fact, and historical (situated in time and space), those of the Apocryphon are abstract and mythological, without a 'Sitz im Leben' [34]. The author seems to be shying back from arriving at the actual creation; all the time he is interposing new entities between the Father and this world.

Finally, Christ the Autogenes brings forth 'the perfect and true Man, the first revelation, and the truth'; he is called 'Adamas' [35]. He too is an archetypal abstraction, not identical with the biblical Adam. "The invisible one (the Father) gave him an intelligible, invincible power" [36]. This power is Knowledge. "Perfect Knowledge was put forth by the Autogenes und united with him (with Adamas); hence he knew him who is above all things (the Father)" [37]. Once again it is made perfectly clear that Knowledge is the key to the higher world.

"From the Man and Knowledge was born the tree, which itself they (the Barbelo-Gnostics) call Knowledge" [38]. This tree is the biblical tree of the knowledge of good and evil, the only element of actual creation mentioned so far. It has the function here of a custom house : only those who 'know' may pass. Adamas has a son, Seth. It is not stated how he came by him; possibly he must be seen as yet another emanation. His abode is not on the earth but with the second light-aeon, Oroiel. Seth too has a progeny, his seed, the saints (= the Barbelo-Gnostics) whose souls are placed in the third light-aeon, Daveithai. In the fourth and lowest aeon, Eleleth, "the souls were placed of those who do not know the Pleroma and who did not repent at once, but who persisted for a while and repented afterwards" [39]. For those who do not 'know' and never see the need of repenting there is, of course, no room in the heavens.

b. Sophia's wilful acting

So far there is nothing but bliss except for a vague suggestion that there might be people who do not 'know'. However, as may be expected in Gnostic cosmogony, things now take a wrong turn. One of the twelve aeons of Christ is Sophia, or Wisdom. She began to act without the approval of the Spirit, the Father. She wanted to have a male consort but could not find one to her taste among the celestial beings. Even in the lower regions she found no suitable companion. Finally, she succeeded in bringing forth, a-sexually that is, an offspring. "A thing came out of her which was imperfect and different from her appearance ... And when she saw (the consequence of) her desire, it had changed into a form of a lion-faced serpent. And its eyes were like lightning fires which flash. She cast it away from her, outside that place (= the heavens), that no one of the immortals might see it, for she had created it in ignorance... And she called his name Jaltabaoth" [40].

    This is a highly charged text. First of all, here the really dualistic oppositions begin, for now Ignorance comes into play as the counterpart of Knowledge. Ignorance's radical difference from the higher world is expressed by the words that "no one of the immortals might see it". The name given to it is already known to us from Ophitic ideology (Jaldabaoth), a name used to denote a lesser, an inferior, even an evil divinity. It seems illogical that it is exactly Sophia who brings it forth; she, of all persons, should have known better. This twist of the screw, however, is needed to explain why there is so much 'wisdom' that is really unwise and has no celestial origin. And this wisdom, that in fact is identical with sheer Ignorance, has an ugly face; it is even full of danger. What is described here is in fact the Fall. As always in Gnostic ideology, the Fall is not the fault of human beings. It happens far above the sphere of the mortals. It seems as though, for Gnostics, the Fall is an event so great that it demands other participants greater than frail human beings.

c. Jaltabaoth the Demiurge

Jaltabaoth "is the first archon (i.e. he is the great ruler of the nether regions - F.), who took a great power from his mother and moved away from the place where he was born (i.e. he deliberately took up his abode in the lower spheres - F.). He became strong and created for himself other aeons with a flame of luminous light which (still) exists now". This signifies that he began to act as the Demiurge of the cosmos. "And he joined with his madness which is in him and begot authorities for himself" [41].

What now follows is a genuine sample of Gnostic ideology; it shows the Gnostics' predilection for a complex mythology. Twelve aeons are created, each with its own name; it is very difficult to detect what names like Kalila-Oumbri or Melchior-Adonein signify. But we recognize Sabaoth (who in this ideology is not the Demiurge) and also Cain and Abel. There is also Belias = Belial who reigns 'over the depth of Hades'. Next there are 'seven kings over the seven heavens' = the seven 'planets' of Antiquity, and five kings 'over the depth of the abyss' = the underworld. The only one who can be pinned down with certainty is Jaltabaoth himself, for he is no other than the Old Testament Jahve; he can be identified because, 'impious in his madness' as he is, he says : "I am God and there is no other God besides me" [42]. This is in accordance with the favourite Gnostic tenet that the Jewish-Christian God is the wicked Demiurge.

The seven lower (planetary) archons create 'seven powers', these too with fantastic names like Atoth and Eloaiou. These are 'the sevenness of the week', in other words, the seven days of the week. One of these is easily recognizable, namely 'Sabbede', the seventh day = the Sabbath. With the exception of Sabbede who has 'a shining fire-face', they all have animal faces, those, for instance, of a donkey, a hyena, a serpent with seven heads, and so on. What does this mean? My guess is that to be subjected to chronology, as human beings are by necessity, is a hallmark of inferiority. In addition, the seven powers created 365 'angels' who, in all probability, must be understood as demons; it will be clear that they represent the days of the year [43].

What we have heard thus far Irenaeus resumes very aptly, but he does not use the name 'Jaltabaoth' calling him instead the 'Proarchon, the creator of the present condition' = the Demiurge. "He stole from his mother a great power, and departed from her into the lower regions, and made the firmament of heaven, in which also they say he dwells. And since he is Ignorance, he made the powers that are under him, angels, and firmament and all terrestrial things" [44]. We may be absolutely sure of one fact : our terrestrial world bears no comparison to the celestial sphere; it is so infinitely inferior that the distinction must be called dualistic.

d. Jaltabaoth's cosmogonic activities

Jaltabaoth's cosmogonic activities must be seen as flawed. He desired to create 'like the indestructible ones' whom he had never seen himself. "For he was ignorant thinking that there was no other, except his mother alone." The names he gave his powers might, in principle, remind us of 'the glory which belongs to heaven' but in reality mean 'destruction and powerlessness' [45]. Or to quote Ireneaeus again : "he united with Presumption and begot Wickedness, Envy, Jealousy, Revenge, and Passion" [46]. The prospect for humanity looks very sombre indeed! The Demiurge himself glorified in his work and said, quoting the Old Testament : "I am a jealous God, and there is no other God beside me". At this point the author of the Apocryphon becomes critical of the Demiurge. By saying this, the Demiurge indicated that there was indeed another God, "for if there were no other one, of whom could he be jealous?" [47].

e. Sophia repents what she has done

The already enormous distance between the higher and lower worlds was made still greater because Sophia came to realize how wrongly she had acted. She saw that the light she had brought with her had become weak, because it had got mixed with darkness [48]. "She became aware of the deficiency when the brightness of the light had diminished ... When she had seen the wickedness which had happened, and the theft which her son had committed (i.e. of creational power - F.), she repented for she recognized that the cover of darkness was imperfect." The Pleroma, that is the total of the celestial beings, pitied her and implored the Spirit for her. He came down over her "in order that he might correct her deficiency. And she was taken up, not to her own aeon but above her son (Jaltabaoth), that she might be in the ninth (heaven) until she has corrected her deficiency" [49].

What is happening here presents no problem. The first stages of the ascent of the Gnostic soul are pictured. This soul first of all has to realize that it is 'deficient', ignorant, wrapped in darkness. Then it can accept the Spirit, enlightenment, Knowledge; in consequence it is able to rise 'above Jaltabaoth', that is, to distance itself from this our world and to experience itself as elect and different from the unknowing mass.

f. The creation of Adam

The reader will remember that, earlier in the Apocryphon, there has been talk of the First Man, Adamas, an emanation from the Father and an archetypal prototype. It is probably in opposition to this Adamas that Jaltabaoth decides to create his own man, Adam. Collaborating with his powers, he fashioned "a man according to the image of God and according to our likeness", that is, to the likeness of Jaltabaoth, not to that of the Father. However, the text is confusing here since at the same time it is stated that Adam was created "to the likeness of the First Perfect Man". The chief archon and his cronies, having seen the reflection of the First Man in the water, obviously tried to ape it [50].

The fashioning of Adam proved a highly complicated affair. First the seven (planetary) powers came into action by each of them infusing a soul (psuchê) into Adam - a sinew-soul, a blood-soul, a marrow-soul, and so on. This means that Adam falls under the competence of the astrological bodies and not under that of the highest Father. These 'souls' must be understood as vital forces active in the body and directly related to the planetary spheres, which is in strict accordance with Hellenistic astrological belief.

Next, 'the multitude of angels' took a hand in the creational process. Using 'the seven substances of the psychic (form) as their 'material', they composed the rump and the limbs and connected the parts with each other [51]. Working from the head downward, each angel fashioned his own part of the body, the right eye, the left eye, the navel, the right hip, the left hip, the nails of the feet, and so on, and also the interior, the heart, the liver, the arteries, and so on. The name of each modelling angel is given; strange names they are that do not inspire confidence, products of the luscious mythological fantasy of the Gnostics : Menigesstroeth, Akioreim, Archan, Treneu, Kriman, Gormakaiochlabar [52]. Since the 'angels' represent the days of the year, the parts of the body, in this view, are also related to chronology; this means that human existence is at once finite and changeable and, moreover subject to planetary influences.

We are not yet out of demonology. For each of the main parts of the body, mainly exterior, with the exception of the womb, are placed under the guidance or dominance of special angels who bear just as exotic names : Diolimodraza, Yammeax, Charcharb, Marephnounth [53].

Over these are placed seven overseers plus four others who control the main elements of the whole fabric : Aarmouriam, Richram, Olemmaa, and their colleagues [54].

If the reader's brain begins to reel now, he or she may begin to breath more freely because we suddenly reach safety on solid ground. "The origin of the demons which are in the whole body is ordained to be four(fold) : heat, cold, wetness, and dryness. And the mother of all them is matter" [55]. This number four is a peculiarity of this author; it resembles, but is not identical with, the four main elements or the four temperaments. Its meaning, however, is clear : man is matter, and nothing but matter, subject to the whims of the climate. Each of these four has its own demon; their mother "is truly matter, for they (the demons) are nourished through her" [56].

The great human impulses, pleasure, desire, grief, and fear, have their own special demons. Each impulse generates passions : from grief come envy, jealousy, distress, anxiety, and sorrow, from pleasure much wickedness and empty pride, from desire anger, wrath, and other vices, from fear fawning, agony, and shame [57]. Man's emotional life looks very gloomy indeed; there is nothing but misery in it. By way of conclusion it is stated that the 365 angels "all worked on it until, limb for limb, the psychic and material body was completed by them". The reader who wants to know more is referred to 'the Book of Zoroaster', whatever that may be. But let us make no mistake! The human body is composed of matter and psyche but there is as yet no 'pneuma' in it : "their product was completely inactive and motionless for a long time" [58].

g. The Pneuma

This pneuma, the really life-giving spirit, had to come from above; the nether world does not contain it. At the request of the Mother, Sophia, the Father sends down five 'lights' (= luminous spirits); these 'lights' persuaded Jaltabaoth to 'blow' his own spirit (pneuma) into the motionless human body, which he did, the result being that "the body moved and gained strength, and it was luminous". It may seem somewhat incongruous that it is exactly the ill-disposed Jaltabaoth who makes the body 'luminous' since he finds himself on the wrong side of the dualistic dividing line that runs through the universe. But we must not forget that it was "the power of the Mother (that) went out of Jaltabaoth into the psychic soul". The reader will remember that the Demiurge had succeeded in keeping to himself some part of Sophia's light. This does not mean that he wholeheartedly cooperated in the operation. Far from it! "He did not know (this) for he exists in ignorance" [59].

h. The second Fall

Then again a Fall takes place - the second one, the first being Sophia's blunder of generating Jaltabaoth. "The powers (planets, angels) became jealous because his (man's) intelligence was greater than that of those who made him, and greater than that of the chief archon (the Demiurge Jaltabaoth). And when they recognized that he (man) was luminous, and that he could think better than they, and that he was free from wickedness, they took him and threw him into the lowest region of all matter" [60].

Man is portrayed here as basically a part of the divine sphere, at least with regard to his spirit; his body and psyche, however, belong to the material sphere. So man is really a hybrid being. The rulers of the nether sphere do not suffer his presence there gladly; they consider him not only an exile from the higher sphere but still more a threat to themselves. The fierce dualism of both spheres has to some extent been broken through by the creation of luminous man. The wicked powers attempt to restore the situation by throwing him into the lowest pit, that is as far as possible from the upper realm. Once again we see that the Fall is not the fault of man but is effected by higher, non-human beings.

j. Redemption

What is pictured here is the general situation of mankind : man is brought down very low, he is wholly miserable, subject to wicked forces, and forgetful of his origin. But now the theme of redemption is sounded. The great celestial Father of all sent a helper to Adam in his misery, namely "luminous Epinoia which comes out of him, who was called Life ... And the luminous Epinoia was hidden in Adam, in order that the archons might not know her". Here begins, so to speak, a covert rescue operation. 'Epinoia' is thought, notion, intelligence; it is equivalent to knowledge. Her function is to restore Adam to his 'fulness', teach him 'about the descent of his seed' (i.e. that he is of divine origin) and "about the way of ascent, (which is) the way he came down"[61]. This, to all intents and purposes, is an authentic Gnostic program.

k. The counter-offensive

We must not expect that the 'powers' leaned back and peacefully waited on events that would happen. When they began to suspect that man was coming into his own, they held a council of war on how they might overthrow him again. They partly succeeded in this by turning all the material elements against him and by, to a certain extent, creating him anew; they infused their own material spirit into him with the ignorance of darkness and desire, so that "he became a mortal man", that is, the notion that he was no more than mortal overwhelmed him. But their victory was not complete, for "the Epinoia of the light which was in him, she is the one who will awaken his thinking"[62].

  The author then makes his own use of the Paradise story in Genesis. The archons place Adam in the Garden and exhort him to eat freely from all the trees, including the tree of life. Close reading is necessary, for the text does not speak of the tree of life but of 'the tree of their life'. And what is their life? "The root of this tree and its branches are death, its shadow is hate and deception is in its leaves." It is not a tree of life at all!

It is the same, indeed, with all the other trees. "Their luxury is deception and their (the archons') trees are godlessness and their fruit is deadly poison". There is one notable exception : the tree of knowledge of good and evil, which is 'the Epinoia of the light'. But this tree is situated in such a way that Adam is unable to realize its potency. For the chief archon brought 'a forgetfulness' over him [63]. This Barbelo-Gnostic Eden is a prototype of human existence : nothing but deception and ignorance, with death as the outcome, and with an almost undetectable spark of light only.

Unlike in the Paradise story in Genesis, Adam does not succomb to the seduction to eat from the trees. Epinoia had hidden herself in him, and the chief archon's attempts to chase her out of him were in vain. Angry at his failure, he, the Demiurge Jaltabaoth, "made another creature in the form of a woman according to the likeness of Epinoia". This too was a means of deception in order to lead Adam astray. But when he saw this woman, a luminous appearance, "she lifted the veil which lay over his mind (i.e. the forgetfulness - F.) ... And he recognized his counterpart" repeating the biblical words of the man leaving his parents in order to cling to his wife. Nevertheless, this woman is, after all, a product of the wicked Demiurge. But Sophia came down "in order to rectify her deficiency. Therefore, she (Eve) was called Life which is the mother of the living" [64].

l. The fallen state

The Barbelo-Gnostic author does not relate or paraphrase the Genesis story of the Fall. This is impossible for him because in Genesis the Fall is caused by the first couple's eating from the tree of knowledge. The effect of eating from the author's tree of knowledge would have been quite the reverse. There is no Fall, there never is a human Fall in the Gnosis. But there is a 'fallen state', in the sense that the first human beings dwell in a fools' Paradise. The tree of knowledge plays a role to the extent that an eagle appeared on it and awakened them 'out of the depth of sleep (= ignorance)', and now they recognized their nakedness"

(= how miserable they were in their ignorance - F.)". It was through Sophia that "they tasted the perfect knowledge". And "the Epinoia appeared to them as a light (and) she awakened their thinking" [65].

The reader, who by now will have become quite used to the notion that in Gnostic doctrine the woman most of the time is not a help but an obstacle on the path to salvation, will be astonished to read that here the woman is the counterpart of the male and shares his enlightenment. But soon enough the scene changes! The woman proves a liability. As soon as Jaltabaoth saw that he had been fooled, "he cursed his earth ..., he cast them out of Paradise and he clothed them in gloomy darkness". This means that he is trying to reduce them once again to their fallen state. But "when the foreknowledge of the All (Sophia) noticed (it), she sent some angels and they snatched Life out of Eve" [66].

By this trick the woman is turned into the secondary and inferior being that most Gnostics wanted her to be. That 'the Life' went out of her did not, of course, mean that she died, but that she lost her knowledge and insight and became dumb and ignorant. The chief archon now regains full sway over her, seduces her, and begets two sons with her. In this way sexuality was introduced into the world. "Up to the present day sexual intercourse continued due to the chief archon. And he planted sexual desire into her who belongs to Adam. And he (the Demiurge) produced through intercourse the copies of the bodies, and he inspired them with his opposing spirit" [67]. The hallmark of man's fallen state is sexual desire that forces people to have sexual intercourse; this leads to offspring with a negative spirit and subject to the wicked Demiurge. This is the downright condemnation of sexuality that we may expect in a Gnostic text.

m. Eloim and Yave

The two beings who were born from Eve are Eloim and Yave. It is not difficult to recognize in them the two names of the deity in Genesis, Jahve and Elohim, sometimes combined into Jahve-Elohim, which is usually rendered as 'the Lord God'. In Genesis they are identical but not in the Apocryphon where they are two different beings. Yave is righteous and has a cat-face; Eloim is unrighteous and has a bear-face. Obviously they are gods of nature, for "Yave he (the Demiurge) set over the fire and the wind, and Eloim he set over the water and the earth". In other words, he divided the elements between them. That the one is righteous whereas the other is not reminds us of Cain and Abel. And indeed, "he (the Demiurge) called them with the names of Cain and Abel with a view to deceive" [68].

What we see here is the picture of a closed universe that is wholly physical, without the spirit, and, in consequence doomed to die. "The two archons (Yave and Eloim) he (the Demiurge) set over the principalities so that they might rule over the tomb" [69]. 'The tomb' is at once the symbol and the end of human existence.

n. The origin of Seth

It may seem that, in his dualistic duel with the higher powers, the Demiurge is already close to the final victory. But he has reckoned without Adam. "When Adam recognized the likeness of his own foreknowledge (= became aware of his real identity - F.), he begot the likeness of the son of man. He called him Seth according to the way of the race of the aeons." In this context it deserves attention that there is no mention of Eve; it is evident that Adam begets his son in an a-sexual way. The meaning of this is to stress that Seth has a superior origin. His superiority is also emphasized by the sending down by the Mother (Sophia) of her spirit, on Seth obviously. Her spirit is "a copy of those who are in the Pleroma" [70].

o. A promise

Let us not assume too readily that all is well now! Once again the Demiurge attacks. If the weapon of the powers from above is 'enlightenment', his is 'forgetfulness'. "He made them (Adam, Seth, their progeny) drink water of forgetfulness ... in order that they might not know from where they came. Thus the seed (the progeny of Seth) remained for a while assisting (him, the Demiurge) in order that, when the Spirit comes forth from the holy aeons, he may raise him (Seth) up from the deficiency, that the whole Pleroma may (again) become holy and faultless" [71]. For by making Seth forgetful, the Demiurge had succeeded in breaking in into the upper sphere.

Bad as the situation may look, a promise is held out, albeit not to all mankind. It is a mysterious message, "difficult to explain ..., except to those who are from the immovable race (= the Gnostics who do not belong to fickle humanity but are 'perennial' people - F.). "Immovability", writes Williams, "is a hallmark not only of the Pleroma and all its constituents but also of the race of the elect ... We have an **ascetic contest** (Williams' emphasis) waged by those on whom the Spirit has been poured out, against the restless and chaotic movements of the passions and the archontic powers who arouse them ... One who has been 'set right' (= who has become a Gnostic - F.) is properly aligned, as it were, with the noetic, the realm of the 'standing aeons'. This alignment produces enormous power to be used against the unstable, disruptive cosmic powers who control the realm of constant change and movement outside the Pleroma" [72]. Among the many dualisms with which the Gnosis abounds, there is also one of immovability (the Pleroma with the aeons, the Gnostics) and movement (the cosmos, the cosmic powers, mankind).

"Those on whom the Spirit of life will descend ..., they will be saved and become perfect ... and be purified from all wickedness and the involvements of evil." Their life may be troublesome enough but "they endure everything ..., that they may finish the good fight and inherit eternal life. They are not affected by anything except by being in the state of flesh alone" [73]. This communication gives a very adequate idea of the Gnostic attitude to life and its inherent predicament : the only thing that worries a Gnostic is that he is human.

p. The destiny of the souls

"Where will the souls of those go who have come out of their flesh?" Once again it is pointed out that there is no heavenly future for the body. "The soul in which the power (of Sophia) will become superior to the despicable spirit (the Demiurge), she (the soul) is strong and she flees from evil, and through the intervention of the incorruptible one (the highest Father) she is saved and she is taken up to the rest of the aeons" [74]. Others, more stupid, may have gone astray. Their lot, it goes without saying, is worse but even for them there is hope. The Demiurge "draws her (a soul like this) to the works of evil and casts her down into forgetfulness. And after she comes out (of the body), she is handed over to the authorities (the demons) who came into being through the archon, and they bind her with chains and cast her into prison ..., until she is liberated from the forgetfulness and acquire knowledge." The instrument of redemption, as always, is knowledge, or rather, the knowledge is the redemption. How the imprisoned soul will come by this knowledge is not revealed. "If she thus becomes perfect, she is saved" [75]. Judging from the 'if', this acquirement of knowledge is not guaranteed but only possible for people of this sort.

The worst fate is reserved for lapsed Gnostics, for "those who did know but have turned away ... To that place where the angels of poverty go they will be taken, the place where there is no repentance. And they will be kept for the day on which those who have blasphemed the Spirit will be tortured, and they will be punished with eternal punishment" [76].

q. A bad, bad world

In the concluding sections of the Apocryphon, the author recapitulates what has been expounded so far. First of all, it is stated that it was the highest power, "the one who is merciful", who "raised up the perfect race of man and his thinking and the eternal life of man". This is the well-known picture of the elect race that stands wholly, dualistically, apart from the rest of mankind. They even "are exalted above him in the height (= the chief archon Jaltabaoth, the Demiurge), they surpass him in thinking." They simply do not belong to this creation. In his anger the chief archon poured out over the world "every sin and injustice and blasphemy and the chain of forgetfulness and ignorance and every difficult command (perhaps the injunctions of Mosaic Law are meant - F.) and serious sins and great fear. And thus the whole creation was made blind, in order that they may not know God who is above all of them" [77].

Once again the story of Noah is repeated, not the story of the Ark, there having been no Ark. One of the reasons for rejecting this feature is doubtless that the Ark was too concrete, too material - too well carpented - for the Gnostic taste; another is that not only Noah and his family are to be saved but all the elect with him. Instead of entering into the Ark, all of them "hid themselves in a luminous cloud" [78].

Next we find a story that seems to have enjoyed a certain popularity, that of the sexual relations between celestial beings and earthly women; it is not impossible that both the Gnostic version and the biblical one in Gen. 6:1-4 [79] go back on an ancient myth current in the Middle East. The Barbelo-Gnostic rendering of this story differs from that in Genesis. Here it is the Demiurge who sends "his angels to the daughters of men, that they might take some of them for themselves, and raise offspring for their enjoyment."

In Genesis, where the angels are not sent out but go by themselves, they indeed have children. But in the Apocryphon "they have no success". I suppose this highlights the notion that celestial and terrestrial cannot combine. First, the angels have to create "a despicable spirit ... so as to pollute the souls with it". Then they assume the likeness of human males, closely resembling the husbands of those women, and fill them 'with the spirit of darkness ... and with evil'. Only then were they able to seduce the women and have children with them.

It is not stated in this report, as in Genesis, that the offspring were giants. Instead, it is related that "they (the angels) steered the people who had followed them into great troubles, by leading them astray with many deceptions. They (these people) became old without having any enjoyment. They died, not having found truth and without knowing the God of truth. And thus the whole creation became enslaved forever from the foundation of the world until now" [80]. Here we find the well-known theme of the utter depravity of the world and its subsequent rejection by the Gnostics.

r. The Saviour

It all ends with the redemption of the holy ones. The Saviour is nobody less than Barbelo, "the Pronoia of the All, ... the richness of the light, ... the remembrance of the Pleroma". Of course, she does not descend into the darkness in order to redeem the whole world or even mankind as such. She comes only for those who 'hear'. Having arrived 'in the middle of darkness', she says : "He who hears let him get up from the deep sleep". And someone answers : "Who is that who calls my name, and from where has hope come to me, while I am in the chains of prison?" [81]. What we witness here is the Gnostic process of inner enlightenment, which is spiritual, personal and a privilege, and of the redemption by knowledge.

The 'Pronoia of the pure light' makes herself known as "the thinking of the virginal spirit (the Father of the All), he who raised you up to the honoured place. Arise and remember that it is you who harked and follow your root, which is I, the merciful one". 'Following the root' betokens that awareness of self, that taking possession of one's real self that is so central an idea in Gnostic thought. Through knowledge the Gnostic becomes identical with his real self, whereas most people, so to speak, live besides themselves.

The state of election that goes with this fundamental self-awareness is expressed in these terms. "Guard yourselves against the angels of poverty and the demons of chaos and all those who ensnare you, and beware of the deep sleep (i.e. of ignorance) and the enclosure of the inside of Hades (i.e. of physical existence)." Finally, he who is elected and redeemed is made immortal. "I (Pronoia) raised him up and sealed him in the light of the water with five seals, in order that death might not have power over him from this time on" [82].

The first who has 'heard' Barbelo-Pronoia and was 'sealed' by her is the (anonymous) prophet of Barbelo-Gnosis. Barbelo orders him to write everything down and divulge it secretly to his fellow-spirits, "for this is the mystery of the immortal race (the Gnostics)". The prophet did what he was told; "he went to his fellow disciples and related to them what the Saviour had told him" [83].

s. Dualism

Is it really necessary to point out that all the usual dualistic elements of the Gnosis are present here too? The most basic of these elements is the sharp distinction between the upper and nether worlds, then the opposition of light and darkness, equivalent to knowledge and ignorance, the depravity of all creation, the rejection of this world, and finally the race of the elect as opposed to the rest of mankind, the 'massa damnata'.

9. Other Barbelo-Gnostic sects

a. Which sects there were

As I said in the beginning, there are several other Gnostic sects that are more or less closely related to the Barbelo-Gnosis. In the present state of affairs nobody will be able to describe with scholarly exactitude the affiliations between all those sects.

Epiphanius speaks of Phibionites, followers of Epiphanes, Stratiotics, Levitics, Borborians, and the rest [84]; among this rest we must probably count the Coddaeans, Zacchaeans, and Barberites [85], while there was perhaps also a connection with the Nicolaites. Of most of these sects we know next to nothing. Deprecatingly this Father of the Church says : "Each of these has contrived his own sect to suit his own passions and has devised thousand ways of evil" [86], thereby suggesting that we have to do with libertine Gnostics.

b. The role of Barbelo

"Some of these", he goes on to say, "glorify in a certain Barbelo who they say is above in the eighth heaven ... She was produced by the Father, and she is the mother of Jaldaboath according to some, of Sabaoth according to others" [87]. Then came the dualistic split of the upper and nether regions. "Her son violently and tyrannously possessed himself of the seventh heaven, and says to those below (to mankind) 'I am the first ...; apart from me there is no other god."

Because Jaldaboath is a 'son' (an emanation) of Barbelo and through her of the first Father of All, he was able to abscond with some of the light which he distributed downward. Barbelo tries to recover it; her efforts are described in sexual terms which, in all probability, present a clue for the understanding of the libertine practices of some of these sects. "When they indulge their passions", writes Epiphanius, "(they) have recourse to a myth to give this pretext to their shameful deeds" [88]. "She (Barbelo) always appears to the archons in beauty (that is, she seduces them - F.) and takes from them their seed through pleasure (causing) its emission." With this is intended that she robs the lower powers of the supernatural element they are usurping. In doing so she hopes to "recover again her own power that was inseminated into these various beings" [89]. Her action results in making the two worlds ever more dualistically apart. After all, the archons smuggled some elements of the heavenly sphere into the cosmos but these are now recuperated by Barbelo.

c. The two spheres

In these sects too the doctrine of the spheres flourished. "In the first heaven is the archon Iao, and so on, and in the third Seth, in the sixth heaven is, some say, Jaldaboath, but others Elilaeus. And they suppose that there is another, seventh, heaven, in which they say is Sabaoth; but others say no, Jaldaboath is in the seventh. In the eight heaven is the (female) power who is called Barbelo and the Father of the Universe, its

Lord, who is also called 'Autopater' (= 'self-father'); and another one, Christ, who brought himself to birth, and this Christ is the one who descended and showed men this knowledge whom they call also Jesus. And he was not born from Mary, but he was manifested through Mary. And he has not assumed flesh, unless it be a mere appearance. And some say that Sabaoth has the face of an ass, others that of a swine; for this reason he commanded the Jews not to eat swine. And he (Sabaoth) is the maker of heaven and earth and of the heavens after him and of his own angels. And the soul as it leaves this (world) passes by these Archons but cannot pass unless it is in full possession (pleroma) of this knowledge, or rather condemnation (= of the wicked angels and their corrupted world - F.), and being carried (past) (it) escapes the hands of the Archons and authorities. And the Archon who possesses this world has the shape of a serpent, and he devours the souls which are not in a state of knowledge and brings them again into the world through his tail, where they are sent into swine and other beasts and brought up again by the same means ... And they (these Gnostics) say that he (the saved soul) comes to Sabaoth and tramples upon his head ... and so passes over into the higher region, where there is the Mother of the Living, Barbero, or Barbelo, and so the soul is saved" [90]. This looks very much like a recapitulation of all the foregoing! I don't think explanation is needed.

d. The two battling forces

The basic Gnostic idea of two forces dualistically doing battle with each other is expounded in the following passage from Epiphanius. "There was darkness and abyss and water, and the Pneuma was between them and made a division between them (= the Spirit began to create order in the primeval chaos - F.). But the Darkness was hostile and jealous of the Spirit; and this Darkness ran up and embraced the Spirit ... and engendered a so-called Womb (mētra) which when it was engendered became engendered by that same Spirit. And from the Womb four Aeons were produced, and from the four Aeons came fourteen, and there came into being the right side and the left, the Light and the Dark. And afterwards after all these there was produced a loathsome Aeon (= the Demiurge), and he had intercourse with the Womb formerly described, and from this loathsome Aeon there originated gods and angels and demons and seven spirits" [91].

We can sum this up in the words of Leisegang : "In this way two powers stem themselves against each other in the world : the pure divine force with which Barbelo was fecundated and from which all life originated, and the force of evil, the Demiurge who fell away from God" [92].

e. Libertinism

We now come to an highly unsavoury section of our disquisition, a part that I for one find utterly repellent. I have seriously considered omitting it but on second thoughts I decided against it since the happenings to be described constitute an integral part of Barbelo-Gnostic and/or Nicolaite doctrine. These people celebrated a ritual that was downright sexual. Now, first of all, I want to stress that most Gnostics deeply abhorred sexuality, abstained from it as much as they could, and did not practice it during their liturgical gatherings. But a minority did. It has been often supposed that the early Fathers of the Church who report these things were happily slinging mud at the Gnostics, or perhaps were celibates with a dirty mind, a well-known topos in anti-clerical polemics.

But in this case there can be no doubt that we really are among libertine Gnostics, since we have a witness, Epiphanius. This later bishop of Salamis on Cyprus and Father of the Church, as a young man not yet twenty years old, visited Egypt as I have already related. For some time he must have been fairly close to a Barbelo-Gnostic community. He shows himself so well up in the matter that the conclusion is justified that, at least for a short period, he was an aspirant or perhaps even an member. He gives such a graphic description of this group's ritual that he must have been present and, who knows, took part in it.

When the celebration begins, they recognize members who are new to their group by a certain secret sign. "When they stretch out their hand, by way of the usual greeting, they make a tickling stroke beneath the palm of the hand, indicating by this means that the new arrival belongs to their cult." Then they begin to dine lavishly on meat and wine. When they are all more or less drunk, the moment for promiscuity has come. "They have their women in common." Husbands even exhort their wives to make love 'with the brother'.

When they have had intercourse, "the man and the woman take the man's emission in their own hands ... offering to the natural Father of the universe that which is in their hands, saying ... : 'This is the body of Christ, and this is the Passover; hence our bodies are given over to passion and compelled to confess the passion of Christ'" [93]. There is more of this in the same vein - or still worse [94] - but I think this suffices.

Now the great question is, why did they do such things? Out of sheer lust, some will say. But why then did they make a ritual of it? Because of the ideology behind it. In the Pleroma - and this, of course, is its essential characteristic - nothing is apart but everything is connected with everything. In particular, Sophia and the Saviour form a pair, or suzugê, as bride and bridegroom, and "their bridal chamber is the entire Pleroma" [95]. Irenaeus, who also shortly reports on these libertine practices, says that, whereas everyone receives grace on loan, so that it can be taken away, they, these Gnostics, "have grace as their own possession, which has come down from above with them from the unalterable and unnamable conjunction ('suzugê')". And he concludes : "Therefore, they must always in every possible way practice the mystery of the Conjunction" [96].

This Conjunction cannot be celebrated in a normal marriage, because the marital bond is seen as a form of apartheid incompatible with the notion of Pleroma. So marital fidelity has to be sacrificed to promiscuity which is the true image of the heavenly Conjunction as well as of the Pleroma. The quintessence of this ritual is found in the Barbelo-Gnostic belief that the "Spirit (Pneuma) is nothing more or less than sperm, the life-giving stuff that created the world and mankind. The pneuma is thus the Godhead self, possessed by man in his own seed ... To be united with God means that one's seed is fused into one with the seed of the universe. To be redeemed means to release one's seed from its earthly destiny and to return it to the divine source of all seed" [97]. And Gerhard Zacharias adds to this quotation from Leisegang that "by offering the sperm to the Omnipresent Father, whose wholeness, or Pleroma, embraces the Earth Mother, the might of the Archon, who stole the divine powers from Heaven, is broken ... The act of redemption is completed when the Gnostics, communicating with the sperm, receive back the divine powers and are only then truly redeemed" [98].

Since these Barbelo-Gnostics are firmly founded in grace, they are incapable of sinning; what is wrong in others is not wrong in them. On the contrary, "they call us (non-Gnostics) 'psychics' ('psuchikoi', or 'soul-people' with no pneuma, the Christians are meant - F.) and say that we are from the world, and that continence and virtuous conduct are necessary for us ... but by no means (necessary) for themselves whom they call 'spiritual' ('pneumatikoi') and 'perfect'. For it is not conduct that brings men into the Pleroma but the seed which was sent out from its infancy and is made perfect in this world" [99].

These libertines enable themselves to enter the Pleroma by leaving nothing undone. By committing acts that commonly are considered forbidden, they showed that they were triumphing over matter and were absolutely immune against the world. Not doing these forbidden things would mean that they were afraid and, for that reason, kept their distance from them. But every form of apartheid, even apartheid from evil, was abhorrent to them, since it detracted from the Pleroma. "Just as gold does not lose its beauty in filth and reserves its nature, undammaged by the filth, they (these Gnostics) are never injured neither do they lose their spiritual essence because material actions have no impact on them" [100].

Yet another reason for this ritual is that the male semen (and the menstrual blood) are supposed to contain the spark of light. From a Gnostic viewpoint this is only logical because the sparks of light are transmitted from one generation to the other by means of sexual intercourse. In order to be able to make these sparks return to their origin, one must dispose of the male seed and the blood of the period (which also plays its part in the ritual). "They say : 'We are collecting the power of Prunicus (Sophia) from their bodies by their fluids"[101]. "And the powers which reside in the periods and in the semen, they say, is the soul, which we collect and eat. And whatever we eat, be it meat, vegetables, bread, or anything else, we are doing a kindness to created things, in that we collect the soul from all things and transmit it with ourselves to the heavenly world"[102]. All the time these Barbelo-Gnostics are engaged in liberating the sparks of light from the material husks that envelop them.

NOTES TO CHAPTER VI

1. Leisegang, Gnosis 186.
2. Theodor., Haer.fab.comp. 1.13.
3. Bousset, Hauptprobl. 14.
4. Epiph., Panarion 45.2.1-3. According to Bousset, "the step from 'barthenos' to 'barbelo' is explained most easily in handwriting". We find indeed this name spelled as Barbelo, Barbelos, Barbero, Barberoth.
5. Leisegang, Gnosis 186.
6. Epiph., Panarion 21.2.5.
7. Epiph., Panarion 26.17.
8. Ir., Adv.haer. 1.29.1.
9. Epiph., Panarion 26.8.
10. It is called "up to the present the best-attested original gnostic document". It is extant in four copies, three of which in NHL, II.1., III.1., and IV.1, introduced and translated by Frederik Wisse. See Foerster/Wilson, 100. Sevrin, Le dossier 9 concludes from the existence of four copies (the fourth in Codex Berolinensis 8502 (BG)) that the Apocryphon must have enjoyed a considerable credit in the Gnostic world.
11. NHL 2.1.1.30-2.10.
12. NHL 2.1.2.19-26.
13. NHL 98.
14. NHL 2.1.2.28-35.
15. NHL 2.1.4.1-5.
16. NHL 2.1.3.28-31.

17. NHL 2.1.3.
18. NHL 98. Bousset, Hauptprobl. 85 : "Diese Spekulation über den hochsten, unbekannten Gott, der im Gegensatz namentlich auch zu den weltschöpferischen Mächten steht, kann nicht irgendwie auf jüdischemn Einfluss zurückgeführt werden ... Aber ihre Wurzel kann... diese Spekulation auch nicht im Christentum gehabt haben."
19. NHL 2.1.4.
20. NHL 2.1.4.
21. NHL 2.1.5.
22. NHL 2.1.5.
23. BG 28.5, in Foerster/Wilson 108.
24. Ir., Adv.haer. 1.29.1.
25. NHL 2.1.6.
26. Ir., Adv.haer. 1.29.1; BG 30.1.
27. BG 30.5, Foerster/Wilson, Gnosis 109.
28. NHL 2.1.6.
29. BG 30.15, Foerster/Wilson, Gnosis 109; Ir., Adv.haer. 1.29.1.
30. NHL 2.1.7; Ir., Adv.haer. 1.29.1.
31. NHL 2.1.7.
32. NHL 2.1.7.
33. NHL 2.1.,7,8. Ir., Adv.haer. 1.29.2.
34. For the inconsistencies in the Apocryphon (which I have somewhat glossed over in order not to confuse the uninformed reader) and for the differences between it and the report by Irenaeus, one should consult Foerster/Wilson, Gnosis 100-103 (text by Martin Krause).
35. In the Apocryphon 'Pigeraadama(s)', NHL 2.1.8; Ir., Adv. haer. 1.29.3.
36. NHL 2.1.9.
37. Ir., Adv.haer. 1.29.3.
38. Ir., Adv.haer. 1.29.3.
39. NHL 2.1.9.
40. NHL 2.1.9-10; Ir., Adv.haer. 1.29.4.
41. NHL 2.1.10.20-29.
42. NHL 2.1.11.
43. NHL 2.1.11.

44. Ir., Adv.haer. 1.29.4.
45. NHL 2.1.9.
46. Ir., Adv.haer. 1.29.4.
47. NHL 2.1.13.
48. NHL 2.1.11.
49. NHL 2.1.13-14.
50. NHL 2.1.15.
51. NHL 2.1.15.
52. NHL 2.1.15-17.
53. NHL 2.1.17.
54. NHL 2.1.17-18.
55. NHL 2.1.18.
56. NHL 2.1.18.
57. NHL 2.1.18.
58. NHL 2.1.19.
59. NHL 2.1.19.
60. NHL 2.1.20.
61. NHL 2.1.20.
62. NHL 2.1.21.
63. NHL 2.1.21-22.
64. NHL 2.1.22.
65. NHL 2.1.22-23.
66. NHL 2.1.23-24.
67. NHL 2.1.24.
68. NHL 2.1.24.
69. NHL 2.1.24.
70. NHL 2.1.24-25.
71. NHL 2.1.25.
72. Williams, Immov. race 139/140.
73. NHL 2.1.25-26.
74. NHL 2.1.26.
75. NHL 2.1.27.
76. NHL 2.1.27.
77. NHL 21.28.

78. NHL 2.1.29.
79. See Vol. IV, Ch. II.11b.
80. NHL 21.29-30.
81. NHL 2.1.30-31.
82. NHL 2.1.31.
83. NHL 2.1.31-32. The ending of the Apocryphon seems to have been modelled on that of the Revelation of John. For instance, the Apocryphon closes on 'Jesus Christ, Amen", the Revelation on 'Amen. Come, Lord Jesus'. If this is correct, then the Apocryphon must be dated after A.D. 90. As its time of origination, usually ca. A.D. 150 is assumed.
84. Epiph., Panarion 25.2.1.
85. Epiph., Panarion 26.3.6-7.
86. Epiph., Panarion 25.2.1.
87. Epiph., Panarion 25.2.2.
88. Epiph., Panarion 25.3.2.
89. Epiph., Panarion 25.3.2.
90. Epiph., Panarion 26.10.1-10.
91. Epiph., Panarion 25.5.1-3.
92. Leisegang, Gnosis 188.
93. Epiph., Panarion 26.4.1-8.
94. Epiph., Panarion 26.5.1-7.
95. Ir., Adv.haer. 1.7.1.
96. Ir., Adv.haer. 1.6.3.
97. Leisegang, Gnosis 195.
98. Zacharias, Satanic cult 30.
99. Ir., Adv.haer. 1.6.4.
100. Ir., Adv.haer. 1.6.2.
101. Epiph., Panarion 25.3.2.
102. Epiph., Panarion 26.9.4

CHAPTER VII

THE BASILIDIANS

1. Basilides and his work

Bardy begins his article on Basilides, one of the greatest Gnostic teachers, in the following not very promising way : "Basilides is the first of the Gnostics about whom we have positive information. However, this information amounts to very little" [1]. We know neither when he was born nor when he died; he must have seen the light towards the end of the first century A.D. so that he 'flourished' around 130/140. Was he, like his contemporary and fellow-Gnostic Valentinus, an Egyptian? Probably not. The scarce information we have points in the direction of Palestine and Syria. He himself is reported to have said that he was taught by Glaukias, who is referred to as the interpreter of the apostle Peter [2]. Taught what? Must we infer from this scant information that Basilides was a Jew who was converted to Christianity?

If he was ever an orthodox Christian, we may suspect that he did not remain so for long. For, together with Saturnilos, another Gnostic teacher [3], he sat at the feet of Menander [4] on whom the mantle of Simon the Magician [5] had fallen [6]. He himself claimed - and this is typical of many a Gnostic teacher - to have been in the possession of secret teachings by Jesus; he had these from the apostle Matthias who had received them from Jesus himself [7]. There exists an (unwarranted?) tradition that Basilides went to Persia in order to teach there "not long after the time of our Apostles". The same source goes on to say that when Basilides saw that everything had already been taken possession of (that everyone was Christian already? - F.), he, being sly, began to preach 'duality' which in all probability means some sort of dualism [8].

But one thing, at least, is certain : he went to Alexandria and taught there. He lived in this city during the reign of the Roman emperor Hadrianus (117-138) and was still there during that of Antoninus Pius (138-161) [9]; he roamed through several Egyptian cities before establishing himself in the capital [10]. He was married and had a son called Isidore who was his disciple and successor [11].

2. The heresiologues on Basilides

We have a tangled mass of information on Basilides' doctrines in which it is very hard to distinguish between what is original Basidilianism and what are later accretions. One thing is certain : the linchpin of the whole system is dualism. As Bousset wrote : "An outspoken dualist of oriental provenance is Basilides" [12]. It is an irreparable loss that we no longer possess the oldest work directed against the Basilidians, the "Elengchos kata Basileidou', by a certain Agrippa Castor, a contemporary of the founder himself [13]. Clement who used it calls it a very able work [14].

In the absence of original Basilidian documents - the jar of Nag Hammadi contained nothing of this kind [15] - we shall have to rely on the expositions of the heresiologues, the early Fathers of the Church; they offer us two extensive disquisitions, those of Irenaeus and Hippolytus, and a few less important ones. The tricky problem is that the former accounts considerably differ from each other. For some scholars this has been a sufficient reason to dismiss both of them altogether, as least as testimonies of early Basilidianism. This would leave us with hardly any information at all about the teaching of the founder himself. It seems improbable to me that nothing of it would have been preserved in the writings of the early Fathers.

Of the two larger reports that of Irenaeus is the oldest; it has the disadvantage of being rather imprecise. Where he certainly went wrong is in accusing Basilides and his immediate followers of gross immorality. For Clement cites ascetic, strictly moral, even somewhat puritanical utterances of Basilides and Isidore to confound later Basilidians who were not so particular [16]. In the same line we find the accounts of Epiphanius (more orderly) [17] and some others [18].

3. What remains of Basilides' writings

I feel the best thing we can do is to follw the approach of Leisegang who begins his disquisition with the few authentically Basilidian texts we have [19]. The first fragment comes from the thirteenth book of Basilides' 'Gospel Commentary'. This book began as follows. "As we begin the thirteenth book of our Treatises, the salutary saying (= the Gospel text) will provide a necessary and fruitful saying (= the Commentary). It shows, in the parable of the poor man (Lazarus) and the rich man [20], whence sprouted the nature without root and place, which has come upon the things" [21].

An enigmatic text! For the ordinary Bible reader this parable suggests a more practical interpretation. Leisegang proposes the idea that this text has something to do with theodicy, the question of divine justice. After all, the poor good man is rewarded, the bad rich one punished. Perhaps the problem of the origin of evil is looming in the background. And what can 'nature without root and place' mean? We shall have to come back to this.

After this opening phrase, as quoted in the 'Acta Archelai', five hundred lines are omitted, and then comes a somewhat longer authentic citation. First Basilides says contemptuously that he will "cease from the empty and curious diversity", by which in all probability Greek philosophical opinions are meant. Having swept these out of the way, he says that he will rather turn to the barbarians - an utterly unhellenic proposition! - in order to hear what they have to say "about good things and bad, and what conclusions they have reached on all those things" [22]. This confirms the opinion that Basilides was wrestling with the question of the origin of evil. Greek philosophy had not enlightened him on this point.

"Some of them (the barbarians) have said that there are two origins of all things, and with them they have associated good and evil; they say that the origins themselves are without origin and unoriginated; that is, in the beginning there were light and darkness, which existed of themselves" [23]. It is not difficult, of course, to recognize in this description the doctrine of Zoroaster, or rather its Zervanite derivation [24]. This is the radical or absolute dualism of two opposed and unconnected worlds.

The literal quotation goes on to explain that darkness tried to encroach upon the light but failed, the light remaining as pure as it was. Nevertheless, darkness succeeded in catching a glimpse of the light, no more than a reflection, a lustre. "Hence there is no perfect good in this world, and what (good) there is is very weak, because of what was received in the beginning (= only a glimpse - F.) But still, through this little light, or rather through a certain lustre from the light, what was created was able to create something similar; this goes back to the mixture it had received from the light. And that is the creation which we see" [25].

Leisegang thinks that it would be rash to conclude from this fragment that it reflects Basilides' own view; it could be that he intended to confront it with his own, different opinion [26]. This is, of course, conceivable. But why then did the Acta Archelai leave out the refutation? It should, for honesty's sake, have presented it. I feel that the author of the Acta must have believed (or known) that Basilides agreed with what is written here. Anyhow, this fragment fits admirably into the general trend of Gnostic thought, in the respect that it explains that there is 'no perfect good' in the world, that there is only some weak light in it, and that this light can hardly hold its own. Whether or not Basilides wholly agreed with this radical Persian dualism [27] is an open question, but it supplied him with an answer where evil came from [28].

In another equally authentic fragment, this time taken from the twenty-third book of the Gospel commentary and reported by Clement, Basilides is speaking of the Christian martyrs. Common opinion has it that they died because they were Christians. This is wrong. They have sinned, albeit undetected. It was God's privilege for them that they were actually accused of quite different things [29]. But in fact the martyrs were punished for their sins. Nobody is really sinless. Even a little child has sinfulness in him, although it does not actually sin. Perhaps we might imagine a sinless man but although he did not sin, he nevertheless wanted to. "Even if he has done nothing bad, I will call him bad because he wanted to sin" [30]. Basilides seems to include even Jesus in this rigorous censure. "I will say that whatever man you name is man ... For as some one says : 'Nobody is free from dirt'" [31]. Clement states expressly that Basilides was speaking here of Jesus who, in his eyes, was a sinner too [32].

Why did Basilides stretch his argument to this extremity? Because he wanted to safeguard God against any suspicion that he could be the source of evil. "I will say anything rather than call Providence bad" [33]. The consequence is a dualistic separation of God and man : "Man is man but God is just" [34]. Evil remains confined in the nether, the human world; God, being totally outside this world, can in no way be associated with it. As Leisegang says, this is deep pessimism, a pessimism that is not rare in Greek thought [35] : all grief in the world is in fact a punishment for a guilt (the guilt of being world, of being human) that is ineluctable, even for Jesus. I have argued earlier that such pessimism is one of the roadways leading to dualism [36].

4. The report of Irenaeus

a. The Pleroma

Let us now turn first to Irenaeus and also to Epiphanius for a more or less systematic account of Basilidian doctrine. Epiphanius begins with an unequivocal statement : " There was un ungenerated principle that alone is the Father of all things" [37]. This unambiguously rules out a dualistic starting-point by positing a single one [38]. Then follows a series of emanations. "From this (the first principle) proceeds Nous, from Nous Logos, from this Phronêsis (Prudence), and from this came Dynamis

(Force) and Sophia." These two caused the powers, potentialities, and angels to be.

b. The heavens

What now comes is a feature characteristic of Basilidian doctrine. The angels made a heaven, the first one, and peopled it with other angels, emanating from the first group. This second group made another heaven, the second one, within it yet another group of angels. And so on, and so forth, until there were 365 heavens in all. "That is why the year has that number of days, in accordance with the number of heavens" [39]. Seized by a poetic furor, says Epiphanius, Basilides assigned names to each of the rulers of all these heavens [40].

The great chief (archon) of all those heavens together is Abraxas, says Irenaeus. Because there are 365 heavens, "he has 365 numbers in him" [41] which means that the sum of the numerical values of the letters of his name is 365 [42]. The background of this idea of there being as many heavens as days in the year is, of course, the Greek notion of the correspondence of the macro- and microcosmos. For the same reason the Basilidians held that the human body counted 365 parts [43].

c. The world

The reader will by now be sufficiently acquainted with Gnostic thought to guess that, the further we descend, the less the quality of the aeons becomes. The very last heaven is the vault of heaven, the dome of the fixed stars, as we see it. The angels who rule this dome "set up everything in the world, and divided between them the earth and the nations upon it" [44]. Each nation on the world, therefore, has its own angel who is more like a stern ruler than a guardian angel. It will strike the reader that there is no Demiurge; all the angels together act as 'demiurges', as creators, without being called so. The ungenerated first principle of all has no direct part in the creative process; it is only by proxy of his umpteenth emanation that he is represented. I know of no other Gnostic system in which the first principle is so hermetically sealed off from the world; the number of interposed aeons in the Basilidian system is ten times greater than in Valentinianism, as we shall see in the next chapter. The dualistic distance between the first principle and mankind is immense.

d. The God of the Jews

Just as the celestial aeons have their own supreme chief in Abraxas, the nations of the world have as their sovereign prince the God of the Jews. What the Jews call their prophecies come from the ones who made the world; the Law derives from the Jewish God [45]. In other words, there is no good in it. The God of this world was enormously ambitious; he tried to subject all other nations to the Jews. But "all the other principalities (= the angels of the nations) opposed him and worked against him" [46]. Am I wrong if I believe I can detect here, for the very first time in history, the idea of a Jewish conspiracy to rule the world - an indictment that lives on till in our own time, for instance in the ill-famed (spurious) 'Protocols of the Sages of Sion'? Anyhow, this passage has a decidedly anti-Jewish ring.

It should be noted that, just as there is no real Demiurge, there is no real Fall. The substitute for the Fall is the seizure of power by the Jewish God; from then on everything goes wrong on earth. The whole world was in turmoil now, apparently through the fault of the Jews.

e. Christ

The unoriginated Father, perceiving 'their (the nations') disastrous plight', sent his first-born Son, the one "who is called Christ". His task was "to liberate those who believe in him from the power of those who made the world" [47]. Christ appeared in the shape of a man, in a human body, and is identical with Jesus. The problems about his nature which so beset the Valentinians (see next chapter) are entirely absent here.

Nothing is said of his birth and his life, except that he performed miracles; the name of Mary is not mentioned nor are the apostles.

The paramount interest seems to have been whether or not Christ suffered on the cross. The Basilidians think he didn't. It was Simon of Cyrene who carried the cross on which he was to die. The problem why nobody noticed why Jesus was no longer there is solved by stating that he transformed Simon of Cyrene into himself. "Jesus took on the form of Simon, and stood laughing at them" [48]. The reason why Basilides took recourse to such a cheap trick will be evident. Coming from the first principle Christ was essentially incorporeal and, in consequence, could not suffer. Before the crucifixion he disentangled himself from this world and "ascended to him who has sent him, since he could not be held (down here) and was invisible to all" [49].

Then comes the almost obligatory attack on Christian belief. "It is not right to confess him who was crucified (= the Jesus of the Gospels) ... If anyone confesses the crucified (as orthodox Christians do - F.), he is still a slave, and under the power of those who made the bodies" [50]. To be free means to deny the crucified Jesus.

f. 'Those who know'

It is at this point that the redeeming gnoosis appears. "Those who 'know' these things have been set free from the rulers who made this world ... (They) 'know' the (saving) dispensation made by the unoriginate Father" [51]. "Only to us, says he (Basilides), has he (the Saviour) revealed the truth of this matter" [52]. Once again the Gnostics parade as a privileged race, set apart from the common run of the unknowing. "We, he (Basilides) says, are the men; the rest are all pigs and dogs. That is why he (Jesus) said : 'Do not throw your pearls before the swine and do not give the holy things to the dogs'" [53].

The privileged are few in number. "Not many can know these (doctrines), but one in a thousand, and two in (ten thousand) ... Just as the Son (Christ) was unknown to all, so they (the Gnostics) also should be recognized by none; but whereas they ... pass through them all (= the angels of this world - F.), they are themselves invisible and unknown to all ... They say they are no longer Jews, but yet not Christians; and their secrets must not be uttered at all, but they must keep them concealed by silence" [54]. Just as in other Gnostic systems, salvation is not for the body; "the body is by nature corruptible" [55].

g. Conclusions

It is time for a few conclusions. First of all, this text throws a perhaps unexpected light on the often repeated notion that Gnostics are really Christians. These Basilidians categorically state that they are neither Jews nor Christians. Epiphanius expressed this even more pointedly : 'no longer Jews, no longer Christians' [56].

Next, we often hear that whereas the Basilidian system is presented as monistic by Hippolytus, it is dualistic in the version of Irenaeus. But Irenaeus too sees only a single starting-point, the unoriginate Father from whom everything emanates. It is true that already with these emanations a principle of division is to be recognized, and also that the quality of the emanations deteriorates the further down we come, so that, in the lowest echelon, a Fall or a fatal Error, becomes possible. One could, therefore, maintain à la rigueur that the principle of evil, operating in the lower world, was latently present in the Father too, since it, with everything else, must have proceeded from him. But there is not a word in the text to make this explicit. Futhermore, the 365 heavens, interposed between the blameless Father and the wicked world, form an almost impregnable barrier shielding off the Father from evil.

There is no talk of the Fall in definite terms. But the text, such as we have it, suggests that something untoward occurred in the lowest heaven, that nearest to earth; anyhow, there, all of a sudden, the ambitious and arrogant Jewish God appears. There is a clear dualism between the upper and nether worlds, the last one being the realm of ignorance. Then there is also the dualistic separation of those who know and are saved by Knowledge and the rest.

5. The Hippolytan version

Let us now turn to the version of Basilidian theology as given by Hippolytus; in many respects it differs from the report by Irenaeus.

a. Rootless nature

Perhaps the reader will remember the phrase found in the Acta Archelai that "nature sprouted without root and place". What may this mean? Nothingness, and the 'creatio ex nihilo' [57]? Quoted by Hippolytus, Basilides says indeed that "there was a time ..., when there was nothing; not even nothing was there, but simply, clearly, and without any sophistry, there was nothing at all" [58]. We see Basilides struggling here with the fundamental problem that the human mind is incapable of imagining 'nothing'; it always becomes 'something', however vague or diffuse.

This text speaks of God in terms of the 'theologia negativa' which can only speak of him in terms of what he is not. His 'nothingness' is "above every name that is named". Names are confusing and inappropriate, even for the things of this world that needs must bear names. How then could a proper name be found for the ineffable "that is not even ineffable"; even the slightest suggestion of bringing it into contact with a name must be dropped [59].

Hippolytus then defines the Basilidian starting-point in emphatic but wholly negative terms. "There was nothing, no matter, no substance, nothing insubstantial, nothing simple, nothing composite, nothing imperceptible, no man, no angel, no god, nothing at all that could be named." Was there a God? There was one, indeed! But a 'non-existent God' [60]. The bewildered reader may ask who is somebody who is not. However, it should be clear that Basilides does not mean at all that God does not exist; he is very far from being an atheist. On the contrary, he expresses himself in this way, "because he wants to safeguard God from all criticism and all attacks" [61]. Not the remotest thought of God being the source of evil should take form in a human mind.

b. God the cause of this world?

God certainly is the cause of this world : "(he) wished to make a world". But then again the Basilidian author falls over backwards in order to make God's part in the creational work infinitesimally small. He uses the word 'wished' only because he feels constrained to use some word or other. This 'wish' is described once again in negative terms, for it was "without intelligence, without perception, without will, without resolve, without impulse, without desire, (that God) wished to make a world" [62]. Just as the author wanted to postulate a God who existed and did not exist at the same time, he needed a God who was a creator and not a creator by the same token.

c. The world-seed

In this line of reasoning it is perfectly logical that God did not make the world as it is, but only provided its very first beginning, a 'world-seed' [63]. Just as small mustard-seed has all the elements of the later large plant already in it, or as an egg contains the beginning of the fowl that will come from it, so "the non-existent (sic) seed deposited by the non-existent God has (within it) the multiform and heterogeneous seed-mixture of the world" [64]. Bardy is correct in saying that "it is the uppermost preoccupation of Basilides to enlarge as much as possible the distance separating God from the world" [65]. I therefore do not understand why the version that is presented by Hippolytus is so glibly called monistic, for instance by Foerster who states that Basilides is "the one who harnessed his Gnosis in the most consistent way to a monistic system" [66]. It is as dualistic as is imaginable; the non-existent God treats the world-seed as a foundling.

The Basilidian author repeats once again : "the seed of the world came from the non-existent" [67]. This effectively rules out the idea of 'emanations', of celestial entities that form an ontological ladder reaching down to the cosmos and connecting it, albeit in the very last resort, with the primal God. "Basilides shuns and abhors the essence of things produced by emanations"[68]; in consequence, the world-seed must not be seen as an emanation either. All the created things lay stored up in it, and, with regard to what was contained in it, we should not ask where it came from, "since it had been previously determined by the non-existent that it should come into being"[69]. So the origin of creation has to remain shrouded in mystery, with the result that we can in no way ascribe the origin of evil to God.

d. The threefold Sonship and the Spirit

The main element that was in the all-containing seed, the 'panspermia', is "a three-fold Sonship, in all respects the same as the non-existent God, which came into being from the non-existent". This 'Sonship' consists of three parts, a light one, a coarser one, and one in need of purification[70]. True to its nature, the light part strives upwards back to God[71]. The coarser part would like to do the same but is unable to effect this because it has no 'wing'[72]. This 'wing' is the Holy Spirit, originating from nowhere, but needed to carry the coarser part aloft.

This Spirit was not allowed to remain near God, 'for it was not of the same substance and had no nature (in common) with the Sonship"[73]. Although it was relegated to a lower sphere and "remained without any part of the Sonship and separated from it, (it) has within itself ... a fragrance of the Sonship"[74]. The place of the Spirit is near "the place where we are", the world that is[75]. The Spirit, therefore, serves as a mediator, or a trait d'union, between the upper and nether world.

e. Two worlds

For a moment we shall have to leave aside the third part of the Sonship, that which is in need of purification. Basilides now first posits two worlds. "The things that exist are divided (by him) into two adjacent and principal divisions; the one is called according to him Cosmos and the other the Supermundane, and the limit between the world and the Supermundane is the Spirit"[76].

f. The Great Ruler of the Cosmos

Out of the cosmic seed, out of what was still in it, there arose another being, the Great Ruler, the archon of the cosmos, "the head of the world, of a beauty and power which cannot be spoken of ..., superior to any beautiful thing whatever you might mention" [77]. He soared up as high as he could, but then hit on the firmament, the frontier between both worlds that he could not pass. Since he could not go further, he thought he was on top of everything, supposing "that nothing whatever existed beyond (and was) surpassing everything you might call good, excepting only the Sonship which was still left behind in the world-seed" [78]. We are in the presence here of a world-ruler but not of a wicked one; he is expressly stated to be 'great and wise' [79]. It should, however, not be lost sight of that he is fundamentally ignorant; he knows nothing of the upper world.

g. The Son of the Demiurge

"Deeming himself to be lord and master and wise architect he (the Demiurge) turned to the detailed construction of the world." But obviously he felt unequal to his task and therefore "begot a Son much better and wiser than himself ... When he saw his Son, he was filled with astonishment, admiration, and consternation" [80]. There certainly was some reason for consternation, for the new entity is superior to its father. But this must not upset us, "for the non-existent God has purposed all these things in advance, when he deposited the world seed" [81].

How the roles in the creational act were divided between father and son remains somewhat unclear. "The whole celestial ... creation was the achievement of the great and wise Demiurge himself. But the Son born from him was effective in this and proposed it to him, being much wiser than the Demiurge himself" [82]. We may well ask whose work it really was. And also why the Demiurge, great and wise as he is, needed a counsellor who is superlatively wise. According to Hippolytus, Basilides explained this by making use of Aristotelian philosophy : the body of itself can achieve nothing, it needs the soul to make it effective. This notion is applied to the Demiurge and his Son. The Demiurge is compared to the physical, organic body, and the Son to the soul that works and accomplishes. "The Son manages the God (the Demiurge)", states Basilides [83]. Perhaps we must see the Demiurge as organic matter, and the Son as the evolutionary, finalistic principle working in it. This principle is the really divine part in creation.

h. The lower archons

What the Great Ruler and his Son accomplished was the creation of the dome of the fixed stars, the eighth heaven or Ogdoad [84]. Their creational activity did not extend further than this. For the rest a second Ruler is needed, also arising from the world-seed but much inferior to the first archon and Demiurge. He too begets a son more prudent and wise than himself. What they accomplished between them is the creation of the Hebdomad, or the seven planetary spheres, and all that is underneath it [85]. There is no doubt that this second and lower archon is identical with the Jewish God : "This is the ruler of the Hebdomad who spoke to Moses" [86].

j. The third Sonship and his Gospel

The reader will remember that in the world-seed there was a threefold Sonship. Two of these Sonships have been mentioned; the third is still in the seed. Now that "the whole world and the supermundane things were ... finished, and nothing was lacking", the time has come for the third Sonship to be revealed [87]. This revelation is provided by the Gospel that goes out from the Sonship, and, through the Son of the Great Ruler, reaches the Demiurge himself. What the Great Ruler now learns is that he is not, as he thought, the supreme godhead of all but was generated himself. "He was converted and became afraid, for he perceived what ignorance he was in" [88]. After the Great Ruler had been instructed, "the whole creation of the Ogdoad (= the sphere of the fixed stars) was instructed and taught, and the mystery was made known to the heavenly spheres" [89].

The Gospel, therefore, is the source of illuminating and redeeming Knowledge. It clearly is not be thought of as 'scripture' but rather as a divine message or a light sent from above. It is something entirely different from what orthodox Christians understand by it; it is infinitely more than a book for human beings. Next the Gospel descends to the Hebdomad, the planetary spheres. In handing down the Gospel the Son of the Great Ruler was active; somewhat unexpectedly we hear that he is the Christ [90]. He poured the light that he himself had received from the third Sonship and with which this Sonship had illumined the Great Ruler, on the Son of the Ruler of the Hebdomad, the second and lower Ruler that is. He too was illumined in his turn by his Son and repented [91].

Finally, the Gospel will reach the still formless sphere, dark and unknowing, where humanity lives [92]. The light that came from above now shone on Mary and through her on her son Jesus [93]. Basilides accpted all that was said of the biography of Jesus in the Gospels : "All that concerns the Saviour happened in a similar way to what is written in the Gospels" [94]. But in all probability he interpreted the events of Jesus' life in his own way. "These things happened", says he, "so that Jesus might become the first fruit of the distinction of kinds among which was confused" [95].

Now what are these 'kinds' that must be distinguished? Remember that the cosmos is divided into the Sphere of the Eight, into the Sphere of the Seven, and into the sublunar terrestrial sphere. Whereas the two upper spheres are beautifully ordered and have their own Rulers, the terrestrial sphere is characterized by formlessness. It is in this formlessness and indistinctness that the third Sonship resides [96]. This is an image of the unredeemed state of humankind; there is a divine element in it, a parcel of the light, but it goes unheeded and has still to be delivered.

This delivery was effected by the passion of Jesus (who in this version is not identified with Christ). After and through his resurrection the 'distinction of kinds' took place. His bodily part had come from formlessness and had to remain there. When he rose up he surrendered its psychic part to the Sphere of the Seven from which it had originated. He left a third, unspecified part of his being with the Ruler of the Ogdoad. What finally remains was his real self, the knowing part, that leaves all the spheres behind it and soars on to the first Father of all, taking the purified third Sonship with him [97].

k. The fate of the world

Once the threefold Sonship has been reunited in the Pleroma, "all the men of the Sonship may follow", by which is meant the Gnostics who have accepted the Gospel of the light [98]. When these too have gone up, not a single parcel of light remains in the terrestrial sphere. The whole world will be given over then to the 'great ignorance' that, from then on, will prove incurable. The souls of the unknowing will stay here below without having any idea of the Pleroma. They may live on forever, but if such a soul oversteps the limits of its nature, destruction will be its lot [99].

Even the two Rulers, those of the Ogdoad and the Hebdomad, will be gripped by the great ignorance, "so that they may in no way strive for what is contrary to their nature and feel pain" [100]. Their ignorance, therefore, is a blessing in disguise; by keeping them in their allotted places it makes life tolerable for them. This contains a warning to non-Gnostics not to strive after knowledge that they are viscerally incapable of attaining. The final result of this re-ordering is "the restoration of all things, which were founded in the beginning according to nature in the seed of the universe" [101]. In other words, only then is the creation definitely completed.

l. Some conclusions

It is time to look back. Very probably we shall never know which of the two versions, that of Irenaeus or that Hippolytus, is the original one. It is possible that Hippolytus had access to primary sources that were not known to Irenaeus so that he was able to present the more complete and precise account. Anyhow, it is remarkable that, although he is nearly always dependent on Irenaeus, he this time steers his own course.

As I have pointed out, the Hippolytan version is sometimes called monistic. This would be appropriate only if, descending from the first Father to the smallest particle of life on earth, all that is were to form part of one uniform system, or, in other words, if there existed one long chain of being or a great hierarchy of existents in which each element partook in the divine essence of the first particle. But we have seen that this chain broke off between the Father, the first principle, and the 'world-seed'. After depositing this seed and providing it with a part of his own power, the Father lost all interest in what was going to happen; he indeed is no longer even mentioned. Henceforward we must think of him as the deus ignotus et absconditus of all the Gnostics.

Furthermore, there is a well-defined boundary between the supermundane or pleromic world and the cosmos. This boundary is the firmament of the fixed stars over which the Holy Spirit stands guard; or rather, "the limit between the world and the Supermundane is that Spirit" [102]. This frontier can only be passed by Jesus and by those who have acquired the redeeming Knowledge. The terrestrial world, below the firmament, is the abode of the third Sonship as long as he unpurified. Here we have the usual Gnostic rejection of all that is material; since the third Sonship dwells in this material world, he can, in consequence, only be cleansed by leaving it.

The same applies to the elect. The fact that both Rulers, that of the Ogdoad and that of the Hebdomad, are, for a time, provided with Knowledge, forms part of the saving action for the third Sonship, for the light that is imprisoned in matter, in bodies. As soon as this liberation has been effected, the Rulers no longer need the Knowledge; it would only harm them. The result is that the upper and nether worlds are hermetically and dualistically sealed off from each other. The celestial world is that of light and Knowledge, the cosmos that of ignorance and darkness. The only contact that ever existed between them had the purpose of making the liberation of the light possible. After that the safety-curtain goes down between the two worlds.

6. The Basilidian community

We know hardly anything of the followers of Basilides, the Basilidians. Isidore, his son, is the only disciple we know by name. The sect was at home in lower Egypt, with its base at Alexandria. Whether there were also adherents in Rome or in southern Spain is a moot point; it is generally held not to be very probable. In the first half of the third century Origen often spoke of them, which proves that he must have known them. But after that little or nothing is heard of Basilidians. In the later part of the fourth century they were, according to Epiphanius, still flourishing in Egypt [103].

Basilides certainly did not enjoy the same popularity as Valentinus [104]. Peake ascribes this lack of popularity to the following reasons: "His (Basilides') abstruse speculations as to the non-existent God, the universal seed, and the third Sonship, were too exalted for many of his followers; and the system quickly experienced a moral and speculative degradation" [105].

NOTES TO CHAPTER VII

1. G. Bardy s.v. 'Basilide", Dict.Hist.Géogr.Eccl. 6 (Paris, 1932), 1128. This Basilides is not to be confused with Saint Basilides, an Egyptian, who died a martyr's death in Alexandria in 202/203. It is a curious fact that Jonas, in his 'Gnosis und spätantiker Geist' as well as in his 'The Gnostic Religion' passes over Basilides and his sect almost in silence.
2. Clem.Al., Strom. 7.106.1.
3. See Vol. VII, Ch. III.3.
4. See Vol. VII, Ch. III.2.
5. See Vol. VII, Ch. III.1.
6. Epiph., Panarion 22.1. Ir., Adv.haer. 1.24.1, too vaguely suggests that there was a doctrinal relation between Simon/Menander and Basilides.

7. Hipp., Ref. 7.20.
8. Hegemonius, Acta 67.4. The same text says that this dualism was sustained by a certain Scythianus; I have not been able to find out who this man was. Scholars hold different views of the trustworthiness of Bas.' stay in Persia. Antonio Ferrua, Enc.catt. 2, 970, says that it "non sembra attentibile", whereas G. Krüger, Realenz.prot.Theol.u.Kirche 2, 431, thinks that it is "uncontrollable, but not really improbable".
9. Clem.Al., Strom. 7.106.1; Ir., Adv.haer. 1.24.1; Eus., Hist.eccl. 4.7.3.
10. Epiph., Panarion 24.7.1.
11. Hipp., Ref. 7.20.1. Quispel s.v. 'Gnosticism', Enc.Rel. 5, 571, states that Basilides "was never excommunicated and remained a respected member of the Church of Alexandria until his death". I nowhere found any evidence in the sources to corroborate this statement. Perhaps it is a consequence of this scholar's tendency to turn all Gnostics into good Christians.
12. Bousset, Hauptprobl. 61.
13. G. Krüger s.v. 'Agrippa Castor', Realenz,prot.Theol.u.Kirche 1, 257.
14. Clem.Al., Strom. 4.7.6; what Hier., Viris ill. 21 and Theodor., Fab.haer. 1.4 have to report on Bas. goes back on Eus.
15. Only once in NHC the name of Basilides is mentioned, as the father of Isidore, without any further information, Testimony of Truth, NHC 9.3.57.8.
16. Clem., Al., Strom. 3.1-3.
17. Epiph., Panarion 24.1.
18. We find a good account of the sources for Basilides' life and doctrine in Hendrix, Basilides Ch. III, section 2, 25-33.
19. Leisegang, Gnosis 203.
20. Lc.16:19-31.
21. Hegemonius, Acta 67.5.
22. Hegemonius, Acta 67.7.
23. Hegemonius, Acta 67.7.
24. See Vol. IV, Ch. IV.8-12, and Vol. V, Ch. I.5.
25. Hegemonius, Acta 67.8-11.
26. Leisegang, Gnosis 204.
27. Hendrix, Basilides 45/46, thinks that Basilides' dualism must be ascribed to Persian influence. In some sources, he writes, Bas. clearly is a precursor of Mani.

28. The fact that Bas. shows himself so well acquainted with Iranian doctrine might lend some force to the disputable assertion that he was a teacher in Persia once. There has been scholarly discussion around this fragment, triggered off by the fact that its dualism does not agree with the alleged monism of the report of Hipp. "There can be no doubt", writes A.S. Peake in Enc.Rel.Eth. 2, 428 (Edinburgh, 1909), s.v. 'Basilides, Basilidians", "that the author of the Acts understood him to be a dualist, but that, of course, does not settle the question. He may have misunderstood Bas., especially since his (Hegemonius') preoccupation with Manichaeism made such an interpretation of the Gnostic doctrine not unnatural to him". As though the whole Gnosis was not thoroughly dualistic!

29. Clem., Al., Strom. 4.81.1.
30. Clem.Al., Strom. 4.82.1.
31. Job 14:4.
32. Clem.Al., Strom. 4.83.1.
33. Clem.Al., Strom. 4.821.
34. Clem.Al., Strom. 4.83.1.
35. Leisegang, Gnosis 206.
36. See Vol. I, p. 133; Vol. II, p. 113; Vol. III, Ch. I.8n.
37. Epiph., Panarion 24.1.
38. Ir., Adv.haer. 1.24.3, too knows only the 'unoriginate Father'.
39. Ir., Adv.haer. 1.24.3; Epiph., panarion 24.1.
40. Epiph., Panarion 24.2.
41. Ir., Adv.haer. 1.24.7.
42. From the Basilidians his name was transferred through the ages to medieval magicians and alchimists, Hendrix, Basilides 63.
43. Epiph., Panarion 24.7.6.
44. Ir., Adv.haer. 1.24.4.
45. Ir., Adv.haer. 1.24.5.
46. Ir., Adv.haer. 1.24.4; Epiph., Panarion 24.2.
47. Ir., Adv.haer. 1.24.4.
48. Ir., Adv.haer. 1.24.4; Epiph., Panarion 24.3.
49. Ir., Adv.haer. 1,24.4; Epiph., Panarion 24.3.
50. Ir., Adv.haer. 1.24.4.
51. Ir., Adv.haer. 1.24.4.
52. Epiph., Panarion 24.3.

53. Epiph., Panarion 24.5.2.
54. Ir., Adv.haer. 1.24.6; Epiph., Panarion 24.5.4.
55. Ir., Adv.haer. 1.24.5; Epiph., Panarion 24.5.
56. Epiph., Panarion 24.5.5.
57. Leisegang, Gnosis 204.
58. Hipp., Ref. 7.20.2.
59. Hipp., Ref. 7.20.3.
60. Hipp., Ref. 7.21.1.
61. G. Bardy s.v. 'Basilide', Dict.Hist.Géogr.eccl. 6, 1171 (Paris, 1932).
62. Hipp., Ref. 7.21.1.
63. Hipp., Ref. 7.21.2.
64. Hipp., Ref. 7.21.3-4.
65. G. Bardy s.v. 'Basilide', Dict.Hist.Géogr.eccl. 6,1171 (Paris, 1932).
66. Foerster/Wilson, Gnosis 62.
67. Hipp., Ref. 7.22.4.
68. Hipp., Ref. 7.22.2.
69. Hipp. Ref. 7.22.6.
70. Hipp., Ref. 7.22.7.
71. Hipp., Ref. 7.22.8.
72. Hipp., Ref. 7.22.9.
73. Hipp., Ref. 7.22.12.
74. Hipp., Ref. 7.22.14.
75. Hipp. Ref. 7.22.15.
76. Hipp., Ref. 7.23.1.
77. Hipp., Ref. 7.23.3.
78. Hipp., Ref. 7.23.4.
79. Hipp. Ref. 7.23.7.
80. Hipp., Ref. 7.23.5-6.
81. Hipp., Ref. 7.23.6.
82. Hipp., Ref. 7.23.7.
83. Hipp., Ref. 7.24.1-2.
84. Hipp., Ref. 7.24..3.
85. Hipp., Ref. 7.24.3-4.

86. Hipp., Ref. 7.25.4.
87. Hipp., Ref. 7.25.1.
88. Hipp., Ref. 7.26.1.
89. Hipp., Ref. 7.26.4.
90. Hipp. Ref. 7.26.2.
91. Hipp., Ref. 7.26.4-5.
92. Hipp. Ref. 7.26.7.
93. Hipp., Ref. 7.26.8-9.
94. Hipp., Ref. 7.26.8.
95. Hipp. Ref. 7.27.8.
96. Hipp., Ref. 7.27.9.
97. Hipp., Ref. 7.27.10-11.
98. Hipp. 7.27.1.
99. Hipp., Ref. 7.27.2-3.
100. Hipp. Ref. 7.27.3-4.
101. Hipp., Ref. 7.27.4.
102. Hipp., Ref. 7.23.2.
103. Epiph., Panarion 24.1. Hendrix, Basilides 93, says that, generally spoken, their sect was not be found outside Egypt.
104. G. Bardy s..v. 'Basilidiens', Dict.Hist.Géogr.eccl. 6, 1178-1180 (Paris, 1932).
105. A.S. Peake s.v. 'Basilides, Basilidians', Enc.Rel.Eth. 2, 432 (Edinburgh, 1909).

CHAPTER VIII

THE VALENTINIANS

1. The founder

In his book on the Gnostic religion Hans Jonas begins his chapter on the Valentinian Gnosis in this way. "Valentinus and his school represent the culmination of what in want of a better word we have been calling in this study the Syrian-Egyptian type of Gnostic speculation" [1]. Who was this Valentinus?

Of his life very little is known. He was born an Egyptian (probably around 100 A.D.) in that hotbed of creeds, Alexandria, where he was grounded in Greek scholarship [2] by a certain Theodas (or Theudas), it is said. Clement has it that this man had been a disciple of the Apostle Paul [3]. Hippolytus says that his heresy was based on the doctrines of Pythagoras and Plato [4], so that Tertullian could call him 'Platonicus Valentinus' [5]. Anyhow, he must have been a highly gifted and well-educated man. Jerome says this of him : "No one can bring a heresy into being unless he is possessed, by nature, of an outstanding intellect and has gifts provided by God. Such a person was Valentinus" [6]. There can be no doubt that he was "one of the most gifted and versatile minds of the early Church" [7].

After a first spell of professional life in Alexandria, Valentinus went to Rome, arriving there during the pontificate of Hyginus (136/138-142/143); he stayed in the capital during that of Pius I (143-154/155), and was still there when Anicetus was bishop of Rome (154/155-166) [8].

Tertullian reports a story that Valentinus aspired to become bishop of Rome, to which office he felt his brains and his eloquence entitled him. But, so the story goes, he was passed over by somebody else, probably Pius; because of this rebuff, he is said to have broken with the Church [9]. In all probability this is only legend; it is not very likely that such a brilliant man as Valentinus was would have turned heretic overnight just because he felt slighted. A long period of gestation must have preceded the last move. Scott even says that "it is more than probable that he never formally detached himself from the orthodox Church" [10]. What seems probable is that, at least nominally, he was still a Christian when he arrived in Rome.

It is far from clear what he did after he had left the Church, apart from composing a number of writings. If we believe Epiphanius, he preached his new creed when still in Rome. But he was also active in Egypt and in Cyprus where he is said to have died leaving behind many disciples [11]. Epiphanius, however, is not the most reliable of the early Fathers of the Church. Irenaeus seems to contradict him when he writes that he died in Rome [12]. If this is correct, Valentinus never left Rome. The exact date of his death remains unknown.

2. The literary output of Valentinus

What did Valentinus write [13]? Irenaeus mentions a 'Gospel of Truth' : "(The Valentinians) have gone so far in their audacity that they call a recently composed work of theirs 'Gospel of Truth', although it corresponds in nothing with the gospels of the apostles" [14]. Now in the Nag Hammadi Library, as part of the Codex Jung, an 'Evangelium Veritatis', a 'Gospel of Truth', written in Subachmimic Coptic, is to be found [15]. This work is anonymous but unmistakingly Valentinian [16]. The two great questions are : is this the book meant by Irenaeus, and was its author Valentinus? First of all, the book bears no resemblance to the biblical gospels, not being a biography of Jesus.

These two questions, it goes without saying, have elicited a lot of discussion and controversy. Let me restrict myself to the well-pondered opinion of the Dutch scholar R. van den Broek, Quispel's successor in Utrecht State University. With regard to the first question he writes that Irenaeus' "report contains nothing to suggest that the Gospel of Truth to which he is alluding, is another book than that found back in Nag Hammadi" [17]. It would indeed be strange should there have been two Valentinian Gospels of Truth.

Respecting the second question, the problem is that the (Nag Hammadi) Gospel's doctrine is not yet vintage Gnosis. There is, for instance, no wicked Demiurge; his place is taken by Error. However, we know for certain that there existed a Valentinian Gospel of Truth, and also that Valentinus had his own Gospel. This leads almost automatically to the conclusion that the great Gnosticus himself was the author. Furthermore, the text is stylistically identical with the authentic Valentinian fragments that we know of old. For these reasons, Van den Broek ascribes the authorship of the Gospel to Valentinus [18].

The problem that the Gospel does not contain a fully developed Valentinianism he solves in this way. The fact that Valentinus was passed over in the episcopal election radicalised his thought; after that he became an out and out Gnostic. But he must have been 'gnosticizing' already before that fatal moment; it is to this gnosticizing that the Gospel bears witness. Van den Broek thinks that its contents must have seemed acceptable to many Christians in Rome after A.D. 140; the tone of the work is restrained and hardly Gnostic [19]. It distressed Irenaeus that many Christians were so easily misled and did not see a heresy in the Gnosis (by which he meant the Valentinian doctrine in particular), just like people who are unable to distinguish between costly emeralds and an artful glass imitation [20]. Epiphanius seems to suggest that Valentinus was acquainted with earlier Gnostic systems [21]; if we understand Irenaeus correctly, then the Sethian and Ophitic doctrines must be meant [22].

Of the other works of Valentinus we possess only fragments [23]. There are also fragments of a few letters [24]; of his homilies only a few lines have been handed down to us [25]. Valentinus was also the author of psalms of which only seven lines survive [26]; although their author is sometimes celebrated as a great poet, Bardy finds these lines, from a poetical point of view, 'rather mediocre' [27]. Finally, Valentinus reportedly wrote a book called 'On the three natures' of which nothing but the title is known [28].

3. What Valentinus intended to do

In spite of this all in all rather meagre harvest, it is, perhaps, possible to penetrate somewhat further into the mind and mentality of this eminent Gnostic. He attempted something great. The reader who has followed me so far, throughout Chapters IV, V, and VI, will probably have become somewhat confused. So many Gnostic prophets, groups, doctrines have filed past, all of them different and not rarely contradictory among each other. This fragmentation was doubtless one of the main reasons why the Gnosis as such proved incapable of holding its own against orthodox Christianity. What Valentinus set out to do was to construct "out of the chaotic materials of Gnostic tradition ... a harmonious body of thought in which there are not a few elements of real speculative value" [29]. Because of his importance it is necessary to get as clear a picture of the workings of his mind as possible.

Valentinus tells us that he once had a vision in which he saw a very young boy. Asked who he was, the boy replied that he was the Logos [30]. In a psalm fragment he reports that he saw in the spirit how all things hang together [31]; this was, to use a modern term, a 'holistic' vision. These few instances make it clear that this Gnostic prophet had a "visionary character that puts him along the prophets of the oldest Gnosticism" [32].

4. The first stage : the Gospel of Truth

a. The necessity of Knowledge

Let us begin our quest of Valentinianism with an analysis of the Gospel of Truth which in all probability represents its first stage [33]. Already the very first paragraph contains the typical Gnostic key-words. "The Gospel of Truth is a joy for those who have received from the Father of truth the gift of knowing him." The implication is that 'Knowledge' is only to be had as a gift from above, not by human means. One receives the Knowledge "through the power of the Logos that came forth from the Pleroma". The Logos is not brought forth or created but is an emanation of the Fulness. It is "in the thought and mind of the Father"; it is set "to perform the work of redemption of those who were ignorant of the Father" [34]. The problem of mankind is not sin but ignorance; celestial knowledge and human ignorance form the great contrast.

b. The Father and the Son

The Father is, as is customary, sketched as 'incomprehensible, inconceivable, and superior to every thought' [35]. The supernal godhead remains entirely beyond the human ken. The Father is indicated as 'Nous', thought, or mind. From his Nous the Word emanates, the Logos, "the first to come revealed". Nobody can know why this is so, because the Father's will is incomprehensible [36]. The Logos is also called 'Son', and is the same as Christ. Very probably the Logos-Son must not be seen as a really new being but rather as an aspect of the Father. "Now the name of the Father is the Son ... who was himself ... The Father's name is not spoken, but it is apparent through a Son" [37].

c. The aeons

If I understand the text well, all the other 'aeons' (or 'logoi', by which term other supranatural entities are meant) are brought forth by the Son [38]. They too are aspects of the divine Nous [39]. I believe the Gospel is very intent on keeping the Pleroma really 'full'; separate creations, even if they occur in the supreme sphere, seem to suggest a sort of split. The leading idea is that there can be no 'apartheid', no dualism of any kind in the supernal realm; dualism remains reserved for the lower regions only.

"All the emanations of the Father are pleromas, and the root of all emanations is in the one (=the Father) who made them all grow in **himself** (my emphasis)" [40]. So obsessed is the author with his 'full' fulness that he accepts a certain illogicality by speaking of 'pleromas' in the plural, as though there could be more than one. The Son is sent to proclaim the Pleroma as the resting-place and to glorify it and the name of the Father [41].

d. Error

Outside or under the Pleroma "ignorance of the Father brought about anguish and terror. And the anguish grew solid like a fog so that no one was able to see." A new opposition arises, that between the luminous upper world and the murky nether world. In this world "Error became powerful". It is typical for the Gospel that there is no mention of a Fall but, instead, of Error. "It set about making a figure ('plasma'), with (all its) might preparing, in beauty, the substitute for the Truth". This opposition between the world of Truth and its mendacious substitue would be yet another example of dualistic contrast.

Of course, Error was unable to hurt the Father at all, because the anguish and the oblivion and the lying caused by it (the hallmarks of the nether world) were nothing, "while the established Truth is immutable, imperturbable, perfect in beauty" [42]. "Oblivion (obviously equated with Ignorance - F.) did not come into existence because of him (= the Father)" [43]. This means that, although the Father is the ground of all that is, the existence of oblivion or Error must not be directly imputed to him. But the Father is the immediate cause of the existence of Knowledge. Knowledge and oblivion are mortal enemies : "If the Father comes to be known, oblivion will not exist from that moment on" [44].

For this reason the creature that was mentioned above, is 'without any root'. "It (Error) fell into a fog regarding the Father" [45], that is, it was without any cognizance of the higher world. "Error tried to entice those of the middle and capture them" [46]. Who are 'those of the middle'? If we follow the well-known Gnostic division of mankind into three groups, the 'pneumatics' or 'spirit-people', the 'psychics' or 'soul-people', and the 'hylics' or 'matter-people', then the term 'middle' refers to the 'soul-people'. The 'spirit-people, having the Knowledge, are certain of salvation; the 'matter-people', being hopelessly ignorant, are doomed to perdition. But the 'soul-people' may be redeemed if they are able to choose between salvation and doom [47]. It could be that with 'those of the middle' orthodox Christians are meant.

e. What is wrong with the world

The present world is seen as a deficiency, "for the place where there is envy and strife is a deficiency". It is contrasted with the Pleroma, for "the place where (there is) Unity is a perfection". "The deficiency came into being because the Father was not known; therefore, when the Father is known, from that moment on the deficiency will no longer exist." What is wrong with the world is its ignorance. However, the Son is sent to blot out the deficiency. This will also mean the end of the present state of the world, even of the world itself, because there is no talk of a re-creation [48].

Now follows a highly telling passage. What is wrong with the world is not only its ignorance but still more its multiplicity. This multiplicity is seen not only as an imperfection but even as an impurity. "Within Unity he (the Valentinian Gnostic) will purify himself from multiplicity into Unity, consuming matter within himself like fire, and darkness by night, death by life ... Deficiency vanishes into the perfection ... The form (of this world) will vanish in the fusion of Unity, for now their works (i.e. of Ignorance and darkness - F.) lie scattered. In time Unity will perfect the spaces. It is within Unity that each one will attain himself" [49].

This offers us an insight into the basically puritanical Gnostic mind. Puritans are people who want to have things nicer than they really are. Gnostics are mentally incapable of standing (and understanding) the multiple state of the world and its material basis. For this reason, they postulate a spotless, immaterial, spiritual world, dualistically opposed to our concrete world. To this world the opprobrious terms 'deficient, impure, dark, dead' are used as equivalents of multiple.

f. Jesus the Christ

It is evident that the Gospel is not intended for everybody; it is "revealed to those who are perfect through the mercies of the Father". With the 'perfect' the spirit-people, the pneumatics are meant, the Valentinian Gnostics, that is. The phrase is somewhat inconclusive : do they become perfect through divine mercy, or are they already perfect before they receive it? What, however, is crystal-clear is who brought these mercies, or perhaps rather, who is mercy himself. He is 'Jesus the Christ, the hidden mystery'. As far as I know, this is the first time that Jesus and Christ are identified in a Gnostic text. But are they identified without any reserve? I feel that, as to the relationship between Jesus and Christ, some remarks would be in place since the later Valentinus manifestly had problems with it. I shall come back to this when we are speaking of full-fledged Valentinianism.

Jesus Christ "enlightened those who were in darkness. Out of oblivion (= ignorance) he enlightened them; he showed them a way. And the way is the truth which he taught them" [50]. But "Error grew angry at him (and) persecuted him ... He was nailed to a tree". This is one of the few biographical details of Jesus' life in the Gospel (the tree is the cross, of course); nothing, however, is said of a resurrection and an ascension. Instead, we find that "he became a fruit of the Knowledge of the Father ...; to those who ate it it gave (cause) to become glad in the discovery" [51]. I don't believe that this 'eating' is a reminiscence of the Eucharist; it rather means that the believer makes himself spiritually one with Christ and with Knowledge [52].

g. The 'book'

Jesus acted as a teacher. "He became a guide ...; he went into the midst of schools (and) he spoke the word as a teacher. Then came the wise men - in their own estimation - putting him to the test. But he confounded them because they were foolish. They hated him because they were not really wise". This alludes to Jesus' battles with the scribes and Pharisees who are seen here as the representatives of Ignorance. Those who are really receptive to Knowledge are the little children : "They knew, they were known" [53].

The teaching of Jesus is described as a 'book', 'the living book of the living'. We must not think here of the New Testament or of a Gnostic document, for it was written "in the thought and the mind of the Father" [54]. This book was destined only for Jesus. It will be evident that with it the secret Knowledge is meant which was initially in the possession of Jesus alone. "No one was able to take it since it is reserved for the one who will take it and will be slain (= Jesus)." Once again the Gospel is speaking of a Knowledge that is utterly different from all kinds of human knowledge, a divine Knowledge. It is the only means of salvation, for "no one could have appeared among those who believed in salvation unless that book had intervened" [55]. The consequence is that the 'book', not being material, is unaccessible to those to whom it has not been disclosed.

h. Sleep and awakening

Listening to the Gospel of Truth is described as a process of awakening. "This is the way each one has acted, as though he were asleep at the time when he was ignorant. And this is the way he has come to Knowledge, as if he had awakened. (And) Good for the man who will come to and awaken" [56]. This is similar to the difference between being and non-being, equivalent to the fundamental opposition of Knowledge and Ignorance. They "have cast Ignorance aside from them like sleep ... The Knowledge of the Father they value like the dawn" [57]. Now they become wisdom themselves. "The Knowledge given by the Gospel of Truth is also self-knowledge, that is to say, a re-cognizing by the spiritual one of his divine origins" [58]. This self-knowledge entails that the chosen ones realize that there is a dualistic distance between the world of the

Pleroma and the cosmos, and an equally dualistic one between them and the matter-people [59]. "Speak of the Truth with those who search for it, and (of) Knowledge to those who committed sin in their error ... For you are the wisdom that is drawn forth" [60].

The condition of the ignorant is not enviable. "They were ignorant of the Father, he being the one whom they did not see. Since there were terror and disturbance and instability and doubt and division, there were many illusions at work because of these, and (there were) empty fictions, as if they were sunk in sleep and found themselves in disturbing dreams" [61]. Those who never accept the Gnosis are destined for doom. "He who is ignorant until the end is a creature of oblivion, and he will vanish along with it" [62]. This is the dualistic division of mankind into the knowing who will be saved and the unkowing who are doomed to extinction.

The situation of the knowing is very different from that of the ignorant. They (the knowing) "possess (something) from above the immeasurable greatness, as they stretch out after the one alone and the perfect one, the one who is there for them. And they do not go down to the underworld nor have they envy nor groaning nor death within them, but they rest in him who is at rest ... They themselves are the Truth, and the Father is within them and they are in the Father, being perfect, being undivided in the truly good one" [63]. "This is the word of the gospel of the discovery of the Pleroma" [64].

j. The true nature of Jesus

It was precisely his death on the cross that revealed Jesus in his essential nature. "Having stripped himself of the perishable rags (= the body), he put on imperishability which no one can possibly take away from him". We encounter here the common Gnostic tenet that there is no resurrection of the body. At the same time we discover the equally common contempt of the body lovingly indicated as 'rags'. "Having entered the spaces of terror, he passed through those who were stripped naked by oblivion." This very probably means that he was able to leave unscathed the horrible nether world that is peopled with hopeless ignorants; he could do this since he himself is 'knowledge' and 'perfection' [65].

k. The Gospel of Truth as a Gnostic tract

In conclusion of our disquisition on the Gospel of Truth something must be said of its status as a Gnostic-dualistic tract. We are justified in not seeing it as full-blown Valentinianism. True enough, one of the most characteristic Gnostic notions is playing a conspicuous role throughout the text, namely the notion of Knowledge, as 'gnoosis', as the beginning and end of everything, as the means of redemption. Ménard counted almost sixty occurrences of the words 'to know' and 'knowledge' in this text; for this reason he says that the tract presents itself as a disquisition on knowledge, but then on a knowledge that refers above all to knowledge of God who is identified with Truth [66].

Furthermore, there is a pronounced dualistic distinction between the upper and nether worlds, a feature that is common to all Gnostic systems; the author does not hold what is material and corporeal in high esteem, to put it mildly. As always, the human body is not destined to enter celestial bliss. It is only the Spirit, the pneuma, that counts.

The Fall, however, is not strongly emphasized; the term itself is not used, instead we find 'Error'. How this Error originated is not explained but in any case it should not be imputed to the Father. "The deficiency of matter has not arisen through the limitlessness of the Father ...; the thought of error did not exist within him" [67]. This is a marked difference with fully developed Valentinianism where the crisis occurs within the Pleroma itself, that is, within the divine sphere, and among the direct emanations from the Father. Here there is no talk of splits within the Pleroma.

There is also no wicked Demiurge who creates a bad world, apart from some vague talk of Error "fashioning its own matter foolishly" [68]. Although the created world is far from perfect, it is not rejected in such fierce terms as we have become used to. It is as though the author is still somewhat reticent on this issue. If he is Valentinus, he is obviously no longer an orthodox Christian but he has not yet gone over to the Gnosis lock, stock and barrel [69].

5. Vintage Valentinianism

From the somewhat confusing fact that we possess no less than six not wholly identical renderings of the Valentinian system [70], it has sometimes been concluded that there simply was no Valentinian doctrine. This seems a somewhat rash conclusion since, as Rudolph rightly remarks, a number of basic tenets are to be discovered in all Valentinian schools of thought. Gnostics are not dogmatic; they did not acknowledge a magisterium. The differences between the various schools can easily be explained by their letting the spirit blow where it wanted [71].

The following quotation from Epiphanius who is citing literally a Valentinian text, introduces us to the mystical atmosphere of the sect. "Indestructible Nous greets the indestructible ones! To you I make mention of secrets nameless, ineffable, super-celestial, which cannot be comprehended either by the dominions or the powers of the lower beings, nor by the entire mixture (= the cosmos), but have been revealed to the Ennoia (Thought) of the Immutable alone" [72]. Then follow the mysteries of the first beginnings.

a. The Depth

"Before the beginning of all beginnings, there exists", asserts Irenaeus, "in the invisible and ineffable heights a pre-existent, perfect aeon whom they (the Valentinians) also call Pre-beginning, Forefather and Depth (Bythos). Incomprehensible and invisible, eternal and unbegotten, he was throughout endless ages in serenity and quiescence. And with him was Silence (Sigē)" [73]. This sounds to me like the mysterious beginning of Bruckner's Fourth Symphony.

The term 'Depth' must be interpreted as the Primal Cause of all that is. In all the variants of the Valentinian doctrine, "the beginning of all things is a monad, which is unbegotten, imperishable, inconceivable, incomprehensible, productive, and a cause of the generation of all created things. (This) monad is called ... Father"[74]. This sounds very much like monism, or even undiluted monotheism, but there is reason for doubt. The attentive reader will doubtless have remarked that the Father is not alone but is 'with Silence'; the significance of the existence of Silence is that it reminds the Gnostics of the necessity to remain quiet and silent in their innermost self, which is the only means to escape from Multiplicity and to return to the Unity[75].

Bousset wrote that "Valentinus and his disciples tried to overcome oriental dualism (with which he meant Iranian dualism - F.) by a speculative monism - with the help of the idea of emanations". But he added somewhat ruefully that "the traces of the basic gnostic-dualistic concepts everywhere shine through"[76]. Much later Jonas commented that, indeed, "the introduction of a 'monism' seems totally to contradict the basic dualistic position of all Gnosis". "The ground of being (= the Father) generates its own dualism", for the concrete, phenomenal world, material as it is, is the absolute opposite of the Spirit, erring, lost, and lapsed as it is[77]. The notion of an absolute Spirit, the monist principle, and that of a bad cosmos do not bear with each other! Jonas concludes that in the chain of emanations whose purport it is to connect the initial monism with the Gnostic world view, dualism uncurtailedly reappears[78].

b. Ennoia

Right at the start, Irenaeus presents a remarkable thing. Along with the Father, he writes, "there existed also Ennoia (Thought), whom they (the Valentinians) also name Grace ('Charis') and Silence ('Sigê')"[79]. Does this signify that we have to do with a dyad instead of a monad? It can hardly be doubted. Anyway, he contradicts Hippolytus who wrote that "the Father was without any other entity capable of being thought in any way. He was alone ... and reposing in isolation within himself"[80]. Since Hippolytus speaks of a monad and Irenaeus suggests a dyad, there is a contradiction here between the two reports; it could be that Irenaeus is referring to a later system, that of Ptolemaeus. "As to whether the Fore-Father or Abyss (Depth) was originally alone or was matched from the outset with Silence there was great difference of opinion among the Valentinians", says Jonas [81]. Utterly self-contained and self-sufficient as it is, the Bythos (Depth) can hardly be believed to have also been the source of generation. To become really a Father, he needed a second being who, in all probability, was co-existent and co-eternal with him.

c. Emanation

"Since he was productive, he (the Father) decided once to generate, and bring forth the fairest and most perfect that he had in himself, for he was not fond of solitariness" [82]. The Father having it 'in himself', what came forth was an emanation from him. However, the process is described in sexual terms. "Like a seed, he deposited this production which he resolved to bring forth, as in a womb, in that Sigê that was with him. She then, on receiving this seed, became pregnant and gave birth to Nous (Mind)" [83].

Epiphanius is still more explicit. "The imperishable Ennoia (Grace, Silence) wanted to spring the eternal fetters and stir up inclination for a woman in the Greatness (the Father) so that he desired to lie with her" [84]. What a revealing passage this is! Not so much because of its blatantly sexual imagery but rather because the first principle here clearly is dual. There even is an inkling of dualism, of breach within the Greatness, since the Father does not want to tread out of himself but has to be goaded into this by means of feminine wiles.

The Nous "was both like and equal to him who produced him, and who alone comprehended the greatness of the Father", says Irenaeus; in other words, he too is an emanation. "This Nous they (the Valentinians) also call Only-begotten (the Son, that is) and Father and Beginning of all. Along with him there was produced Truth ('Alêtheia')" [85]. We see here the first of the 'suzugiai' or pairs (unless the original couple 'Father-Sigê' is one of the suzugiai) that are needed to connect the Father with all the worlds lower down.

d. The Pleroma

The Son, the Only-begotten, is rightly called 'Father' too, because he is "the father of all things that come into being after him, as well as the beginning and forming of the whole Pleroma" [86]. Hippolytus, however, has it that Nous (male) and Truth (female) form "a Dyad, which was mistress, beginning, and mother of all the aeons which they (the Valentinians) number within the Pleroma" [87]. The really important thing is not who or what fathered or mothered the Pleroma but that the Pleroma did not start with the Depth or Primal Cause. In Valentinian theology this does not constitute a part of the Pleroma but is beyond and above it. Once again, the first godhead is kept at a safe distance from all that may resemble creation.

With the Pleroma we are already one stage further down in fact. It is "a means to bring the abstract and inaccessible God into relation to the actual world. The Pleroma is the first outgoing of God from himself, the manifestation of the Absolute in a sphere of being which is still, in some sense, one with Him. This process of self-unfolding is continued on an ever-descending scale until at last the divine principle is merged in the depths of matter" [88].

Valentinus himself presents us with some sort of a 'chain of being'. "I behold all things suspended by Spirit; I see how in the ether all is mixed with Spirit; I perceive all things borne on by Spirit - flesh suspended from soul, soul upheld by air, air suspended from ether, and fruits produced from Depth, and the child born from the womb" [89]. Hippolytus who quotes this fragment explains that 'flesh' means matter in general. Matter is born by air, and air hangs on ether. The ether is the highest level of the created cosmos; here we find the Demiurge who is suspended from the Spirit or Pneuma. This Pneuma, however, must not be confused with the Father of all. Hippolytus says expressly that the Pneuma remains **outside** the Pleroma.

Having reached this level, we hit on the dividing line, the frontier, or 'horos', between the upper and nether worlds. Above this line the Pleroma arises, the realm of the pure and immaterial. It is beyond argument that the difference between the Pleroma and the cosmos is dualistic in nature. But like all national frontiers here on earth, this frontier too is not impregnable; in other words, the in-built dualism is not radical or absolute. Valentinus expresses this by the words "fruits produced from the depth, child born from the womb"; Hippolytus elucidates these somewhat mysterious terms by stating : "This is the whole emanation of the aeons from the Father" [90].

In the last resort, when all is said and done, all that is is dependent on the Father. "Thus the whole universe is conceived as an infinite gradation of being, instinct, though ever more faintly, with the power which has called it forth" [91]. But we shall see yet that by no means all is said and done. "The spirit of the visionary (Valentinus) has surged upward till into the Pleroma. From on high he is looking downward, he sees the Pneuma and ether, and also how the soul of the world struggles to free itself from the burden of matter" [92].

e. All the aeons

Let us remain with Valentinus for some moments on his lofty viewpoint in the Pleroma. With the pairs 'Father-Silence' and 'Nous-Truth' we have a Tetrad, a quaternity, called 'Pythagorean' by Irenaeus [93]; the Valentinians saw this Tetrad as 'the root of all things'. Nous came together with his consort Truth and produced with her another pair, Logos (Word) and Life, respectively male and female. Logos "was the Father of all things that come into being after him as well as the beginning and forming of the whole Pleroma" [94]. These two consorted with one another and brought forth the fourth pair, Man and Church (Ekklesia). By now we have four pairs together forming an Ogdoad. "This constitutes the primordial Ogdoad, the root and substance of all things" [95].

I can imagine that the reader has become somewhat confused. What then is 'the root of all things', the Father, the Pleroma, the Tetrad, the Ogdoad, the Logos? Let us ask Sagnard to explain this to us in his characteristically Gallic way. "This is like a successive manifestation of the infinite and hidden Principle. One goes from within to without. The Depth, the unknowable, manifests itself first of all as Intelligence (Nous, Mind), the principle of all knowledge, and also of all existence which must correspond to an Idea. Intelligence, in its turn, will express itself in profoundly harmonious liaison in the womb of the world, that is to say, as Logos. These liaisons in effect make it possible to catch what is characteristic in all things ... The first of the concepts designed by the Logos is Man, the most perfect image of the most perfect aeon ... He will be like a summary of the Universe; he will assume in himself matter and animal life and will also consist of a divine part ... This ideal Man is made for the Church, that is to say, for the ideal Assembly of the elect, of the initiated in the Gnosis" [96]. Since Sagnard also explains that the Logos is the Idea of all things and classifies them each in their particularity, we detect a definite Platonic turn of thought here. But this must not mislead us, because Valentinus is a theologian rather than a philosopher.

The two pairs of the second Tetrad produce other aeons (entities) in pairs, the pair Logos and Life ten of them, and the pair Man and Church another twelve, the last of these being Sophia [97]. The Pleroma, therefore, is divided into an Ogdoad (consisting of two Tetrads), a Decad, and a Dodecad, counting in all thirty aeons between them [98]. All the aeons beneath the Father of all are inferior to him, since they can only procreate in pairs of male and female, whereas "in the Unbegotten all things exist simultaneously", so that he does not need a paredra. "In the begotten the female brings forth the substance, while the male gives form to the substance" [99]. Since Sophia, the youngest of all aeons, was just as imperfect as them all, she could not procreate alone but, in order to have offspring, she needed her male partner, called Desired. At this point the trouble begins.

f. The Fall

Sophia was fatuous enough not to desire her natural partner but, instead, nobody less than the Father himself. This was not love at all, says Irenaeus, but temerity, "because she had no communion with the Father such as Nous shared" [100]. This shows that, although we are still in the Pleroma, the ontological distance between the highest and the lowest aeons is already considerable. Sopha "wished to comprehend his (the Father's) greatness" [101]. An impossible task, of course, for the Father is unknowable; but Sophia was not wise enough to realize this. "She wished to emulate the Father and to produce offspring of herself alone, without a partner, in order that she might achieve a work in which she would not be in any way inferior to the Father" [102]. In other words, she wanted to bring forth emanations instead of creations. As Foerster writes, "this perverse attempt is in fact lack of knowledge concerning God, and from it flows everything else" [103].

Here the accounts of Irenaeus and Hippolytus differ. According to the last mentioned, Sophia "brought forth that of which she was capable, an unformed and incomplete substance" [104]; this is what was to be expected, since, according to Aristotle, it is the male who gives form to the substance, and there was no male involved. In Irenaeus' account, Sophia was on the brink of losing her identity totally in the Father becoming "absorbed in the sweetness and dissolved in the total essence". In the nick of time, however, Sophia is saved by a special aeon, called 'Horos', the Limit. It was brought forth by the Father through the Nous as his image [105] - looking very much like a 'deus ex machina'. But its function is clear : "By it she (Sophia) was halted, supported, and, with difficulty, brought back to herself and convinced that the Father is incomprehensible" [106]. She had learned the hard way that there is an impassable barrier in front of the Father.

It is conceivable that, in this way, Valentinus sought to condemn all attempts by Hellenic philosophy to comprehend God [107]. If this supposition is correct, I feel that, remaining on Valentinian ground, we should include all Christian theology. What Valentinus means is that it is no use to speculate on God's essence. That the Limit is the Father's image means that incomprehensiblity is part and parcel of his being.

g. Matter

The reports about Sophia bringing forth something 'unformed' were known to Irenaeus too; he calls them 'mythical'. This 'unformed' thing, to all intents and purposes, is the earth as it is depicted in Gen. 1, the 'tohu wabohu', or else it is matter tout court. Right from the start it is made clear that matter, as the product of foolishness, is highly imperfect. Sophia was afraid of its imperfection. She even tried to hide it, just like a servant-girl who, having given birth to an illegitimate baby, becomes afraid and ashamed, and tries to get rid of it. "From here, from ignorance, from suffering and fear, matter had its inception" [108].

Irenaeus has this to add with regard to the nature of matter. Once cured of her senseless passion, Sophia was allowed to stay in the Pleroma, but her desire, with her passion, was cut off from her and left outside the Pleroma. "Although in itself a spiritual substance, since it was the natural instinct of an aeon, it (passion) was without shape and form, because it understood nothing. Therefore, they (the Valentinians) call it a frail and female fruit" [109]. Passion, as something irregular and ignorant, was banished from the upper world and firmly located in the nether, material world; we must not overlook the fact that it is dubbed 'female'.

h. Uproar in the Pleroma

Peace was not yet fully restored. The other aeons were horrified by Sophia's ignorance and by her bringing forth formlessness. "Uproar broke out in the Pleroma. The aeons, seeing what had happened, greatly feared that their own offspring would be just such an abortion as that of Sophia. She had by her stupidity jeopardized the whole Pleroma. But at the aeons' request and moved by Sophia's tears, the Father of all ordered an additional pair to be brought forth" [110]. This additional pair is constituted by Christ (male) and the Holy Spirit (female). They were engendered not by the Father of all himself but by Nous and Truth [111].

The task of the new couple was to set the Pleroma at rest. First of all, they took care that the other aeons did not set eyes on the 'abortion', since it would embarrass them 'because of its shapelessness' [112]. The dualistic dividing line between the upper and nether worlds flares up ever more distinctly! Christ restored rest to the Pleroma by imparting knowledge of the Father to the aeons. This knowledge actually consisted in their realizing that there is no knowledge of him. "The reason for the eternal permanence of the aeons is the fact that the Father is incomprehensible" [113]. This means that the stability of the Pleroma is guaranteed only by its ontological ignorance of the Father's essence. There is, in consequence, also a dividing line between the Father and the aeons but it does not signify dualism. The difference between the ignorance of the aeons and that of the earthly philosophers, exegetes, and theologians is that, whereas the aeons quietly and reverently accept it, their human counterparts do not. They constantly repeat Sophia's initial blunder with the same dire results.

Although order now reigns again in the Pleroma, nothing is as before. It looks now like a damaged painting that has been restored most carefully : on close inspection the slices made by the vandal's bowie knife can still be detected. The Pleroma, says Jonas, "possesses its integrity no longer simply and unquestionably but only in contrast to a negatively posited without". This 'negatively posited' is Sophia's 'abortion'. "The Limit was not planned in the original constitution of the Fullness, i.e. of the free and adequate self-expression of the godhead, but was necessitated by the crisis as a principle of consolidation and protective separation. The appearance of the figure itself (the Limit) is therefore a symbol of the beginning dualism as it dialectically arises out of original Being itself" [114]. We must realize that within the Pleroma there should be no Limit at all.

j. Jesus, the joint fruit of the Pleroma

The Holy Spirit too is a new emanation. Her (remember she is female!) task is it to make all the aeons "equal in form and perception, and they become all Noes (plural of Nous), all Logoi, all Men, and all Christs; similarly the female ones became all Truths, all Lives, all Spirits, and all Churches. When everything was thus established and had attained perfect rest, with great joy ... they praised the Forefather, for they had become very glad." Harmoniously united as they now were, they brought forth the most perfect beauty and star of the Pleroma, its perfect fruit Jesus, "whom they also call Saviour and Christ and Logos, after his Father, and All, because he is derived from all" [115]. Hippolytus adds that Jesus too is an aeon and the "joint fruit of the Pleroma, in order that he might be the proof of their unity, agreement, and peace". Here he is called 'the Great High Priest' [116].

k. Esoteric knowledge

That we are treading on sacred ground, in fact that we are trespassing, is indicated by Irenaeus. "This is not openly spoken of, they (the Valentinians) say, because not all are capable of knowledge of these things, but it is revealed, as in a mystery, by the Saviour through parables to those who are able to understand." Such a parable is, for instance, that "the thirty aeons are indicated by the thirty years during which they say the Saviour performed no public work" [117]. Here, as usual, the line is drawn between those who know and those who do not.

l. Sophia's offspring

We now return to the nether world where Sophia's rejected offspring, the 'abortion', dwells. It soon turns out to be a "Sophia' too, the 'lower Sophia', in contrast to the 'higher Sophia' who was converted from her error. She is also called 'Achamoth', a word derived from the Hebrew 'chokmah' = wisdom [118]; this means that there is some worldy wisdom in her, of no great value, "since she comprehended nothing (= of the higher things)". This entity is needed to show why there is so much folly and fatuity in the world. But Christ and the Holy Spirit make a rapid excursion, almost a sally, from the Pleroma towards Achamoth who is outside it; Christ gives her a form, a 'Gestalt' so to speak, "but only in respect of substance, not of knowledge" [119]. Once she has received 'form and security' [120], she has become an independent entity, a no longer formless but recognizable being.

However, she does not feel secure at all, quite the contrary! For Christ and the Holy Spirit immediately return to the superior regions, leaving her alone and without their help and protection [121]. This is a kind of punishment for her so "that she might become aware of the passion that belonged to her by reason of her severance from the Pleroma and might strive after better things, since she possessed a certain aroma of immortality which has been left in her by Christ and the Holy Spirit" [122].

The hasty departure of Christ and the Spirit made Achamoth fall "into a state of great terror ... She experienced grief and great distress" [123]. Because she was now intelligent but nevertheless deserted by the Logos, "she strained herself to search after the light which had departed from her, but she was not able to comprehend it, because she was prevented by Limit (= she was forbidden to enter the Pleroma - F.)" [124]. This faithfully portrays the situation of one who has realized that he is alone and without real knowledge; he has already progressed so far that he is aware of the higher urge in him. He sadly comes to understand that the higher world is debarred from him; he is incapable of entering it of his own accord. I suppose that this is the meaning of the curious communication by Irenaeus that, at the frontier between both worlds, Limit "prevented her (Achamoth) from striving any further:, saying "'Iao' and thus the name 'Iao' is said to have originated" [125]. Now Iao is one of the Gnostic names for the wicked Demiurge; what Limit wants to convey is that the celestial realm is that of the Father and the Pleroma, whereas the lower one is left to this Demiurge.

Having been rebuffed at the impassible frontier, Achamoth "fell into all sorts of sufferings ...; she experienced sorrow, because she had not comprehended; fear, lest life might abandon her, as light had done; in addition, perplexity; but all these (she suffered) in ignorance" [126]. These are the basic elements of the unenlightened human condition.

"From her fear and sorrow all the rest took its beginning" [127]. As all other Gnostics, the Valentinians took a gloomy view of the human condition.

m. A glimmer of hope

But in spite of all this, there remains a glimmer of hope. For there is in the lower Sophia also "another disposition, namely that of turning to him who gave her life ... From that returning (or : conversion) of hers every soul in the world and that of the Demiurge had its origin" [128]. She (the lower Sophia) "turned her attention to supplicate the light which had left her, that is Christ" [129]. This is in fact a description of the conditio humana. Humanity is dualistically torn apart between a downward urge and an upward surge. It is solidly encased in the nether world but after all it has a higher origin and faintly remember this.

The impulse towards the better, as we shall see, is not in itself sufficient to effect the return to the Pleroma. For the 'substance' that came forth from lower Sophia's (Achamoth's) 'conversion' is the 'psychic'. 'Psychic' is more than 'material' ('hylic') but less than 'spiritual' ('pneumatic'), and it is exactly the spiritual that is really necessary for the redemption. For the time being the spiritual remained beyond the reach of Achamoth. She implored Christ to return to her, but "he was naturally reluctant to descend a second time, and so he sent to her the Paraclete, that is, the Saviour" [130]. Hippolytus calls this Saviour 'the Joint Fruit of the Pleroma'; he was sent "as a marriage-partner for Sophia outside (= Achamoth), that he might rectify the sufferings (or : passions) which she experienced whilst she sought for Christ" [131].

n. The Saviour

To the Saviour who is nobody else than Jesus - we shall yet see wether we must distinguish Jesus from Christ - "the Father gave all power and put all things under his authority, and the aeons too" [132]. In other words, Jesus is made the universal ruler. What the Saviour does for

Achamoth is to give her knowledge and heal her of her passions. But with these passions the Saviour had his troubles. What had been possible for the higher Sophia - to rid her of her passions - proved not feasible for Sophia-Achamoth, because in her "the passions had already become fixed by habit and powerful"[133]. But on the other hand, "she could not continue with such passions"[134]. "Therefore he separated them (from her) and made them solid and transformed them from an incorporeal passion into (an) incorporeal matter"[135].

Another source, the 'Excerpta ex Theodoto', preserved by Clement of Alexandria, renders very clearly what happened. "From incorporeal and contingent passion he (the Saviour) moulded them (the passions) into a still incorporeal matter and then, in the same way, changed them into compounds and bodies - for it was not possible to turn the passions into substances at once - and he created in the bodies a capability according to (their) nature"[136].

o. Substances and bodies

Who is able to tell what 'incorporeal matter' is? Hippolytus makes a brave attempt; he speaks of 'substance-possessing essences'[137]. Should we think here of something like Platonic ideas that enable concrete things to exist? This seems to follow from Irenaeus' communication that the Saviour "implanted in them an aptitude and nature such that they could come together in (= result in) compounds and bodies so that two substances (= two kinds of substances) might come into being, the one evil, resulting from the passions, the other passible, resulting from the conversion"[138]. The dualistic split is carefully maintained.

At this point the accounts of Irenaeus and Hippolytus differ somewhat, the first mentioned speaking of three resulting basic substances, the second of four. One of the substances is matter, resulting from passion (Irenaeus) or sorrow (Hippolytus); the difference does not count. Hippolytus adds that distress led to a demonic substance, although there is no reference to this in Irenaeus; fear, says Hippolytus, leads to the psychic, whereas Irenaeus has it that the psychic came from conversion.

The difference is not so great as it may seem, for Hippolytus adds that the conversion, the entreaty (for something higher), and the supplication (of the soul) were made "into repentance and the power of psychic substance" [139]. Perhaps we should assume that fear leads to conversion.

p. The Demiurge

The first and principal formation made by Achamoth is the Demiurge. He is called Demiurge as well as Father, or even Father-Mother and Fatherless. This means that he has at least a twofold appearance, more simply stated, he is Right as well as Left. Formed from the psychic substance, from fear, says Hippolytus (not from the spiritual, that is!), he is "king of all those things which are of the same nature as he is, that is the psychics, which they (the Valentinians) call the Right, and of those things which sprang from passion and matter which they call the Left". Right and Left mean, as of old, that there is a better side and a worse one.

The 'creator of this world' [140] is Father to those of the Right, the psychics, that is to those who might be saved (probably the Christians), but the Demiurge to those of the Left, the hylics, the material ones, who are irrevocably lost [141]. "If it (the psuchê) becomes like those above (i.e. the higher Sophia and the Saviour - F.), then it is immortal ..., but if it becomes like matter, that is, the corporeal passions, then it is perishable and goes to destruction" [142]. This entails that a psychic may still become a hylic and share his fate. There must be no misunderstanding : initially, the Demiurge is "king of all ... because he was the creator of all that is psychic and material" [143].

But what about the creation of the pneumatics, the spiritual ones? It goes without saying that these cannot possibly have been created by the Demiurge; he is incapable of creating anything spiritual. We shall have to come back to this.

Hippolytus is very outspoken on the Demiurge. "The power of the material essence is an image of the Demiurge, and he is the Devil, the ruler of this world" [144]. Irenaeus entirely agrees with him, but he is more specific. The Valentinians, he writes, call the Devil 'the world-ruler'; he is a creation of the Demiurge. We now have to do with three ascending layers of entities, that must be carefully kept apart. The world-ruler, or Devil, "who dwells in this world of ours", is the lowest; he "knows what is above him, since he is a spirit of wickedness". What is above him is the Demiurge himself and the seven heavens made by him, the Hebdomad (as usual the seven planetary spheres - F.) in which he lives.

Atop of the planetary spheres Achamoth lives 'in the supra-heavenly place', called the Ogdoad. Irenaeus dubs this topmost and somewhat incongruous part of the nether world 'the Middle'[145], suggesting thereby that this sphere is intermediate between the upper and nether worlds; it links the two realms together, at least to a certain extent, because of the kinship between the higher and lower Sophias. Hippolytus adds a fourth nether-world sphere, the underworld, or Hades, ruled by Beelzebul[146].

q. The creation of man

The Demiurge made the visible world from the four elements[147]. After this, he made man, "not of this present dry land (as in Gen. 2 -F.) =, but out of the invisible substance, the liquid and flowing part of matter, and into him he bred then the psychic; finally, there was put on him the coat of skin by which is meant ... the flesh that is subject to sense-perception"[148]. It should be noted that the story of Gen. 2 is told here in the reversed order : there the Creator first fashions the human body and then breathes the life-spirit into it.

Hippolytus states expressly that "the Demiurge made bodies for the souls"; he made them "from the material and devilish essence". This is the usual Gnostic contempt of the body, in fact for all that is physical and material. The body will have no part in salvation. There is also a dualistic distinction between soul and body. "The material man ... is like an inn, or residence, either of the soul alone, or of the soul and demons, or even of the soul and Logoi." A psychic man has two possibilities : he may permit his soul to cohabitate either with demons or with Logoi. These "Logoi have been sown from above by the Joint Fruit of the Pleroma (Christ) and by (the higher) Sophia into this world, and they dwell in an earthly body if no demons reside with the soul" [149]. This makes it perfectly clear what is meant by 'Logoi' : it is Wisdom, Knowledge.

But how is it conceivable that elements of redemptive Knowledge trickle down into the human soul, the creation of the wicked and ignorant Demiurge? Foolishness is his hallmark. The line between Knowledge and Ignorance runs between the Ogdoad and the Hebdomad, between Achamoth and the Demiurge. He is totally ignorant of the existence of Achamoth [150]; in fact, he "knows nothing whatsoever, but is ... without understanding and silly, and does not know what he is doing or bringing to pass" [151].

"He was foolish and without understanding, and believed that he himself was creating the world, unaware that Sophia ... was accomplishing everything for the creation of the world, without his knowledge" [152]. Achamoth, who was "spiritual like the mother herself (the higher Sophia) ... was secretly inserted into him (the Demiurge) without him knowing it, in order that through him it (the pneuma, the spark of light) might be sown into the soul ... and into the material body, and having been born and increased there might be prepared to receive the perfect Logos (= to receive the redeeming Knowledge - F.)". This remarkable trick is needed to explain why there are also pneumatics in this world.

It was in the last resort Achamoth who made them. Irenaeus mentions that "what she brought forth ... was the spiritual" [153]. "Freed from her passions, (she) received with joy her vision of the lights coming with him (the Saviour), that is the angels with him, became pregnant ... and gave birth to progeny after their image, a spiritual offspring which was formed after the likeness of the Saviour's bodyguards" [154]. As Jonas writes, "this is the origin of the pneumatic element in the lower world" [155]. In this element the Gnostics in general, and the Valentinians in particular, participate.

The conclusion is that there exist two, or perhaps, three, races of human beings, the first being the pneumatics, the second the hylics, and lastly the psychics who can move in either direction. The difference between pneumatics and hylics is dualistic, not only with regard to their final destination but also respecting their origin, because the pneumatics stem from Achamoth and the hylics from the Demiurge. Since both Achamoth and the Saviour's angels have their root in the Pleroma, the pneumatics are of higher descent than the hylics whose progenitor is the ruler of the nether world.

The pneumatics are the seed of Achamoth, "known by them (the Valentinians) as the Church (the Valentinian sect), the image of the Church above; and they believe that this is the man (i.e. the real man, the pneuma) who is in them. Thus they have their soul (psuchê) from the Demiurge, the body from the dust, flesh from matter, and the spiritual man from the mother, Achamoth" [156]. The psychics and hylics concur in this that they both are unknowing. Jews (and probably also Christians) are ignorant. "All the prophets and the Law spoke from the Demiurge, a silly god ... For none of the prophets said anything at all concerning the things of which we speak (Hippolytus is obviously quoting Valentinus himself - F.). For everything was unknown because it was spoken by the Demiurge (who is the Jahve of the Old Testament - F.)" [157].

The Excerpta describe the final destination of the three races as follows. "The spiritual is saved by nature (= of itself, by being what it is); the psychic, being possessed of free will, has an inclination towards faith and towards incorruptibility, but also towards unbelief and destruction, but the material perishes by nature" [158].

r. Christ and Jesus

The Saviour of mankind is Jesus. Regarding his person there are three important questions : are Christ and Jesus the same person, what was the nature of the body of Jesus, and who underwent the passion?

The answer to the first question must remain ambiguous. The heavenly Christ was one of the aeons and was paired with the Holy

Ghost. But Jesus was also one of the aeons, the last one, brought forth after unity had been restored in the Pleroma. This means that, in the Pleroma, Jesus and Christ are different persons. It is Jesus who becomes the Saviour on earth, but since inclusiveness is the hallmark of the Pleroma, and since, as the last aeon, Jesus derives from the whole Pleroma, he is also Christ.

Are we to believe Hippolytus, then there were no less than three Christs : "1. the one brought forth by Nous and Truth along with the Holy Spirit (Christ and the Holy Spirit being one of the fifteen pairs of aeons - F.); 2. the Joint Fruit of the Pleroma, the husband of the Sophia outside (= the lower Sophia or Achamoth), who is also called Holy Spirit but is inferior to the first and higher one (in the top layer of the nether world the pair Achamoth-Spirit is a kind of replica of the Pleromic pair Sophia-Holy Spirit but necessarily of a lesser quality - F.); 3. the one born through Mary for the purpose of rectifying this creation of ours" [159].

It does not become quite clear in which way and in how far these Christs were interrelated, but interrelated they were. Anyhow, we have heard with sufficient clarity that the Saviour, the Christ from the Pleroma, descended into the body of Jesus. This does not mean at all that Jesus and Christ formed an integral whole so that we are allowed to speak of 'Jesus Christ', just as the orthodox Church does. "They (the Valentinians) hold that Jesus spoke partly under the influence of the Saviour, partly of the mother (not Mary but Achamoth), and partly of the Demiurge" [160].

The second question presented considerable difficulties to the Valentinians. They agree that he has a double origin. His mother was the Virgin Mary by means of the overshadowing by the Holy Spirit. From this one would conclude that the father of Jesus is the Holy Spirit. But once again the doctrine gives a most curious twist to a Gospel text. "The Holy Spirit will come upon thee (Mary) and the power of the Most High will overshadow thee" [161]. Hippolytus explains : "The Spirit is Sophia ... (and) the Most High is the Demiurge." For Jesus is not like other human beings who were "created by the Most High alone, that is by the Demiurge. Rather, Jesus is the New Man, (created) by the Holy Spirit and by the Most High, that is, by Sophia and the Demiurge, in order that the Demiurge might complete the formation and the equipment of his body, but the Holy Spirit provided his essence, and a heavenly Logos proceeds from the Ogdoad, born from Mary" [162].

Jesus the Saviour, therefore, has his origin both in the Pleroma, from where he derives his real self, his 'essence', and from the nether world, from where he has his body. This is wholly in keeping with the basic dualism of the Valentinians, of all Gnostics indeed, that nothing 'essential' can constitute an integral part of creation. Irenaeus provides a further explanation by saying that the body of the Saviour "was constructed by ineffable art (so) that it was visible, tangible, and capable of suffering" [163].

On the question of the Saviour's nature and origin a split arose in the Valentinian school. "Those from the (Middle) East - to whom Axionicus and Ardesianes belong - affirm that the body of the Saviour was pneumatic. For there came upon Mary the Holy Spirit, that is Sophia, and the power of the Most High, the creative art, in order that what was given to Mary by the Spirit might be formed" [164]. I feel that this may be understood in this way : the demiurgic art of fashioning bodies was for once delegated to Mary, so that the Demiurge would have nothing to do with the formation. If this supposition is correct, the Saviour to all intents and purposes would have an origin only from above [165].

The Jesus who came to redeem mankind was born from Mary but in a non-biological manner. For, because the text of Irenaeus states that "he passed through Mary as water passes through a pipe" [166], we are forced to assume that his body was non-material. This would imply that Mary is not Jesus' biological mother; she served only as an instrument. His real mother is Sophia. This probably is original Valentinianism. As a consequence of this, the Valentinians were ready to put up with the contradiction in terms of a 'pneumatic body'.

There can be no doubt that, in the view of Valentinus himself, Jesus only had a pneumatic, a spiritual body. Tertullian asserts that to the founder Christ's body was 'spiritalis' [167], whereas others saw it as 'materialis' [168]. However, the fact that Jesus was born through (and not from) Mary does not immediately mean that he was perfect. What was still lacking in him was Knowledge [169]. In a curious passage which he ascribes to Marc the Magician, a Valentinian Gnostic, Irenaeus reports that "the one who passed through the womb (of Mary) was chosen by the Father of all, through the intermediary of the Logos, with regard to the Knowledge of which he (the Father) must be the object" [170].

Marc added that this happened 'through the economy' ('kat' oikonomian'). According to Kaestli, this 'economy' does not designate the reign of the Demiurge but refers to the will of the supreme God who wanted to destroy death and lead mankind to Knowledge [171]. It will be evident that Jesus is a prefiguration of the Gnostics who, although from their birth selected as a chosen race, did not come into the world in full possession of the redeeming Knowledge.

It was only at the moment of his baptism that Jesus came into full posesion of the Gnosis through which, in the first place, he himself realized, or rather became, what he was intended to be. The Spirit who descended on Jesus is "the Spirit who spoke through Jesus, indicated him as the Son of Man, revealed the Father and came down on Jesus to unite himself with him" [172]. This too prefigures the situation of the Gnostic who, as soon as he acquires full Knowledge, becomes an elated person, living far more in the higher world than on this earth.

The straits into which Valentinus was driven by the question of how corporeal the Redeemer was is properly demonstrated by a quotation from a letter he wrote to a certain Agathophus. It says that "Jesus sustained everything and was self-controlled; he strove to possess divinity. He ate and he drank in a way that was peculiar to him because he did not secrete the food again (in other words, he did not need to use the toilet - F.). So great was the power of his self-control that the food in him was not subject to putrefaction, since he himself was not subject to decay" [173].

But difference of opinion arose. "Those of Italy - and to this group Heracleon and Ptolemaeus belong - say that the body of Jesus was psychic (i.e. of this earth - F.) and that because of his baptism the Spirit came upon him like a dove - that is the Logos of Sophia, his mother from above - and entered into his psychic body, and also raised him from the dead" [174]. This entails that Jesus was not born as the Saviour but only became so at the moment of his baptism in the Jordan, when he was already thirty years old. Irenaeus states this expressly : "There descended upon him at baptism, in the form of a dove, the Saviour from the Pleroma" [175].

The difference between the two branches of Valentinianism may seem smaller than it really is. In original Valentinianism Jesus has a far more elated origin and nature than the Italian group was prepared to admit. Both branches agreed on the central importance of Jesus' baptism. But the easterners held that Jesus, who was born as the Saviour, realized who he was through this particular event, whereas the Italians assumed that Jesus was not born as the Saviour but only became so when the Spirit descended on him. In consequence, they were far more prepared to concede that Jesus had a material body, in contrast to the easterners to whom it seemed inconceivable that the one who was born from the Pleroma as the Saviour would have a physical nature.

The foregoing discussion has in fact already provided us with an answer to the third question : who it was that suffered on the cross. The Saviour "is said to have remained far from suffering - for it was impossible that he should suffer, since he was unconquerable (i.e. by decay and death - F.) and invisible - and accordingly, when he was brought before Pilate, the Spirit of Christ placed in him (Jesus) was taken way" [176]. This is sufficient proof that the one who was nailed to the cross was not identical with the Christ Saviour. That the Saviour did not possess a real physical body is made clear by Valentinus' opinion that "Christ received nothing whatever material, for matter is not capable of being saved" [177]. The usual dualistic distinction of spirit and matter is strictly maintained in the Christ-Jesus relation too.

We must yet probe somewhat deeper, and, at the same time, round off our disquistion on this confusing problem. Valentinus obviously had considerable difficulties with the Christ-Jesus relationship. His

Christ is a complex being composed of four parts He is spiritual (his heritage from Achamoth), he is psychic (from the Demiurge), he is material (since he belongs to creation too), and, finally, he was endowed by the Saviour with a special gift that descended upon him from the upper world in the shape of a dove. The spiritual part of Christ, as the 'seed of his mother', was incapable of suffering, being invisible even to the Demiurge himself. What, however, could undergo the passion was the psychic part, but only after, when he stood before Pilate, the spirit was taken away. The departure of the spirit was the actual cause of his death. "He died when the Spirit which had come upon him in (the river) Jordan departed from him ...; it withdrew in order that death might operate .... But death was outwitted by craftiness. For when the body had died the Saviour sent forth the ray of power which had come upon him and destroyed death, and he raised the mortal body after he had scattered the passions. The psychic part is raised in this way and is saved" [178].

6. A different view of the Demiurge and his work

With regard to the Demiurge and his work a somewhat different stance is taken in the so-called 'Letter to Flora' written either by Valentinus himself or by some other prominent sage of the sect to a lady, Flora, probably a Christian, who wanted to be instructed in Valentinian doctrine; it has been preserved for us by Epiphanius. The writer states expressly that the world was created by a God "who is just and hates evil" [179]. This God must not be confused with the 'perfect God and father', the first godhead. This lower divinity is "the Demiurge and Maker of this entire universe and of what is in it".

He must certainly not be confounded with the Devil. "He is different from these two realities (the perfect God and the Devil) and since he stands in the midst between them, he rightly bears the name 'Middle'. And if the perfect God is good by his own nature ... and if the one of the opposite nature (the Devil) is evil and wicked ..., then the one who is situated in the midst of the two and who is neither good nor evil ..., can be properly called just" [180].

Should we now rush to the conclusion, as, for instance, Foerster does, that "the special position of Valentinianism is ... clear from the fact that the world is the work not of the Devil, but of a righteous God, who hates evil'" [181]? In other words, that the usual dualistic rejection of the cosmos and of all that is material is failing in this particular case? I feel this would be rather overhasty. First of all, the author of the Letter to Flora is guilty of contradicting himself when he first states that the Demiurge is righteous and hates evil, and then, later on, that he is neither good nor evil.

We have a remarkable quotation directly from Valentinus about the essence of the world. "The form is not exactly to the life, but the name supplies what is wanting in the effigy; the invisibility of God cooperates with what has been fashioned" [182]. What this signifies is this. "Valentinus compares the world to an imperfect image of God, which is inscribed, however, with the name of him whom it represents so as to authenticate it". In this way "he seeks to bring the abstract and inaccessible God into a relation to the actual world" [183].

This looks like an unwieldy attempt to revalue the cosmos somewhat, a cosmos that, although in this version it is an image of God, nevertheless is a very imperfect image. The clumsiness of the attempt is proved by the fact that first we have a cosmos that is not created by the first God but by the Demiurge, while only afterwards the first God came into it to put his seal onto it, although what all this adds up to is far from clear. The question is what could yet be repaired in an imperfect world that, although perhaps not created by a downright evil power, nevertheless is made by one who is as ignorant (about the Pleroma) as he is arrogant (since he imagines himself to be the sole God).

The ontological relation between Sophia and the Demiurge, as Jonas says [184] - we leave the Letter to Flora for one moment aside - is best expressed by a phrase in which she is called Spirit (pneuma) and he soul (psuchê) [185], which is a qualitative difference. Add to this that, although Epiphanius is not joined by Irenaeus in identifying the Demiurge as the Devil, the last mentioned author expressly states that the 'world-ruler', the Devil, is a creature of the Demiurge. He also writes that the cosmos is a highly imperfect imitation of the perfection of the Pleroma; the Demiurge was viscerally incapable of expressing what is great in the Fulness. "In consequence, truth eluded him, and he followed the lie. And for this reason his work will be dissolved at the end of times" [186]. It is in accordance with this that no good word can be said of this world, of mankind, and in particular not of the body. It is all doomed to perdition.

Returning now to the Letter to Flora, we may agree with Jonas that what it says of the Demiurge "is the most charitable view taken of the Creator in all the Sophia-gnosis, inside and outside the Valentinian school". The Letter looks very much like an erratic block, at variance with the main body of Valentinian doctrine. How can this be explained? Jonas continues by saying that its contents "are no more than variations of mood in the development of a basic theme". He even supposes that it was a matter of policy, because Valentinus did not want to yield up his real insights to one who was not a member of his sect - and, let me add, to a lady who was still a Christian and might easily be put off by the blasphemous idea of a wicked Creator. Jonas concludes that "by and large the traits we have met all along in connection with the 'gnostic' theology of the world-god are those of the Valentinian demiurge too" [187].

7. Heracleon's view

Heracleon was a rather independent disciple of Valentinus [188], even the most respected of all, says Clement [189]. He was active in Italy, maybe in Rome, during the latter half of the second century of our era; this is all we know of him. Of his writings only fragments remain, forty-eight in Origen's 'Commentary on John', and two more in Clement's 'Stromateis'. Origen drew the passages he is quoting from a book by Heracleon called 'Hypomnêmata'(= 'Memoirs'). This book itself is lost. Origen adds that Heracleon himself drew on an apocryphal book, the 'Praedicatio

Petri' (also lost), and that he had much of his doctrine from Valentinus and Marcion [190].

In Heracleon we have the very first author "of whom a coherent exegesis of a New Testament book has been preserved" [191]; we should take this 'preserved' as meaning that we know that he wrote it. That this book was a commentary on John will not surprise us if we know how liberally Gnostics quoted from this apostle whom they considered one of themselves [192].

There has also been discussion on the place of Heracleon in the general context of the Gnosis, and more in particular in that of Valentinian doctrine. This discussion is kindled by, for instance, the remarkable fact that Heracleon nowhere refers to the Pleroma with its aeons; in his upperworld only God is dwelling. This induced some scholars to suggest that Heracleon cannot be seen as a genuine representant of Valentinianism [193]. Is this verdict related to the fact that we do not have Heracleon's complete text? Or did he consider the Pleroma a senseless myth? Perhaps he felt more congenial with the 'Gospel of Truth', the early version of Valentinianism in which also no Pleroma figures. Pagels asks : "Could they (the Pleroma and the Gospel) represent, not a more 'highly developed' Valentinianism, but, on the contrary, an earlier and more original version" [194]?

However this may be, Pagels draws our attention to a quotation from Heracleon [195] where, commenting on Jesus' parable of the sower, he explains who is the sower and who is the reaper. He makes it entirely clear that the sower and the reaper are different persons. The apostles are not the sowers, they are the reapers. The seed itself was sown by the Son of Man 'beyond the place, beyond the Topos' [196]. Since the Topos can hardly mean anything else than the cosmos, the inference is that the sowing takes place in the upper world and is a pre-cosmic event.

Pagels concludes that "such references indicate that Heracleon ... does regard the pre-cosmic myth (i.e. the myth of the Pleroma - F.) as the presupposition of his theological exposition". But why then did he not expound this further? Pagels supposes that the commentary formed part of Heracleon's exoteric teaching, destined for outsiders, while the esoteric teaching, including the mythology of the Pleroma, remained reserved for the initiates [197].

Neither does Heracleon mention the pairs of emanations which, of course, does not mean that he did not acknowledge them. But he fully recognized the wicked Demiurge who fashioned this evil world. He also knew of the Logos, the Word. The fragments do not inform us where the Logos came from, although it must be assumed that its place of origin was the Pleroma. But then Heracleon makes a very remarkable statement. "Neither the aeon (the Pleroma is meant) nor what is in the aeon (the emanations) came into being through the Logos". This clearly restricts the activities of the Logos to the nether world.

As Gnostics often do, Heracleon amplifies a Gospel text, in this case one of John, for he adds to the words of Jo. 1:2 :"And without him noothing came into being" these words : "of the things in the cosmos and the creation". Origen comments that the aeon came into being before the Logos [198]. This stupifying text is 'uncharacteristic of Valentinian theology', although Pagels cautiously adds : 'at first glance' [199]. The Logos is the Saviour, states Heracleon [200], and the Saviour is Christ. However, we learn that the Logos-Saviour-Christ is not the same as the Demiurge [201].

Maybe Pagels is right in supposing that Heracleon did not intend at all to refer to the Pleroma but limited himself to a theology of the cosmos. According to her, this would not imply that, in Heracleon's view, there was no pleromic Logos-Christ but only that Heracleon wanted to speak of "the Logos who manifests himself as the creator of the cosmos and as the Saviour" [202].

Commenting on John's phrase in 1:4 "what was made in him was life", Heracleon wrote that this 'in him' must be understood as meaning 'for spiritual people' = for the Gnostics [203]. The redemption brought by the Saviour is for the 'spirituals' alone. 'Life' must not be interpreted as biological life but as something divine, a sort of life granted to the elect who, as a consequence, "stand in a special relation to the Logos" [204]. This does not look as though the Logos took a great interest in creating the less happy part of mankind. And in fact, he left a great deal of the creational work to the Demiurge, so that, after all, the Logos is not the direct creator of this world.

Instead, he "provided the Demiurge with the cause for creating the world ...; he gave the energy and another created" [205]. In another fragment, Heracleon plainly calls the Demiurge 'the creator of this world', but one 'inferior to Christ' [206]. This inferiority is graphically expressed by this same Gnostic author in this way : "The Demiurge is only a kinglet (not a 'basileus' but a 'basiliskos' - F.), for he too has authority over his subjects, but his realm is small and only temporary since he is installed by the universal king (the first godhead) over a little kingdom" [207].

This is a text rich in consequence. What immediately strikes the reader is the deprecating tone that characterizes references to the cosmos and the world (for this is the Demiurge's small and temporary kingdom). It is also remarkable that he is not only suffered but actually installed by the highest godhead. This does, of course, not mean that the primal godhead admired the work of the Demiurge but rather that this potentate does not exist by his own will. His realm will only last as long as it is tolerated and until it is definitely abrogated by Christ.

Our conclusion, with regard to the main theme of this work, is that we hit here on a very peculiar dualism. Two creators are at work here who do not exactly see eye to eye. The principal and only task of the Logos-Christ seems to be to give the pneuma to the elect thus redeeming them. This creates a dualistic division from all the rest of mankind which is left to the discretion of the Demiurge and apparently does not have much of a future. In this respect the doctrine of Heracleon does not differ at all from main line Valentinianism.

Heracleon's notion of the nature of Christ differs somewhat from that of the oriental Valentinians. On this point he rather agrees with Ptolemaeus, another prophet of the Italian school of Valentinianism; of whom too nothing is known biographically. According to both of them, Jesus did not become 'pneumatic' and the Saviour at the moment of his birth so that there was a period in which he was, so to speak, only latently pneumatic. As we saw, he was only assumed by the Logos-Saviour when he was baptized in the Jordan, and when he appeared before Pilate, the Logos left him. It was not his pneumatic but his psychic part that underwent the passion.

It is possible that the idea of the division of mankind, not into two groups, the pneumatics and the hylics, but into three, with the psychics added, was more at home in Italy than in the Orient. It is also possible that the category of the psychics was inserted into the original system in order to attract Christians by assuring them that they were not hopeless cases.

8. The Tripartite Tractate

There is in the Nag Hammadi Library a document entitled 'The Tripartite Tractate' [208], by an anonymous author, that may or may not be Valentinian. If it is Valentinian, then it is much nearer to the Italian school than to the Egyptian. This tract too presents the division of humankind into "three essential types, the spiritual, the psychic, and the material, conforming to the triple arrangement of the Logos". While the spiritual race is "like light from light ..., the psychic race is like light from a fire, since it hesitated to accept knowledge from him (the Saviour) who appeared to it. (It hesitated) even more to run towards him in faith" [209].

a. The Father, the Son, and the Church

It all begins with "the Father who is the root of everything" [210]. He is unbegotten and immutable, and "as to the universe, he is the one who begot it and created it" [211]. "He is the one who knows himself as he is" [212], that is, he is the fountain-head of real knowledge. "He alone is the good ..., the completely perfect one ...; there is no evil in him" [213]. The Father, in no sense different from the primal godhead of the Valentinian schools, is the first of the three primary members of this system.

The second is the Son, the first-born of the Father, existing like him 'in the fullest sense' [214]. The third of the three primary members is the Church; just like the Father and the Son, it exists from the beginning "in the conditions and the properties in which the Father and the Son exist" [215]. The notion of the Church as a root, as one of the primal elements of the Pleroma, is peculiar to this tract; according to Tertullian, this 'theological innovation' stems from Heracleon [216]. The Church must not be understood as the Catholic Church or even as the Valentinian community but as the celestial prototype of that community.

b. The Logos

"The text goes on", says the introduction by Attridge and Pagels, "to relate the process of devolution and procreation known from Valentinian sources in the form of the myth of Sophia" [217]. But then again there is a deviation from orthodox Valentianism. In this tract it is the lowest aeon, the Logos, who gets into trouble of his own making by wanting to do something that is beyond his own power. Here the Logos is identical with Sophia. In the Pleroma everyone is duly "silent about the incomprehensibility of the Father." But "it came to one of the aeons (the Logos) that it should attempt to grasp the incomprehensibility ... Therefore he took a nature of wisdom in order to examine the hidden establishment." In other words, he imagined himself to be wise enough to probe the mystery of the Father. Perhaps he did this because he "was the last aeon to have been brought forth ..., and he was very young in age".

The author stresses that "the intent of the Logos was something good", and he adds that it is "not fitting to criticize the movement which is the Logos". This because the Logos "is a cause of the system, which has been destined to come about" [218]. This means that the Logos was acting in harmony with the Father. This too differs considerably from the orthodox version in which Sophia is acting contrary to the will of the Father. This might signify that the theology of this text is less dualistic than that of the others.

c. The lower sphere

This does not mean that what the Logos brought forth, the nether world, was as perfect as the Father of all. Far from it! He bungled the whole affair so that the result was not different from Sophia's nether world. The dualistic male-female opposition crops up when the author writes that the Logos "became weak like a female nature which has abandoned its virility" [219]. "The Logos was a cause of these (who) came into being", but what came into being made him "embarrassed and astonished : instead of perfection, he saw a defect, instead of unification, he saw division, instead of stability, he (saw) disturbances, instead of (rest), tumults". The beings peopling this imperfect world are "fighters, warriors, troublemakers, apostates, lovers of power" [220]. This sub-Pleroma is the prototype of political strife on earth. "They were brought to a lust for power over one another ... each imagining that he is superior to the others" [221].

It is stated, indeed, that "the things which came into being from the arrogant thought (= of the Logos)" resemble the entities in the Pleroma : "it was the imitation of the system which was a unity" [222]. The Pleroma is confronted here with a kind of sub-Pleroma. But at the same time it is added that it contains "only shadows, and phantasms, lacking reason and light ..., since they are not products of anything ... Their end will be like their beginning : (they are) from that which did not exist, (and are) to return to that which will not be" [223]. Their arrogance was exemplified by the fact that "they thought about themselves that they were beings originating from themselves alone and were without a source" [224]. There is an ontological dualism here of being and not-being.

The quarrelling powers of the lower sphere conform in one thing only : their lust for power. The Logos was perfectly aware of this and "graciously granted their desire to them ... As a result, there are commanders and subordinates in positions of domination ... None (of the archons) lacks a command, and none is without a kingship from the end of the heavens to the end of the (earth), even to the foundations of the (earth) and to the places beneath the earth. There are kings, there are lords, and those who give commands, some for administering punishment, some for administering justice, still others to give rest and healing, others for teaching, others for guarding" [225]. Since we know that political power does not stem from the Pleroma but is a prerequisite of the lower sphere, this conclusion is somewhat surprising. The effects of political power are presented as, on the whole, beneficial. Could it be that the author was unconsciously thinking of the Pax Romana? Nevertheless, we must not forget that political power was a product of a very imperfect world.

However good the intentions of the Logos may have been, the cosmos became the exact opposite of the Pleroma, for it was characterized by ignorance. "The things which had come into being unaware of themselves both did not know the Pleroma from which they came forth, and did not know the one who was the cause of their existence" [226]. The difference is perhaps not so much of an ontological nature - "it (the cosmos) was the imitation of that which was a unity (= the Pleroma)" [227] - but rather epistemological (Knowledge versus Ignorance).

d. The Logos, the Demiurge, and the world

Just as in orthodox Valentinianism we find the conversion of the Logos and its return to the Pleroma. "When the Logos which was defective was illumined, his Pleroma began. He escaped those who had disturbed him at first. He became unmixed with them. He stripped off that arrogant thought" [228]. This is exactly the road the Gnostic has to go : from ignorance and arrogance through illumination to the Pleroma.

The return of the Logos to the upper world does not imply that he abandoned the lower one. Quite the contrary! "The Logos received the vision of all things, those which preexist and those which are now and those which will be, since he has been entrusted with all things" [229]. To be his lieutenant in the cosmos, the Logos "over all the images established an Archon ..., the lord of all of them"; he even is "a representation of the Father of the Totalities (= the Pleroma) ... He too is called 'father' and 'god' and 'demiurge' .... The Logos used him as a hand, to beautify and work on the things below" [230]. This constitutes a remarkable departure from common Gnostic doctrine, since this Demiurge is not wicked at all! "He established a rest for those who obey him, but for those who disobey him he also established punishment. With him too there is a paradise and a kingdom" [231]. This Demiurge closely resembles the God of the New Testament.

It looks as though the Logos installed this supreme Archon to create some order among the warring factions of the sub-Pleroma. "The whole establishment of matter (is divided) into three. The (strong) powers which the spiritual Logos brought forth from fantasy and arrogance, he established in the first spiritual rank. Then those (powers) which these produced by their lust for power, he set in the middle area, since they are powers of ambition, so that they might exercise dominion and give commands with compulsion and force to the establishment which is beneath them. Those which came into being through envy and jealousy and all the other offspring of this sort, he (the Archon) set in a servile order controlling the extremities, commanding all those which exist and all (the realm of) generation, from whom came rapidly destroying illnesses" [232]. This picture already considerably differs from that presented earlier : political power is now painted in a far more sombre hue. It can only be hoped that the supreme Archon will be able to keep the servile order somewhat in check.

I believe that the conclusion may be that the idea the Tripartite Tract has of political power and its exercise agrees with notions found earlier, in the Book of Daniel [233], in the Revelation of John [234], and in Essenian doctrine [235]. Political power is not so starkly reviled here as elsewhere, but, all the same, its origin is defective and it tends to oppressiveness and anarchy. At best, it is a necessary evil.

e. The creation of man

In this context we must speak of the creation of man. "The first man is a mixed formation, and a deposit of those of the left and those of the right, ... (and his) attention is divided between each of the substances of which he takes his being" [236]. Which are those substances that go into the making of man? The Tractate's account is somewhat garbled here, but so much is clear that the components are a spiritual and a material one. The combination obviously leaves much to be desired. And who is the creator of this first man (who is nowhere called Adam, while there is no mention of Eve)? The soul of the first man comes from the spiritual Logos. But "the creator (the Demiurge) also sent down souls from his substance, since he too has power of procreation." Finally, those of the left (= the less-well intended archons - F.) brought forth ... men of their own, since they have a likeness of being" [237]. This tends to there being three different races of human beings with three different origins.

This is exemplified in Paradise in which there are not two special trees but three. It is not specified what these tree represent, except that there was a tree of life. Anyhow, an evil power, called 'the serpent', enticed the first man to eat from the wrong tree. "He made him transgress the command, so that he would die." Death is not so much physical extinction as "the complete Ignorance of the Totality (the Pleroma)". Man thereby lost his future that "after the deprivations which are in these (evils = of existence on earth - F.), he should receive of the greatest good, which is life eternal, that is firm knowledge of the Totalities, and the reception of all good things" [238]. The dilemma of human existence is pictured here in the form of the dualism of Knowledge and Ignorance.

f. A confusing moral perspective

It must be admitted that the moral perspective is rather confusing for an ordinary human being. There are the powers of the right and the left, the one being good and the other bad. One would expect that this would give some guidance, but no! "It happens that they both act with the same emulation of their deeds, with those of the right resembling those of the left and those of the left resembling those of the right." The wise may commit evil, just as the foolish may sometimes attempt to do some good. This is, of course, meant to highlight the significance of Knowledge. "Those who were not instructed are unable to know the course of things which exist" [239].

There are no human means to make head or tail of this. Some say helplessly that it is the pre-ordained course of the world; others assume that it is just fate or put forward still other solutions. Such people do not attempt to go further than 'the visible elements'. Those who do are the philosophers and the sages, both Greek and barbarian; arrogant as they are, they fancy that they have attained the truth, whereas what they attained is error. Having thus successfully dealt with all possible forms of purely human knowledge, the author concludes that philosophy, medicine, rhetoric, music, and logic - in short, the whole gamut of Greek paideia - are nothing but opinions and theories. With this verdict all Hellenic and Hellenistic scholarship is refuted.

But could it be that the Bible contains a really higher form of wisdom? At this point the author begins to proceed very cautiously, obviously not wanting to alienate Jews and Christians. First of all, being a Jew is not in itself a guarantee for possessing the truth [240]. Among the Jews there are righteous ones and prophets; "each one by the power which was at work in him, and while listening to the things which he saw and heard (= things of a higher order - F.), spoke of them in faith" [241]. "The prophets (of Israel) did not say anything of their own accord, but each of them (spoke) of the things which he had seen and heard through the proclamation of the Saviour" [242].

So far so good. The Old Testament undoubtedly contains a germ of truth, in particular in the announcement of the Saviour. But where it goes hopelessly wrong, according to this author, is in teaching the Law. What the scribes produced led only to a 'multitude of ideas'. As a result, "many have accepted the Scriptures in an altered way. By interpreting them they established many heresies which have existed to the present day among the Jews" [243].

g. The Saviour

With all competitors for wisdom safely out of the way - it must have struck the reader that the author has said nothing at all of Christians -, he is now ready to present his own doctrine of Redemption. His Saviour has a most exalted origin. His Father is the invisible, unknowable, incomprehensible God; it is "from the spiritual Logos who is the cause of the things which have come into being, from whom the Savior receives his flesh". In the view of the author the Saviour is not identical with the Logos, since "the one who exists (the Saviour) is not a seed (= cause or origin) of the things which exist, since he was begotten at the end", whereas the Logos is unbegotten. All the same, the Father "ordained the manifestation of salvation" through him; he is "the fulfillment of the promise"[244].

The Saviour's appearance is human. "He had let himself be conceived without sin, stain, or defilement". No mention is made of Mary or of the virgin birth. He was alike other people, for "he accepted their smallness" and did "take upon himself the death of those whom he thought to save". But this does not mean at all that he was just as human as everybody else. Quite the contrary! "The Saviour was a bodily image of the unitary one. He is the Totality (Pleroma) in bodily form. Therefore, he preserved the form of indivisibility, from which comes impassibility." The difference with other people is that "they are images of each thing which became manifest"[245]. In other words, they represent multiplicity.

Here we meet once again the dualistic opposition of unity and multiplicity, of the One and the Many which, to the author of the Tripartite Tract, is just as important as, or perhaps even more important than that of Knowledge and Ignorance. Be this as it may, the importance of Knowledge is also unambiguously stated. "The freedom is the knowledge of the truth which existed before ignorance came to be, (the truth) ruling forever without beginning and without end, being something good and a salvation of things and a release from the servile nature in which they have suffered"[246].

h. The fate of mankind

The author then presents his threefold division of mankind into spirit-people, soul-people, and matter-people. "Each of the three essential types is known by its fruits" [247], and therefore, they will have different fates : "Some will perish (the hylics), while others benefit (the pneumatics) and still others (the psychics) are set apart" [248]. However, it is only their existential relation to the Saviour that makes their fundamental stance apparent. "They were not known at first but only at the coming of the Savior ... who revealed what each was" [249].

"The spiritual race, being like light from light and spirit from spirit, when its head (the Saviour) appeared, it ran to him immediately ... It suddenly received knowledge in the revelation" [250]. Something remains unexplained here. If the pneumatics receive knowledge by revelation (suddenly), how then will they be able, having no previous knowledge, to recognize the Saviour? Is it because of their special origin that is unlike that of other people, for they are light from light? However this may be, "the spiritual race will receive complete salvation in every way" [251].

As with Ptolemaeus and Heracleon, there is hope for the psychics, the soul-people, whom the author calls 'those of the thought', which means that they are not hopelessly ignorant. This 'psychic race' (the Christians, to all intents and purposes) is 'in the middle', because it is "double in its determination for good and evil". It hesitates to accept knowledge, and even more "to run towards him (the Saviour) in faith". For this reason it needs instruction; through the acceptance of this instruction (offered by Gnostic teachers, it goes without saying) "it takes its appointed departure suddenly and its complete escape to those who are good ... It will be saved completely (because of) the salvific thought" [252]. This implies that the existence of the second race is only temporary; in the end it will merge with the first race.

For the rest, the matter-people, the 'Dark Ones', there will be no Knowledge. They are disobedient, they will not listen, and, in consequence, they are irrevocably lost. To them the author has menacing words to say. "The material race ... is alien in every way; since it is dark, it shuns the shining of the light, because its appearance destroys it (this race). And since it had not received its unity, it is something excessive and hateful toward the Lord at his revelation" [253]. They are the ones "who are affected with the lust for power and are proud because of the desire of ambition".

But even for them there remains some hope. If they only "will relinquish their wrath, they will receive the reward for their humility, which is to remain forever". If not, woe to them! "They will receive judgment for their ignorance and their senselessness" [254]. "Not only that they denied the Lord and plotted evil against him but also toward the Church (the Gnostic communion) too their hatred and envy and jealosusy is directed; and this is the reason for their condemnation" [255].

j. The Redeemer redeemed

We must now pay attention to a point that, in all ages, has divided the Gnosis from orthodoxy. The Redeemer needs redemption himself, says this tract. For how could he redeem others if he had not been redeemed himself? In fact, everything and everyone that is below the Father needs redemption, not only humans but also the angels and the aeons. "Even the Son himself, who has the position of Redeemer of the Totality, (needed) redemption as well". This is not because he, as a divine being, was not spotless, but because, when he had appeared in the flesh, "he gave himself for each thing which we need, we in the flesh who are his Church ... For those (the elect) who received the one who had received (redemption) also received what was in him" [256]. I feel this makes crystal-clear what is meant : redemption is transmitted to the redeemed by the Redeemer who possesses it as a quality.

k. Christ all in all

The author obviously does not acknowledge a baptism with water but prefers a spiritual one. "There is no other baptism", he states expressly

[257]. It consists in "attaining in an invisible way to the Father, Son, and Holy Spirit in an undoubting faith ... so that the return to them might become the perfection of those who believed in them and (so that) the Father might become one with them, the Father, God, whom they have confessed in faith and who gave them their union with him in knowledge"[258]. In the end there will be only 'a unitary existence' when "Christ is all in all"[259]. The tract ends on an impressive doxology speaking of "the bridal chamber which is the love of God the Father", revealed "through the Lord, the Savior, the Redeemer of all those belonging to the one filled with Love, through his Holy Spirit from now through all generations for ever and ever. Amen"[260].

l. The Tripartite Tract and its relation to Christianity

It will not have escaped the attentive reader that the general tone of 'The Tripartite Tract' differs in many respects from that of both the 'Gospel of Truth' and the doctrine of fully developed Valentianism. This tone sometimes sounds decisively Christian, for instance in the doxology with its seemingly orthodox trinitarian confession. This implies that the end of the tract is at variance with its beginning since it does not begin with proclaiming the Trinity. On the contrary! The 'root of everything' is the Father, and he alone. He then engenders the Son, and together they bring forth, not the Holy Ghost but the Church.

Then there is no 'myth of Sophia' but, instead, the story of the Logos. True enough, the Logos gets into a predicament and undergoes suffering. The notion of the Fall is far less pronounced here (if it occurs at all), while there is also no wicked Demiurge. Quite the reverse : the Logos is clearly fulfilling the wishes of the Father, and although by no means all is for the best in the cosmos, he installs an Archon to restore and keep some order. What is wanting too is the total rejection of all that is matter, physical, world, human. The opposition of Knowledge and Ignorance is emphasized less strongly than, for instance, in the Gospel of Truth; it is paired with that of unity and multiplicity.

In between the usual races of the pneumatics and the hylics we find the psychics to whom the choice of either side is open. This lessens the dualism within mankind considerably, since, according to my own definition of the phenomenon, when there is a connecting middle term, there is no dualism. However, the psychic element is only provisional; it is destined to disappear, leaving in the end only the two original and totally opposed orders. At the same time, the dualism of the upper and nether worlds is not so heavily accentuated as elsewhere. Although the two worlds are very different, there is, nevertheless, a sort of osmosis going on between them. The announcement of the fate of the wicked and of the destruction of the world is spirited away, while it is also not said in as many words that there will be no resurrection of the body.

The conclusion must be drawn that this tractate is much closer to Christian teaching than the common run of Gnostic tracts. Why is this so? Could it be that the author remained more attached to his (supposedly original) Christian moorings than he himself realized or even wanted? Or was this tract meant to be 'exoteric', destined not for the initiated but for the psychics, implying here the orthodox Christians? Since they could fall on either side, they were in principle capable of becoming good Valentinians. Possibly the author's intention was to demonstrate that Valentinianism did not really differ so much from ecclesiastical Christianity, that it was a refinement and a deepening of it rather than an opposed doctrine. Once won over to Valentinianism, the converted Christian could yet be exposed to the full blast of the Gnosis. I for one would opt for the second possibility.

9. The extent of Valentinianism

In its Valentinian garb the Gnosis must have been highly popular and widespread. An irritated Irenaeus complained that their communities sprang from the ground like mushrooms, while in Tertullian's view they were by far the largest heretical school [261]. It was not for nothing that so many Fathers of the Church polemiced so extensively, and not without vehemence, against them; they must have seen in them a serious threat, and considered them as people very well equipped to lure Christians away from the Church. To Irenaeus they were the heretics par excellence; he begins his great work with a long disquisition on Valentinianism.

Valentinianism experienced its heyday around A.D. 200 [262]. At that time, Valentinian communities flourished in North Africa and Egypt, in Syria and Asia Minor, in Greece, Rome, and Gallia. By then the movement had already split into its oriental and Italian branches, divided as they were on the question of the nature of Christ. It is often thought that after 210 Valentinianism began to wane and soon almost completely disappeared. However, around 375 Epiphanius still found it worthwhile to mention it; he knew of its presence in Egypt [263]. We know that in the fourth century Valentinian groups were active in Egypt, Syria, and in certain regions of Asia Minor. Klaus Koschorke to whose article on the spread of later Valentinianism I am much indebted for this section [264] mentions an ancient author, Didymus the Blind (+ 389), who wrote that in Alexandria many followed the christological insights of the Gnostics.

Athanasius as well as Chrysostomus knew of, among others, Valentinians in Antiochia in the second half of the fourth century. Athanasius describes the conditions on which repentant Valentinians may again be admitted to the Church, while Chrysostomus warns Christians against the alluring theses of the Valentinians. At the same time riots of Arians against Valentinians in Syria occurred to which the emperor, Julian the Apostate, reacted by seizing the assets of the Arian Church. In 388 a Valentinian church in Kallinikon on the Euphrates was reduced to ashes by fanatical monks.

In the fifth century the eastern emperor Theodosius II in an imperial decree of 428 mentioned among heretics in Rome Valentinians; twenty years later a letter by bishop Theodoretus of Cyrus (near Antiochia) testifies to their presence in Syria. Even much later, around 600, Timotheus, a presbyter in Constantinople, discusses how converted Valentinians might be readmitted to the Church. The very last mention of them that Koschorke delved up in patristic literature dates from 692, when the synod called 'Trullanum II', in Constantinople, stipulated on which conditions converted Valentinians might be reconciled with the Church.

NOTES TO CHAPTER VIII

1. Jonas, Gnost.Rel. 174.
2. Epiph., Panarion 31.2.1.
3. Clem.Al., Strom. 7.1.106.4.
4. Hipp., Ref. 6.21.
5. Tert., De carne Christi 20.1.; in De praescr. 40 he calls him 'platonicae sectator'.
6. Hieronymus, Comm. in Osee 2.10 (106).
7. E.F. Scott s..v. 'Valentinianism', Enc.Rel.Eth. 12, 572.
8. Ir., Adv.haer. 3.4.3.
9. Tert., Adv.Val. 4.
10. E.F. Scott s.v. 'Valentinianism', Enc.Rel.Eth. 12, 572.
11. Epiph., Panarion 31.7.2.
12. Ir., Adv.haer. 3.4.3; the verb 'paremeinen' that he uses can mean 'lived on, survived'.
13. A still highly useful review of Valentinus' writings (before the Nag Hammadi find, of course) is found in Harnack, Gesch.altchrist.Lit. 1. Th., 174-183. According to Edwin Preuschen s.v. 'Valentinus', Realenc.prot.Theol.u.Kirche 20, 393, we should not regard Val. as a (sort of professional) author but rather as a man fully occupied with practical affairs. Useful summaries of the three Valentinian treatises in NHC in Quispel, De Codex Jung.
14. Ir., Adv.haer. 3.11.9.
15. NHC 1.3 (and NHC 12.2 in Sahidic).
16. Arai, Christologie 122 thinks that the Gospel was written in Egypt.
17. Van den Broek, Taal v.d. Gnosis 106. As far as I know there is no English translation of this book which is a pity.
18. Arai, Christologie 13, writing much earlier than Van den Broek, said that the possibility that Valentinus himself wrote a treatise resembling the Gospel must remain open; pp. 5-13 he reviews the research on the question of the authorship (as it stood in 1964).
19. Van den Broek, Taal v.d. Gnosis 144/115; see also Standaert, L'Évangile, and Van Unnik, Het kort geleden ontdekte Ev.. Van Unnik's final conclusion, p. 86, is that "the Gospel of Truth ...

was written by Valentinus in Rome about 140-145, before the development of his typically Gnostic tenets".

20. Ir., Adv.haer. Praef. 2. See for a short discussion of the scholars' opinions with regard to the authorship Wilson, Valentinianism. Rediscovery of Val. I, 132/133. The notable exceptions are Schenke and Haenchen who do not view the Gospel as Valentinian.

21. Epiph., Panarion 37.5.1.

22. Ir., Adv.haer. 1.30.14; see Van Unnik, Het kort geleden ontdekte Evangelie 78.

23. These haven been assembled and published several times, for instance in Völker, Quellen V.1 Die Fragmente.

24. Clem.Al., Strom. 2.36.2-4, 2.114.3-6, 3.59.3, 4.89.1-3, 4.89.6-4.90..1.

25. Clem.Al., Strom. 6.52.3-4.

26. Hipp., Ref. 6.37.6-8.

27. G. Bardy s.v. 'Valentin'. Dict.théol.cath. 15, 250.

28. Marcellus of Ancyra, De sancta ecclesia 9 (formerly attributed to Anthimus of Nicomedia) = Völker, Quellen fr. 9, p. 60. Leisegang, Gnosis 282

29. E.F. Scott s.v. 'Valentinianism', Enc.Rel.Eth. 12, 572.

30. Hipp., Ref. 6.42.2.

31. Hipp., Ref. 6.37.7.

32. Erik Peterson s.v. 'Valentino', Enc.catt. 12, 979.

33. NHC 1.3. and 12.2. Arai, Christologie 13/14, states that most scholars (with the exception of Rudolph) agree that the Gospel has the literary form of a homily; in consequence, it has no strictly logical construction. On pp. 20/21 Arai presents a short but very useful summary of the text, and a more detailed one on pp. 15/16.

34. NHL 1.3.16-17.

35. NHL 1.2.17.

36. NHL 1.3.37.

37. NHL 1.3.38.

38. NHL 1.3.37.

39. Van den Broek, Taal 113.

40. NHL 1.3.41.

41. NHL 1.3.40-41.

42. NHL 1.3.17.

43. NHL 1.3.18.
44. NHL 1.3.18.
45. NHL 1.3.17.
46. NHL 1.3.17.
47. Van den Broek, Taal 133, n. 5. This scholar adds that possibly the term is used less specifically and refers to people hovering between Truth and Error.
48. NHL 1.3.24.
49. NHL 1.3.25. The 'spaces', comments Van den Broek, Taal 138, n. 25, are identical with the emanations of Error, darkness and death.
50. N.H.L. 3.1.18.
51. NHL 1.3.18.
52. But perhaps it is an allusion to the tree of the knowledge of good and evil in Genesis 3; the words 'tree' and 'fruit' that recur here may indicate that the cross on which Christ hung was the true tree of knowledge, and Christ its fruit.
53. NHL 1.3.19.
54. NHL 1.3.23 : "They are not vowels nor are they consonants so that one may read them ..., but they are letters of the truth ... They are letters written by the Unity, the Father having written them for the aeons that by means of his letters they should know the Father."
55. NHL 1.3.20.
56. NHL 1.3.30.
57. NHL 1.3.29-30.
58. Ménard, Évangile 18.
59. Ménard, Évangile 34.
60. NHL 1.3.32-33.
61. NHL 1.30.29.
62. NHL 1.3.21.
63. NHL 1.3.42.
64. NHL 1.3.34.
65. NHL 1.3.20.
66. Ménard, Évangile 17. He adds therefore that "the Gospel of Truth is doubtless the one that best illustrates the phenomenon of the Gnosis."
67. NHL 1.3.35.

68. NHL 1.3.17.
69. Helderman, Anapausis 88/91 is of the opinion that the Gospel of Truth is a Valentinian-Gnostic text. Arai, Christologie 17/18, quotes the opinion of Van Unnik that (in the time of the Gospel) Valentinus had Gnostic leanings, but had not yet moved fully over to the Gnostic position.
70. Gospel of Truth; Ir., Adv.haer. 1.1-8, 11-12, 13-21; Hipp., Ref. 6.29-36; Clem.Al. who had his report from Theodotus (the fragments 'ex Theodoto' in Foester/Wilson, Gnosis, Ch. 12); Epiph., Panarion 31.5-8, 35.4. The fragments of Valentinus himself we find assembled in Foerster/Wilson, Gnos, Ch. 13. To the report by Origen in his Commentary on John I shall come back later since this is concerned with Heracleon rather than Valentinus himself.
71. Rudolph, Gnosis 341/342; on pp. 342/343 this scholar describes what is common to all Valentinians. Quispel, Orig.doctr. 43 states that "the antiheretic authors transmit ample and very contradictory accounts of their systems. How much of their opinions go back to the founder of the sect is still uncertain." On pp. 45/46 he presents a useful list in rubrics of the principal tenets of the different schools.
72. Epiph., Panarion 31.5.1-2.
73. Ir., Adv.haer. 1.1.1.
74. Hipp., Ref. 6.29.2; Epiph., Panarion 31.5.2.
75. Ménard, Évangile 19.
76. Bousset, Hauptprobl. 106.
77. Jonas, Gnosis u. spätant. Geist II, 154.
78. Jonas, Gnosis u. spätant. Geist II, 155.
79. Ir., Adv.haer. 1.1.1.
80. Hipp., Ref. 6.29.5.
81. Jonas, Gnost.Rel. 180, n. 7; ib. he remarks that the names of Ennoia, Charis, and Sigê are all of the feminine gender. The Father, of course, is male. Perhaps there is a vague idea of Sigê being the paredra of the Father.
82. Hipp., Ref. 6.29.5.
83. Ir., Adv.haer. 1.1.1.
84. Epiph., Panarion 31.5.3.
85. Ir., Adv.haer. 1.1.1.
86. Ir., Adv.haer. 1.1.1.
87. Hipp., Ref. 6.29.6.
88. E.F. Scott s.v. 'Valentinianism', Enc.Rel.Eth. 12, 524.

89. Hipp. Ref. 6.36.7.
90. Hipp., Ref. 6.36.8.
91. E.F. Scott s.v. 'Valentianism'. Enc.Rel.Eth. 12, 575.
92. Leisegang, Gnosis 283.
93. Ir., Adv.haer. 1.1.1. This refers to Pythagorean number speculation, in particular to his predilection for the number 'four', the symbol of completeness, see Vol. I, Ch. I.10.
94. Ir., Adv.haer. 1.1.1.
95. Ir., Adv.haer. 1.1.1.
96. Sagnard, Gnose val. 302.
97. Ir., Adv.haer. 1.1.2.
98. Ir., Adv.haer. 1.1.3.
99. Hipp., Ref. 6.30.7.
100. Ir., Adv.haer. 1.2.1.
101. Ir., Adv.haer. 1.2.1.
102. Hipp., Ref. 6.30.7.
103. Foerster/Wilson, Gnosis 124.
104. Hipp., Ref. 6.30.8.
105. Ir., Adv.haer. 1.2.3.
106. Ir., Adv.haer. 1.2.2.
107. Quispel, Gnosis Weltrel. 87-89.
108. Ir., Adv.haer. 1.2.3.
109. Ir., Adv.haer. 1.2.4.
110. Hipp., Ref. 6.31.1-2.
111. Hipp., Ref. 6.31.1.
112. Hipp., Ref. 6.31.4.
113. Ir., Adv.haer. 1.2.5.
114. Jonas, Gnost.Rel. 184.
115. Ir., Adv.haer. 1.2.6.
116. Hipp., Ref. 6.32.1.
117. Ir., Adv.haer. 1.3.1.
118. Jonas, Gnost.Rel. 186.
119. Ir., Adv.haer. 1.4.1.
120. Hipp., Ref. 6.32.2.
121. Ir., Adv.haer. 1.4.1.

122. Ir., Adv.haer. 1.4.1.
123. Hipp., Ref. 6.32.2-3.
124. Ir., Adv.haer. 1.4.1.
125. Ir., Adv.haer. 1.4.1.
126. Ir., Adv.haer. 1.4.2.
127. Ir., Adv.haer. 1.4.2.
128. Ir., Adv.haer. 1.4.1-2.
129. Ir., Adv.haer. 1.4.5.
130. Ir., Adv.haer. 1.4.5.
131. Hipp., Ref. 6.32.4.
132. Ir., Adv.haer. 1.4.5.
133. Ir., Adv.haer. 1.4.5.
134. Hipp., Ref. 6.32.5.
135. Ir., Adv.haer. 1.4.5.
136. Clem.Al., Exc. ex Theod. 46.
137. Hipp., Ref. 6.32.6.
138. Ir., Adv.haer. 1.4.5.
139. Ir., Adv.haer. 1.5.1; Hipp., Ref. 6.32.6.
140. Hipp., Ref. 6.32.7.
141. Ir., Adv.haer. 1.5.1.
142. Hipp., Ref. 6.32.9.
143. Ir., Adv.haer. 1.5.1.
144. Hipp. Ref. 6.33.
145. Ir., Adv.haer. 1.5.4.
146. Hipp., Ref. 6.34.1.
147. Ir., Adv.haer. 1.5.4.
148. Ir., Adv.haer. 1.5.5.
149. Hipp., Ref. 6.33.6.
150. Ir., Adv.haer. 1.5.6.
151. Hipp., Ref. 6.33.
152. Hipp., Ref. 6.34.8.
153. Ir., Adv.haer. 1..5.1.
154. Ir., Adv.haer. 1.4.5.
155. Jonas, Gnost.Rel. 189.

156. Ir., Adv.haer. 1.5.6.
157. Ir., Adv.haer. 1.5.6.
158. Clem.Al., Exc. 55.3.
159. Hipp., Ref. 6.36.4.
160. Ir., Adv.haer. 1.7.3.
161. Lc. 1:35.
162. Hipp., Ref. 6.35.1.
163. Ir., Adv.haer. 1.6.1.
164. Hipp., Ref. 6.35.5.
165. Kaestli, La nature 396 : "Les puissances qui interviennent dans la création du Jésus visible n'ont rien à voir avec le Démiurge et les réalités psychiques qu'il gouverne".
166. Ir., Adv.haer. 1..7.2.
167. Tert., De carne 15.1.
168. Tert., De carne 10.1.
169. Kaestli, La nature 396.
170. Ir., Adv.haer. 1.15.3.
171. Kaestli, La nature 396.
172. Ir., Adv.haer. 1.15.3, according to Marc the Magician.
173. Clem.Al., Strom, 3.7.59.3. For a balanced discussion of this difficult question consult Kaestli, Valentinisme.
174. Hipp., Ref. 6.35.6.
175. Ir., Ad.vhaer. 1.7.2.
176. Ir., Adv.haer. 1.7.3.
177. Ir., Adv.haer. 1.6.1.
178. Clem.Al., Exc. 61.6-8.
179. Epiph., Panarion 33.3.6.
180. Epiph., Panarion 33.7.4-5.
181. Foerster/Wilson, Gnosis 155.
182. Clem.Al., Strom. 4.13.
183. E.F. Scott s.v. 'Valentinianism', Enc.Rel.Eth. 12, 574.
184. Jonas, Gnosis u. spätant. Geist I, 273.
185. Hipp., Ref. 6.34.1.
186. Ir., Adv.haer. 1.17.2.
187. Jonas, Gnost.Rel. 193.

188. Orig., Comm. 66.
189. Clem.Al., Strom. 4.9.
190. Or., Comm. 226 (13.17).
191. Caroline Bammel s.v. 'Heracleon', Theol.Realenz. XV, 55 (New York, 1986).
192. I discussed the question whether or not John was a Gnostic or a predecessor of the Gnostics in my Vol. VII, Ch. IV.7.b; my answer was negative.
193. Pagels, Joh.Gosp. 17.
194. Pagels, Joh.Gosp. 18.
195. Orig., Comm. 13.49.
196. Orig., Comm. 13.48-49.
197. Pagels, Joh.Gosp. 18/19.
198. Orig., Comm. 2.13.
199. Pagels, Joh.Gosp. 47.
200. Orig., Comm. 6.20.
201. Orig., Comm. Jo.6.19.
202. Pagels, Joh.Gospel 48.
203. Orig., Comm. 2.19.
204. Pagels, Joh.Gosp. 48.
205. Orig., Comm. 2.3.
206. Orig., Comm. 2.8; 6.23; 20.30.
207. Orig., Comm. 13.59.
208. NHC 1.5, in the Jung Codex.
209. NHC 1.5.118-119.
210. NHC 1.5.51.
211. NHC 1.51.53.
212. NHC 1.5.52.
213. NHC 1.5.54.
214. NHC 1.5.57.
215. NHC 1.5.58-60.
216. NHL 54.
217. NHL 54.
218. NHC 1.5.76.
219. NHC 1.5.78.

220. NHC 1.5.80.
221. NHC 1.5.79.
222. NHC 1.5.81.
223. NHC 1.5.79.
224. NHC 1.5.84.
225. NHC 1.5.99-100.
226. NHC 1.5.80.
227. NHC 1.5.81.
228. NHC 1.5.90.
229. NHC 1.5.95.
230. NHC 1.5.100.
231. NHC 1.5.101.
232. NHC 1.5.104.
233. See Vol. IV, Ch. II.7c,d.
234. See Vol. VII, Ch. IV.5d.
235. See Vol. VII, Ch. V.9h.
236. NHC 1.5.106.
237. NHC 1.5.105-106.
238. NHC 1.5.107-108.
239. NHC 1.5.108-109.
240. NHC 1.5.110.
241. NHC 1.5.111.
242. NHC 1.5.113.
243. NHC 1.5.112-113.
244. NHC 1.5.114.
245. NHC 1.5.116.
246. NHC 1.5.117.
247. NHC 1.5.118.
248. NHC 1.5.96.
249. NHC 1..5.118.
250. NHC 1.5.118.
251. NHC 1..5.199.
252. NHC 1.5.118-119.
253. NHC 1..5.119.

254. NHC 1.5.120-121.
255. NHC 1.5.122.
256. NHC 1.5.125.
257. NHC 1..5.127.
258. NHC 1.5.128.
259. NHC 1.5.132.
260. NHC 1.5.138.
261. Tert., Adv.Val.1.1.
262. As far as I know, the doctoral thesis of E.H. Jensen, An examination of the history and teachings of Valentinus and his school, Diss. Oxford, 1975, exists only in the British Dissertation Abstracts; I have not seen it.
263. Epiph., Panarion 31.7.1.
264. Koschorke, Patrist.Materialien passim (see Biblography).

CHAPTER IX

GNOSTIC POLEMICS AGAINST JUDAISM
AND CHRISTIANITY

1. Were the earliest Fathers of the Church 'heresy-hunters'?

It is a well-known topic of present-day gnoseology that the early Fathers of the Church vehemently polemized against the Gnosis and the Gnostics. This is certainly true. The Fathers of the first centuries A.D. saw the Gnosis as an almost mortal threat to the Church. For this reason, they did not mince their words when they spoke of it, and this they frequently did. Polemizing was not a gentleman's sport in those days, not even for a long time afterwards. Hitting below the belt was considered a perfectly permissible device in the acrimonious word-battles, in which arguments ad personam were the most normal thing in the world. And have these totally disappeared nowadays?

It has often been suggested that those Fathers, in their wrath, horribly distorted Gnostic ideology so that we did not possess an approximately objective picture of what Gnostics taught. Since the discovery of the Nag Hammadi Library, however, we know that at any rate Irenaeus and Hippolytus were fairly accurate in their descriptions but Epiphanius less so.

The Fathers in question - not only these three, but also Clement, Origen, Tertullian, and others - are often referred to as 'heresy-hunters' or 'witch-hunters', terms that put them in a bad light, associated as they are with denouncements and persecution, perhaps even with burning people at the stake. What those who use such terms so easily conveniently forget is that in the centuries under consideration in this volume the Fathers were not in a position to undertake anything against Gnostics, even if they had wanted to. The Roman-Catholic Church of the first centuries went through one persecution after another; bishops could not claim the assistance of the secular arm, as they did in the Middle Ages. The only corrective measure they had at their disposal was to exclude people from the Church; of this I know only one instance, that of Epiphanius denouncing Gnostics in or near Alexandria to the bishop of that city whereupon eighty of them were excommunicated. For the rest, the polemics remained restricted to words.

Since the discovery of the Nag Hammadi Library we know that such polemics were not a one-sided affair. The Gnostics paid back in kind hitting right in the eye of the orthodox. And of the Jews! The Fathers in their works react to what Gnostics wrote, quoting from their texts and paraphrasing their doctrine; for this reason we may suppose that Gnostics were the first to attack. What I am going to expound now is based on my own careful reading of the Nag Hammadi documents and on research mainly by Klaus Koschorke. In this context it should not be overlooked that Gnostics polemized also against other Gnostics [1].

2. Gnostic syncretism?

Martin Krause tried to diffuse the polemical charge of many a Gnostic document by explaining it away. He wrote that the discussion between Christianity and the Gnosis was conducted mainly in a non-polemical way. The reason for this, he said, was that the Gnostics inherited from Pharaonic Egypt a syncretistic manner of thinking. The Egyptian state arose out of a great number of cantons each with its own regional divinity. When these cantons were united, their divinities were brought into a certain relationship to one another, for instance in families of gods. The Gnostics did not act differently. Their way of thinking, Krause admits, differed fundamentally from Jewish monotheistic thought. The Gnostics tried to win over orthodox Christians by presenting a Christian-coloured Gnosis in their writings. This they hoped to achieve by adapting and allegorizing Bible passages and by adopting and re-explaining Christian sacraments. This is what this scholar means by Gnostic syncretism [2].

The problem is that the Gnosis was not, like the well-peopled Egyptian pantheon, polytheistic. Gnostics acknowledged only one primal divinity. In this respect they did not take their cue from Egyptian paganism but were in basic agreement with Judaism and Christianity. But they differed from the monotheistic concept of these two religions in this that this primal godhead was impersonal and abstract, was not a creator, and kept aloof from cosmos and mankind. It is true that the Gnosis was syncretistic (and eclectic), but Egyptian syncretism was not its paradigm.

3. Gnostic polemizing

a. The anti-Jewish attitude of the Gnostics

The Gnostics did indeed polemize, often in a bitter vein, against both Judaism and Christianity. In order to conquer a place in the sun, they had to fight up against these two religions, in particular against Christianity that in this same period was rapidly gaining ground in the ancient world. But for a long time the Jews too had been proselytizing, not without results. The Gnostics were faced with strong competitors, and this explains the not rarely hateful tone they adopt. I have already presented a fair instance of this in Chapter IV of the present volume where a Sethian Gnostic author first derides the Bible and the whole Jewish religion and then fiercely attacks the New Testament [3]. In the same context I mentioned Sethian antinomianism in which the Bible is turned upside down by glorifying the Sodomites [4]. The Cainites proclaimed all the dark figures of the Old Testament as their heroes, first and foremost their patron-saint Cain, but also Cham, the Sodomites, Esau, and Datan and Abiram; they praised Judas too, because he was 'admirable and great' [5].

It is true, of course, as Tröger wrote, that "only part of the (Gnostic) writings display an anti-Jewish attitude". But this "does not necessarily mean that anti-Jewish elements were not typical of the Gnostic religion" [6]. Sometimes there is open anti-Judaism; one might even dub it anti-Semitism when the Jewish people is 'condemned and spurned', but oftener the attack is made more indirectly. "Central Jewish-biblical traditions are turned upside down ... The Jewish traditions are twisted and turned to ridicule." Tröger concludes that in many texts "the whole concept is an anti-Jewish one" [7]. New Testament Christianity is often accused of being anti-Semitic, but in an earlier volume I demonstrated that the New Testament cannot be thought of as being an anti-Jewish or anti-Semitic document [8]. I should rather say that the real hotbed of religious anti-Semitism in the first centuries A.D. was the Gnosis.

b. Anti-Christian polemizing

The Gnostics also freely attacked Christianity, Christians, and the Roman-Catholic Church. In particular, the 'hierarchically structured, established Church' was a favourite object for attacks [9]. Koschorke, who has very thoroughly researched this subject, presents many instances of this. In his opinion, the 'Apocalypse of Peter', a Nag Hammadi text from the first half of the third century, takes "a uniformly frontal stand against Catholic Christianity". This document reproaches orthodox Christians that they have defected from the truth : "The Christianity of the multitude is ... apostasy from the beginning" [10]. What, according to the Gnostics, makes Catholic Christians into heretics is their belief in a 'dead man', in the Jesus who died on the cross in order to redeem mankind. In consequence, Christians are 'dead souls'. Since the Catholic Church is based on this Jesus and his teaching, it is no more than an imitation-Church. By falsely pretending to be in sole possession of the truth, it leads people astray. The Catholics have their 'root' not in the Pleroma but in the created world, and this is no recommendation [11].

The Apocalypse of Peter also attacks the Catholic hierarchy. In vain, bishops and deacons appeal to a 'warrant from God', for they are 'channels without water'. The real rulers in the Church are the Archonts; no wonder, then, that Catholics venerate the wicked Demiurge, the Jewish God. In consequence, Gnostics and Catholics can have nothing to do with one another [12].

The attitude of the Gospel of Truth vis-à-vis the Catholic Church is equally dualistic. Whereas the Gnostics unvariably find themselves on the side of light, life, knowledge, and purity, orthodox Christians unfailingly stand on that of darkness, death, ignorance, and pollution [13]. The fundamental objection to the Church is that it does not reject the world. In consequence, it remains imprisoned in the world and is incapable of working salvation [14]. Its sacraments are only surrogate [15].

The Catholic Church is especially accused of propagating marriage and the bringing forth of children, which necessarily implies the use of sexual capacities. Catholics are libidinous in this view. The body is material and, therefore, worthless; it is nonsense to hope for its resurrection [16].

Koschorke very clearly points out the dualistic distance between the Gnostics and the Catholic Christians by stating that the Gnosis "did not constitute itself as opposition against but rather as a higher stage over ecclesiastical Christianity" [17]. The Gnosis belongs to the pleromic world of light and life where the Father of all reigns, the Church, on the other hand, to the nether world that is in the grip of the Demiurge and the Archonts. Orthodox Christians serve the Jewish God who is blind and makes blind.

NOTES TO CHAPTER IX

1. Pearson, Anti-heretical warnings 145/146.
2. Krause, Christl.-Gnost. Texte (see Bibliography).
3. Pp. 113-116.
4. Pp. 113/114.
5. Ch. V.19.
6. Tröger, Attitude 91.
7. Tröger, Attitude 91/92.
8. Vol. VII, Ch. IV.5.j-n.

9. Tröger, Attitude 89?90.
10. Koschorke, Polemik, 14, 17 and 37.
11. Koschorke, Polemik 38 and 63.
12. Koschorke, Polemik 63.
13. Koschorke, Polemik 97.
14. Koschorke, Polemik 110.
15. Koschorke, Polemik 104.
16. Koschorke, Polemik 110.
17. Koschorke, Polemik 204.

SIMONIANISM

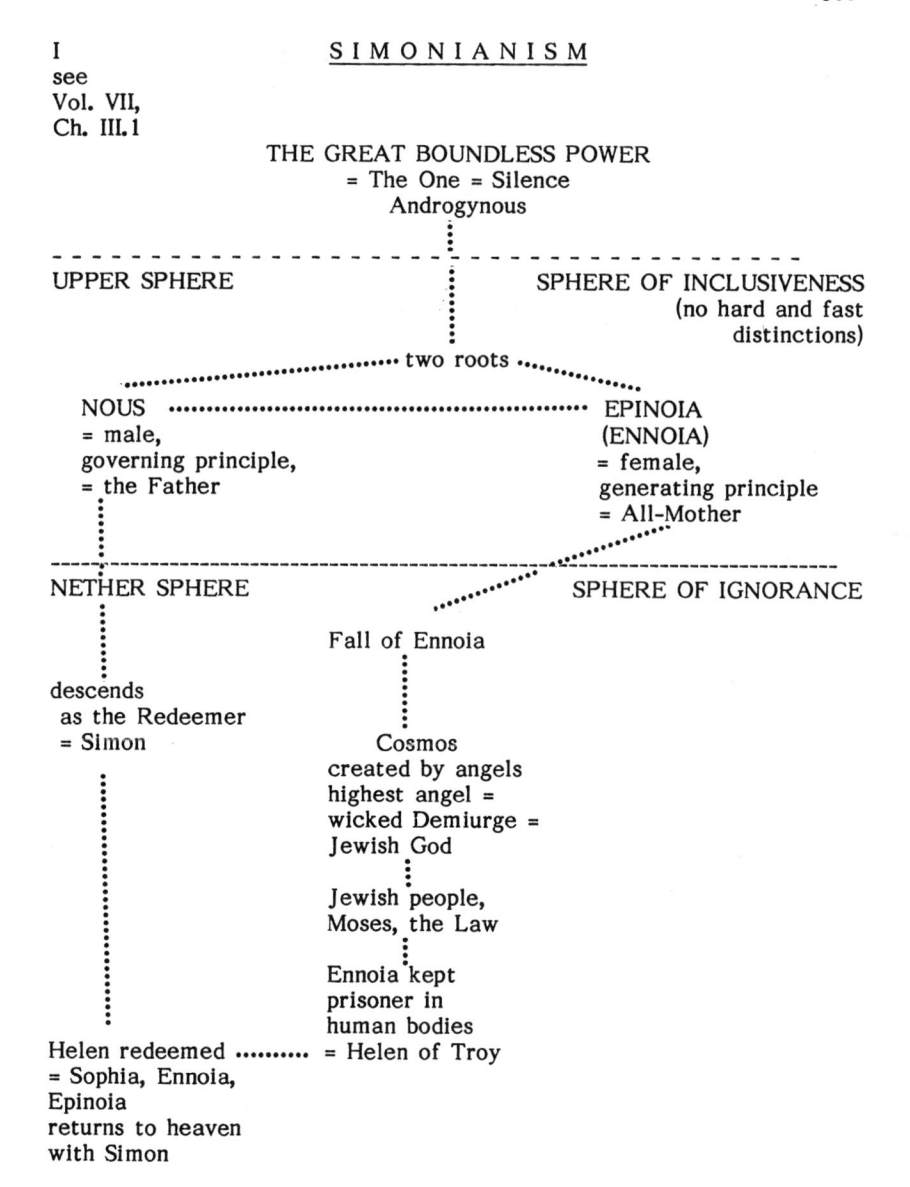

I
see
Vol. VII,
Ch. III.1

THE GREAT BOUNDLESS POWER
= The One = Silence
Androgynous

UPPER SPHERE | SPHERE OF INCLUSIVENESS
(no hard and fast distinctions)

.... two roots ....

NOUS .... EPINOIA
= male, (ENNOIA)
governing principle, = female,
= the Father generating principle
 = All-Mother

NETHER SPHERE | SPHERE OF IGNORANCE

Fall of Ennoia

descends
as the Redeemer
= Simon

Cosmos
created by angels
highest angel =
wicked Demiurge =
Jewish God

Jewish people,
Moses, the Law

Ennoia kept
prisoner in
human bodies

Helen redeemed .... = Helen of Troy
= Sophia, Ennoia,
Epinoia
returns to heaven
with Simon

II
see
Vol. VII,
Ch. III.2

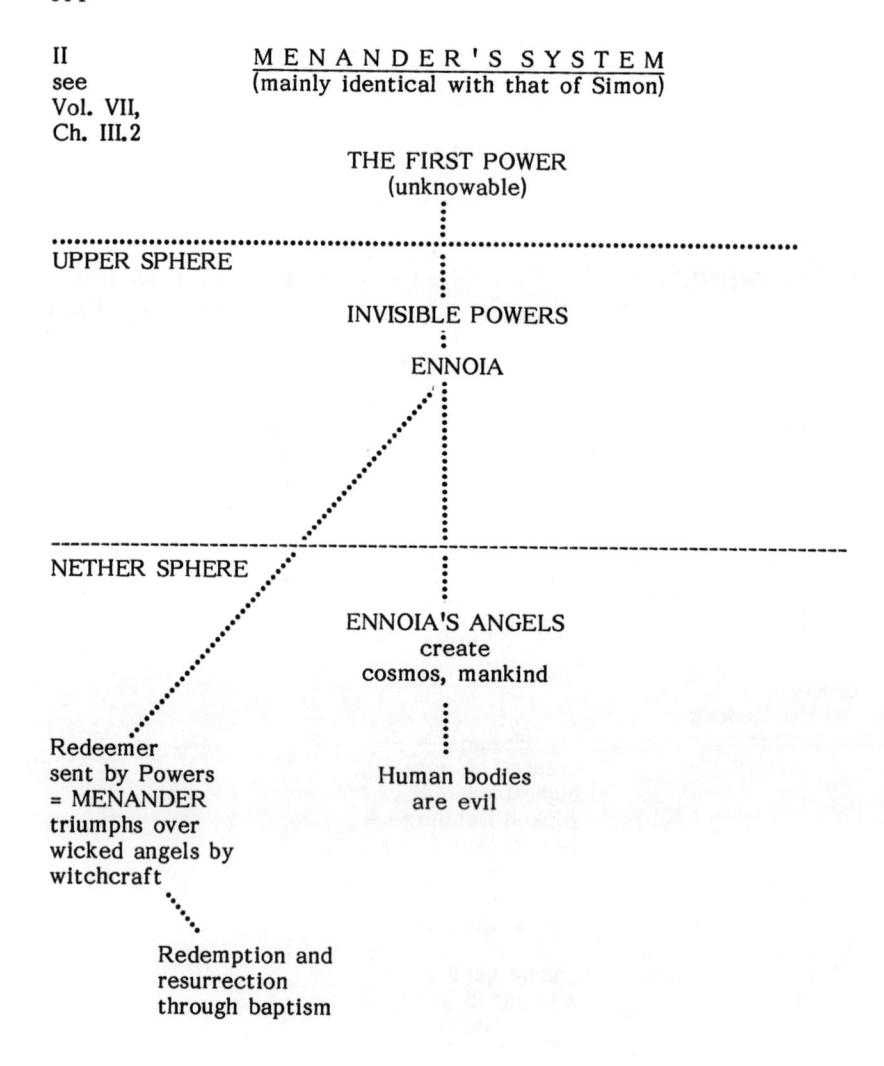

MENANDER'S SYSTEM
(mainly identical with that of Simon)

THE FIRST POWER
(unknowable)

UPPER SPHERE

INVISIBLE POWERS

ENNOIA

NETHER SPHERE

ENNOIA'S ANGELS
create
cosmos, mankind

Redeemer
sent by Powers
= MENANDER
triumphs over
wicked angels by
witchcraft

Human bodies
are evil

Redemption and
resurrection
through baptism

III
see
Vol. VII,
Ch. III.3

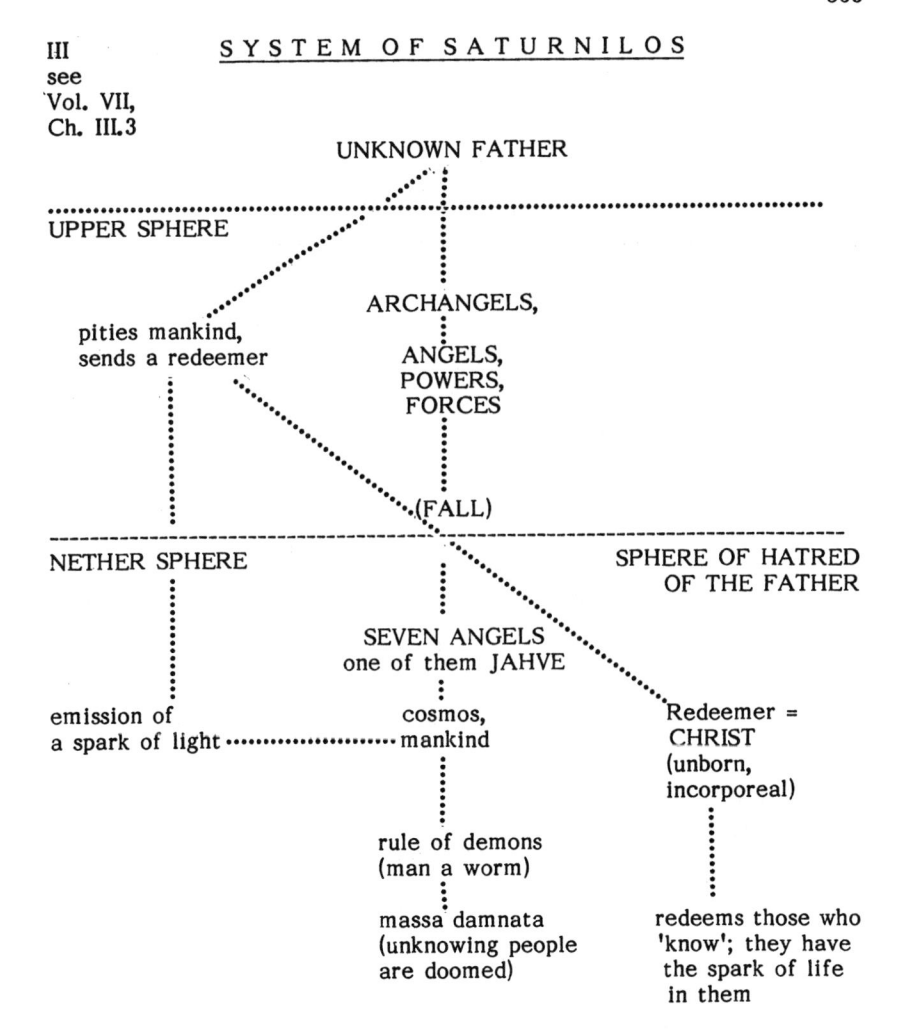

SYSTEM OF SATURNILOS

UNKNOWN FATHER

UPPER SPHERE

pities mankind,
sends a redeemer

ARCHANGELS,
ANGELS,
POWERS,
FORCES

(FALL)

NETHER SPHERE

SPHERE OF HATRED
OF THE FATHER

SEVEN ANGELS
one of them JAHVE

emission of
a spark of light ·········· cosmos,
mankind

Redeemer =
CHRIST
(unborn,
incorporeal)

rule of demons
(man a worm)

massa damnata
(unknowing people
are doomed)

redeems those who
'know'; they have
the spark of life
in them

IV
See
Vol. VII
Ch. III.4

SYSTEM OF CERINTHUS

FIRST GOD,
PRIME PRINCIPLE,
UNKNOWN FATHER

UPPER SPHERE

SPIRIT
sent out
by Father

strict dualism of upper and nether spheres

NETHER SPHERE

DEMIURGE
(wicked, unknowing)
creator of

cosmos,
mankind

SPIRIT
descends on ·············· JESUS
spiritual   Jewish son
union of   of
JESUS   Joseph and Mary
and CHRIST ·························· 'KINGDOM OF CHRIST'
                                    = terrestrial,
                                    Jewish independence

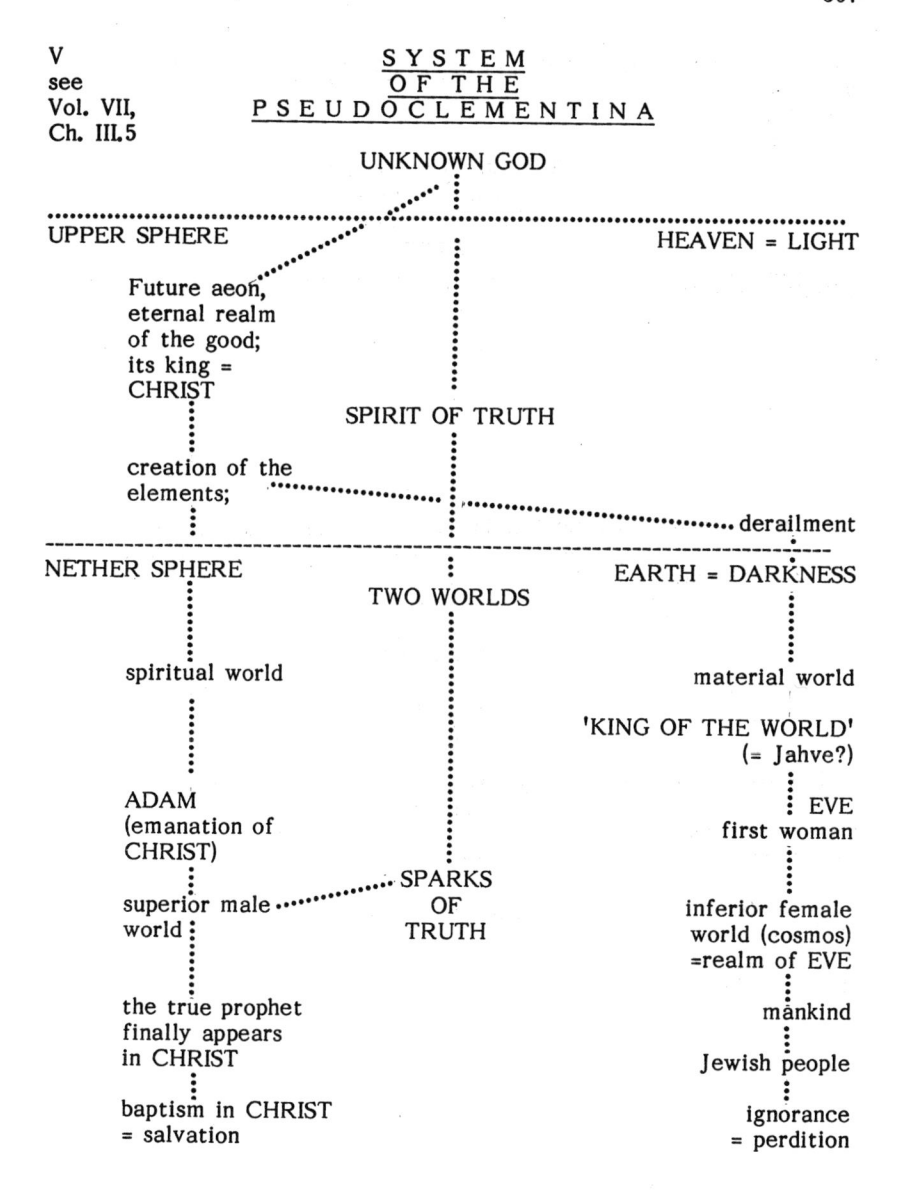

V
see
Vol. VII,
Ch. III.5

SYSTEM OF THE PSEUDOCLEMENTINA

UNKNOWN GOD

UPPER SPHERE .... HEAVEN = LIGHT

Future aeon,
eternal realm
of the good;
its king =
CHRIST

SPIRIT OF TRUTH

creation of the
elements; .... derailment

NETHER SPHERE .... EARTH = DARKNESS

TWO WORLDS

spiritual world   material world

'KING OF THE WORLD'
(= Jahve?)

ADAM   EVE
(emanation of   first woman
CHRIST)

superior male .... SPARKS   inferior female
world   OF   world (cosmos)
                       TRUTH   =realm of EVE

the true prophet   mankind
finally appears
in CHRIST   Jewish people

baptism in CHRIST   ignorance
= salvation   = perdition

VI   THE CARPOCRATIAN SYSTEM
see
Vol. VII,
Ch. III.6

SUPREME GODHEAD
unborn Father
primordial ground
of being

UPPER SPHERE

EMANATIONS

Knowledge enables the elect to break through the sphere of the powers

NETHER SPHERE

POWERS
(dunameis)
= fallen angels

COSMOS

JESUS .... Jewish people
Judaism
his soul returns
to heaven   The Law

souls of the .... the body a prison
elect return
to heaven after
many migrations

VII   THE SETHIAN SYSTEM
see
Vol. VIII,
Ch. IV.1-18

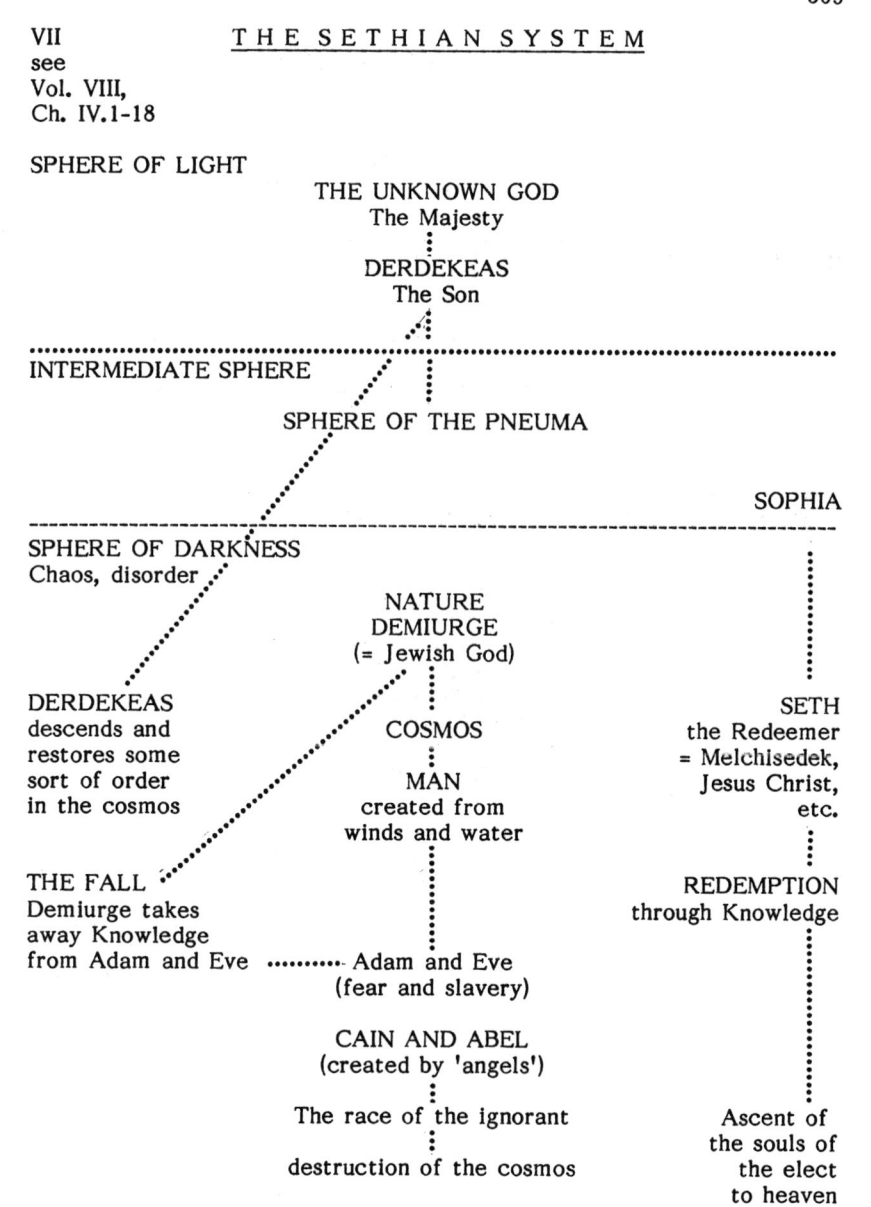

SPHERE OF LIGHT

           THE UNKNOWN GOD
           The Majesty

           DERDEKEAS
           The Son

INTERMEDIATE SPHERE

           SPHERE OF THE PNEUMA

                                                SOPHIA

SPHERE OF DARKNESS
Chaos, disorder

           NATURE
           DEMIURGE
           (= Jewish God)

DERDEKEAS   SETH
descends and   COSMOS   the Redeemer
restores some   = Melchisedek,
sort of order   MAN   Jesus Christ,
in the cosmos   created from   etc.
                   winds and water

THE FALL   REDEMPTION
Demiurge takes   through Knowledge
away Knowledge
from Adam and Eve   Adam and Eve
                   (fear and slavery)

           CAIN AND ABEL
           (created by 'angels')

      The race of the ignorant   Ascent of
                                                  the souls of
     destruction of the cosmos   the elect
                                                  to heaven

VIII
See
Vol. VIII,
Ch. IV.19

THE ARCHONTIC SYSTEM

Dual supreme godhead
THE FATHER AND THE MOTHER

....

SUPERIOR HEAVEN   THE OGDOAS

ruled by
ARCHONS

supreme archon =
THE MOTHER

INFERIOR HEAVEN   THE HEBDOMAS

ruled by seven
ARCHONS

supreme archon =
SABAOTH
the Demiurge
(the Jewish God)
⋮
THE DEVIL
(Sabaoth's son)
⋮
EVE .... ADAM AND EVE
⋮   ⋮
CAIN AND ABEL   SETH
                                the Redeemer
                                   ⋮
                              THE ARCHONTICS

IX   THE OPHITIC SYSTEM
see
Vol. VIII,
Ch. III.1-17

UPPER SPHERE   FATHER OF ALL
sphere of the   the First Man
Depth
                            ENNOIA
                         the Second Man
THE IMPERISHABLE
AEON   HOLY SPIRIT
                         the First Woman

INVISIBLE   CHRIST ·························· CHRIST
CHURCH   begot by First and second Man   sent down
                      with First Woman   to mankind

                         SOPHIA ················· CHRIST unites
                    = emanation of Light   himself
                                                    with SOPHIA

NETHER SPHERE   SOPHIA
                      becomes physical,
THE FALL   Light enclosed in matter
                       but Sophia
                   returns to heaven later

                         JALDABAOTH
                       Sophia's son = Jahve

                       hierarchy of sons

                            NOUS
                      = Serpent, Demiurge

                       ADAM AND EVE
              CAIN   ABEL   SETH   NOREA
              CAINITES   OPHITES

                            MARY

                         JESUS ············ CHRIST/SOPHIA
                                              the Redeemer

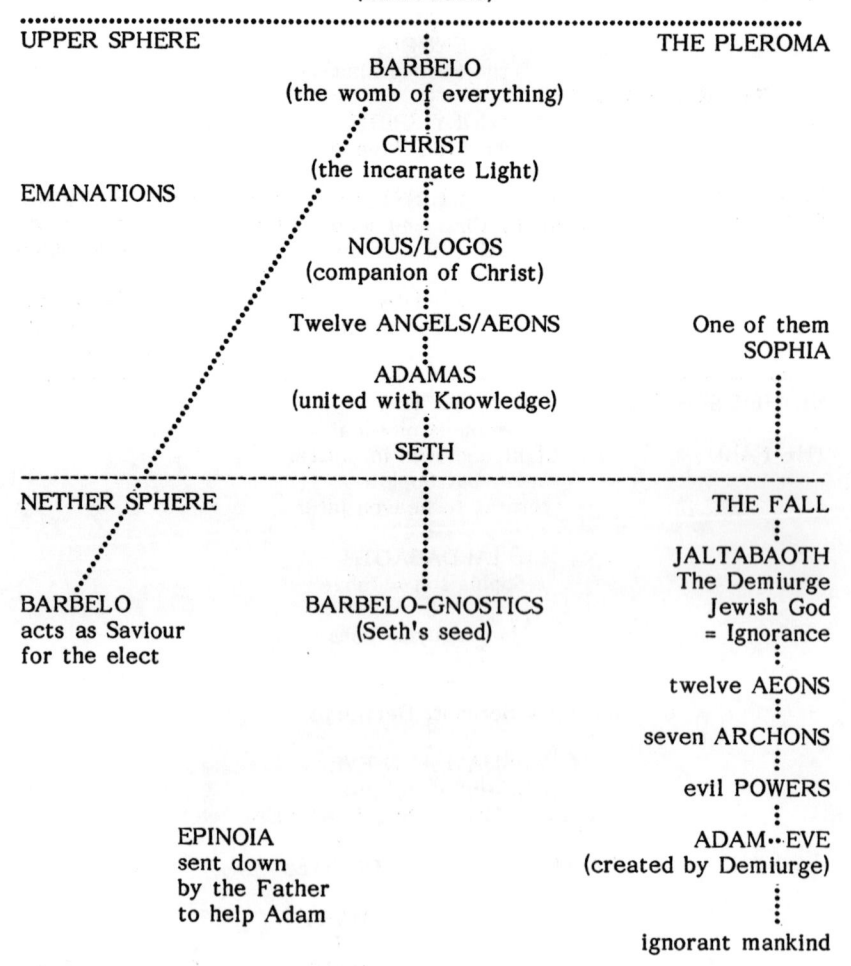

X
see
Vol. VIII,
Ch. VI

THE BARBELO-GNOSTIC SYSTEM

THE MONAD
The Father of All
(unknowable)

UPPER SPHERE   THE PLEROMA

BARBELO
(the womb of everything)

CHRIST
(the incarnate Light)

EMANATIONS

NOUS/LOGOS
(companion of Christ)

Twelve ANGELS/AEONS   One of them
                                              SOPHIA

ADAMAS
(united with Knowledge)

SETH

NETHER SPHERE   THE FALL

JALTABAOTH
The Demiurge
BARBELO   BARBELO-GNOSTICS   Jewish God
acts as Saviour   (Seth's seed)   = Ignorance
for the elect

twelve AEONS

seven ARCHONS

evil POWERS

EPINOIA   ADAM••EVE
sent down   (created by Demiurge)
by the Father
to help Adam

ignorant mankind

XI
Vol. VIII,
Ch. VII.4

THE SYSTEM OF THE GOSPEL OF TRUTH

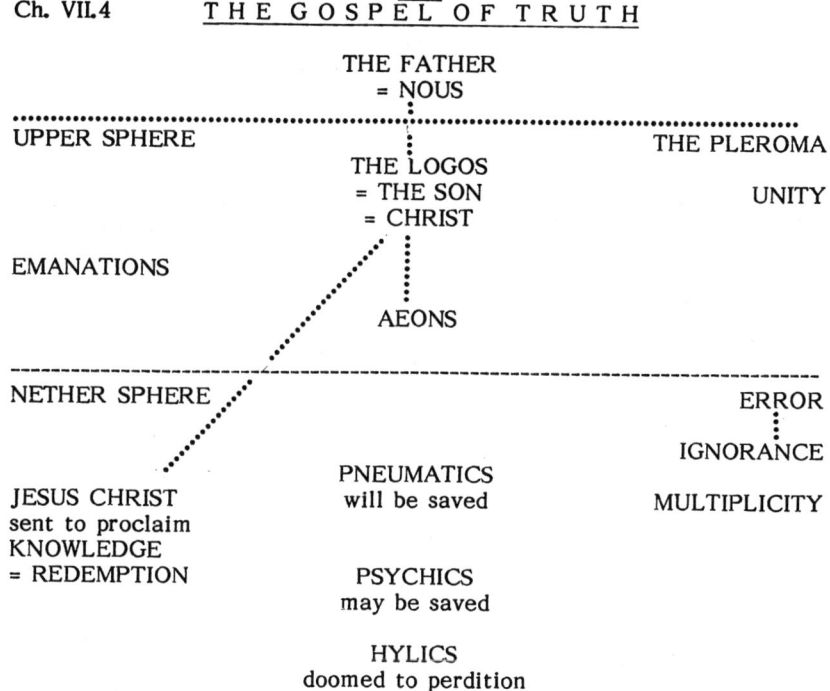

THE FATHER
= NOUS

UPPER SPHERE   THE PLEROMA

THE LOGOS
= THE SON   UNITY
= CHRIST

EMANATIONS

AEONS

NETHER SPHERE   ERROR

                                                            IGNORANCE

                        PNEUMATICS
JESUS CHRIST   will be saved   MULTIPLICITY
sent to proclaim
KNOWLEDGE
= REDEMPTION
                        PSYCHICS
                        may be saved

                        HYLICS
                        doomed to perdition

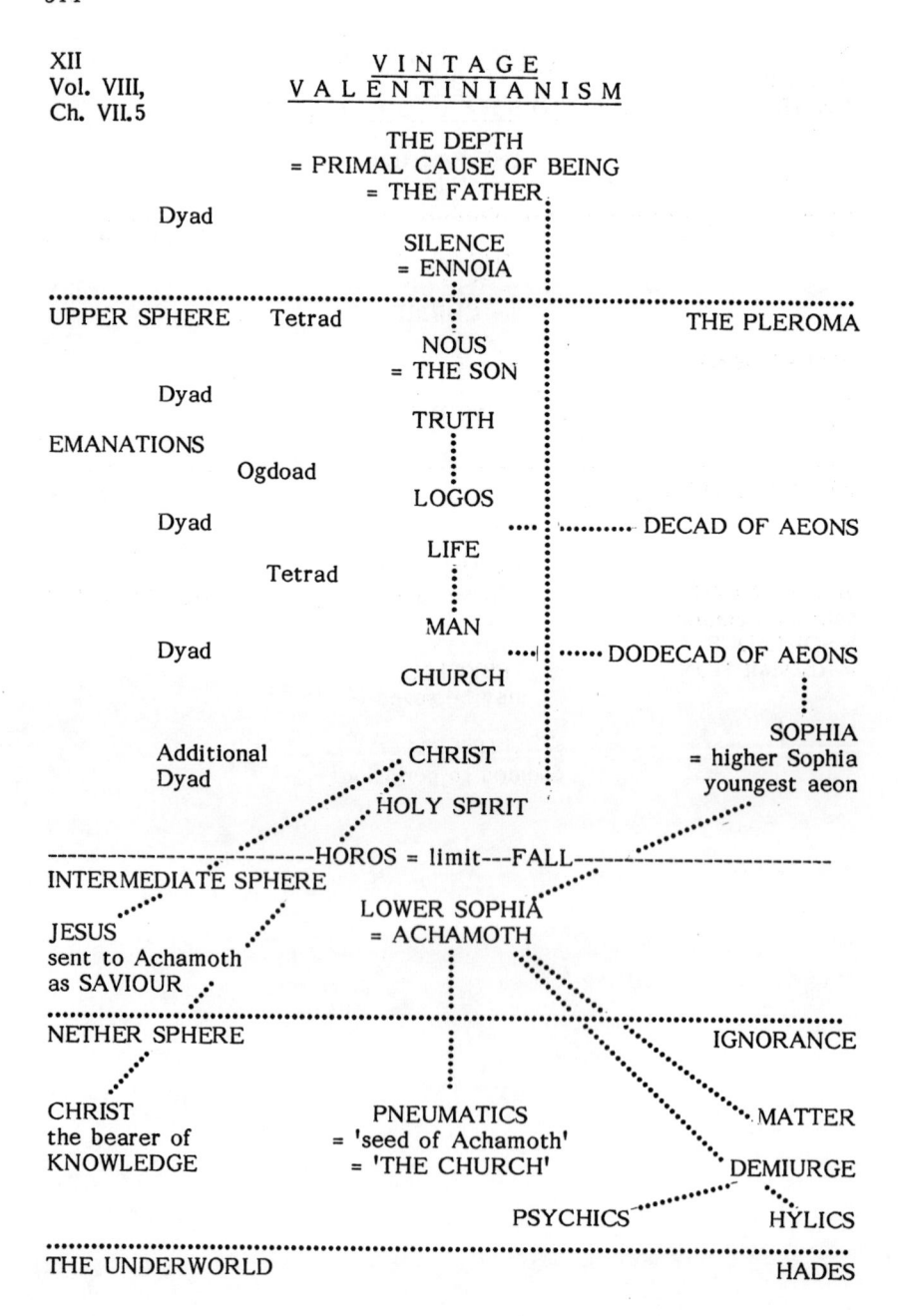

XII
Vol. VIII,
Ch. VII.5

VINTAGE VALENTINIANISM

```
                              THE DEPTH
                          = PRIMAL CAUSE OF BEING
                              = THE FATHER
         Dyad
                                 SILENCE
                                 = ENNOIA
.............................................................................
UPPER SPHERE      Tetrad                                    THE PLEROMA
                                  NOUS
                                = THE SON
         Dyad
                                  TRUTH
EMANATIONS
                   Ogdoad
                                  LOGOS
         Dyad                                  ......... DECAD OF AEONS
                                  LIFE
                   Tetrad
                                   MAN
         Dyad                                  ...... DODECAD OF AEONS
                                 CHURCH
                                                             SOPHIA
         Additional          CHRIST                      = higher Sophia
         Dyad                                              youngest aeon
                            HOLY SPIRIT
----------------------------HOROS = limit---FALL-----------------------
INTERMEDIATE SPHERE
                             LOWER SOPHIA
JESUS                        = ACHAMOTH
sent to Achamoth
as SAVIOUR
.............................................................................
NETHER SPHERE                                             IGNORANCE

CHRIST                     PNEUMATICS                    MATTER
the bearer of             = 'seed of Achamoth'
KNOWLEDGE                 = 'THE CHURCH'                  DEMIURGE

                             PSYCHICS                     HYLICS
.............................................................................
THE UNDERWORLD                                              HADES
```

XIII   THE TRIPARTITE SYSTEM
Vol. VIII,
Ch. VII.8

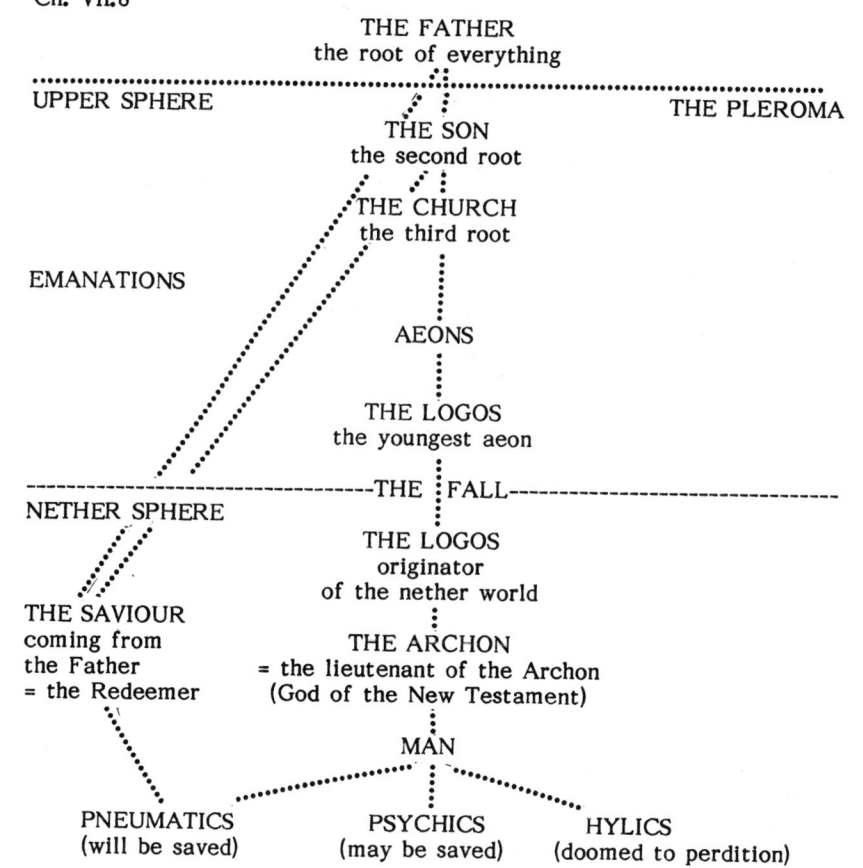

THE FATHER
the root of everything

UPPER SPHERE   THE PLEROMA

THE SON
the second root

THE CHURCH
the third root

EMANATIONS

AEONS

THE LOGOS
the youngest aeon

------------------------------- THE FALL -------------------------------
NETHER SPHERE

THE LOGOS
originator
of the nether world

THE SAVIOUR
coming from   THE ARCHON
the Father   = the lieutenant of the Archon
= the Redeemer   (God of the New Testament)

MAN

PNEUMATICS   PSYCHICS   HYLICS
(will be saved)   (may be saved)   (doomed to perdition)

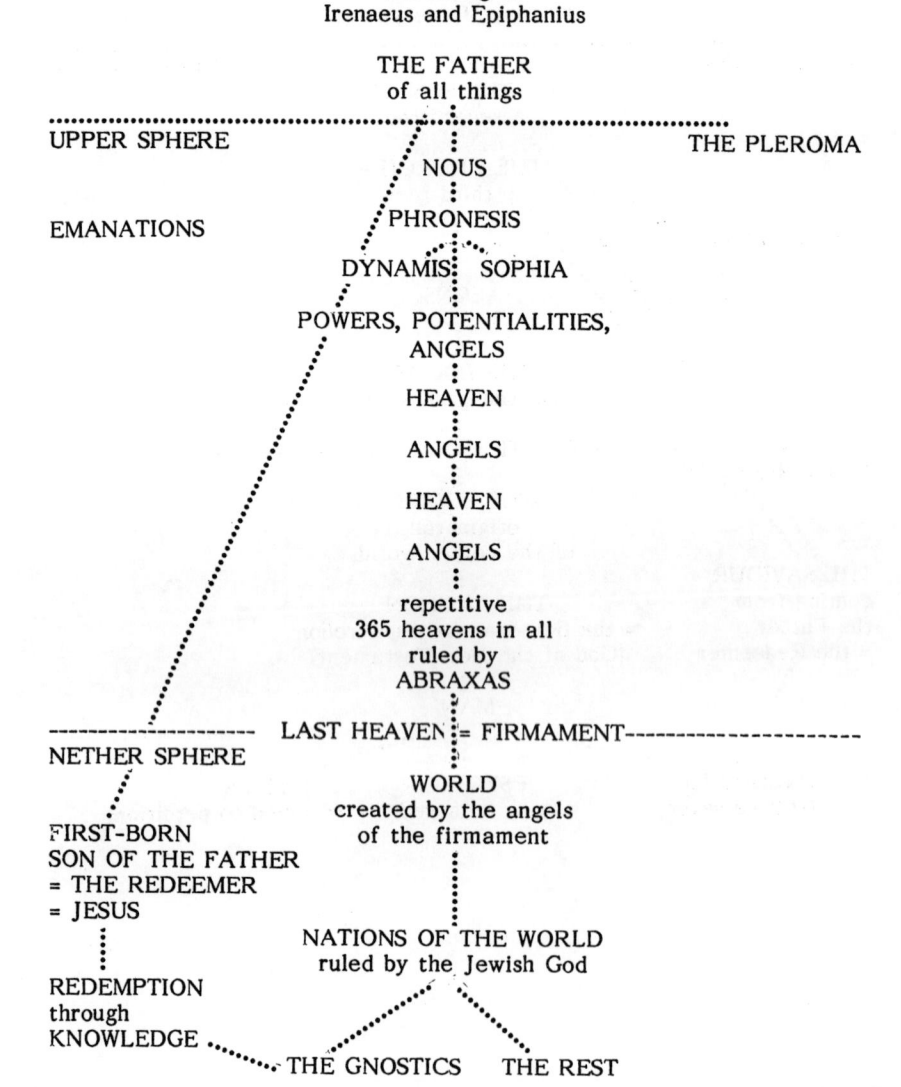

XIV
Vol. VIII,
Ch. VIII.4

THE SYSTEM OF BASILIDES
according to
Irenaeus and Epiphanius

```
                         THE FATHER
                         of all things
UPPER SPHERE ·····················:·····················      THE PLEROMA
                              ╱   NOUS
                             ╱     :
EMANATIONS                  ╱  PHRONESIS
                           ╱    ..:..
                          ╱  DYNAMIS : SOPHIA
                         ╱       :
                        ╱  POWERS, POTENTIALITIES,
                       ╱         ANGELS
                      ╱           :
                     ╱          HEAVEN
                    ╱             :
                   ╱            ANGELS
                  ╱               :
                 ╱              HEAVEN
                ╱                 :
               ╱                ANGELS
              ╱                   :
             ╱                repetitive
            ╱               365 heavens in all
           ╱                    ruled by
          ╱                     ABRAXAS
         ╱                        :
--------╱---------- LAST HEAVEN := FIRMAMENT---------------------
NETHER SPHERE                     :
       ╱                        WORLD
      ╱                   created by the angels
  FIRST-BORN               of the firmament
  SON OF THE FATHER               :
  = THE REDEEMER                  :
  = JESUS                         :
      :                   NATIONS OF THE WORLD
      :                   ruled by the Jewish God
  REDEMPTION                  ..·'    ·..
  through                 ..··           ··..
  KNOWLEDGE ·······  ..··                   ··..
                 ····· THE GNOSTICS        THE REST
```

XV
Vol. VIII,
Ch. VIII.5

THE SYSTEM OF BASILIDES
according to Hippolytus

THE NON-EXISTENT GOD
= the cause of the world

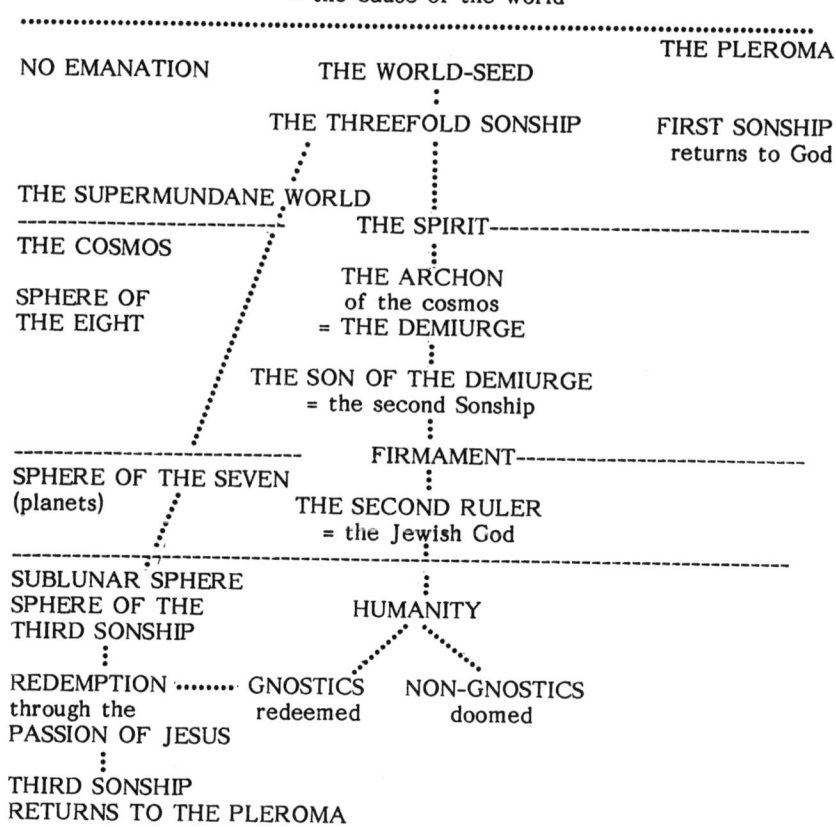

NO EMANATION   THE WORLD-SEED   THE PLEROMA

THE THREEFOLD SONSHIP   FIRST SONSHIP
returns to God

THE SUPERMUNDANE WORLD

THE COSMOS   THE SPIRIT

SPHERE OF
THE EIGHT

THE ARCHON
of the cosmos
= THE DEMIURGE

THE SON OF THE DEMIURGE
= the second Sonship

SPHERE OF THE SEVEN   FIRMAMENT
(planets)

THE SECOND RULER
= the Jewish God

SUBLUNAR SPHERE
SPHERE OF THE   HUMANITY
THIRD SONSHIP

REDEMPTION ········ GNOSTICS   NON-GNOSTICS
through the   redeemed   doomed
PASSION OF JESUS

THIRD SONSHIP
RETURNS TO THE PLEROMA

BIBLIOGRAPHY

I ORIGINAL SOURCES
A COLLECTIONS

CORPUS HERMETICUM. Hermès Trismégiste. Edited by A.D. Nock and A.-J. Festugière. 4 Vols. Collection Budé. Paris, 1954 (réimpression photoméchanique de l'édition 1938).

CORPUS HERMETICUM, ingeleid, vertaald en toegelicht door R. van den Broek en G.Quispel. Amsterdam, 1990.

GNOSIS. A selection of Gnostic texts. Original German edition by Werner Foerster. Translation by Robert Machlachlan Wilson. Vol. I Patristic evidence. Oxford, 1972. (Cit. as Foerster/Wilson).

GOSPEL OF THE EGYPTIANS. NHC III.2 and IV.2, NHL III.2. Introduced and translated by Alexander Böhlig and Frederik Wisse.

THE NAG HAMMADI LIBRARY IN ENGLISH. Ed. James M. Robinson. Leiden, 1977 (cited as NHL, the codices themselves cited as NHC).

PHILO
1. Edition in Greek with English translations by F.H. Colson and G.H. Whitaker. Loeb Classical Library, 10 vols. (1929-1962) + 2 vols. translations from the Armenian by Ralph Marcus (1953).
2. Edition in Greek by Leopoldus Cohn and Paulus Wendland (Eds.), Philonis Alexandrini Opera Omnia quae supersunt. Berolini, 1896-1915 (photostatischer Nachdruck Vol. I-VI, Berlin, 1962). Vol. VII 1 and 2 Indices, composuit Ioannes Leisegang. Berolini, 1926-1930).
3. German translation (without the Greek) by Leopold Cohn, Isaac Heinemann, Maximilian Adler and Willy Theiler. 7 vols. Berlin, 1962-1964 2 (1908 1).
4. Index Philoneus von Günther Maier. Berlin/New York, 1974.

STOBAEUS
Ioannis Stobaei Anthologium. Vol. I Ed. Curtius Wachsmuth. Berolini, 1884. Vol. III. Ed. Otto Hense. Berolini, 1894.

VÖLKER, Walther,   Quellen zur Geschichte der christlichen Gnosis.

Sammlung ausgewählter kirchen- und dogmengeschichtlicher Quellenschriften. Tübingen, 1932.

B INDIVIDUAL AUTHORS

ALLOGENES. NHC IX.3, NHL IX.3. Introduced by Antoinette Clark Wire and translated by John D. Turner and Orval S. Wintermute.

THE APOCALYPSE OF ADAM. NHC V.5. NHL V.5. Introduced and translated by George W. MacRae.

MORARD, Françoise, L'Apocalypse d'Adam. Bibliothèque copte de Nag Hammadi. Section 'Textes' 15. Québec, 1985.

THE APOCALYPSE OF PETER. NHC VII.3. NHL VII.3. Introduced by James Brashler and translated by Roger A. Bullard.

THE APOCRYPHON OF JOHN. NHC II.1, NHL II.1. Introduced and translated by Frederik Wisse.

ARISTOTELES
Aristotelis De Mundo. Ed. W. Lorimer. Paris, 1933. English translation E.S. Forster De Mundo. The Works of Aristotle translated into English. Ed. W.D. Ross. Vol. III. Oxford, 1951 (lithographic reprint of 1931 1).

AUGUSTINUS
De haeresibus ad Quodvultdeum. Patrologia latina 42. Paris, 1861.

CLAUDE, Paul, Les trois stèles de Seth. Hymne gnostique à la triade (NH VII, 5). Bibliothèque copte de Nag Hammadi. Section 'Textes' 8. Québec, 1985.

CLEMENS OF ALEXANDRIA
1. Excerpta ex Theodoto. Patrologia graeca 9. Paris, 1857.
2a. Stromateis. Die griechischen Schriftsteller der ersten drei Jahrhunderte. Clemens Alexandrinus. Herausg. Otto Staehlin. Leipzig, 1906.
2b. Des Clemens van Alexandrien Teppiche. Herausg. Otto Staehlin. Bibliothek der Kirchenväter. 2. Reihe, Bd. XVII. Clemens van Alexandreia, Bd. III. München, 1936.

DIDYMUS ALEXANDRINUS
In Epistolam Beati Apostoli Judae Enarratio. Patrologia graeca XXXIX. Paris, 1863.

THE DISCOURSE OF THE EIGHTH AND THE NINTH. NHC VI.6. NHL VI.6, introduction and translation by James Brashler, Peter A. Dirkse, and Douglas M. Parrott.

EPIPHANIUS OF SALAMIS
Panarion haereseoon. Die griechischen christlichen Schriftsteller der

ersten drei Jahrhunderte. Ed. Karl Holl. Leipzig, 1922.
(New Translation) The Panarion of Epiphanius of Salamis. Book I (sects 1-46). Translated by Frank Williams. Nag Hammadi Studies. Vol. XXXV. Ed. James M. Robinson. Leiden, 1987.

EUSEBIUS OF CAESAREA
Historia ecclesiastica. Die griechischen christlichen Schrifsteller der ersten drei Jahrhunderte. Eusebius II.1, herausgegeben von Eduard Schwartz. Leipzig, 1903.

EVANGELIUM VERITATIS. NHC I.3 and XII.2 (in Sahidic). NHL I.3 and XII.2, introduced and translated by George W. MacRae.

HEGEMONIUS
Acta Archelai. Ed. Charles Henry Beeson. Die griechischen christlichen Schrifsteller der ersten drei Jahrhunderte. Teil 16. Leipzig, 1906.

HIERONYMUS
De viris illustribus. Patrologia latina 22. Paris, 1845.

HIPPOLYTUS
Refutatio omnium haeresium. Die griechischen christlichen Schriftsteller der ersten drei Jahrhunderte. Bd. 26. Hippolytus, 3. Bd. Ed. Paul Wendland. Leipzig, 1916.

IRENAEUS LUGDUNENSIS
Adversus haereses. Contre les héresies. Eds. Adelin Rousseau and Louis Doutreleau. Vol 2 Textes latin et grec et traduction. Paris, 1982.

JOHANNES DAMASCENUS
De haeresibus liber. Patrologia graeca 93. Paris, 1864.

JOSEPHUS, Flavius
Jewish Antiquities. Translated by Ralph Marcus. 7 vols. Loeb Classical Library 365. London/Cambridge (Mass.), 1943 6.

MELCHIZEDEK. NHC IX.1, NHL IX.1. Introduced by Birger A. Pearson, translated by Soren Giversen and Birger A. Pearson.

ORIGENES
1. Commentaria in Evangelium Joannis. Patrologia graeca 14. Paris, 1862.
2. Contra Celsum. Patrologia graeca 11. Paris, 1857.
3. Homiliae in Lucam. Patrologia graeca 13. Paris, 1862.

PARAPHRASIS SHEM. NHC VII.1, NHL VII.1. Introduced and translated by Frederik Wisse.

PAINCHAUD, Louis, Le Deuxième Traité du Grand Seth. Bibliothèque copte de Nag Hammadi. Section 'Textes' 6. Québec, 1982.

PHILO
De Abrahamo (On Abraham). Philo VI (Loeb).
De cherubim (On the Cherubs). Cohn-Wendland I.
Contra Flaccum (Against Flaccus). Philo IX (Loeb).
De confusione linguarum (On the Confusion of Tongues). Philo IV (Loeb).
De congressu quaerendae eruditionis gratia (On Mating with Preliminary Studies). Philo IV (Loeb).
De decalogo (On the Decalogue). Philo VII (Loeb).
Quod deterius potiori insidiari solet (The Worse Attacks the Better). Philo II (Loeb).
Quod Deus immutabilis (On the Unchangeableness of God). Philo III (Loeb).
De ebrietate (On Drunkenness). Philo III (Loeb).
De fuga et inventione (On Flight and Finding). Philo V (Loeb).
De gigantibus (On the Giants). Philo II (Loeb).
Legatio ad Gaium (On the Embassy to Gaius). Philo X (Loeb).
Legum Allegoria (Allegorical Interpretation). Philo I (Loeb).
De migratione Abrahami (On the Migration of Abraham). Philo IV (Loeb).
De opificio mundi (On the Creation). Philo I (Loeb).
De posteritate Caini (On the Posterity and Exile of Cain). Philo II (Loeb).
De praemiis et poenis (On Rewards and Punishments). Philo VIII (Loeb).
Quis rerum divinarum heres? (Who is the Heir of Divine Things?). Philo IV (Loeb).
De sacrificiis Abeli et Caini (The sacrificies of Abel and Cain). Philo II (Loeb).
De sobrietate (On Sobriety). Philo III (Loeb).
De somniis (On Dreams). Philo V (Loeb).
De specialibus legibus (On the Special Laws). Philo VII and VIII (Loeb).
De virtutibus (On the Virtues). Philo VIII (Loeb).
De vita Mosis (The Life of Moses). Philo VI (Loeb).

PLINIUS
Natural History.
Translated by H. Rackham. Loeb Classical Library. London/Cambridge (Mass.), 1942 4.

PSEUDOCHRYSOSTOMUS
Opus imperfectum in Matthaeum. Patrologia graeca 56. Paris, 1861.

PSEUDOTERTULLIANUS
Adversus omnes haereses. Tertulliani Opera, Pars III. Ed. Aemilius Kroymann. Corpus Scriptorum Ecclesiasticorum Latinorum XXXXVII. Wien/Leipzig, 1906.

THE SECOND TREATISE OF THE GREAT SETH. NHC VII.2, NHL VII.2.
Introduced by Joseph A. Gibbons. Translated by Roger A. Bullard.

Edited by Frederik Wisse.

SERAPION OF TMUIS
Against the Manichees. Ed. Robert Pierce Casey. Harvard Theological Studies 15. Cambridge, 1931.

TERTULLIANUS
De carne Christi. Patrologia latina 2. Paris, 1844.
De praescriptionibus. Patrologia latina 2. Paris, 1844.
Adversus Valentianos. Patrologia latina 2. Paris, 1844.

TESTIMONIUM VERITATIS. NHC IX.3, NHL IX.3. Introduced by Birger A. Pearson. Translated by Soren Giversen and Birger A. Pearson.

THE THOUGHT OF NOREA. NHC IX.2, NHL IX.2. Introduced by Birger A. Pearson. Translated by Soren Giversen and Birger A. Pearson.

THEODORETUS
Haereticarum fabularum compendium. Patrologia graeca 83. Paris, 1864.

THE TRIPARTITE TRACTATE. NHC I.5. NHL I.5. Introduced by Harold W. Attridge and Elaine H. Pagels, translated by Harold W. Attridge and Dieter Müller.

ZOSTRIANOS. NHC VIII.1, NHL VIII.1. Introduced and translated by John H. Sieber.

I I S E C O N D A R Y W O R K S

A   W O R K S O F R E F E R E N C E

Dictionnaire d'histoire et géographie ecclésiastiques. Paris, 1932.

Dictionnaire de théologie catholique. Paris, 1931, 1950.

Enciclopedia cattolica. Città del Vaticano, 1953, 1954.

Encyclopaedia Judaica. Jerusalem, 1974 2 (1972 1) (cited as Enc.Jud.).

The Encyclopaedia of Religion. New York/London (1987).

Encyclopaedia of Religion and Ethics. Edinburg, 1909, 1912, 1913, 1917, 1921.

Paulys Real-Encyclopädie der classischen Altertumswissenschaft. Neue Bearbeitung von Georg Wissowa. Stuttgart (cited as PW).

Realenzyclopädie für protestantische Theologie und Kirche. Leipzig, 1897, 1908 3.

Reallexikon für Antike und Christentum. Stuttgart, 1950.

Theologische Realenzyklopädie. Berlin/New York, 1986.

B COLLECTIONS

THE REDISCOVERY OF GNOSTICISM. Proceedings of the International Conference on Gnosticism at Yale, Newhaven, Connecticut, March 28-31, 1978. Ed. Bentley Layton. Studies in the History of Religions. Supplements to Numen, Vol. XLI. Leiden, 1981. (Cit. as Rediscovery). Vol. II Sethian Gnosticism.

SCHOLER, David, Nag Hammadi Library 1948-1969. Nag Hammadi Studies I. Ed. George W. MacRae. Leiden, 1971.

SLOTERDIJK, Peter/MACHO, Thomas H. (Eds.), Weltrevolution der Seele. Ein Lese- und Arbeitsbuch der Gnosis von der Spätantike bis zur Gegenwart. 2 Vols. Artemis & Winkler Verlag, 1991.

C MONOGRAPHS

ALAND, Barbara, Die Paraphrase als Form gnostischer Verkündigung. Nag Hammadi Studies XIV. Ed. R.McL. Wilson. Nag Hammadi and Gnosis. Papers read at the First International Congress of Coptology (Cairo, December 1976). Leiden, 1978.

ARAI, Sasagu, Die Christologie des Evangelium Veritatis. Eine religionsgeschichtliche Untersuchung. Leiden, 1964.

BAER Jr., Richard A., Philo's Use of the Categories Male and Female. Arbeiten zur Literatur und Geschichte des hellenistischen Judentums III. Leiden, 1970.

BERTRAND, Daniel Alain, 'Paraphrase de Sem' et 'Paraphrase de Seth'. Nag Hammadi Studies VII. Ed. Martin Krause. Les textes de Nag Hammadi. Colloque du Centre de l'histoire des religions (Strasbourg, 23-25 octobre 1974). Ed. Jacques-É. Ménard. Leiden, 1975.

BILLINGS, Thomas H., The Platonism of Philo Judaeus. New York & London, 1979 (photomechanic reprint of edition Chicago, 1919).

BOUSSET, Wilhelm,
1. Hauptprobleme der Gnosis. Göttingen, 1907.
2. Die Religion des Judentums im späthellenistischen Zeitalter. Handbuch zum Neuen Testament 24.Tübingen, 1926 (3. verbesserte Auflage, herausgegeben von Hugo Gressmann).

BRÉHIER, Émile, Les idées philosophiques et religieuses de Philon d'Alexandrie. Études de philosophie médiévale VIII. Paris, 1950 3.

BROEK, R. van den, De taal van de Gnosis (The Language of the Gnosis). Gnostische teksten uit Nag Hammadi. Baarn (NL), 1986.

COULIANO, Ioan P., Les Gnoses dualistes d'occident. Histoire et mythes. Paris, 1989.

DART, John, The Laughing Savior. The Discovery and Significance of the Nag Hammadi Gnostic Library. New York, Hagerstown, San Francisco, London (1976).

DODD, C.H., The Bible and the Greeks. London (1935).

DORESSE, Jean, Les livres secrets des Gnostiques d'Égypte. Introduction aux écrits gnostiques coptes découverts à Knenoboskion. Paris, 1958.

DRUMMOND, James, Philo Judaeus, or the Jewish-Alexandrian Philosophy in its Development and Completion. Amsterdam, 1969 (reprinted from the first edition, London, 1888).

FARANDOS, Georgios D., Kosmos und Logos nach Philon von Alexandrien. Elementa. Schriften zur Philosophie und ihrer Problemgeschichte IV. Amsterdam, 1976.

FESTUGIÈRE, A.-J., La révelation d'Hermès Trismégiste.
I. L'astrologie et les sciences occultes.
II. Le dieu cosmique.
Collection d'études anciennes. Études bibliques. Paris, 1983 (réimpression de l'edition 1949).

FILORAMO, Giovanni, A History of Gnosticism. Translated by Anthony Alcock (L'attesa della fine. Storia della Gnosi). London, 1991 (1990).

FISCHER, Karl Martin, Die Paraphrase des Seem. Nag Hammadi Studies VI. Ed. Martin Krause. Essays on the Nag Hammadi texts in honor of Pahor Lahib. Berliner Arbeitskreis für koptisch-gnostische Schriften. Exegetische Probleme der Schriften von Nag Hammadi Codex VII. Leiden, 1975.

FOWDEN, Garth, The Egyptian Hermes. A historical approach to the late pagan mind. Cambridge (1986).

GOODENOUGH, Erwin R., An Introduction to Philo Judaeus. New Haven, 1940.

HAENCHEN, Ernst, Das Buch Baruch. Ein Beitrag zum Problem der christlichen Gnosis. Gott und Mensch. Gesammelte Aufsätze. Tübingen, 1965.

HARNACK, Adolf von, Geschichte der altchristlichen Literatur. Erster Theil. Die Überlieferung und der Bestand der altchristlichen Literatur bis Eusebius. Leipzig, 1893.

HEINEMANN, Isaac, Philons griechische und jüdische Bildung. Kulturvergleichende Untersuchungen zu Philons Darstellung der jüdischen Gesetze. Hildesheim, 1962 (photomechanischer Nachdruck von 1929-1932 1).

HELDERMAN, Jan, Die Anapausis im Evangelium Veritatis. Eine vergleichende Untersuchung des valentinisch-gnostischen Heilsgutes im Evangelium Veritatis und anderen Schriften der Nag Hammadi-Bibliothek. Nag Hammadi Studies XVIII. Eds. Martin Krause and Jan Zandee. Leiden, 1984.

HENDRIX, Petrus (Pjotr) J.G.A., De Alexandrijnse Haeresiarch Basilides. Een bijdrage tot de geschiedenis der Gnosis. Doctoral thesis Leiden State University. Amsterdam, 1926.

HÖNIG, Adolf, Die Ophiten. Ein Beitrag zur Geschichte des judischen Gnostizismus. Berlin, 1889.

IVERSEN, Erik, Egyptian and Hermetic Doctrine. Opuscula graeco-latina (Supplementa Musei Tusculani), Vol. 27. Copenhagen, 1984.

JONAS, Hans,
1. Gnosis und spätantiker Geist. Teil I Die mythologische Gnosis. Göttingen, 1934.
2. The Gnostic Religion. The Message of the Alien God and the Beginnings of Christianity. London, 1992 (second edition, revised) (1958 1).

KAESTLI, Jean-Daniel, Valentinisme italien et Valentinisme oriental : leurs divergences à propos de la nature du corps de Jésus. The Rediscovery of Gnosticism. Proceedings of the International Conference on Gnosticism at Yale New Haven, Connecticut, March 28-31, 1978. Vol. I. The School of Valentinus. Ed. Bentley Layton. Sudies in the History of Religions (Supplements to Numen XLI). Leiden, 1980.

KLIJN, A.F.J., Seth in Jewish, Christian and Gnostic Literature. Supplements to Novum Testamentum, Vol. XLVI. Leiden, 1977.

KOSCHORKE, Klaus,
1. Patristische Materialien zur Spätgeschichte der valentinianischen Gnosis. Nag Hammadi Studies XVII. Ed. Martin Krause. Gnosis and Gnosticism. Papers read at the Eighth International Conference on Patristic Studies. Oxford, September 3d-8th, 1979. Leiden, 1981.
2. Die Polemik der Gnostiker gegen das kirchliche Christentum. Skizziert am Beispiel des Nag-Hammadi-Traktates Testimonium Veritatis. Nag Hammadi Studies. Vol. VIII. Ed. Martin Krause. Gnosis and Gnosticism. Papers read at the Seventh International Conference on Patristic Studies (Oxford, September 8th-13th, 1975). Leiden, 1977.

3. Die Polemik der Gnostiker gegen das kirchliche Christentum. Unter besonderer Berücksichtigung des Nag-Hammadi-Traktate 'Apokalypse des Petrus' (NHC VII,3) und 'Testimonium Veritatis' (NHC IX, 3). Nag Hammadi Studies. Vol. XII. Ed. Martin Krause. Leiden, 1978.

KRAUSE, Martin, Christlich-gnostische Texte aus Quellen für die Auseinandersetzung von Gnosis und Christentum. Nag Hammadi Studies. Vol. XVII. Ed. Martin Krause. Gnosis and Gnosticism Papers read at the Eighth International Conference on Patristic Studies (Oxford, September 3d-8th 1979). Leiden, 1981.

LEISEGANG, Hans, Die Gnosis. Stuttgart, 1955 4 (1924 1).

MAHÉ, Jean-Pierre, Le sens des symboles sexuels dans quelques textes hermétiques et gnostiques. Nag Hammadi Studies. Vol. VII. Ed. Jacques-É. Ménard. Les textes de Nag Hammadi. Colloque du centre de l'histoire des religions (Strasbourg, 23-25 octobre 1974). Leiden, 1975.

MOORSEL, Gerard van, The Mysteries of Hermes Trismegistus. A phenomenological study in the process of spiritualisation in the Corpus Hermeticum and the Latin Asclepius. Utrecht, 1955.

MÉNARD, Jacques-É., L'Évangile de Vérité. Traduction et commentaire. Nag Hammadi Studies II. Ed. Martin Krause. Leiden, 1972.

MORARD, Françoise,
1. L'Apocalypse d'Adam de Nag Hammadi. Un essai d'interprétation. Nag Hammadi Studies VIII. Gnosis and Gnosticism. Papers read at the Seventh International Conference of Patristic Studies (Oxford, September 8th-13th, 1975. Ed. Martin Krause. Leiden, 1977.
2. Christlich-gnostische Texte als Quellen für die Auseinandersetzung von Gnosis und Christentum. Nag Hammadi Studies XVII. Gnosis and Gnosticism. Papers read the the Eighth International Conference on Patristic Studies (Oxford, September 3d-8th 1979). Ed. Martin Krause. Leiden, 1981.
3. Thématique de l'Apocalypse d'Adam du Codex V. Bibliothèque copte de Nag Hammadi. Section 'Études' 1. Colloque international sur les textes de Nag Hammadi (Québec 22-25 août 1978). Ed. Bernard Barc. Québec/Louvain, 1981.

NIKIPROWETZKY, V., Le commentaire de l'écriture chez Philon d'Alexandrie. Son caractère et sa portée. Observations philologiques. Arbeiten zur Geschichte des hellenistischen Judentums XI. Leiden, 1977.

PAGELS, Elaine,
1. The Gnostic Gospels. London, 1980 (Am. ed. 1979).
2. The Johannine Gospel in Gnostic Exegesis : Heracleon's Commentary on John. Nashville, NY (1973).

PAINCHAUD, Louis, Fragment de la République de Platon (NH VI,5).

Bibliothèque copte de Nag Hammadi. Section 'Textes', 11. Québec, 1983.

PEARSON, Birger A.,
1. Anti-heretical warnings in Codex IX from Nag Hammadi. Nag Hammadi Studies VI. Ed. Martin Krause. Essays on the Nag Hammadi texts in honor of Pahor Lahib. Leiden, 1975.
2. The Figure of Seth in Gnostic Literature. In : Rediscovery II.
3. Philo and the New Testament. In : The New Testament and the Gnosis. Essays in honour of Robert McL. Wilson. A.H.B. Logan & A.J.M. Wedderburn, Eds. Edinburgh, 1983.

POHLENZ, Max, Philon von Alexandrien. Nachrichten von der Akademie der Wissenschaften in Göttingen. Philologisch-historische Klasse. Jg. 1942.

PRÜMM, Karl, Gnosis an der Wurzel des Christentums? Grundlagenkritik der Entmythologisierung. Salzburg (1971).

PUECH, H.C. and QUISPEL, G., Op zoek naar het Evangelie der Waarheid (In Search of the Gospel of Truth). Nijkerk (NL), w.d.

QUISPEL, Gilles,
1. De Codex Jung. H.C. Puech and G. Quispel, Op zoek naar het Evangelie der waarheid (In Search of the Gospel of Truth). Nijkerk (NL), w.d.
2. Hermes Trismegistus and the origins of Gnosticism. In : Vigiliae Christianae 46 (1992).

REITZENSTEIN, Richard, Poimandres. Studien zur griechisch-ägyptischen und frühchristlichen Literatur. Leipzig, 1904.

ROBINSON, James M.,
1. From the Cliff to Cairo. The story of the discovery and the middlemen of the Nag Hammadi Codices. Bibliothèque copte de Nag Hammadi 1. Colloque international sur les textes de Nag Hammadi (Québec, 22-25 août 1978). Ed. Bernard Barc. Québec/Louvain, 1981.
2. The Jung Codex. The Rise and Fall of a Monopoly. Religious Studies Review. Vol. 3, no. 1 (January 1977).

RUDOLPH, Kurt,
1. Die Gnosis. Wesen und Geschichte einer spätantiken Religion. Göttingen (1980 2, 1977 1).
2. Die Sethianische Gnosis - eine häresiologische Fiktion? In : Rediscovery II.

RUNIA, David T., Philo of Alexandria and the Timaeus of Plato. Philosophia antiqua XLIV. Leiden, 1986.

SÄVE-SÖDERBERGH, Torgny, Holy Scriptures or Apologetic Documentations? The 'Sitz im Leben' of the Nag Hammadi Library. Nag Hammadi Studies. XII. Les textes de Nag Hammadi Colloque du Centre d'Histoire des religions (Strasbourg, 23-25 octobre 1974). Ed. Jacques-É. Ménard. Leiden, 1974.

SAGNARD, François-M.-M., La Gnose valentinienne et le témoignage de Saint Irenée. Paris, 1947.

SCHENKE, Hans-Martin, The Phenomenon and Significance of Sethian Gnosticism. In : Rediscovery II.

SEVRIN, Jean-Marie, Le dossier baptismal séthien. Études sur le sacramentaire gnostique. Bibliothèque copte de Nag Hammadi. Section 'Études' 2. Québec, 1986.

SLOTERDIJK, Peter, Die wahre Irrlehre. Über die Weltreligion der Weltlosigkeit. In : Weltrevolution der Seele. Ein Lese- und Arbeitsbuch der Gnosis von der Spätantike bis zur Gegenwart I. Peter Sloterdijk and Thomas H. Macho (Hg.). 1991 Artemis & Winkler Verlag.

STANDAERT, Benoit, 'L'Évangile de la vérité' : critique et lecture. New Testament Studies 22 (1976).

STONE, Michael E., Report on Seth Traditions in Armenian Adam Books. In : Rediscovery II.

STROUMSA, Gedaliahu A.G., Another seed : studies in Gnostic mythology. Nag Hammadi Studies. Vol. XXIV. Ed. Frederik Wisse. Leiden, 1984.

TARDIEU, Michel, Les livres mis sous le nom de Seth et les Séthiens de l'hérésiologie. Nag Hammadi Studies VIII. Ed. Martin Krause. Gnosis and Gnosticism. Papers read at the Seventh International Conference on Patristic Studies (Oxford, September 8th-13th 1975). Leiden, 1977.

TRÖGER, Karl-Wolfgang,
1. The attitude of the Gnostic religion towards Judaism as viewed in a variety of perspectives. Bibliothèque copte de Nag Hammadi. Section 'Études' 1. Colloque international sur les textes de Nag Hammadi (Québec, 22-25 août 1978). Ed. Bernard Barc. Québec/Louvain, 1981.
2. Mysterienglaube und Gnosis im Corpus Hermeticum XIII. Texte und Untersuchungen zur Geschichte der altchristlichen Literatur. Bd. 110. Berlin, 1971.
3. Der zweite Logos des grossen Seth. Gedanken zur Christologie in der zweiten Schrift des Codex VII (p.49,10-70,12). Nag Hammadi Studies VI. Ed. Martin Krause. Essays on the Nag Hammadi Texts. In honour of Pahor Labib. Leiden, 1975.

UNNIK, W.C. van, Het kort geleden ontdekte 'Evangelie der waarheid' en het Nieuwe Testament (The Gospel of Truth and the New Testament). Mededelingen van de Koninklijke Akademie van Wetenschappen. Nieuwe Reeks 17.3. Amsterdam, 1954.

WERSCH, Stefan van, De gnostisch-occulte vloedgolf. Van Simon de Tovenaar tot New Age. Een kritische beschouwing. (The Gnostic-occult tide. From Simon the Magician to New Age). Kampen (NL), 1990.

WILLIAMS, Michael Allen, The Immovable Race. A Gnostic designation and the theme of stability in late Antiquity. Nag Hammadi Studies XXIX. Ed. Frederik Wisse. Leiden, 1985.

WILSON, Robert MacLachlan,
1. The Gnostic problem. A Study of the Relations between Hellenistic Judaism and the Gnostic Heresy. London (1958).
2. Philo and Gnostiscism. Kairos 14. 1972.
3. Valentinianism and the Gospel of Truth. The Rediscovery of Gnosticism. Proceedings of the International Conference on Gnosticism at Yale, New Haven, Conn., March 28-31, 1978. Vol. I The School of Valentinus. Ed. Bentley Layton. Leiden, 1980.

WINDEN, J.C.M. van, The world of ideas in Philo of Alexandria. An interpretation of De opificio mundi. Vigiliae christianae 37 (1983).

WISSE, Frederik, Stalking Those Elusive Sethians. In: Rediscovery II.

WOLFSON, Harry Austyn, Philo. Foundations of Religious Philosophy in Judaism, Christianity and Islam. 2 vols. Cambridge (Mass.), 1948.

ZACHARIAS, Gerhard, The Satanic Cult. Translated (from the German) by Christine Trollope. London (1980) (first German edition Wiesbaden, 1964).

ZELLER, Eduard, Die Philosophie der Griechen in ihrer geschichtlichen Entwicklung. Bd. III.2. Hildesheim, 1963 (photomechanischer Nachdruck von Leipzig, 1923).

ZIELINSKI, Th., Hermes und die Hermetik. Archiv für Religionswissenschaft 8 (1905).

GENERAL INDEX

Aarmouriam, 193
Abel, 95, 96, 106, 107-110, 121-122, 123, 144, 155, 189, 198
Abiram, 155, 176, 298
Abraham, 113, 145, 154
Abraxas, 218, 219
Achamoth, 255-256, 257, 258, 259, 260, 261, 262, 263, 267
Achilles, 159
Achmounein see Khomonou
Acts of the Apostles, 156, 171
Adam, 22, 64, 95, 96, 97, 98, 105-106, 107, 109, 110, 113, 122, 125, 126, 143, 144, 155, 167, 173, 174, 192, 195, 196, 197, 198, 278
Adamas, 109, 110, 112, 187, 188, 191
Agathopus (correspondent of Valentinus), 267
Agrippa Castor, 214
Ainon, 109
Akioreim, 192
'Al-Qasr (Egypt), 86, 87
Aland, Barbara, 128
Alchemy, 45, 51
Alexandria(n), 1, 2, 3, 4, 5, 6, 49, 50, 90, 136, 214, 230, 231, 235, 285, 297
Allogeneis (Gnostic treatise), 119, 130
American, 88
Amir, Yehoshua (Neumark), 4, 38
Androgyny, androgynous, 64, 66, 67
Angels (in Philo), 18-19, 24
Anicetus, 235
Anthimus of Nicomedia, 287
Anthropomorphism, anthropomorphic, 8, 9, 184
Antinomian(ism), 113, 122, 153-158, 298

Antiquity, 85
Anti-Semitism, anti-Semitic, 299
Antoninus Pius (Roman emperor), 214
Aphrodite, 73, 153, 167, 170
Apocalypse of Adam, 105-106, 183
Apocalypse of Peter, 299-300
Apocryphal gospels, 34
Apocryphon of John, 183, 184, 185, 186, 187, 191, 198, 200, 201, 209, 210, 212
Apostles, 213, 220
Arab, 86
Arai, Sasagu, 286, 287
Archan, 192
Archontic(s), 91, 118-123, 134
Ardesianes, 264
Ares, 73
Arians, 285
Aristippus of Cyrene, 157
Aristotle, Aristotelian, 4, 8, 13, 35, 153, 225, 252
Ark of Noah, 201
Armenia(n), 4, 38, 119, 126
Armstrong, A.H., 41
Astrology, 51, 60
Ascension of Isaiah (Gnostic tractate), 119
Ascent of Paul, 156
Asclepius (hermetic text), 53, 79, 88, 91
Asia Minor, 156, 285
Astaphaios, 152
Athanasius, patriarch of Alexandria, 90, 285
Athens, 3, 153
Atoth, 190
Augustinus, 132
Austrian, 34
Axionicus, 264

Babylonian, 159
Baer, 42, 43
Balaam, 157, 176
Balak, 157, 176
Bammel, Caroline, 293
Barbarian(s), 47, 215, 216, 279
Barbelites, Barberites, 181, 203
Barbelo, 108, 109, 110, 116, 129, 181, 184-185, 186, 202-203, 204, 205, 206, 209
Barbelo-Gnostic(s), 91, 94, 134, Ch. VI passim
Barbero(s), 181
Bardy, G., 213, 223, 230, 233, 234, 238, 287
Bareille, G., 153, 175
Barth, Karl, 8
Baruch (biblical prophet), 179
Baruch (Justin's book), 165-170, 179, 181
Basilides (Gnostic), 115, Ch. VII passim
Basilides (Saint), 230
Basilidians, Basilidianism, Ch. VII passim
Baur, F.C., 143
Beelzebul, 260
Behemoth, 150, 152
Belial, Belias, 189
Belgian, 87
Bertrand, Daniel Alain, 127, 132
Bible, biblical, 5, 6, 8, 10, 11, 12, 14, 17, 20, 22, 26, 28, 33, 34, 36,, 67, 70, 90, 113-114, 122, 145, 150, 153, 159, 169, 171, 186, 188, 279, 298
Billings, Thomas H., 41, 42
Book of Jaldabaoth, 183
Book of Noreah, 183
Books of Seth, 183
Book of Zoroaster, 193
Borborites, 181, 203
Bousset, Wilhelm, 4, 38, 70, 74, 79, 82, 83, 124, 125, 174, 175, 181, 209, 210, 214, 231, 247, 289
Brahmans, 47
Brashler, James, 93
Bräuninger, 79
Bréhier, Émile, 9, 13, 22, 31, 40, 42, 43
Broek, R. van den, 78, 79, 237, 286, 287, 288
Bruckner, Anton, 246

Cain, 95, 96, 106, 107-110, 121-122, 123, 144, 155, 156, 189, 198, 298
Cainite(s), 134, 144, 153-156, 172, 176, 298
Cairo, 87, 88
Caligula, 2, 3
Catholic see Roman-Catholic
Celbes, 159
Celsus, 148, 149, 151, 172, 174, 175
Chaldaean, 47, 50
Cham, 107, 155, 298
Charaxio, 97
Charcharb, 192
Chenoboskion, 85, 86, 89
Christ (Gnostic), 109, 113, 114, 118, 123, 131, 138, 139, 145, 147, 155, 186, 187, 188, 205, 207, 219-220, 227, 229, 239, 253, 254, 255, 256, 257, 261, 262-267, 271, 272, 282-283, 285, 288
Christian(s), 35, 48, 62, 72, 79, 81, 85, 86, 89, 90, 91, 114, 115, 116, 123, 125, 126, 136, 139, 142, 147, 154, 155, 156, 158, 159, 163, 164, 165, 174, 175, 184, 190, 208, 213, 214, 216, 220, 221, 227, 231, 236, 237, 240, 241, 246, 252, 259, 267, 269, 273, 279, 280, 281, 283, 284, 285, 297, 299-300
Christianity, 4, 90, 95, 115, 116, 123, 148, 154, 210, 213, 283, 284, 297, 298, 299, 299-300
Chrysostomus, Johannes, 285
Claremont, Ca., 88
Claudel, Paul, 129
Claudius, 2
Clement of Alexandria, 157, 177, 214, 215, 216, 230, 231, 232, 235, 258, 269, 286, 287, 291, 292, 293, 296
Coddaeans, 181, 203
Colpe, Carsten 79
Constantinople, 285
Coptic, 85, 86, 87, 88, 89, 109, 236
Coptic Museum of Cairo, 87, 88

Corpus Hermeticum, 45
Cypriote, 87
Cyprus, 182, 206, 236

Daniel, Book of, 277
Dart, John, 92, 93
Datan, 155, 176, 298
Daveithai, 187, 188
Davithe, 110, 129
Dead Sea Scrolls, 90
Demeter, 153
Demiurge, 14, 28, 37, 53, 55, 58, 59, 60, 61, 63, 64-65, 65, 71, 77, 103, 105, 108, 114, 117, 123, 141, 143, 155, 158, 162, 163, 178, 189, 190-191, 194, 197, 198, 199, 200, 206, 218, 219, 225, 226, 237, 245, 249, 256, 257, 259-262, 263, 264, 267, 268, 269, 271, 272, 275-276, 283, 292, 300
Dendera, 78
Derdekeas, 98, 100, 101, 102, 103
Diaspora, 1, 5
Didymus of Alexandria (the Blind), 94, 95, 125,
Diogenes, 153
Diolimodraza, 192
Discourse of the Eighth and the Ninth (Gnostic treatise), 91
Docetism, Docetist(s), 123, 131
Dodd, Ch., 39
Domedon Doxemedon, 109
Dominican, 5
Doresse, Jean, 87, 88, 92, 93
Doresse, Marianne, 87
Dositheus, 95
Drummond, James, 23, 39, 42
Dualism, dualistic, 10, 13, 14, 15, 17, 18, 19, 20, 21, 22, 23, 24, 25, 29, 34, 35, 41, 42, 52, 53, 54, 55, 56, 57, 65, 68, 73, 75, 76, 77, 79, 81, 91, 98, 100, 101, 102, 106, 120, 121, 124, 125, 126, 139, 141, 146, 148, 151, 153, 154, 155, 158, 160, 161, 164, 166, 169, 172, 184, 190, 194, 198, 199, 200, 201, 203, 204, 205, 213, 216, 217, 219, 221, 223, 229, 231, 232, 239, 240, 241, 244, 245, 247, 248, 250, 254, 257, 262, 264, 266, 268, 272, 274, 275, 278, 280, 284

Dual(ity), 139, 146, 214, 248
Dutch, 79, 236

École biblique, Jerusalem, 87
Edom, 155
Egypt(ian)(s), 1, 5, 6, 45, 47, 48, 49, 50, 52, 69, 70, 79, 81, 85, 86, 87, 89, 94, 95, 119, 136, 159, 160, 163, 165, 182, 206, 213, 214, 230, 235, 236, 273, 285, 297, 298
Eid, Joseph Albert, 87, 88
Eleleth, 110, 129, 187, 188
Elilaeus, 204
Elizabeth (mother of John the Baptist), 146
Eloaiou, 190
Eloim (Gnostic son of Eve), 197, 198
English, 45, 48, 121
Ephesus, 156
Epinoia, 195, 196, 197
Epiphanes, 203
Epiphanius, 94, 95, 97, 107-108, 119, 122, 124, 125, 126, 132, 133, 136, 141, 142, 143, 158, 171, 172, 173, 176, 177, 180, 181, 182, 183, 203, 204, 205, 206, 209, 212, 215, 217, 218, 221, 230, 231, 232, 233, 234, 236, 237, 246, 267, 285, 286, 287, 289, 292, 295, 296, 297
Es-Sayyad, 86
Esau, 155, 298
Esephech, 109
Essenian(s), 47, 277
Essenianism, 34, 44
Euboea, 159
Eucharist, 137, 242
Eugnostos, 97
Euphrates (Gnostic), 159
Euphrates (river), 285
Europe, 87
Eusebius of Caesarea, 37, 171, 180, 231
Eutactus, 119
Evangelium veritatis see Gospel of Truth
Eve, 95, 96, 97, 105-106, 107, 110, 121, 122, 143, 144, 154, 163, 167, 197, 198, 278
Excerpta ex Theodoto, 258, 262, 289

Exodus, Book of, 6, 7

Farandos, Georgios D., 40
Father of All, 137
Father(s) of the Church, 90, 94, 136, 157, 165, 206, 214, 236, 284, 296-297
Ferguson, 83
Ferrua, Antonio, 231
Festugière, A.-J., 4, 5, 13, 38, 44, 46, 48, 49, 50, 54, 58, 67, 72, 75, 76, 77, 78, 79, 80, 83, 84
Fikri Jibra'il, 87
Filastrius, 158, 172, 176, 177
First Man, 137
Fischer, Karl Martin, 127, 128
Flaccus, 2
Flood, the, 145
Flora (correspondent of Valentinus), 267
Foerster, Werner, 143, 147, 148, 149, 151, 172, 174, 175, 177, 223, 233, 252, 268
Forms see Ideas
Fowden, Garth, 78, 79
French, 79, 82, 250

Gafni, Isaiah, 37
Gallia, 285
Gebel al-Tarif, 86
Genesis, Book of, 8, 9, 12, 15, 16, 21, 22, 27, 39, 40, 58, 67, 70, 96, 110, 113, 137, 142, 143, 144, 166, 168, 187, 195, 196, 198, 201, 253, 260, 288
Glaukias, 213
Gnosis, 14, 26-34, 37, 47, 54, 66, 67, 116, 149, 151, 196, 223, 232, 235, 237, 243, 246, 247, 251, 267, 269, 284, 288, 296, 297, 298, 299
Gnostic(s), 12, 14; 27, 28, 29, 30, 31, 32, 33, 34, 37, 44, 52, 57, 59, 61, 63, 73, 76, 77, 79, 90, 91, 93, 94, 95, 96, 99, 100, 105, 106, 108, 110, 112, 113, 114, 115, 116, 117, 119, 120, 122, 123, 124, 125, 127, 131, 132, 134, 135, 137, 139, 140, 141, 142, 143, 144, 146, 151, 153, 156, 159, 160, 161, 163, 164, 165, 166, 168, 169, 170, 172, 176, 181, 182, 183, 184, 185, 186, 187, 188,

189, 190, 191, 192, 195, 197, 198, 199, 200, 201, 202, 203, 205, 206, 207, 208, 209, 213, 216, 219, 220, 221, 229, 231, 232, 235, 237, 238, 239, 240, 242, 243, 244, 245, 246, 247, 257, 260, 261, 264, 267, 269, 270, 271, 272, 276, 277, 281, 282, 284, 285, 287, 289, 293, Ch. IX passim
Gnosticizing, 12, 30, 51, 65, 237
'Gnostikoi' (Irenaeus), 134, 137
Goodenough, Erwin R., 38
Gormakaiochlabar, 192
Gospel of the Apostles, 183
Gospel of Completion, 183
Gospel of the Egyptians, 97, 108-110
Gospel of Eve, 183
Gospel of John, 16, 187
Gospel of Judas, 156
Gospel of Philip, 183
Gospel of Truth, 236, 237, 238-246, 270, 283, 286, 287, 288, 289, 300
Great and Little Symphonies (Gnostic tractate), 119
Greece, 285
Greek(s), 2, 3, 4, 5, 6, 7, 12, 15, 24, 28, 31, 45, 46, 47, 48, 49, 50, 52, 54, 56, 70, 79, 85, 86, 88, 89, 94, 95, 109, 123, 136, 137, 156, 159, 163, 173, 180, 181, 184, 215, 218, 235, 252, 279

Hadrianus (Roman emperor), 214
Haenchen, Ernst, 166, 178, 179, 287
Harmozel, 110, 129, 187
Harnack, Adolf von, 286
Hebdomad, 120, 121, 123, 144, 145, 146, 226, 227, 228, 229
Hebrew, 3, 6, 38, 39, 136, 173, 181, 255
Hegemonius, 231, 232
Heinemann, Isaac, 10, 39
Helderman, Jan, 288
Hellenic see Greek
Hellenism, Hellenistic, 3, 5, 6, 7, 8, 10, 13, 15, 26, 29, 31, 32, 34, 35, 36, 44, 45, 46, 47, 49, 50, 51, 60, 79, 136, 153, 279

Hellenization, hellenized, 1, 2, 10, 49, 69
Hendrix, Petrus, 231, 232, 234
Hera, 31
Heracleon, 267, 269-273, 274, 281, 289
Heracles, Hercules, 170, 178, 179, 180
Hermes Trismegistos, 45, 46, 49, 50, 52, 70, 73, 74, 75, 76, 77, 83, 91
Hermetic, 45, 90, 91
Hermetica, 34, Ch. II passim
Hermopolis (Khomonou), 49
Herodian princes, 2
Herodotus, 178
Hippolytus, 94, 95, 98, 102, 103, 104-105, 124, 125, 126, 128, 129, 136, 137, 159, 160, 161, 162, 164, 165, 166, 172, 177, 178, 179, 180,, 214, 221, 220-230, 231, 232, 233,, 234, 235, 247, 249, 252, 255, 257, 258, 259, 260, 262, 263, 286, 287, 289, 290, 291, 292, 296
Hiw (Egypt), 85
Hönig, Adolf, 135, 142, 143, 172, 173, 174
Homer, 7
Homeric gods, 7
Horaios, 152
Horus, 69, 70
Hyginus, 235

Iao, 204, 256
Ideas (Philonic), 18, 20
Ideas (Platonic), 161
Indian, 31, 50
Institute for Antiquity and Christianity, Claremont, 88
Interrogations of Mary, 183
Iranian, 45, 50, 56, 57, 79, 81, 124, 125, 174, 216, 231, 232, 247
Irenaeus, 94, 95, 125, 126, 131, 132, 134, 137, 141, 148, 156, 157, 158, 172, 173, 174, 176, 177, 182, 183, 185, 186, 190, 207, 209, 210, 211, 212, 214, 217-221, 222, 228, 229, 230, 231, 232, 233, 236, 237, 246, 247, 250, 251, 252, 253, 255, 256, 258, 259, 260, 266, 268, 284, 285, 286, 287, 289, 290, 291, 292, 296
Isaac, 113
Isidore (son of Basilides), 214, 215, 230, 231
Isis, 69, 70, 75, 76, 81, 82, 83
Israel (kingdom), 174
Israel (people), 4, 145, 157, 160, 169, 279
Italy, Italian, 266, 269, 273, 285
Iversen, Erik, 79

Jacob, 113
Jahve, 6, 7, 8, 38, 142, 262
Jaldabaoth, Jaltabaoth, 140-148, 151, 171, 188, 189-191, 191, 192, 193, 194, 196, 197, 201, 204
Jensen, E.H., 295
Jeremiah, 179
Jerome (Father of the Church), 157, 177, 231, 235, 286
Jerusalem, 3, 156, 179
Jesus of Nazareth, Jesus Christ, 2, 16, 95, 97, 98, 110, 111, 113, 114, 115, 125, 131, 138, 146, 147, 154, 158, 164, 170, 175, 178, 183, 186, 205, 213, 217, 220, 236, 242-243, 244-245, 254-255, 257, 270, 299
Jew(s), Jewish, Jewry, 1, 2, 3, 5, 6, 9, 10, 11, 13, 14, 31, 32, 34, 35, 49, 50, 62, 72, 79, 96, 113, 114, 115, 116, 120, 121, 125, 126, 138, 142, 145, 156, 158, 166, 174, 184, 190, 205, 210, 213, 219, 221,, 226, 262, 279, 297, 298, 299, 300
Johannes Damascenus, 132
John the Baptist, 113, 146, 154
John (the disciple), 98, 183, 270, 271, 293
Jonas, Hans, 33, 44, 56, 58, 62, 64, 65, 66, 67, 80, 81, 82, 105, 125, 129, 160, 177, 178, 230, 235, 247, 248, 254, 261, 268, 269, 286, 289, 290, 291, 292
Jordan, 266, 267, 273
Josephus, Flavius, 2, 4, 37, 96, 125
Joshua, 145
Juda (kingdom), 174
Judaism, judaistic, 5, 6, 10, 15, 19, 95, 113-114, 115, 116, 125,

148, 154, 156, 298-299
Judas, 155, 156, 298
Judea, 174
Julian the Apostate, 285
Jung, Carl, 88
Jung Codex (Codex I NHL), 87-88, 236
Jung Institute
Justin (Gnostic author), 165-170, 178
Justin the Martyr, 165
Justinians, 134, 165-170

Kaestli, Jean-Daniel, 292
Kalila-Oumbri, 189
Kallinikon, 285
Kant, Immanuel, 153
Kaphar Barucha, 119
Karystos, 159
Khomonou (Egypt) = Hermopolis, 49
Klein, J., 175
Klijn, A.F.J., 125, 126
Korah, 155
Koré Kosmou (hermetic text), 69-77
Koschorke, Klaus, 285, 295, 297, 299-300, 301
Krause, Martin, 210, 297, 300
Kriman, 192
Kronos, 73, 162
Krüger, G., 231

Latin, 80, 88, 94
Law of Moses, 3, 10, 25, 39, 145, 153, 201, 219, 262, 279
Leisegang, Hans, 16, 19, 32, 37, 136, 149, 175, 177, 178, 181, 206, 208, 209, 212, 215, 216, 217, 231, 232, 233, 290
Letter to Flora (Valentinian), 267-269
Letter to the Galatians, 187
Letter to the Philippians, 187
Leviathan, 150, 151, 152
Levitics, 181, 203
Leviticus, Book of, 23
Logos, 15, 16, 17, 18, 19, 20, 22, 31, 32, 40, 41, 49, 58-59, 59, 60-61, 61, 62, 63, 64, 65, 66, 138, 161, 186, 187, 217, 238, 239, 250,

251, 261, 264, 267, 268, 271, 272, 273, 274-277, 280, 283
Lurker, Manfred, 172
Luxor, 85
Lydia, 180
Lyons, 182

Magi (Iranian), 45, 47
Magic, 51
Mani, 231
Manichaean, Manichaeism, 79, 232
Marc the Magician (Valentinian Gnostic), 267, 292
Marcellus of Ancyra, 287
Marcion, 270
Marephnounth, 192
Marsianos, 119
Martiades, 119
Mary (mother of Jesus), 146, 205, 220, 227, 263, 264, 266, 280
Matthias (apostle), 213
Mayer, Ulrich, 16
Mediterranean, 85
Meier, C., 88
Melchior-Adonein, 189
Melchizedek, 110-111
Melchizedek (Gnostic tractate), 111
Menander, 213, 230
Ménard, Jacques-É., 288, 289
Menigsstroeth, 192
Mesopotamia, 176
Messiah, 138, 173
Middle Ages, 85, 297
Middle East, 201, 264
Mina, Togo, 87
Mirothoe, 109
Moab, 176
Momus, 74-75
Monad-Dyad, 17, 17-18, 247, 249
Monism, monistic, 41, 79, 160, 164, 221, 229, 223, 232, 247
Monotheism, monotheistic, 8, 247, 297, 298
Moorsel, G. van, 78, 79
Morard, Françoise, 126
Moses, 7, 14, 113, 155, 163, 166, 169, 176, 179, 226
Moslems, 62
Muhammad 'Ali 'al-Shamman Muhammad Halifah, 86

Musil, Robert, 34, 44
Mysticism, Jewish, 14, 34, 44

Naassenes, 134, 136, 137, 138, 172
Nag' Hammâdi (town), 85, 91
Nag Hammadi Library, 34, ch. III passim, 95, 96, 98, 111, 119, 125, 126, 130, 136, 182, 183, 236, 237, 273, 286, 296, 297, 299
Narcissus-motif, 185
Netherlands, the, 134
Neumark see Amir
New Testament, 5, 8, 16, 34, 44, 90, 95, 113, 114-116, 146, 243, 270, 277, 298
Nicolaites, 156-159, 181, 203, 206
Nicolas (Gnostic), 156-159, 177
Nikiprowetzky, V., 38
Nile, 45, 48, 85, 89, 182
Noah, 107, 145, 155, 181, 201
Nock, A.D., 79, 80
Norden, Eduard, 83
Norea, 144, 145
North Africa, 285

Occultism, 51
Ogdoad, 68, 120, 121, 123, 151, 226, 228, 229
Old Testament, 3, 5, 6, 8, 10, 16, 21, 27, 34, 38, 44, 70, 90, 95, 113, 116, 126, 136, 137, 145, 150, 155, 183, 189, 191, 262, 279, 298
Olemmaa, 193
Olympian gods, 6, 7, 47, 49
Omphale, 180
One and the Many, problem of the, 16/17, 280
Origen, 269, 271, 293
Oroi(a)el, Oriel, 110, 129, 187, 188
Orphic, 29, 31, 95
Ophian(s), 148-152, 174, 175
Ophites, Ophitic, Ophitism, 91, 94, Ch. V passim, 172, 174, 181, 189, 236
Origen, 148, 151, 172, 175, 230, 289, 296
Osiris, 49, 75, 76, 82

Pachomius, Pachomian, 85, 86, 89
Paganism, 298

Pagels, Elaine, 270-271, 293
Painchaud, Louis, 92
Palestine, Palestinian, 9, 119, 136, 213
Pantheism, pantheistic, 53, 54, 79
Paradise, 97, 136, 143, 149, 150, 167, 278
Paraphrasis Shem, 98-102, 104, 115, 116, 127-128, 132
Paredra, 31, 81, 120
Paul, apostle, 39, 153, 176, 187, 235
Pax Romana, 276
Peake, A.S., 230, 232, 234
Pentateuch, 4, 159, 171, 179
Pearson, Birger A., 43, 44, 110, 111, 125, 130, 300
Perates, Peratic, 134, 158-164, 177
Pergamum, 156
Persia, 36, 213, 231, 232
Persian see Iranian
Peter, apostle, 37, 213
Peter, an Archontic, 119, 132
Peterson, Erik, 95, 124, 287
Pharisees, Pharisaic, 5, 39, 243
Phibionites, 181, 203
Philo Judaeus, Ch. I passim, 49, 59, 67
Phoenicians, 49
Pius I, 235, 236
Plutarch, 39
Plato, Platonic, Platonism, 4, 12, 13, 23, 24, 26, 29, 34, 35, 39, 40, 41, 42, 44, 70, 71, 79, 88, 91, 153, 161, 235, 251, 258
Pliny, 46, 78
Plutarch, 7
Pohlenz, Max, 7, 38, 41
Poimandres (hermetic text), 55-69
Polytheism, polytheistic, 298
Pontius Pilate, 266, 267, 273
Powers (Philonic), 19
Preuschen, Edwin, 286
Prophecies of Barcabbas, 183
Protestant, 139
Protocols of the Sages of Sion, 219
Prunicus (Pruneikos), 97, 181, 209
Pseudochrysostomos, 125
Pseudotertullian, 94, 107, 124,

126, 129, 155, 172, 176
Ptolemaeus (Valentinian Gnostic), 248, 267, 272, 281
Ptolemaeans, Ptolemaic, 1, 50
Puech, Henri, 88, 118, 119, 132
Puritans, puritanical, 241
Pythagoras, Pythagorean(ism), 24, 45, 46, 235, 250, 290

Qena (Egypt), 87
Quintilla, 154
Quispel, Gilles, 78, 79, 88, 231, 237, 286, 289, 290

Reitzenstein, Richard, 79, 80, 81, 82, 83, 156
Red Sea, 160
Revelation of John, 156, 211, 277
Richram, 193
Robinson, James, 89, 90, 91, 92
Roman(s), 2, 46, 47, 48, 85, 91, 179, 214
Roman-Catholic (Church), 139, 148, 154, 171, 172, 182, 235, 236, 263, 274, 285, 286, 296, 297, 299-300
Roman Empire, 1
Rome, 2, 4, 37, 165, 230, 235, 236, 237, 269, 285, 287
Rudolph, Kurt, 92, 93, 117, 125, 131, 175, 246, 287, 289
Runia, David T., 41, 42

Sabaoth, 120-121, 124, 189, 204, 205
Sabbath, 3, 190
Sabbede, 190
Sagnard, F.-M., 250, 251, 290
Salamis, 206
Samaritan, 95, 125
Samuel, 145
Satagh, 119
Saturn, 150
Saturnilos, 213
Säve-Söderbergh, Torgny, 93
Sahidic Coptic, 87, 286
Schenke, Hans-Martin, 96, 124, 125, 287
Scholer, David, 93
Schoolmen, 4
Scott, E.F., 83, 124, 134, 172, 236, 286, 287, 289, 290, 292
Scribes (Jewish), 243
Scythia, 178
Scythianus, 231
Second Man, 137
Second Treatise of the Great Seleucid princes, 9
Semitic, 136
Septuagint, 3, 6, 7, 58
Serapion of Thmuis, 94, 95, 124
Seth (son of Adam), ch. iv passim, 98, 112, 113-116, 116, 118, 134, 144, 154, 188, 198, 199, 204
Seth (Egyptian godhead), 95
Sethian(s), 91, ch.iv passim, 134, 145, 172, 237, 298
Severians, 134, 171-172
Severus, 171
Sevrin, Jean-Marie, 126, 209
Sexual(ity), 27, 53, 65, 66, 67, 101, 102, 103, 104, 116, 117, 166, 168, 171, 197, 201, 204, 206-209, 248, 300
Shem, 98, 100, 113
Shenesit see Chenoboskion
Sibylline oracle, 177
Simon of Cyrene, 115, 220
Simon Magus, 115, 213, 230
Sloterdijk, Peter, 33, 44, 175
Sodom(ites), 113-114, 154, 155, 298
Solomon (king of Israel), 113
Solomon of Basra, 125
Sophia, 49, 97, 108, 110, 118, 139-140, 140, 141, 142, 143, 144, 145, 146, 149, 155, 181, 187, 188-189, 191, 193, 194, 196, 197, 198, 200, 207, 209, 218, 251-259, 259, 260, 261, 263, 264, 268, 269, 274, 283
Spain, 230
Standaert, Benoît, 286
Stephen (deacon), 158
Stobaeus, 54, 55, 69, 80, 82
Stoic philosophy, 9, 10, 14, 26, 28, 29, 30, 32, 36, 40, 79
Stone, Michael E., 126
Stratiotics, 181, 203
Subachmimic Coptic, 87, 236
Switzerland, 88
Syria(n), 213, 235, 285

Talmud, 34, 44
Tano, Phocion J., 87
Tatian, 180
Tardieu, Michel, 125
Tartarus, 150, 152
Tat, son of Hermes Trismegistos, 52
Temple of Jerusalem, 2, 3
Tertullian, 154, 156, 176, 235, 236, 274, 284, 286, 292, 295, 296
Tetragrammaton, 6
Theodas (Theudas), 235
Theodore, Pachomian abbot-general, 90
Theodoretus of Cyrus, 132, 145, 146, 157, 172, 173, 174, 176, 177, 180, 181, 209, 231285
Theodosius II, 285
Thmuis, 94
Three Steles of Seth, 112
Tiberius, 2
Timotheus (presbyter in Constantinople), 285
Torah,, 39 10
Toth, 49, see also Hermes
Tout-Ank-Amon, 88
Treitel, L., 10, 15, 19, 40, 41
Treneu, 192
Tripartite Tractate, 273-284
Tröger, K.-W., 78, 79, 131, 298, 299, 300, 301
Trullanum II (synod), 285

Unnik, W.C. van, 286, 287
Utrecht (NL), 88

Valentinian(s), Valentinianism, 91, 219, Ch. VIII passim
Valentinus, 213, 230, 235-238, 249, 250, 251, 252, 262, 264, 266, 267, 268, 269, 270, 286, 287, 289
Völker, Walther, 287

Wagner, Richard, 173
Williams, Michael Allen, 199, 211
Wilson, Robert McL., 5, 6, 7, 29, 33, 38, 39, 42, 44, 123, 287
Wisdom, Book of, 16, 30
Wisse, Frederik, 116, 124, 183, 184, 209
Wolfson, Harry, 4, 38, 40, 41

Women, attitude to, 26, 27

Yammeax, 192
Yave (Gnostic son of Eve), 197, 198
Yoel, 109

Zacchaeans, 181, 203
Zacharias, Gerhard, 172, 208
Zarathustra see Zoroaster
Zeller, Eduard, 21, 23, 27, 41, 42, 43
Zeno, 153
Zervanism, 81, 216
Zeus, 7, 8, 31, 73
Zielinski, Th., 59, 65, 79, 81, 82, 83
Zodiac, 71, 72, 149, 152
Zoroaster, Zoroastrian, 45, 110, 124, 125, 130, 216
Zostrianos, 110, 117
Zostrianos (Gnostic tractate), 111-112
Zürich, 88